BEFORE THE GARDEN

GOD'S ETERNAL CONTINUUM

PAULA A. PRICE

FLAMING VISION PUBLICATIONS
TULSA, OK

Flaming Vision Publications
7107 S Yale Avenue
Tulsa, OK 74136
www.ppmglobalresources.com

Book Layout ©2013 BookDesignTemplates.com

Ordering Information:
Wholesale Ordering. Special discounts are available on bulk purchases by corporations, associations, and others. For details, contact "Sales" using the address above.

Before the Garden: God's Eternal Continuum/ Paula A. Price. —1st ed.
ISBN-13: 978-1-88628-830-0 ISBN-10: 1-88628-830-5

CONTENTS

DEDICATION

To the precarnate, incarnate and everlasting Jesus Christ, who is my "sugar."

Preface

My reasons for writing this book were triggered by an awareness of today's growing interest in God, Christ, and Christianity by Christians and non-Christians. While spiritual and religious curiosity has always been high, of late it has reached fever pitch, with every sphere of modern society embracing and encouraging it. Revived spirituality urgently nudges people to revisit religion. When they do, their search inevitably leads them to Christianity because it is the world's first global religion and its second monotheistic one. Judaism is the first. The modern world finds it hard to understand the why of Christianity and its exclusivity talk. Seekers and critics want to know what makes Christianity so high minded and why it thinks it is the only true faith. These questions, no matter how they come, have fascinated the masses since His incarnation, departure, and the birth of His church. That they exist, and persist attests to His success. People the world over scrutinize Christianity's Founder, Jesus Christ to learn how He went from being born a lowly carpenter to a religious rebel that was executed as a national criminal. People incessantly ask by what power Jesus Christ managed to displace a polytheistic planet with worldwide monotheism. The biggest question for them is how the man leaves this world crucified and ends up God Almighty. Frankly, the answer is, He began that way. It is this fantastic story that has Jesus' challengers demanding to know what expunged His notorious criminal record to make Him God of all the earth. That anyone would make such a claim is unthinkable. Yet He and His family boldly declare it. And, the challenges do not end with Jesus Himself because as many curiosities surround His homeland and its citizens. Arguers wonder what makes Israel, God's land and the Jews God's chosen people, and why do they get to say so?

Being in ministry for more than three decades gave me occasion to listen to the numerous issues people have with Jesus Christ, His church, and Christianity. Many of the concerns involve gaps in the Bible narratives that document and explain the faith. The most perturbing questions and stinging criticisms surround Jesus Himself. Saved or searching, people want insight on this enigmatic figure. Recently, entertainment, media, science, and history networks, tapping into the growing curiosity have all taken to telling His story earth's way. However, seeing their portrayal of Him, as compared to His self revelation, exposed major flaws in their versions of the stories told. How worldly accounts of the Bible's record lead people to think being a Christian is completely different from how God defines a Christian. Their depiction of The Messiah fuses Him with the deities He dethroned and shows how little is really known about Him and His world. Popular explanations expose human misunderstandings of how things work outside this planet and the extreme influence Christ's world has on this one. These are what Before the Garden: God's Eternal Continuum address. It closes the gap between what people wonder and have heard about Jesus Christ during His brief three and a half year ministry on earth, and discloses what happened behind the scenes before and during it. The book does several other things as well; it unravels His faith from eternity to earth, and back to eternity to unveil a life that spans all ages.

Admittedly and perhaps deliberately controversial, Before the Garden: God's Eternal Continuum takes its readers back to when and where everything about Jesus Christ and Christianity began. That is, to His world where He and everything else started. This seminal work will no doubt breed many others because its subject is far too expansive for any single text to cover. Still, it answers, if only abbreviately, nagging questions many have about Almighty God and His Savior Jesus Christ. Not stopping there, it also takes on gnawing issues people have about salvation, true faith, and the afterlife. Progressively, the book supplies those who speak for God with sage wisdom that separate the false from the true in their generations. It does so by unearthing the fourteen eternal and earthly events that brought Jesus Christ into this world and birthed His church. Nothing in this work seeks to discredit anyone's faith or ministry. It merely aims to provide quality, and practical information to propel the Lord's church forward in its destiny. It is timely because people are jaded. Many of them have abandoned their churches and fallen away from their Redeemer. More than a few believers who were once deeply in love with the Lord now forsake the very Scriptures that once brought them hope and comfort. Before the Garden: God's Eternal Continuum aims to reverse the trend and galvanize people's rediscovery of Christ,

His word, and His faith. It poignancy promises to revive, and supercharge Christian faith in this and future generations.

Prologue

B*efore the Garden: God's Eternal Continuum* elegantly portrays the Christian faith and unearths its most unfathomable truths. It unseals the eternal truths that transported Jesus Christ and Christianity from heaven to earth. Combining eternity's history, Messianic destiny, and the Almighty's indomitable resolve to reproduce after His own kind, the book discloses Jesus' precarnate life and fills in glaring blanks in His narrative. It answers what He did before He became flesh, what happened after He left the world, and what He is doing now. Solomon's words in Ecclesiastes 1:9 and 3:15, make the strongest case for this work. The International Standard Version of the Bible quotes the passages this way, "Whatever has happened, will happen again; whatever has been done, will be done again. There is nothing new on earth." Also "That which was, now is; and that which will be, already is; and God examines what has already taken place". The only wise God providentially endowed Israel's third king, Solomon, with more wisdom than any other person on earth before him. God's first begotten Son Jesus Christ alone surpasses Solomon's wisdom when He enters the world ages later. Despite how cynical the king had become by the time he wrote Ecclesiastes, these two utterances of wisdom say much about the Almighty's existence and expertise. He perpetually controls world events because of the masteries He gained in His world long before creating this one. Whatever earth claims as new is to the Almighty, only recycled and obsolete where He is. The Lord predicts the future because it is His past. Nothing is new under the sun because what is, or what occurs beneath it, happened in God's world before He created the sun. God is God because He has always been, and before His existence, even nothing itself could exist. All of these perspectives, the monarch endowed with otherworldly wisdom discovered.

The principal goal of this work is to discredit the idea that Jesus did not exist before He came into this world. In its place, Before the Garden: God's Eternal Continuum establishes that the implications of the word incarnate infer an immaterial existence extending its form from one place to another place. That is what Jesus did when He became flesh. To investigate His other forms and existences, the discussions explore God's antiquities, probe Jesus' history, and examines creation's sublime architecture. It unravels the Sovereign of sovereigns' lineage from Matthew's royal perspective, based on verse seventeen of the gospel's first chapter. Tracking Jesus as the promised (and prophesied) King of kings, His Messianic Monarchy is traced from Abraham to David to Christ,. Matthew 1:17 says, "So all the generations from Abraham to David are fourteen generations. And from David until the carrying away into Babylon, fourteen generations. And from the carrying away into Babylon until Christ, fourteen generations." What this says about Christians is that in the Creator's geneses, Christ's offspring is the Maker's fourteenth generation. It answers why the number fourteen identifies the last race of people the Almighty created. Thenceforth the Maker's attention turns to getting His final generation from this world into His. Christ's kingly genealogy goes from Abraham, Romans 4's "heir of the world", to King David, The Messiah's royal progenitor, to the Babylonian exile that inseminated the nations, all the way to His incarnation as the Christ. Matthew sees Jesus' journey into this world as divided by fourteen distinct generations. In doing so, he forges the single thread that maps out the Son of God's genetic trail, Davidic kingship, and triumphant return to His Father's right hand. He is David's promised seed and the eternal sire of Abraham's posterity. Moreover, since Jesus is the reason for it all, understanding how He came to be and what makes the Christian Scriptures a reliable record of His existence are a faith imperative. God's word holds the only common thread that follows His life, His exploits, and His experiences. Before the Garden, locates the single strand in the Savior's contiguous life events that runs through the Almighty's Eternal Continuum. Clarifying long standing Christian issues, it resolves concerns Christians have had and will have until the end of time about their salvation, their Savior, their afterlife, and their eternal inheritance. Revelation after revelation teaches readers what the Almighty planned long ago for His deathless progeny.

Over the ages of the Church's existence, Scripture orthodoxy, sound doctrine, and the credibility of Jesus Christ as God repeatedly fell prey to disbelief and discredit. Since His ascension, every generation has vigorously contested His testimony. Believers and unbelievers all speculate on how true the Gospel of Jesus Christ is, while Christians consider how responsible they should be to it, if what it says happens when they die is true. Christian antagonists on the other side, wrestle with His world dominance today as much as they did the day, year, and century after His departure from the earth. The Lord's journey to glory, however, was not an easy one then, and it continues to be a hostile one today. From its inception, His church has been bitterly persecuted for daring to introduce the world to its true and living God. During its formative years, Christ's Ecclesia suffered, as did its Founder, heinous persecution and brutal assaults for the name and testimony of Jesus Christ. Despite its savage treatment, the Most High expelled the ancient world's brutish gods and overthrew polytheism with monotheism. The heavenly operation He initiated with Abraham and Israel saw its prophesied victory through Israel's promised Messiah and the birth of His new creation Ecclesia. Unceremoniously, in many cases, Jesus Christ moved nations from global veneration of many gods to exclusive, worship of a single deity whether or not He is unanimously accepted.

The road to The Messiah's world domination began, with His promise to the serpent in the Garden of Eden, that the seed of the woman would crush his head. His act in fulfillment of His vow was to destroy the antediluvian world. After replenishing the earth with Noah and his sons, to put the next phase in effect, He converted Abram a former Babylonian Prophet from Ur of Chaldea. Several more initiatives brought about Abraham's seed, Israel's birth, Moses' Exodus, and David's kingship. Matthew 1:17 recounts some eventful happenings that culminate in the incarnation of the Son of God. The eternal Lord became a Man by taking upon Himself flesh to complete the project. Briefly, these details introduce the fourteen catalytic events of God's Eternal Continuum, with a few correlating events discussed later in the book omitted for now. Later discussions tell how Jesus came to earth to assume personal responsibility for the souls He made, and to reclaim the lives that Adam sold to another deity. His single objective was to end humanity's atrocious abuse at the hands of otherworldly forces that only He could outmatch and conquer. To save them forever, Christ assumed it all upon Himself. Jesus, as Philippians 2:6 explains, although He was in the form of God, made Himself of no reputation in the divine world to take upon Himself the likeness of flesh to enter this one. Just thinking about any sovereign making such a supreme sacrifice is humbling and quite convicting. Why did He do it? Hebrews 2:15; 1 Corinthians 15:21; and Romans 5:14-17 explain why. Together they tell why the Son of God became the Son of Man. They also uncover to whom He paid that ransom. Read Acts 10:38 and 1 John 3:8 for that answer. What have all of these passages to do with the Continuum? They reveal the plan of salvation and the reasons it is necessary. They show why only God Himself could overhaul the ravages of sin that mercilessly destroyed His earthly creation. As informative as Scripture revelations are, their veracity hinges on a larger issue that Before the Garden: God's Eternal Continuum puts forth. The clue for it is the word continuum.

Before the Garden accesses heaven's archives and rests on eternity's sublime architecture. It unfurls God's histories to communicate how His archetypes predetermined the design and structure of all He created. Scripture states that Jesus Christ is God's first reproduction and consequently the head of all that came after Him. "Through him all things were made, and apart from him nothing was made that has been made." ISV. The Literal Translation of the Holy Bible phrases it this way; its variation is worth mentioning. "All things came into being through Him, and without Him not even one thing came into being that has come into being." The Bible paints Jesus Christ as the head, arche, of all things. He is creation's head cornerstone, humanity's head, the Ecclesia's head, and the head of all rule and dominion. To say that it is all about Jesus is an understatement this work exploits to introduce creation's unending Continuum. The word continuum defines the sequence of connective acts and processes the Almighty implemented to restore humanity to His holiness. It is how He returned the earth to His world's authority and put His Son, on creation's throne, instead of the powers of darkness. As applied to the Almighty's long unbroken history with this world and its inhabitants, Before the Garden: God's Eternal Continuum lifts the veil on the unbroken chain of fourteen events that brought Jesus Christ and Christianity into this world. It declares how He became the highest potentate over it as well.

[1]

Introduction

Before the Garden: God's Eternal Continuum's fourteen events vindicate Jesus Christ and Christianity. It gives sincere messengers of the Lord Jesus Christ the revelatory edge to stem the tide of demonics flooding the world and His church. This book can easily reduce the number of Christians enticed into leaving Christ because of false spirituality and misrepresentation of His righteousness and holiness.

THE PURPOSE OF THIS WISDOM

The purpose of this teaching is to explain at length the Lord's wisdom as it pertains to the following statements. Chosen because they reflect the ongoing curiosities people have about God, they note the most difficult issues regarding His church; God's Son and His deity; Christianity overall and humans' plaguing concerns about the afterlife.

1. How Christianity got to earth
2. Why Christianity is not a classic world religion
3. Eternal events that incited God's plan of redemption
4. Heaven and hell: Where they came from
5. Who is the Holy Spirit
6. What is the Godhead
7. Actions and elements that incarnated the Second Person of the Godhead
8. How to tell if a teaching is of God and Christ or not
9. How to test and verify a declared or populated revelation
10. Why God does not destroy the Devil
11. How to test and validate a prophecy or new doctrine

12. What makes Jesus Christ, God, Lord, Creator, Messiah
13. The origin of war, crime, and the like
14. What makes doctrine, error, heresy or demonic
15. How to become and live as a biblical Christian and why do so

WHAT MAKES THIS WISDOM SO VALUABLE?

The wisdom in this book gives useful reasons for why the Almighty keeps replenishing His church. It answers why He continually revives His body and expounds on His word, explaining pragmatically why He has never had to revise His Scriptures. Furthermore, it justifies His relentless demands that the world convert to His Son's redemptive faith. Learning such information educates the reader with the following:

1. The answers to Christianity's hard questions
2. The answers to what makes a Christian and why Jesus' faith is unique
3. The best ways to learn and use the Holy Bible more precisely
4. How the Christian Bible pre-addressed this world and its trends and seductions
5. The answers to why and how Jesus Christ came to earth
6. The answers to why and how Jesus was doomed to die and go to hell
7. The answers to what makes Jesus Christ, God and why His death enables salvation
8. The answers to what happened in heaven that made humans need salvation
9. The answers to what happened on earth that demands all humanity be saved
10. The story of Jesus Christ from the Godhead's perspective
11. The history of eternity from the Bible's perspective
12. The premises for the new birth and what makes it God's redemption imperative

Before the Garden aims to do for God's modern saints, what David's words in Psalm 18:39 says the Most High did for him as Israel's second king. It arms the Christian with strength for the battle, and make no mistake about it; Christianity is perpetually engaged in an unseen battle for its faith. Beside this is the enablement referred to by Paul, in 2 Corinthians 10:1-6. Before the Garden confronts the hard questions asked about Jesus Christ, Christianity, and His global church in the world. It presents God's attitudes regarding life and death to illustrate how He presolved it all prior to creation. For instance, many saints and scholars cannot say how God, remained outside of earth's time zones at creation and since. Others fail to recognize how God, keeping Himself outside of human time lets Him govern His creation objectively. Speaking of creation, here is a for instance. Although the daylight and night existed, they were static until the Creator did two things to actuate them. First, He commanded a firmament to separate the heavens from the earth (really the sky from the ground) and day from night. Second, He appointed in the heavens, lights to denote the signs of the times. The two acts marked the succession of earth's seasons, days, and years make up, time. Thus, Genesis' time begins marching forward the fourth day despite the Lord, marking His workdays as days one through three before then. The Almighty based His productivity on creation's workdays and not by the rotation of the planets as it has been since creation's fourth day. This example shows how the Creator has always kept Himself and His world outside of the earth's constraints to assure His oversight and intervention in its affairs when necessary. Review the Scripture that records it all from the book of Genesis.

> "And God said, Let there be lights in the firmament of the heaven to divide the day from the night; and let them be for signs, and for seasons, and for days, and years: And let them be for lights in the firmament of the heaven to give light upon the earth: and it was so. And God made two great lights; the greater light to rule the day, and the lesser light to rule the night: he made the stars also. And God set them in the firmament of the heaven to give light upon the earth, to rule over the day and over the night, and to divide the light from the darkness: and God saw that it was good. And the evening and the morning were the fourth day."

To correlate the Genesis account with the New Testament, John discusses the Lord's new city of Jerusalem. In Revelation 21:2, he declares the Almighty is all light, including His own. The Creator lights His world without the luminaries He created on earth relies to illuminate it. The passage says there will be no night there because God's glory and the Lamb's lamp will lighten the new world continually. Revelation 22:5 echoes the verse: "There will be no more night, and they will not need any light from lamps or the sun because the Lord God will shine on them. They will rule forever and ever." The two great luminaries the Maker hung in the sky to light the earth on the creation's fourth day are destroyed and replaced by His very presence after time ends, the way it was before He made them. God's presence, possesses more luminescence than the two luminaries combined and all the stars that shined with them throughout the world's ages. The command "Let there be light" then launches the Lord's Continuum in the terrestrial world, whereas He as eternity's everlasting light concludes it. Between the two epochs, a divine communications vehicle called prophecy steers creation's plan down the Most High's predetermined paths. Its inception begins the Continuum's heaven to earth procession. At times, the Lord boldly declares its journey in Scripture and at other times, when concealing it is to His advantage, He uses parables, allegories, and various symbols to allude to its effects. Either way, prophecy codes and decodes God's concealed mysteries in Scripture.

Prophecy got its earthly start from Adam when he was forbidden to eat from the tree of the knowledge of good and evil. Basically, it is the Lord speaking into this world what He wants to occur in it from His own. The promise that he would surely die is the first consequential prophecy the Lord delivered to the human race in this world. That it took Adam nine hundred and thirty years thereafter to leave his body attests to how powerfully the first man was made. His life span speaks to the original indomitability of his physique prior to surrendering it to the law of sin and death. The mortality that was imposed on his tempter, the Devil that inhabited the serpent's body immediately spreads to Adam when he disobeys his Maker. The moment Adam defied His Maker's edict, the act ejected from his being the indwelling Holy Spirit that brought him into existence. The law of the spirit of life, Adam's life force[1] returned to the world exclusively in the person of Jesus Christ, in whom it abided in the beginning. In turning off the Creator's life force, Adam spread death to all his seed and disseminated the very same condemnation that banished the serpent from heaven and confined him to the earth realm. As such, the first man subjected his entire progeny to the very captivity and doom that cast the old serpent of Revelation 12:9 and 20:2 out of his heavenly abode. Rebellion exiled the Devil from his primordial home and introduced death into all creation. Not so obvious in Scripture this revelatory wisdom fills some compelling narrative gaps. It casts down arguments against Christ that are utilized to lure His people out from His truth. It further counteracts the devious side of this era's spiritual revival attempting to exploit humanity's inherent, though naïve, contempt for its Maker.

The modern world is rife with untempered spirituality, which is nothing new. However, the advent of technology uniting earth's populations makes it more dangerous than ever because it gives everyone twenty-four hour access to everyone else's world. Unclean subject matter is peddled to people's psyches through their communications devices and in seconds saturates them with archaic perversions of former rituals and

---

[1] The breath God gave Adam was that of His natural life, the life that would enable him to live on earth. Eternal life was not granted him then. It had yet to be earned, something Adam failed to do in the Garden and consequentdly forfeited eternal life for himself and all humanity.

sacrifices. Spreading them once took hours, days, months, and years. Where their spiritual practitioners used to roam countrysides to spread their heresies and perversities, today they are big business institutions that peddle them electronically. To get that they mainstreamed into every area of society, entering its gates through the lobby of education, taking their cue from the most successful outreach pattern in history, the global evangelism model of the Church's Great Commission. The Godhead's evangelism that introduced the planet to Jesus Christ was perfected by the Christian church as it went into all the world. Taking in the reverberating success of its global outreach methods, unclean merchants deviously replicated it to blanket the world with wickedness and death. Every day, a new media facilitates their ability to strive with their Maker. Fiendishly, they labor to overturn Christianity's advancement to replace it with antiquity's arcane religions. As it stands now, their efforts seem to have paid off. Piercing the long-standing shields of the Christian faith, their fables and contests against it suggest their overthrow campaigns seem successful. By painting Christianity as old-fashioned and irrelevant, God's adversaries, deceptively, mask their plot to replace it with the archaic beliefs of fallen angels masquerading as new age gods and their faiths. On the surface, it looks as if they have triumphed, especially as modern media reports it. However, that cannot be, given the Savior's words in Matthew 16:18. As God Almighty, He already decreed that "the gates of hell shall never prevail against" His church.

Still, public forums of all kinds continue to celebrate Christian antagonists' greatly exaggerated victory over what they deem to be a stranglehold on human liberties. At first glance, their aims look quite noble. After all, who in their right mind would want to deprive anyone of the basic human right to better themselves and improve their lot in life. In free societies, why should not they be granted the right to choose the religion they want to practice? On the surface, it all sounds like music to the ears of the suffering and oppressed. However, when it comes to spirituality, it is all a sham. Freeing enslaved souls from the captivity that deprives them of their basic human right to education and prosperity, and enlightening them on how to succeed in their societies is noble. Freeing a country to denigrate to its lowest and most degrading depths of depravity is ignoble and that is the undisclosed purpose of today's spiritual mania. Secret wrestles with Jesus Christ and the Christian faith underlie claims to liberate devotees to worship as they see fit, but it is just a ruse. As much as the agenda pretends it is just a matter of faith choices, the tactic really aims to, by disparaging restrictive Christian purities, popularize alternative rituals and debase morality. These are the concealed motives of the culture war. The second verse of Peter's second epistle words it best, "While they promise them liberty, they themselves are the servants of corruption: for of whom a man is overcome, of the same is he brought in bondage." To fend it off, God needs His true believers to know that secularity's core purpose is to snuff out the Christian church's gospel light in the world and free it to fulfill Revelation 9:20.

> "And the rest of the men which were not killed by these plagues yet repented not of the works of their hands, that they should not worship devils, and idols of gold, and silver, and brass, and stone, and of wood: which neither can see, nor hear, nor walk Neither repented they of their murders, nor of their sorceries, nor of their fornication, nor of their thefts."

The whole charade is to draw successive generations into the depths of Satan that Christ condemned in the Thyatira church. It seeks to capture as many souls as possible for the fiery furnace. The only way an attack so deadly can succeed in any era is by dismantling God's truth, discrediting Christ, and confusing their church. Such tactics serve modern spirituality's move to revive the old religions and doctrines that destroyed the ancient worlds that practiced them. Recycling their primitive campaigns allows their modern agents to repeat history in this and future eras, to make exposing the cunning ministers of darkness and their anti-Christ propaganda a priority. While they promise them liberty, as Peter's second epistle says, they shrewdly mislead their cache of deluded followers into destructive captivity. Downplaying the eternal consequences of their ploys, they bring people into a cleverly disguised bondage. In short, seducers deceptively bring to pass Jesus' words in Matthew 23:15: they make their followers "a twofold child of hell". Peter appears to be the most educated in the Lord's differentiation between the child of the Devil and the children of God as his rebuke of Simon the Sorcerer in Acts 13:10 suggests. The cause of their dispute fuels the Almighty's ongoing tussle with His creature hood: the eternal and temporal, heavenly and earthly, spiritual and natural ones.

Bitterly despising the idea of worshipping the true and living God, fallen angels provide what superficially seems to be an appealing substitute for Him and His rigidity. Their tactic is similar to Jeroboam's, the king that succeeded Solomon. Fearing his nation's continued worship of Yahweh would overshadow his human reign, he designed brand new religious traditions for them to worship God without leaving their hometowns, or traveling too far from them. Jeroboam's new religion's appeal was convenience. The people no longer had to travel miles to the country's capital to worship the Lord in His central temple. The self-serving monarch enabled the citizens of his theocratic nation to practice their faith wherever they chose, without the expense and hardship of doing it the old way. No longer did they have to trek all the way to Jerusalem to worship Yahweh or petition His priests. Under Jeroboam, they could craft or select their own deific images and worship them as they saw fit. In corresponding fashion, modern religionists and spiritualists fabricate a disembodied faith to give seekers, and sadly Christians, a pseudo Jesus Christ in place of the true one. The faith they offer is like Jeroboam's, one they can comfortably live with and adapt as convenient. Their alternative, unlike his at the outset, promotes depersonalized deities disguised as iconic worship objects and presented as virtues and benefits instead of what they are, fallen deities. The actual beings as fallen gods manifest themselves later. Isolating rituals from spiritual personages, lets people choose what to worship, believing they are relieved of deciding whom to worship. Deceptively, they end up worshipping they know not what, as Christ says to the woman at the well. The very idols condemned by God's prophets in the Old Testament and ultimately overthrown by the cross are today revived and peddled as surrogates for Jesus Christ in contemporary Christianity. Their detestable rites and destructive devotions are reinvented to suit the modern age, while their initially suppressed effects remain as disease ridden and deadly as they were when the BC people practiced them. Instead of being exclusively religious icons and symbols, they are now portrayed as preferential fashion, politics, and iconic accessories sported to make voiceless statements. To further spiritualize them, Scripture snatches are watered down as slogans and clichés to give the deception a more Christian veneer. Separating God and His truth from His followers diminishes His moral standard and encourages His people to redefine His moral compass at will according to popular culture. Such adherents indulge themselves in wishy-washy sacraments under the pretext of religious liberty, totally unaware that they are pandering to the seductions of Christ destroyed gods.

A brilliant, howbeit devious, strategy, taking advantage of the darkness born within all mankind is why it all works so well generation after generation. It is also why the Lord scripturally exposed their stratagems once in history and never had to rewrite them to forewarn future peoples of their dangers. God knows that arcane religions and their destructive tactics never change because they are nothing more than devilish defaults He permits to accommodate those who reject Him. Stripping idolatry and its rituals from the deities that demand them, contemporary worshippers think they are venerating what appeals to them based on their own imaginations. In reality, they are not, but instead are tricked into serving a being that most at the outset do not even know exists. In reality, they are oblivious to the harms concealed in the hidden deity's rites. For example, by telling people that the universe blesses or curses them, deceivers make worshippers believe they are in charge of their lives and whatever happens to them is largely in their hands. In truth that also is not so. For instance, when one thinks of how vast the universe is and that no corporeal being is discovered to exist there so far, the statement reeks with mockery and fosters delusion. Here is the problem with it. Because no serious plea for help with an issue is made to any one being; it means no one has to respond such petitions, and maybe that is the intent. The scheme has the same effect as that found in the old proverb, "somebody—anybody—nobody." The implication is that if you want something done, assign it to somebody, if you want nothing done assign it to everybody. Entrusting petitions and life outcomes to the impersonal universe is like scattering one's destiny to the wind. Nothing will come of leaving it for any spiritual creature in the universe to handle any more than delegating a task to everyone around gets it done. Such an approach equates to scattering the ashes of a cremated body to the wind for it to become part of everything and recalled by nothing in particular. This example, punctuates ridiculousness of this age's nouveau spirituality in light of God's eternal wisdom.

When one realizes that faith, rituals, and morality all have personified beings fueling them, religion and worship take on a new light. No matter how neutral sounding the mantra is, Jesus' dethronement is at the root of it entirely. His modern wrestles reminisce the age-old battles He has waged against the darkness forever, as cited in the second Psalm: "The kings of the world and their rulers have gathered together against the Lord and His Christ". This clash, John's Apocalypse says, will continue until two hugely momentous things happen. The first one is the kings of the earth give their power to the beast for a season as foretold in Revelation 17:17. The text says that God puts it in the heart of ten nations to agree with each other and with the beast long enough to surrender their power to it. The second thing is declared in Revelation 11:15, "The kingdoms of this world have become the kingdoms of our Lord and His Christ". The two statements show the Almighty's absolute control over world events in John's Apocalypse and above that His planning and execution of them as well. There is a term for these maneuvers on God's part that the Continuum thoroughly explores and explains. It is the word presolve; settling or answering something before it really happens. Synergizing the Lord's predeterminations, predestination, and foreordainment, the word presolve speak to His cohesive application of all three. Together they demonstrate how emerging situations and developments that appear to stall His plans or counter His moves are actually "God's will" at work on earth. Living outside earth's time and formulating creations' outworkings in His world and not this one, the Lord encoded in His revelations of the future, eternal solutions to His temporal obstacles and concerns before they arose. He as would be called today, "vetted" candidates for eternal life and to ensure its heirs can never again mar His eternal world or attempt to overthrow His leadership when they enter it from this one. The second passage, Revelation 11:15, where the kingdoms of this world become the kingdoms of the Lord and His Christ surfaces as the Almighty's ultimate outcome. The concerns voiced in Psalm 2 and the prophecies that foretell this moment in human history converge in the His ultimate triumph. The prophecy says the kingdoms of this world come under the Almighty and His Christ's, supremacy. They are removed from the Beast's control to the Godhead's dominion. Its fulfillment ushers in a glorious time for God and His saints. Before it all happens, He executes preordained tactical maneuvers to rescue His predestined progeny from its inexorable fall into Satan's abyss. Along the way, nonnegotiable taboos sift every generation's wheat and tares to reward the Most High's predestined children with His promised immortality. At the same time, He grants His rejectors their desire also. Those who refuse His way of life He forever banishes from His Presence and providences.

The earth and its inhabitants on the way to their final destination will watch spirituality reach peak in God's kingdom and in the Devil's. Both of their offspring grow up together tussling and clashing at every turn as the gates of hell connive to prevail against the Church of the Lord Jesus Christ. When the iniquity of the world matures, it brings on the judicial destructions that God prescribed before time. These ignites cataclysmic sequences embedded in creation. He enfolded these in the world's ages to compel His presolved end time events to erupt in their preappointed seasons. Prophecies that date back to before time hint at their existence alluding to undetectable divine triggers that actuate specific world events according to the Most High's timelines. As things progress, numerous deviations from divine truth set God's eschatological clock in motion. Every Christian messenger determined to remain faithful to the Lord Jesus Christ and His Continuum heeds it. Although as with Balaam in the book of Numbers, both the darkness and the light perceive God's strategies from time to time. His advocates and adversaries can both declare what they see because all His creatures have the potential (and information) to prophesy some aspect of the world's end as the Creator appointed it. Spiritual and natural, godly and ungodly beings participate in the Most High's prophetic ministrations for their respective realms because all philosophers, preachers, and worshippers veer off course without His thoughts being voiced. Unfortunately, far too many Christian prophesiers and preachers have no idea the Almighty has a Continuum to be guarded, so they recklessly, perhaps inadvertently, sever its links by divining instead of prophesying what He prepared before the foundation of the world. Until prophecy's existence and purposes are learned, false doctrine spread by unwitting ministers of the gospel prevails, and reduces the Continuum's benefit to their generations. This too is according to divine plans that have been in effect since before time. They are what the Lord prophesied through His messengers, saying that heresy and suchlike would steadily increase during the perilous times to come. This must be, for three unyielding reasons. First, God's Scriptures must be carried out; Jesus in the New Testament says it must be thus. Second, as Jesus also said, people do not know the Scriptures that testify of Him and so disseminate error in their ignorance. Third, deeply entrenched godlessness works to neutralize God's power to save the lost. The solution to it all is intelligent, insightful instruction in God's ways and will, and nothing less. Only when wisdom and knowledge upgrade hollow Scripture quotes to sound Redeemer counsel will the effects of these be minimized, and the souls of God's appointed heirs of salvation won.

[2]

The Dire Need for Before the Garden's Continuum Teaching

There is a desperate need for a way to verify secure and true biblical doctrine. It is the only way for believers to distinguish the false from the true. The demand is heightened when it comes to prophecy, making it critical for His faithful ones to discern whom to trust. Of the numerous grounds for such initiatives the Church of Jesus Christ's ongoing grapple with heresy that taints its every new wave surface as the most insistent one. The question of end time revelation sparks the greatest debate. How both sides tell the story of the world's end and explain what God does with those who depart it intrigues all humans, and troubles many. In this regard, the present state of Christ's church makes no subject more deserving of closer attention than the Bible. Answering these hard concerns has been the task of theologians, thinkers, and sages for eons. For the believer in Christ, how the Lord dispensed His truth to Christ's church ignites controversy. What or better yet, who gets to say and confirm what "thus says the Lord", as far as the Christian church is concerned? God's Holy Spirit is who gets to say and confirm eternal truth, that is who. As the very God dispersed throughout the planet, His revelation of the Almighty, their world, and the Redeemer's history and destiny elevates heaven's doctrine from the worldly theologies and the cultural trends laboring to discredit them. It is unfortunate how many believers do not know there is a Holy Spirit and how vital He is to their earthly and eternal life. Those who have heard of Him cannot fathom who or what He is, let alone what He does. Yet, as the Lord Jesus declares in John chapter 5, He passes people from this world's death to God's eternal life. Subsequently, to secure their salvation, the

Christians have to be more than casually acquainted with God's whole word and His Holy Spirit. All believers should know what qualified His handpicked recorders and eyewitnesses to receive and publish the heavenly and earthly chronicles divulged to them.

Today's believers have to comprehend what Scripture writers collected and authenticated as their Savior's truth and grasp what it took for Him to trust humans with His hallowed mysteries. Before that happens though, they should be instructed on what He did within Scripture's genuine authors to enhance them to be deputed to make Him known to this world. They proved their integrity by their fastidious accounts of God's continuing[2] and connective[3] involvement in earthly and human affairs. Their approval yielded them more casual knowledge, it made their testimonies persuasive. Peter and other Scripture notables call those that passed the Lord's qualification tests, holy. They were certified by the Almighty as holy in every respect and therefore trustworthy enough to receive His thoughts and recollections and memorialize them for their own and future generations. He chose them to tell the future the Lord as God.

Holy is a very simple and by now easily trivialized term that back in Scripture's formative period carried enormous weight and respect. Back then, it inspired impressions of truthfulness, loyalty, and a conscientiousness worthy enough to bring to the world the otherwise unknowable and easily perverted revelations of its living God. Being so chosen, took a unique kind of individual. First off, such a scribe had to be in total accord with the Lord's Spirit and convinced of His immutable ways. Scripture's scribes to fulfill their tasks, did more than sit at the Lord's feet to hear what He would say and write it. Stringent lifestyle compliance and life experience assured that they qualified to report on Him accurately. Many of them endured human situations to relate to what He endured. Keenly relatable experiences, conditioned them to word, God's thoughts and experiences accurately. An instance of this is Hosea, who was told by God to marry a prostitute in order to express from the heart Yahweh's emotional struggle with His own wife's infidelity.

---

2 Meaning ceaseless, unbroken, and uninterrupted. Corresponds with later definitions of the word continuum.

3 Adjoining, connective, and adjacent. Corresponds with later expanded definitions of the word continuum.

HOLINESS, THE GOD CRITERIA

To emphasize the Scripture scribe's criteria, turn to Luke's words in Acts 3:21. He consults the holy writ's contributors as the eyewitness reporters that recorded what God spoke. He says that God's thoughts made their way into this world "by the mouth of His holy prophets". The passage's sentiment establishes that God has spoken to earth "since the world began." This repetitive phrase resurfaces variously throughout God's word. Paul underscores Luke's foundation in Ephesians 3:5. There he identifies those whom God entrusted with His ancient (and eternal) thoughts and witness. They are "His holy apostles and prophets." He also fixes the timing of their work, stating that it reaches back to "other ages." In 2 Peter 2:21, that distinguishment continues. There he designates what makes the Scriptures valid, "Holy men of God spoke as they were moved by the Holy Ghost." Collectively, their unsullied character insofar, as God is concerned, adds to the Bible's uniqueness.

WHAT MAKES THE HOLY BIBLE UNIQUE

What makes the Bible superb is that most sacred books used to compete with it were written by a single author, whose lone experience concocted the faith it promotes: not so with the Christian's Holy Bible. It was composed over a period of millennia by dozens and scores of scribes with nothing more in common than the God they served. Yet despite differing cultures, ethnicities, eras, and geographies they all managed to unfold the same story. Contiguously, Scripture scribes relay the same revelations about the one true God, the Judeo-Christian Messiah and His Father, the world's Creator. Now that is an incomparable feat! To depict the Lord as the God of all flesh, numerous scribes unveil Him. To depict Him as the ancient of days, changing cultures and countries record Him. To demonstrate His indomitable power over all the works of His hands, numerous historians narrate His exploits and affirm His redemption. To prove that He is the same yesterday, today, and forever, cascading witnesses preach His faith and righteousness. God's strategy is brilliant and effective. He uses His Scriptures to successfully and progressively, change the world, transforming nations and generations through it. Another thing that makes the Scriptures miraculous is that they are unlike their rival texts. The Christian Bible is for all humanity. They trace all peoples' histories, embrace all nations' lineages, and span ages. Moreover, they did so long before anything God made came into being. Reading the Bible intently fosters a rich appreciation of it that insightful godly teachers increases. Scripture readers who know their God take by faith that it needs no edits or updates.

The everlasting God, who is before and remains outside all time and generations penned His sacred writ when as yet there was no earth or humans. That is why Christians' sacred text can be counted on for enduring truth until the end of every age. Its enduring rationale is its inviolable premise. Christianity's God does not change. Besides that, the Devil He made cannot change. In addition, God's only remedy for what continues to afflict humanity, is the new birth. The Almighty's Scriptures, popularized by Moses and the Ten Commandments, came directly down from heaven. They are inspired by a world that long preexisted this one that controls every one of this world's events. These Bible basics open countless revelations and endless possibilities to those who read it. To sum this up, the capacity for revealing Scripture from heaven, neither begins nor ends with humans. It began with the Lord's holy angels. As it happens, the Continuum reveals them as the founders and maintainers of His first prophetic institution, not on earth but in heaven.

THE PROPHETS OFFICE WAS FIRST STAFFED WITH HOLY ANGELS

Matthew 25:31 says Jesus will return with "all the holy angels". Mark 8:38 notes He will enter His Father's glory along with the glory of "the holy angels". Luke modifies his restatement of The Messiah's advent by saying, *"For whosoever shall be ashamed of me and of my words, of him shall the Son of man be ashamed, when he shall come in his own glory, and in his Father's, and of the holy angels"*. Mark's gospel as received from the Holy Spirit who inspired his words on the glory awaiting Jesus as the Son of Man, presents the Son's glory as equal to His Father's, and that of the "holy angels" too. The Savior and His spiritual ministrants have a future glory into which each will enter as their earned rewards. Revelation 14:10 paints an even crisper picture: the beast and his followers suffer everlasting torment for their crimes against the Creator. Their judgment today is pending until the end of the Lord's disposition of this world and its inhabitants. As instruments of rebellion, they will agonize forever in hell, "in the presence of the holy angels and the presence of the Lamb". The conclusion here is the reality of a stratum of angels that serve as Jesus' prime ministers, and perhaps His prison guards. As members of His celestial court, they participate in the discharge of His Messianic office. These angels, as with the saints on earth, neither labor, nor are loyal in vain. They also have a promised hope, a majestic future in the Lamb's kingdom. The last case to confirm this truth is Revelation 22:9. It is almost a reiteration of Revelation 9:10. Look at it: *"And I fell down before his feet to worship him. And he saith unto me, see thou do it not: I am a fellow-servant with thee and with thy brethren that hold the testimony of Jesus: worship God; for the testimony of Jesus is the spirit of prophecy."* This is one of the strongest affirmations of the prophet's office in the New Testament. Now to address John's encounter with Christ's angel, the first of the two times he does so. As Jesus' apocalypse unfolds to him, John becomes so overwhelmed by the presence of the angel disclosing the revelation that he feels driven to worship him. The angel being the faithful messenger of the Lord that he is, unlike those of Jude, who left their first estate, does not exploit John's awe. Rather than allow the Lord's apostle to idolize (or deify) him, the angel restrains John, using some prophetically pragmatic reasons. He gives three reasons why it is improper for John to succumb to his misplaced veneration.

First, the angel tells John he also is John's fellow servant along with others who are like him. Second, the angel qualifies whom heaven regards as John's fellow servants. They are those of his brothers that hold fast to the "testimony of Jesus". Third, based on these two reasons, the angel commands John to worship God. A fourth comment places his admonitions in godly contexts. The angels affix their collective callings to the prophetic by saying: "The testimony of Jesus is the spirit of prophecy." Preemptively, the angel bounds up the totality of what is to be revealed to the earth in Jesus. This includes whatever is divulged to Christ's ministers and the prophesyings to come from both. Anything said about, from, or through Him, will testify of Him. Whereas Old Testament prophecies foretold Jesus' coming, the New Testament messenger brings forth His present day post Pentecost operations. What the angel is telling John is that whatever Jesus is saying is what His prophets are speaking. It does not matter what the issue, anything He discloses as God's Lion-Lamb is what His prophets are to propagate[1].

John continues to be so awed by the angel that a few chapters later he attempts to worship the messenger again. This time Revelation 22:9 records the angel giving the apostle a bit more awareness. *"And I, John, who have heard and seen these things. And, after I had heard and seen, I fell down to adore before the feet of the angel who shewed me the things. And he said to me: See thou do it not. For I am thy fellow servant, and of thy brethren the prophets and of them that keep the words of the prophecy of this book. Adore God.[4]"* The angel once more relates to John's office, "I am thy fellow servant", only this time he adds another piece to their connection. He too is a prophet[2]. Although the angel is certainly more superior in every way to John and the prophets on earth, and for sure, he has lived eons longer than the aged apostle has, he allies himself with John and the prophets in the world who "hold the testimony of Jesus Christ." As astounding as his disclosure is,

---

4 Revelation 22:8, 9, Douay-Rheims Bible.

it should come as no surprise. After all, the angel speaking to him is Christ's principal messenger, something the Lord reinforces in Revelation 22:16: *"I, Jesus, have sent my angel to give this testimony to you for the Churches. I am the root and the descendant of David, the bright and morning star."*

Obviously, the mere fact that the angel speaks from an eternal document, makes it replete with prophetic content. Its heavenly origin places the celestial messenger and the prophecy alongside John and the prophets. What astonishingly comes through is that angels are appointed to eternity's prophetic office in the same capacity as the humans appointed to it. In addition, the angels know that they collaborate with the Lord's earthly prophets, sharing the weight of their integrity in Christ's service. Angels began the Lord's prophetic institution in heaven before the earth was, which is why the Lord, so quickly instituted the office with Abel after Adam sold his seed and the world to Satan. These explanations further answer why the Lord gives so much credence to prophets and prophecy throughout Scripture. They further clarify why He continually promises His prophets vengeance and immense rewards in return for their abhorrent mistreatment by the world. Both prophecy and prophets have their roots in the Almighty's eternal world. They serve as His living library from which He draws contemporary generations' disclosures and records those it lives out in the flesh. Once He founded this world, He periodically dispatched to the earth Israel's and later the Church's[5] celestial excerpts of eternity's prophecy to advance His agenda and secure His people in the world. The angels that predate earthly prophets oversee Christ's prophetic institution. They are why and how God preserves, perpetuates, and progresses His Continuum. Such phrases in God's word as, "since the world began", "before the world began", "before the foundation of the world," and "since the foundation or creation of the world", all speak to the Continuum. Before the Lord endowed and endued clay people with His word and works, the angels were in His world doing what prophets do in this one. The way heaven inseminated and instituted prophetic ministry in the planet, and how it is discharged by His human offspring through them began in eternity and not on earth. The Lord initially preserved His Continuum by locking humans out of its heavenly secrets until Moses came. Unveiling and unraveling the Continuum increased after Yahweh birthed His earthly nation Israel. Its prophets actuated its disclosures as part of their ministry to His people and continued to do so until the time came for The Messiah's appearance. Later, when Jesus ar-

---

5 Revelation 1:20.

rived, He divulged what God hid in Him to His chosen disciples,[6] ending by His incarnation, a four hundred year prophetic silence. Until then, handpicked prophets spoke to Yahweh's nation and others, steadily releasing to the world the encoded prophecies that ultimately brought Jesus Christ and Christianity into it via the Holy Spirit. Transmitting His future through His angels, the Lord personally saw that His word was performed rightly by uttering it exclusively to His holy prophets. He instructed them to record their messages for His future posterity the generation to come that Isaiah 53:8 identifies as the Christ generation. See below for how important generations[7] are to the Lord. There is so much to glean from Scripture's constant references to generations, most of which assert that Christ has been around forever and will continue until the last generation is born. Not only that, but the Creator took time to plan the lives of every generation and assigned each one prophecies, and angels to see to their maintenance and fulfilled purposes.

---

6 Later discussions add the antediluvian and ancient prophets pre-Abraham and before Moses. See Romans 5:12-14 and 1 Corinthians 15:22.

7 Psalm 71:18; 78:4; 78:6; 102:18; 112:2;145:4.

[3]

Angels The Almighty's First Point of Contact

A ngelic prophets' timeless experience with the Lord qualifies them as His first point of contact when it comes to what He wants to happen in this world. They in turn pass on His will and plans to human vessels, often beginning with His prophets. This is a primary reason why so many prophets come face to face with the Lord's otherworldly powers and agencies. It has to do with how they receive their divine communications, which is typically through angels. The angels are the bridge that connects the Almighty's eternal world with this one, to ensure that what He appointed for it occurs on time. The value of these disclosures to the Continuum is immense and serves to validate the prophet's prominent position in it. They also validate the office's continuance to the end of time. The angels undergird their human counterparts, which is why God holds His prophets accountable through His angels.[8] It is further why prophets are duty bound to the Continuum that was first upheld by angels.

Human prophets must recognize the angels' existence and biblical history shows most of them did. That recognition is what the Angel of the Apocalypse sought to impress upon John. He wanted Christ's apostle to realize the long partnership human messengers shared with the Lord's divine ones. Angels, as celestial messengers also have ministries to fulfill, prophecies to manifest, and missions to answer to the Most High God for on Jesus' behalf. Their initiatives and ongoing involvement demon-

---

[8] Exodus 23:23; 32:34.

strate how the Continuum passes from eternity to time, from angels to people, and from generation to generation. A reality that shows why prophets do not have to make up the word of the Lord and how those that do may be detected as false prophets, or at least how their errant messages can be tagged as false prophecy. Learning and applying the Continuum's gauges is the only reliable way to do so. The angels received everything God appointed for His family in their ages and generations, long before the world began or the need for a redeemed human race arose. Therefore, they above all know what He calls truth. Angels received (and continue to receive) firsthand everything God does, assigns, and executes through them along with the means and methods He planned to bring their messages to pass. Angelic ministerial duties and responsibilities are mirrored by earthly vessels and functioned long before they were sub-delegated to human counterparts. These are what the Lord's angel in the Apocalypse firmly and insightfully imprints on John the Revelator's soul. His stress bears witness with Ephesians 3:15 and explains Ephesians 3:10. A final, yet highly relevant, example of this is Melchizedek's everlasting priesthood. It functioned in heaven and on earth centuries before Levi was born, says Hebrews chapter 7 and several other passages. The Bible contains many such examples to prove how true Solomon's words are. There is indeed "nothing new under the sun and that which is has already been."[9]

CELESTIALS GUARD THE CONTINUUM

In reflecting on the foregoing discussions, three things emerge from the Apocalyptic Angel's assertions. What they all share is continuity. First, angels predate God's physical creation. Second, celestial beings are subrulers in the Most High's realms. Third, what governs this world is but an abstract of what has administrated the Almighty's invisible creation before time. Each angelic prophet's service background and ministry regardless of the era, corroborates and preserves the single thread running throughout the Continuum that encases God's experiences with His invisible creation. Today, faithful prophets brought into the Continuum likewise keep to the same standard. Early prophets, in bringing the world the Scriptures, carefully sought to ensure their words did not unsay a previous prophet's word or discredit his or her ministry and mantleship. Their integrity impressively harmonizes the Scriptures. It is as if their contributors all lived at the same time, in the same place, sharing the

---

[9] Ecclesiastes 3:14, 15. Reading the passage in the context of the Continuum unveils profound revelations concerning this world and God's, and His long time dealings with the earth.

same happenings at once, except they did not. Unanimously, they tell the Lord's story corroboratively, maintaining its commonality and quality. How they did so is a phenomenon that can only be explained by one phrase, God's Eternal Continuum. Their ability to do so could only have come from being briefed on this and the Almighty's world by His angels. Evidently, before God made the earth, His angels administrated His creation wide prophetics. Meaning by this that the Lord's thoughts, will, and governance were disseminated and executed by chosen celestials, when as yet the prophetic had yet to be required on earth. The Lord's angels recorded related excerpts of their world government and culture for this one and stored them in heaven to remain a Creator mystery when this world began.

Despite all of His indisputable achievements, repeatedly throughout the ages God's word, the Scriptures, and the person of Jesus Christ as the word incarnate undergo relentless assaults. Their truths are chronically attacked from every side for various reasons, some practical, and others diabolical. Whichever is the case, the Scriptures, how they came to be, and who made the decisions concerning them grapple with cunningly contrived plots to discredit them. Each new generation perpetuates it. To mitigate some of the effects, the Continuum records how the Almighty's antagonists go all the way back to before the earth's time to embolden present eras to contend with Scripture resistance. Tracing His most formidable antagonists, exposes their long ago, defeats and reports how the Most High ousted their immaterial agencies from His world. Such exposures hide in their core, God's Eternal Continuum to prove to those that believe how and why Jesus Christ is the world's only Savior. The Continuum highlights the very Jesus that many scholars treat as just coming into existence when He appeared on earth. That He is the everlasting eternal God who made all that there is, seen or unseen, escapes many despite what John 1:3 and 10 say. The two references reveal who Jesus is, why He is God, and suggest how He made such reverberating world impact in a brief period of time that, on the surface appears to have ended ignobly for Him. Uncorking these truths strengthen Christian faith to deflect all the controversy routinely surrounding Jesus Christ and Christianity.

The Bible's revelatory potency hinges on what the Almighty's everlasting Continuum purveys and protects as it discloses what God's angels handed off to His prophets and His apostles. [10] Much more can be said about the indomitable and inviolable eternal force the Lord counted on more than He has any human before His incarnated Son or since His return home. The angels that stayed with the Most High through His most

---

[10] Review Ephesians 2:20; 3:15, and Revelation 18:20.

difficult eras resolved that He is forever their one and only God, before the Maker ever said, "Let there be" in this world. Their tests proved their allegiance to Him and their fidelity to His way. Stringent testing that occurred during the first of the Continuum's fourteen events assure the Lord that whatever He entrusts to His holy angels is carried out the way He wants and turns out the way He decreed in His world. For obvious reasons, neither He nor they rely on this creation to fulfill His words, only theirs.

ANGELS' WERE FIRST TO OCCUPY GOD'S ECCLESIAL OFFICES

Hebrews 12:22-24 abounds with eternity's architectural (and infrastructural) wisdom. Almost casually, it discloses profound mysteries about God's world. The phrase that fits here is "an innumerable company of angels" who are citizens of His heavenly world. This comment looks back to Deuteronomy 33:2, "*And he said, The Lord came from Sinai, and rose up from Seir unto them; he shined forth from mount Paran, and he came with ten thousands of saints: from his right hand went a fiery law for them.*"[3] What has been said so far highlights the angels' eternal role in God's world, its governance, and administration. Consequently, they show up in Scripture as messengers more than anything else does.

To paint a vivid picture of God's eternal messaging staff, take as a for instance, the angel Gabriel's New Testament visits to earth. Although he appears out of nowhere, his actions are reported as if they are commonplace as far as the Lord is concerned. Luke's gospel records how Gabriel returns to the planet to ignite two additional phases of the Lord's Continuum plan. He came to enable two impossible pregnancies to set the stage for the planet to rollover from its BC to AD eras. One was an elderly woman and the other a Yahweh verified virgin. Centuries before Gabriel's Jerusalem visit, he shows up in the Old Testament during Israel's Babylonian exile. Daniel's prophecy records this angel's[11] divine assignment on the planet more than once, eons later he shows up to carry out another of the Lord's prophecies. Taking his customary human form while radiating as one from another world, Gabriel appears in the Lord's temple to Zacharias the High Priest.[12] The angel had come to empower Zacharias to impregnate his aged post-menopausal wife Elizabeth, with The Messiah's forerunner, John the Baptist. After doing so, he lingers in the planet for a while. About ninety days later, the angel next visits a young woman, Mary, Elizabeth's relative who is to be The

---

11 Daniel 8:16; 9:21.
12 Luke 1:19, 26.

Messiah's mother. She evidently built a tremendous relationship with Israel's God that rewarded her with becoming the Virgin Mary. Gabriel finds her in the countryside where she must have been accustomed to worshipping the Lord. Presumably caught up in what must have been for her and the Lord, a particularly charged exultant worship, Mary is stunned by his arrival. The Lord timed the moment perfectly. Astounded that an angel appeared to her, Mary learns Yahweh was about to impregnate her with Israel's Messiah. To reiterate, this is the very angel that told Daniel way back in time that what the Lord spoke through him was already written in the Scripture of Truth.[13]

To recall the incident that led him to reveal this to Daniel, God sends the angel Gabriel in answer to his twenty-one day prayer vigil.[14] When he breaks his more than three week fast, Gabriel answers the prophet from a book of Scripture that had yet to be delivered to the earth. At that time, today's Book of Daniel did not exist. The prophet was still living out its transmission through dreams, visions, and angelic visitations predicting unfolding world events. So where did the angel get the prophecies he uttered to Daniel? He said they came from "the Scripture of truth." What Gabriel revealed to Daniel, he implies came from heaven's archives; the same place the angel of the Lord Jesus that visited John got his words from when he appeared to him on the Isle of Patmos. Jesus, being the very God Himself, brought a significant portion of His heavenly library with Him to utter His good news to the planet. Dubbed the gospels, they contained His fulfilled and undivulged prophecy, ecclesial seeds, and global takeover subtleties. All of these were secreted away in heaven's eternal archives dynamically working beneath the surface of the Lord's Continuum. The Author of that same gospel dispatched Gabriel to Zechariah and Mary to set prophecy's wheels in motion once again to fulfill the Lord's eternal word. This insight informs the many people who do not know that what the Church calls Bible stories, the Lord uttered as revelatory engines to propel the future. Prophecy thrusts creation forward into its predestined future with the Most High God. It is amplified by the voices He empowers to detect and decree it.

THE ESSENCE OF PROPHECY

---

13 Daniel 10:21, KJV.
14 See 9 and 10 of his prophecy.

The essence of prophecy is declaring a deity's word before they happen. With the Lord's prophets, it goes way beyond just picking up normally inaudible words and uttering them in the physical world. God's prophecies, as has been shown, come from His extensive library of lives, souls, and preordained events. Excerpts from these writings compiled the Bible, the Christian's sacred text. Prophecy springs from the Almighty's heavenly writ[4] and is engrafted in creation to execute what He wants to produce or perform at preappointed times. God's archival writings are what His angel Gabriel calls the "Scripture or volume of truth". They are what His heavenly and earthly messengers disseminate. Eternity's records are broadcasted to the world as prophecy, revelation, God's laws, and divine commands. Since the Lord does everything by His word, what has been unfolding as divine revelation since before this world was, are priestly extracts from His temple libraries. Classified secrets intelligently and dynamically manifest on earth what is etched in His divine chronicles. Distributed throughout human genetics and cosmic objects, the Lord's angels deliberately discharge His word, often automatically. They in turn impart His prophecies to their assigned human messengers. To equip people to hear and perform His word, God engrafts all divine communicators with His intelligence so they spontaneously declare His foreordained will on earth in their chosen generations. To this end, He either embeds messages in their makeup to release in response to corresponding divine triggers, or He drops them in the prophets' mouths to prophesy when time, circumstance, and hearer converge. Whichever one it is, prophecy is informing the earth, what its God discloses to it.

Humanity's transitoriness, coupled with its frailty and errancy, demands its Maker resort to numerous human-like devices to unveil His divine past and present, and to manifest His world and its inhabitants. To pass His vision for humanity on to them to live out required a recorded prescription of how life will be lived in His created worlds. Such records of His divine revelation (Balaam calls them the visions of the Almighty) constitute prophecy, and spell out the days of every creature's and object's life on earth.[15] It is jolting for people to realize such documents exist anywhere that hold the whole of humanity's existence in it, and that is where their problems with God begin. It is discomforting to think that the entirety of the world's infinitum populations is bound up in one being's will. Living with that reality is hard for everyone, and for some people it is downright impossible. Few want to know that before time, the Lord anticipated every response to His sovereignty and predetermined His reac-

---

15 Psalm 139:16.

tions to them. Living with the knowledge that God detailed for His angels, and voices through His prophets, how everything would be handled in advance challenges many people on earth. Some people find it so unnerving that it drives them to unbelief. In response, these souls devise their own answers to life to spite God, and lo, false prophecy and false religions are born. Yet, there are those who celebrate God's dominion and prudence. They find it encouraging. Coming to terms with God's omniscience settles for them the mystifying answers to life and death.

Every day, prophets renouncing the Lord Jesus, miss how "all that is" came to be. They wade through mountains of error to manufacture believable answers to His presolved issues. In contrast, the prophets that tell God's real story, tap into His mysteries to release well-timed secrets hidden for ages to come. These spokespeople declare what they know about the Lord not just from ancient earthly records, but also from His eternal archives. The Lord teaches these messengers how to confirm what they prophesy is from Him. Those that get their prophecies from the Almighty, never have the questions the world's prophets pose because of the Continuum. They know where their prophecies originate and use that wisdom to verify what they hear in a moment is indeed the word of the Lord. Eternal inside knowledge makes Christian prophets, God's divine guardians along with the angels. For prophets to gain widespread legitimacy has since time immemorial been a formidable obstacle. Almost reflexively, they are excluded from respectable prophetic ministrations. The prophetic's age-old opposition has fueled much of people's love-hate relationship with prophets and prophecy. On the one hand, both wrestle with hostile resistance and backlash. On the other hand, they are sought out for their greatest benefit; tomorrow's answers, today. However, people want a means of testing their prophecies and of assuring what prophesiers claim to speak to them in the name of the Lord is actually so. The need to verify prophets and authenticate their prophecies has proven a stubborn problem for the Lord and His people down through the years. Of course, everyone wants to solve the matter quickly and easily. If only, there was a single instrument to speed up the process a bit. The issue is that the Lord's verifiers are often dismissed in favor of more human or secular resources, believed to be more expedient. Unfortunately, they are not, because truth takes time, and that is what God's prophets bring to the world, truth, His truth. Waiting for evolving human events, actions, and consequences, indeed all of prophecy's sources to prove themselves, takes time. Until the prophet's word comes to pass, the more sure word of prophecy is God's Holy Scriptures. If a prophet is true, the Scriptures are where prophetic audiences are told by God to turn to verify what is prophesied to them, or at least where they should turn. For this advice to be reliable, a prophet must be found faithful to the Lord. In the final analysis, prophet integrity and accuracy start with the messenger's fidelity to God, and that is not automatic. There is no magical, spiritual formula for confirming prophecy other than God's word and His Holy Spirit. Both are intrinsic to His Continuum and serve as its supervising agents and protectants. Having proven that divine communications reach all the way back to eternity and God's staff, Gabriel's Scripture of truth is undeniably the Most High's official writings preordained for His prophets to divulge in their respective eras and spheres. Those writings provide the sole source of trustable future telling. They put forth godly wisdom and disclose normally restricted heavenly counsel. To this end, the Creator prepared ageless compendiums that document His private, public, and sovereign life to be disseminated throughout His worlds.

A preternal canon spells out His thoughts, reveals His will, and articulates His providential operations that served Him prior to His creative acts. Of these, the Christian Bible contains only a fraction. Romans 15:4 and 1 Corinthians 15:4 say why.

> "For whatsoever things were written aforetime were written for our learning, that we through patience and comfort of the scriptures might have hope." Romans 15:4.

> "Now all these things happened unto them for ensamples: and they are written for our admonition, upon whom the ends of the world are come.", 1 Corinthians 10:11.

God leaves it up to the Holy Spirit to fill in Scripture gaps with visions, dreams, trances, and revelations. Here is why the gifts and manifestations of the Holy Spirit are so important to Jesus Christ, His messengers and ministers. The Lord stashed infinite versions of His all-inclusive word in His secret library, with only slivers of it unveiled to the world by His Spirit at pre-appointed times. When appropriate, He unlocks another phase of His plan to usher in a new age in the world to advance His plans. The Lord's starts with through His angels, but it is transmitted to the world by them under His Holy Spirit's auspices, the principal transmitter of God's truth. It is what Acts 2:17, 18 relay, bringing it forward from Joel 2:28 and 29. Such words as *aforetime, predestined*, and *predetermined* had to get their start from somewhere, and according to Romans 15:4; Titus 1:2 and numerous other passages they did. The terms describe the Lord's actions and decisions etched in, and for His creation prior to, its existence that He filed away with a host of books, or scrolls, waiting for their time to speak. For instance, the Book of Life and all of the other books in the Bible substantiate this truth. The largest unveilings of the Lord's eternal word came to Moses, the prophets, the

Lord Jesus, and His apostles. The second most dramatic of them is John's Revelation joined by the Lord Jesus' Gospels. Heavenly texts have always comprised Jehovah's supernal Scripture of truth. Since before all time and before <u>every</u> world their words governed, guided, and oversaw the creation from the beginning of His work.[16] Seemingly endless volumes map out the Lord's movements and actions according to plan. He is not working out His will and outcomes as He goes along. He is performing what He wrote long ago using chronicled foreknowledge as the means, revelation as the method, and prophecy as the media by which He rules the world and redeems His eternal offspring. All of this says His long-standing plan has forever been in effect. Much of what the traditional church models as redemption limits to life under the sun, Scripture proves has been a struggle for the Almighty before any world began. These statements say why, and how, God's sin issue started in heaven and not in Eden as is traditionally taught.

---

[16] See Proverbs 8:12-31.

[4]

God's Redemptive Issues Began in Heaven, Not Eden

The Continuum weaves revelation, prophecy, and the Lord Jesus Christ in all His glory as they are captured in the Scripture. It demonstrates to the world the Most High God's passions and ageless conflicts with His creation. God's Eternal Continuum asserts His struggles began, not in the Garden of Eden as many suppose, but in His own world with His supernal citizens. Moreover, the stories revisited here are not just about the Creator's struggle with the innumerable free wills He granted, but also about the Scriptures that reveal the Christ was alongside Him in it all. The battle that begins the first of the Continuum's Fourteen Events is unrelenting and its agents ruthless. Both sides clash over who shall inherit or disinherit the Lord's eternal life. In this vein, Matthew 11:12 makes greater sense when one realizes that the Lord was speaking of all His worlds' proverbial collision with the evil angels that fought to be liberated from Jesus and His Father's rule. If that were all, perhaps things would not have become as dismal as they did, but that was not all. Heaven's revolutionaries aimed for the Godhead's total dethronement and utter annihilation of its forces. A complete takeover and nothing less than a complete takeover of its citizenry was the objective. Anything short of that would render their efforts null and void. The matter forever settled heaven's conquest in the fight long before Adam's seed populated the earth.

Humans always eye God's foreknowledge suspiciously when they try to make sense of what appears to them to be utterly senseless. How else can one explain the darkness and wickedness of this planet except that its Maker is either destroyed, dense, or completely out of control? Earth's dismality suggests His creatures hold Him captive to their will instead of the reverse. Nonetheless, the reverse is true, God is shrewdly in charge. Despite the myriad of eschatological skepticism to the contrary, the Lord is well in control and working out an eternal plan designed to take this world to the end of time. Take predestination as a for instance. Truly, the question is bigger than this world, and if the Savior's words may be taken at face value, it spans all creation's in-habited realms. The controversy over who makes it into heaven and who does not, how and why, are the crux of the afterlife. The key to predestination hinges on whether or not, God actually knows who will be saved in the end; to which Jesus im-plies He does. The issue extends to whom He decided will or will not reign with Him forever, and is that decision already made too. Again, Jesus asserts that He does, and it is. It does not matter how many opt to believe God wants to be as surprised as hu-mans are at who makes it into heaven and who does not, the truth is that simply can-not be the case. Else, He is not God, but an alien from another world trying to impose itself on this one, the famous sci-fi motif dramatists like to propagate. Is the Almighty the omniscient God that He purports to be by His ministers? Or, is His knowledge of the past, present, and future limited to... what exactly? If He is all the Scripture says about Him, then nothing is unknown to Him. This is consistent with what 1 John 1:5 asserts; "God is light and in Him is no darkness at all." Could that mean He knows the end from the beginning of everything and if so, how does that work with predestina-tion and free will?

God's world has ruled for eons[17] before this one. His invisible civilization—its knowledge, culture, and technologies—outstrip earth's by leagues. If their world moves faster than light, since it originated with them and because this one is drasti-cally slower than theirs, then it would seem the events lived out on earth are well known by their world ages way ahead of earth's time. That being true, whoever dies tomorrow has been known by them for ages, as Samuel's announcement to Saul when he visits the witch of Endor shows.[5] Being roused from the peaceful side of hell, Samuel ends his discourse with Saul by announcing that on the next day (metaphori-cally or perhaps otherworldly speaking) he (Saul) and his sons will join the celebrated prophet they rejected on earth in death. The idea that makes the point is that Samuel knew what Saul with certainty could not know. That is the outcome of the king's im-pending battle with the Philistines, which the long departed from this world knows from his afterlife-resting place. The implications of the boundaries dividing the two worlds back then are immense. It is those boundaries, and God's foreknowledge that

---

17 In addition to the Genesis creation account, see Proverbs 8:22-29.

give predestination its grip. The question then is not if predestination is of God, but rather can God know the whole future or does He merely guess at parts of it?

THE CONTINUUM AND PREDESTINATION

Is predestination valid and binding? Framing the question within the context of God's eternality, omniscience, and omnipresence, the obvious answer to predestination is absolute. God absolutely knows who and what comes and goes out of His planet, which raises another question. Did He choose who is to be saved and live with Him forever; or did He leave that up to chance? If He left it up to chance, then He did so by blinding Himself to what He already knew before life anywhere began outside Him. However, the Continuum addresses that too with the same pragmatism. If God knows all, then He is well able to judge the behaviors and conduct that displeases Him and those that will clash with His makeup in His world. Once more, when posed this way the conclusion is obvious, because there can be no reasonable one other than, He knows. Nevertheless, to support the most logical response calls for seeing the person of God as distinct from the institutions He appointed to oversee His worlds. If one stays with the institutions and ignores their Author and Creator, then any answer to any of earth's issues will suffice. If one instead begins with the Author of those institutions, then a series of other considerations must be taken into account, and to reiterate, that is the work of the Continuum. When it comes to who will live forever with the Lord and who will not, God's position is this. Despite what He knows in His spirit and by the Holy Spirit, those affected by God's inner knowledge are ignorant to His foreknowledge. Just because the Lord knows in heaven those who will accept or reject Him on earth, does not mean everything He gave life and consciousness to share His knowledge. What the Almighty thought through and now comprehends is a mystery to the rest of His creatures. They must see His foreknowledge work out in their realms to appreciate His final judgments. In addition, the free will liberties God grants every intelligent being is merely a spiritual provision until it takes on flesh in this world. Sperms and eggs must become humans to explore their reactions to God, and appreciate His righteousness. To exit earth's mortalities, free will agents must choose to surrender their mortal liberties to the Most High's eternal obediences to pass from death to life because in Adam, all die. People do not know how they feel about the Lord until they encounter Him. They do not know if they approve of His way enough to choose, and live with it on earth or if they prefer the pleasures of this life instead. Such decisions are only appointed to the earth and can only be made by those inhabiting clay vessels. In addition the spiritual agents who must guard God's world and bar those disqualified from it are also precluded from the Most High's foreknowledge. It is their task to maneuver human's salvation opportunities, according to His plan. Remember Peter said that even the angels desired to look into human salvation and Hebrews declared that Jesus did not give aid to angels. Therefore, their ages of experiences aside, the celestial beings are just as in the dark about their human charges' final decisions as the soul making the choices is. Therefore, what God understands from within Himself is only part of it. In the end His justice and mercy must be verified and His judgment vindicated by everything He made. He subjects Himself to the judicial scrutiny of a myriad of guardians, witnesses, and adversaries that subsist on His life. They must all conclude He is just in His final disposition of a soul leaving this world. What shows up in this world must prove beyond a doubt that His dispositions are righteous, according to His Continuum as publicized by those who uphold it. The spiritual ignorance born in people prevents them from otherworldly knowledge and even from penetrating the deep sentiments of their own hearts. As a result, they must act out what they are often unable to think through to confront God's life consequences and their impressions of them. Since they are not born in heaven, what heaven presages about them is irrelevant. What they do in the flesh decrees their eternal choices and proves what the Lord appointed those who make their choices is true and just. So what is this Continuum? The short answer, for the purposes of this work, is the chain of contiguous and indivisible events that brought Jesus Christ and Christianity to this world, and that which will get His offspring into His. When speaking of Christianity, this discussion considers four of its most authoritative components that qualify one to receive the reward of eternal life. The four are entrances into: 1) The Messiah's faith, 2) Jesus' lineage, 3) the Son of God's nation, and 4) naturalized citizenship in its eternal[6] kingdom. Converts to Christ must be whisked from this world, to His, first spiritually and ultimately naturally. All of it begins outside of time and ends when time is no more. How God makes this happen is via the New Creation Church that Hebrews 12 suggests has always existed in another form and place. That revelation explains Ephesians 1:3; 2:6 and 3:10. Using the earth as a kind of molding, filtering, and readiness station, the word *Continuum* best describes what the Almighty deems the most suitable way to extend His kingdom. It further outlines how He prepares His next (and final) generation to populate His new world. Before going any further though, some relevant Scriptures are needed to prime the mind for this teaching's proper consideration.

CONTINUUM HINTS IN SCRIPTURE

The undergirding Scripture for the Fourteen Events Continuum is Matthew 1:17.

> "So all the generations from Abraham to David are fourteen generations; and from David until the carrying away into Babylon are fourteen generations; and from the carrying away into Babylon unto Christ are fourteen generations." KJV.

With this is Matthew 1:1 that traces the kingship of Jesus from Abraham through David to establish Him as the promised Messiah.

> "The book of the generation of Jesus Christ, the son of David, the son of Abraham".

To emphasize the contiguity of the above two passages, there is Luke 21:32 that says,

> "Verily I say unto you, this generation shall not pass away, till all be fulfilled."

As for the Old Testament's foretokens on this subject, there is Isaiah 53:8: "He was taken from prison and from judgment: and who shall declare his generation? For he was cut off out of the land of the living: for the transgression of my people was he stricken". To this add, Acts 8:33: "In his humiliation his judgment was taken away: and who shall declare his generation? For his life is taken from the earth." A passage that intriguingly attaches the three references to the Christ Generation is 1 Peter 2:9: "But ye are a chosen generation, a royal priesthood, an holy nation, a peculiar people; that ye should shew forth the praises of him who hath called you out of darkness into his marvellous light." This passage turns out to be properly related to Genesis 2:4; 5:1 and those below. It reinforces the connecting strands of the Continuum that are reiterated by the Bible's almost two hundred references to the generations. The generations that once were, were to come, to remain forever, and follow successively are what is meant. What could these statements propose except that the Lord is the single common link in His Continuum? The Godhead alone extends its existence and supremacies from age to age, generation to generation, and eternity to eternity, working all things together for its own good. Everything is for the collective glory of manifesting God's eternal righteousness.[18] Several words speak to the Lord's Continuum. They include, but are not limited to:

1. *Ages* – Time winding down
2. *Eternity* – Time that began all time that is without beginning or ending

---

18 Psalm 74:12; John 5:17; Acts 13:55; Acts 3:21; Luke 24:44; Acts 24:14.

3. *Everlasting* – Time with a beginning that never ends

4. *Generations* – Time measured by the birth and prominence of a group of people that make up a cohesive period or life span on earth

5. *Perpetual* – Time that begins and continues due to enactments or similar legislation

6. *Forever* – Time that marks the commencement of something that is designed to repeat or sustain itself without end

7. *Memorial* – Time marked by an event that altered how life, living, or progress began that is revisited or celebrated annually or at some other cyclical period

8. *Never* – The absence of time or any events to record it

A single word that encompasses the full scope of the Continuum in essence and effect is the word **perpetual.** It covers every aspect and intent for the Continuum. The Old Testament Scripture uses the word more than a dozen times for God's ordinances, judgments, statues, generations, and similar objects. The prophets mostly apply the word to various sin related consequences. The New Testament expresses perpetual as forever. What makes it worthy of inclusion in God's Continuum is what Scripture depicts as integral to God's history. Whatever the Lord classified as perpetual is never ending, which makes sense seeing as He is eternal. That means what He classifies as such is not subject to the Old or New Testament dispensations thought to mark or limit their eras, but extends to eternity because everything that exists originated there in some way or another. Think about what the Lord calls perpetual to discover why His choices earned the distinction of being never-ending. Doing so richly enhances appreciation of their value to the Maker's Eternal Continuum. In reviewing them, also consider some relevant Scripture passages that may explain (or substantiate) them from the Old and New Testaments that contain or address what Scripture records as perpetual.

As with the word *perpetual*, so it is with the word *ages*. Numerous passages reflect its connection to the Most High's unending continuity and His Continuum objectives. Using temporal emblems and objects, He was resorted to penetrating the spiritual darkness that prevents His beloved humanity from discerning or comprehending Him. What these all share is their illustration of the Most High's eternal everlastings as typified in fifteen different objects, observances, and activities that span heaven and earth. Right after it, the differences between eternal and everlasting are discussed. Below two Continuum phrases that show what motivated the application of the word perpetual to the Lord's eternality.

Eternal vs. Everlasting

The Continuum teaching would be sorely wanting if the two terms that hold it together were ignored. They are the words *eternal* and *everlasting*. The Continuum is about what began in God's world that sojourned through the earth realm to end it all where it began, in God's world. The eternal part of the journey is the beginning, the sojourning part is the everlasting, and the ending part brings it full circle, back in God's world to merge the two words' meanings and intent. Briefly, that is the Continuum in effect and its inseparable bond with eternity.

In thinking about the word **eternal**, the question is how often does it appear in the Bible and in what ways does the Lord use it in His Scriptures? By its mere definition, the word eternal qualifies for inclusion in God's Continuum string. Scripture attaches many things to the word *eternal* to reflect God's pre-world items and issues. Exploring it is beneficial because a real grasp of the Lord's Continuum rests on a comprehensive understanding His view of the word *eternal*. It is equally important to discern how the Lord distinguishes it from the word *everlasting* so commonly treated as a synonym for it. Beginning logically with God who is eternal, all of the objects of His eternality categorize what began in Him as well as what proceeded from Him. For example, Jesus began in God the Father the way future children get their start from within their parents, especially the babes originating in the father's sperm and growing in the mother's womb. However, everything else proceeds from God. They come into being outside of His person as the work of His hands. It does not matter if something comes from His mind, like for instance His judgments, His expressions, His will, or from His creativity. Everything in one way or another results from His initiatives and is therefore subject to His determined outcomes. This is up to and including hell's fires.

Everlasting

In contrast to the word *eternal*, there is the word **everlasting** that seems to be almost its equivalent. However, looking at its applications below reveals that is not exactly the case. There are marked differences between the two terms. The word *eternal* is not precisely like everlasting even though it means never ending. Likewise, the word everlasting has inferences of eternal in it, but falls short in its beginning. Both words refer to what is never ending, but only one has no beginning. To be more precise one word means outside of time and the other originates in time but extends beyond it. The word <u>everlasting</u> as presented in Scripture is applied below. Its worth to the Continuum is expressed in the statements contained in ways the word is used in the Bible. Research it for all of the things the Lord made outside Himself to last forever.

There are about forty-two everlastings contained in Scripture to lay out what the Lord prepared subsequent to His eternal self and its world. They express what He designed exclusively for His temporal civilizations to enfold them eventually into His eternal one as they conform to or serve Him. Whichever it is, the point to be taken is that everlasting means just what it says and implies. It defines something with a definite beginning that lasts forever being engineered to outlast and function beyond earth's time-bound laws and limits. Hence, both durability and perpetuity are at the heart of everlasting. While eternal, in comparison, innately encompasses both durability and perpetuity, it is not because either one existed before what they apply to was made or born. Eternity stresses predating everything, before time and earth came into being. It is God's actual self and what it produced or projected. Prior to the Continuum's first event, there was no corruption, no cessation; no trouble, sorrow, fear, war, or the like. At the outset, durability and perpetuity were innate to everything the Lord made in heaven. After the first Continuum event, their antithesis and everything else for that matter came into existence, making it necessary for God to create restorative powers and conditions to perpetuate His celestial world. The necessity came from its need to survive the dark atrocities the serpent's rebellion bred in it. Thus, eternality gave way to everlasting; meaning by this that the eternal state of God's world once marred by Continuum number one, caused adaptations to be made until something, or someone brought about the restitution of all things. Once created, those adaptations and consolations, like durability and perpetuity, became implements of the Almighty's corrective works. From their inception onward, God reserved the two powers in anticipation of future need, in case He had to remedy similar inevitable disruptions in His other planetary civilizations. Should later worlds' initial purity be destroyed, these two resources would be drawn on to compensate for their less than pristine condition and keep them running, despite their downgrade. When it came to earth's creation, eternality came off the table and everlasting became the standard because anything everlasting could be repaired; what is eternal must be quarantined; think about hell. Explanations leading to this conclusion are plausible, particularly since heaven's record shows what happened to earth had already happened before in God's world, making the likelihood of history repeating itself predictable and providentially remediable. Examining the words eternal and everlasting strongly surface the Continuum's validity in God's world and every other one He made. Previous discussions already substantiated Scripture writers' deliberate choice of the two words as the best ones to convey God's prelife and afterlife preparations. Their writings lay out the ways eternal and everlasting are applied in His world and imposed on this one.

DELIBERATELY CHOSEN WORDS

Traditional theologians, in preparing their discussions of God's world, often treat the terms eternal and everlasting as synonyms. Doing so superficially characterizes what the Most High appointed as His time zones with those of the earth. In reality, though, the words, despite their synonymic allusions, carry only cursory similarities. In contrast to later theologies, Scripture writers chose both terms to contrast the Almighty's prelife[19] with humanity's afterlife. They were not penned to use interchangeably or synonymically. Just to show the Almighty, as the beginning and the end of all He brought into existence. Eternal and everlasting jointly epitomizes the Most High's jurisdictions over time and timelessness. The most telling value of the difference between the two terms is when a person dies. Take for instance when decedents leave this planet. What immediately brings them under the supernal laws and governors of God's world, and which ones do they come under? The answer has to do with how real God, the real God, was to the person in life and how genuine their desire to spend forever with Him was before they died.

If people are filled with God's eternal Spirit when they die, then they are deemed qualified to live in the light and the life of His eternal world. If on the other hand, they leave planet earth devoid of God's eternal Spirit that is appointed to pass them from death to life,[7] they are doomed to spend their eternity banished from the Godhead's presence because they are void of its light and life and any means of obtaining it. This is the Maker's definition of death. Without the indwelling Holy Spirit, *earthly* life for departed mortals translates to *eternal* death in God's afterlife.[8] With this explanation in mind, it becomes clear why and how everlasting and eternal applies to everything God made, no matter what it is. Still, two isolating factors make the final decision on which side of either one a person lives forever. The first is the status of the human spirit. The second is the condition of the human soul. Both of them determine the eternal destination with the condition of the soul ultimately deciding if everlasting

---

19 A life lived before one's life on earth; earlier than; before; prior to; beforehand, (Onelook Dictionary) (Bible Hub)anterior.

life is in God's light or hell's darkness. Here is how it works. The redeemed life is authorized by the brand new spirit given to betoken eternal life. The new spirit is an exact version of what unites the Godhead; so in a way, the convert is absorbed into it. The new creation spirit is the first and most important eternal life qualifier. It is how Paul can say in Ephesians 2:6 that the Christian is seated in heavenly places in Christ Jesus. The Lord's deposit of the new creation spirit and the indwelling Holy Spirit are the first and most essential afterlife determinants. They are the only way a person inherits eternal life. This determinant is joined by the Spirit's illumination of the human soul. Here, the new creation spirit acts on the dark dead soul to transform it into what God decrees is compatible with His world. This is the second factor, and it governs where and with whom mortal beings departing this world will abide forever.[20] These two requisites decide which dimension of the Lord's eternal and everlasting life those who die in this world enter. None of this is in the decedent's power before or after death. It is only in this world the privilege of rejecting or accepting Jesus Christ is granted. Beyond that, it is all prescribed and prearranged by the Most High. The Lord Jesus is the only way for God's eternal citizens to live, and accepting His Spirit within is the exclusive way for His later civilizations to join Him in their world when they leave theirs. The entire system is secured; safeguarded by an elaborate staff of celestial ministers to whom God delegated responsibility for assuring who abides in His kingdom of life and light, and who resides forever in the doom and gloom of hell. All of it has been resolved and worked out long before the foundation of this world. To carry out these duties, God's unimpeachable guardian force executes every decedent's judgment as He decrees. Heaven's guardians are upheld by celestial inspectors, divine adjudicators, and unimpeachable strata of enforcers, each one guaranteeing deceased humans end up where their earthly life choices dictated. It is how God honors human free will and He does honor it, even if after exiting the body, the person realizes the mistake and regrets it.

Eternal and Everlasting Life Lies in No Man's Hands

No matter how much people maintain their rights or liberties as human citizens of this planet, once they leave here those rights cease, just as they would if one left his native country and entered another. The rights and liberties in the new country may or may not coincide with or extend those of the home country. If they do, an entirely different government administers them in the foreign land that may have little or no inclination to honor or observe the ways of the realm departed. Such is the case

---

20 See Jude 1:9, discussed at length elsewhere in the book.

when one leaves this world and enters God's world. Human rights, even His Law of Moses, are for the people on earth. Since earth's laws pertain to the flesh and its mortality, they are enacted and legislated by the flesh and cover fleshly issues that do not exist in the Almighty's kingdom. Human law and government cannot extend to His realm because there is no mortal flesh there. Doomed souls do not have the celestial capacities to make the trip, which is why dead spirits and souls are by default compelled to another destination. What governs this world cannot show up[9] in God's because those without Christ's nature are barred from it by what separates this life. Life rejuvenating powers keep His eternal citizens from cohabitating with mortals. Just because something is spiritual does not, according to the Almighty's definition of the word, make it immortal. Immorality to humans stems from disobedience to God, to distinguish earthly morality from eternal righteousness. The Most High's domains classify worldliness as a product that accommodates Adam's nature. It is what Scripture plainly voices what humanity lives. In Adam all die, period. Worldliness is not only unwelcome in God's world, it is irreparably incompatible with it. The one who dies filled with the spirit of this world could never survive in the Creator's realm of supernal citizens. Thus, the need for a portion of the Godhead's divine nature is justified. The rules carnal souls snub in this life is, in effect, the construction material of the Lord's eternal constitution. Although Scripture simply calls these barriers God's law and government, as His eternal legislation they are more than writings. The New Testament subtly conveys this reality to express how eternal and immortal governance are completely unlike their terrestrial and mortal counterparts. The same way the earth has guardians, governors, and shields protecting its borders, so too does God. He charged celestial powers with scrutinizing the departed from this world. They inspect the deceased's lives and confirm the presence of the Holy Spirit within them. After verifying a departed soul meets the criteria for eternal life, the person is verified as a spiritual citizen and granted divine access into God's realm. To make it all just, He does it all to oblige the individual human will. Those lacking the redemptive credentials for eternal life are recognized by two things, the absence of the Holy Spirit and the sin that continues to actively corrode the soul. On the grounds of these two, they are disposed of elsewhere.

Rejectors of eternal life are prohibited from abiding where God resides because the laws are different. What sustains and restrains His immortal and celestial citizens is different because they are by nature superior to mortal humans. Each group's sin capacities and outcomes differ drastically, with immortal creatures' sinful acts ominously affecting more than this world. Moreover, each group's appetites, impulses, and influences are drastically different from each other as well. Where the Lord lives, the laws are for immortal beings that cannot die; whose sins, errors, and transgressions have incalculable and ineradicable consequences with the power to pervade all of creation. Such was the case with the first Continuum event, "The Great War in Heaven".[21] Jude, in verse six of his epistle, further reinforces this truth as a throwback to Genesis 6:2, 4. In both examples, when the immortals presume to take upon themselves the privileges and compulsions of the mortal world, devastating calamities befall both that the Most High must judge. His judgment condemns and corrects the resultant calamities and yields tragic outcomes for everyone affected by the transgression. Remember the antediluvian civilization. The fusion of immortal with mortal bred a type of creature the Lord had to obliterate from the planet completely. Recall with the flood, as another, for instance, Sodom, and Gomorrah. Jude's recollection of these judgments unmasks the spiritual world's rebels and renegades responsible for both atrocities. Aside from the permeating damages that came from spiritual citizens melding with humans in an ungodly manner, there is the divinely delegated power and authority inherent in spiritual beings to legislate in earthly governments' constitutions and cultures. Illegal blending of the two only means to steer mortals away from the Lord Almighty. Otherworldly edicts and agendas generated by the super powerful spirit beings cause God's generations, over time, to denounce Him as God in succeeding eras. After a while, godless laws intended to erode the His hold on His people, are passed to guarantee they inherit His eternal damnation. It is against this historical backdrop that Jesus decreed "the gates of hell would not prevail against" His church. He says it as if hell's attempts to do so are inevitable, but He has already neutralized their efforts before they begin. Several of the prophets of old recognized and denounced this practice as a cyclical scheme that affects every civilization the Lord creates.

- Isaiah 51:8: "For the moth shall eat them up like a garment, and the worm shall eat them like wool: but my righteousness shall be forever and my salvation from generation to generation."
- Isaiah 53:8: "He was taken from prison and from judgment: and who shall declare his generation? For he was cut off out of the land of the living: for the transgression of my people was he stricken". (Cf. Acts 8:33).
- Lamentations 5:19: "Thou, O Lord, remainest forever; thy throne from generation to generation."

---

21 See Revelation chapter 12.

- Daniel 4:3: "How great is his signs! And how mighty are his wonders! His kingdom is an everlasting kingdom, and his dominion is from generation to generation."

It is impossible to think about Scripture's recurring word *generation* and not include in its inferences the tenor of the Continuum. The very word itself speaks to a future shaped by a past that sketches what is to follow it successively to the end. The very heart and soul of the Continuum emphasizes future generations and the Lord's pre-determinations for them. Accepting Him as Creator says they somehow know and understand what He wants from His handiwork. That acceptance instills in each generation an inexplicable predisposition that manifests His predestiny decrees. It does not matter if humans hear His voice or believe in Him at all. An instinctual knowledge informs every person by nature, construction, and impulse they exist for God's will to be done. Why? The answer is because all the earth is the work of His hands. Every behavior and thought stem from His preprogrammed control. He set the stage for the lives lived on His planet, the choices made, and the attitudes that motivate the actions taken in order to remain in control and to intervene when necessary. Hebrews 4:12 and 13 mean to make this very point. The Lord thereby brings about His desired outcomes at[10] predesignated[11] points in time. All of the details concerning His creation, from before time, are encased in His Continuum.

- Isaiah 45:11, 12 "This is what the Lord says, the Creator of the signs: "Question me about my children? Or, give me orders about the work of my hands? I myself made the earth and personally created humankind upon it. My own hands stretched out the skies; I marshaled all their starry hosts." ISV
- Isaiah 45:11, 12 Thus saith the Lord, the Holy One of Israel, and his Maker, Ask me of things to come concerning my sons, and concerning the work of my hands command ye me. I have made the earth, and created man upon it: I, even my hands, have stretched out the heavens, and all their host have I commanded. KJV
- Isaiah 45:11, 12 "For thus says the Lord God, the holy one of Israel, the one making the coming things, Ask me concerning my sons. And concerning the works of my hands, shall you give charge to me! I made the earth, and man upon it. I by my hand solidified the heaven. I to all the stars gave charge." Apostolic Bible Polyglot.

The above passages are mentioned because of their allusions to the Christ being active in the Almighty's plans as precipitated by His Father's preordained dealings with

His creation. The phrase *"and His Maker"* indicates as much. Other versions identify The Messiah as a member of the Godhead in the following passages. The language of verse 13 settles the matter.

What all the above Scripture versions share, is their confirmation of God as the Maker. They reinforce His predestiny for everything He made. Everything exists according to His eternal purposes and functions as prescribed by His foreordained will. This especially applies to His Eternal Continuum. It exists because it contains all the Lord envisioned, crafted, ordained and arranged, decreed and encoded to fulfill His will throughout His emerging generations. It sees that events appointed to perform His will do so at their predesignated points in time and history. From the heavenly luminaries to the DNA coding of every creature's genetics, all that is and will be are redesigned to achieve the Maker's prefixed outcomes. With respect to human free will, the reality is, its options are framed within the contexts of God's "will be done on earth as it is in heaven." In this regard, the average person lives unaware of, or shuns awareness of the fact that the earth's present is the Almighty's past and this world's future is the outcome of His history rewound to dole out people's destiny. More precisely humanity's destiny is enjoined to His own world's present. Thus, Jesus is because He has always been; the Holy Spirit dominates because He comprises everything that is and ever was. Look at Isaiah 45:13's foretelling of Christ's predesignated purposes; purposes that He jointly designed with His Father in heaven as the Second Person of the Godhead before anything began along with the Holy Spirit. The entire chapter is worth reading to gain insight into the Lord's perspective on His worlds and His dominion over them all; however, verses 12 and 13 make the point. Isaiah 45:9-13:

> *"Woe unto him that striveth with his Maker! Let the potsherd strive with the potsherds of the earth. Shall the clay say to him that fashioneth it, What makest thou? Or thy work, He hath no hands? Woe unto him that saith unto his father, What begettest thou? Or to the woman, What hast thou brought forth? Thus saith the Lord, the Holy One of Israel, and his Maker, Ask me of things to come concerning my sons, and concerning the work of my hands command ye me. I have made the earth, and created man upon it: I, even my hands, have stretched out the heavens, and all their host have I commanded. I have raised him up in righteousness, and I will direct all his ways: he shall build my city, and he shall let go my captives, not for price nor reward, saith the Lord of hosts."*

The very existence of prophecy establishes the predesign, pre-appointment, and prior purposes of God. Prophecy overall predicts and preprograms how His world will function and advance toward His predestined end. It exists to let earth know that the future is not left up to chance. This world is not left to humanity's discretion or the disagreeable, unseen forces seeking to bring their will to pass on it. In the end, they too bow to the Most High's supervention.[12] His beforehand initiatives are fail-safes that guard what He wants to come out of whatever He does. His predeterminations immutably manage and dictate human and terrestrial limits, set boundaries, grant privileges and permits liberties. He also remedied creation's adversity and contradictions in advance. What was settled before ever there was an earth is what prophecy impresses upon generations of audiences. God spoke before time to inform the world that the future has never been the domain of its human inhabitants. Despite their superficial independence from Him and presupposed dominance over His will, He resolved from eternity that no matter how it looks today, things always turn out His way in the end.

Prophecy, angelic and human, prevents the creature from countermanding its Creator's will. What makes it appear otherwise is the Lord's long-suffering, shrewdness, and familiarity with His earthly program. Collectively, they give the impression He is utterly out of control when in fact He rules His handiwork with a tight hand. See Revelation 2:27; 12:5; 19:15, passages that say why. After long spates of seeming indifference God's absolutes suddenly erupt and shock humanity with crises it is powerless to reverse. As the Maker and Possessor of heaven and earth, the Most High predetermined people's brief life spans and embedded the physical frailties that limit how long they can remain on earth, prosper, and strive with Him while they are here. His sovereignty installed the blindness of the human heart and mind to restrict them to the present and past. Being shut out of what will be tomorrow or next year forces people to trust their outcomes to an uncertain future and for many an unknown power, no matter how much they dislike it. The supremacy gap between the Maker and His creatures is broad and invincible. Inwardly, as frustrating as it is, people on earth—especially leaders—know it and it gnaws at them. Helplessly with the rest of the world, powerful people cringe every time they must face these truths or fall victim to them. Strong-willed, decisive leaders detest the notion that they are not really the masters of their own destiny or determiners of their own fates whenever something unconquerable reminds them of it. To appear otherwise, they contrive a facade of boastful illusions, knowing at heart that the most they can do is guess and hope for the best with those they lead, something else the Lord counted on when He said "let there be".

So what assures God's will is done on earth as it is in heaven? The Continuum is what. His Eternal Continuum encases and imposes His will, while all along, capturing and conforming earthly events to it. Beyond that the Continuum regulates eternity's godly agents, trusting them to fulfill His predestined design. In addition, because they are not subject to the earth's laws of sin and death, the Lord does not find Himself, having to clean up the messes they make due to their being vulnerable to demonic seductions. The Lord's holy angels are His personal ministering spirits, they are His palace guards; His celestial cabinet. Select angels are entrusted with His innermost secrets and most sensitive kingship tasks. Christ's royal ministrants take the lead in seeing that His will is uncompromisingly done, the way He envisions it verbatim. Most impressively, the Lord's celestial agents do their jobs in a way that seems to pit humanity against its Maker while subliminally keeping the Godhead in charge. Consider the angelic response of the warring angel that introduced himself to Joshua in Joshua chapter 5. He told Moses' successor that he was neither for nor against him, but came as the commander of the Lord of hosts to see His will was done. In modern terms, he essentially said I am with you as long as God is; when He shifts, I go. I am here exclusively doing His will on earth, not yours.

[5]

Anatomizing The Continuum

The Continuum, God's "unbroken chain of events " incarnated the second person of the Godhead and transported Him to earth. The same contiguity likewise deposited Christianity into the world." As God's unbroken procession, its stratum is replete with captivating implications that exemplify it. First, the Continuum is an unbroken series of sequences that unravel what the Father appointed as His Son's responsibilities. What can that mean except that when it comes to the Lord Jesus, and Christianity, some ceaseless heavenly program decreed He extend His kingdom to earth, and regulates how He administrates it? Second, a calculated string of precise events brought Jesus Christ into this world. Nothing in human history could take credit for such a masterful achievement. Third, those events also managed to bring Christianity into the world. Could it be that some outside agency was responsible for getting it from another world into this one? If so, what is that agency, are there more of them, and do they suggest Christ's church has origins and sources beyond this universe? The answer to all three is yes. Even if subconsciously for most people, the thought of other worlds outside this one answering to a world higher than it, is typical. Few people want to think that this planet and this life are all there is. Most people on earth are worn out by life's ups and downs and inwardly hope there is a better place with a better life. God's Eternal Continuum holds the key to that hope.

The word continuum as an identifier raises profound questions that hold some staggering inferences regarding the Godhead's world and the life it led before to the Garden, Israel, and the Church. Once explained, the revelations promise to transform church doctrine in explosive ways. As has been said already, the Continuum contains prophecy, revelation, the Church's eternal structure, and its endless future. Its archives hold the mysteries of how the Most High brought all into existence. For these reasons, God's Eternal Continuum emphasizes Christ's kingdom with the Church at the center of it rather than the reverse. The church is eternity's kingdom hub, so to speak. The kingdom surrounds and therefore protects the Church, not the other way around. That is why Jesus promoted the kingdom more than the Ecclesia; He left that part to those who founded His church. Also for this reason, the apostles emerged before the Church in the way that Israel as a nation precedes its spiritual counterpart the New Creation body of Christ. All of this says why the kingdom does not answer to the Ecclesia, as it appears to do today on earth. If that were the case, then the Lord's High Priestly office brings His kingship under the church on earth. That would put His church leaders in charge, not of His Ecclesia, but of His kingdom. The imprudence of the order goes to the comments made above. The text says "kings and priests" not "priests and kings" for good reason. Kings beget kingdoms and populate them with worshippers. Jesus was a King long before He became the Shepherd of God's earthly flock. Based on this, the kingdom hosts every kind of thing, the proverbial good, bad, and ugly. The church in comparison should only house the hallowed and holy. The profane may exist in the kingdom, but should not be in the Church. The Lord made his priests more suited to serving the sanctified while the King is well able to rule the rest. Furthermore, remember Jesus established His kingship long before He became the High Priest of our profession, the prophet, shepherd, apostle, or bishop that He became after Calvary. It is why His followers, recognized Him as the King, most notably, David the King. Elevating the Church above the kingdom limits the Lord to His liturgical duties and exposes His church to invasion and overthrow. It removes Him from most of secularity and confines His authority to spirituality alone. Meaning, that when it comes to Jesus' official power and authority, in the natural realm both appear more abstract and allegorical than temporal which suggests He is impotent on earth. In Scripture, though, The Messiah's kingdom attributes outnumber His priestly ones for excellent reasons.

The New Testament depicts in many parables, God's kingdom as housing and hosting numerous things, some good, and others not so good. Christ disclosed when He was on earth that His kingdom hosts the hallowed and profane, the wheat, and the tares. In God's mind, that is not the case with His church. He expects it to be holy, godly, righteous, and sanctified by His Spirit. Think of it like the human body. In the workplace and elsewhere outside the home, the outer self attracts the clean and the unclean. Different environments contain a mixture of all kinds of substances, people, and influences. That however is not how the typical person wants it to be at home, or on their person. When it comes to both the average person wants the body and the home to be free of anything that offends, what Jesus says will happen, when He returns to take over the world.[22] The Ecclesia is to incorporate God's offspring exclusively. The only entity He wants to come near His person is the body of new creation converts that replicate the divine nature to express the Godhead's character. That is how it is with the true church, earthly and spiritual marauders and infiltrating imposters aside.

To elaborate further, the Continuum is representative of the Lord's *logos*.[13] It comprises His logic, rationale, and mentality. The Logos divulges all God is and characterizes how He behaves. The word defines the Almighty's divine nature, articulates His reasons for initiating and responding to His worlds the way He does. The word puts forth the logic that assures the outcomes He expects from what He sets in motion.[23] Logos mostly speaks to God's intelligences, especially as they are demonstrated in the person of the Lord Jesus Christ. As God's incarnation and Personified Word, He embodies and exemplifies it. Without logic, intelligence is impossible. Therefore, the Lord's logos encompass His pragmatisms worked out through Christ's activities. These include His government, administration, and oversight of His Father's worlds. Logos intellectualizes God's orders. It defines and guides His institutions and regulates His organisms. In comparison, the *Rhema* aspect of the Continuum relates to its published communications. Rhema's[14] meanings are best understood by the word rhetoric. Rhetoric[15] writes and speaks to bring people around to a communicator's way of thinking and acting, or at the least, it aims to motivate them to take in a communication as intended. It is persuasive because its main ingredients include the wise use of language and impassioned oratory skills. The rules and principles of speech composition come under Rhema. The Continuum is how the Lord gets His Logos mind and will to His worlds and their inhabitants. The way logic finds its roots in logos, so too does rhetoric find its roots in Rhema. Impressively, both are integral to the Continuum reflecting the two predominant sides of the Almighty's divine communications.

God weaves His intelligence and persuasiveness throughout His Continuum. It is how He tempers His messengers' emotionality with His wisdom and prudence. The Continuum aligns their doctrinal span and filters out dubious teachings, disproving and disapproving them. It frankly restricts and discredits error by pitting its logic against human sensationalism. In this respect, the Continuum flags and judges false

---

[22] See Matthew 13:41.
[23] Refer to Isaiah 55:11 and Luke 1:37, ASV.

doctrine as heresy simply because it has no link to its fourteen corroborating events. Awareness of this standard inspired Scripture authors to guard their words' future. It taught them to compose their writings to comply with the Lord's Eternal Continuum. In doing so, they effectively nullify biblical misteachings. Dedication to the Lord's truth and realization of its inevitable wrangling by the unscrupulous, guided Scripture recorders. That realization admonished them to phrase their words precisely enough to transmit God's wisdom and expertise to His world accurately. However, it is not the literal language alone that motivated them, but that which properly reflects the mind of Christ. Their correct word usage portrayed God's will in the earth. Both standardardize what the Holy Spirit can confirm or deny.

DEFINING THE CONTINUUM

For clarification purposes, early definitions of the word *continuum* are enlarged to include the following meanings. Etymologically, the word continuum is the Latin, neuter of *continuus*, from the word contineō that means, "To contain in order to enclose". Academically, a continuum is generally understood as:

1. A continuous non-spatial *whole*, extent, or succession in which no part or portion is distinct or distinguishable from adjacent parts
2. A coherent *whole* characterized as a collection, sequence, or progression
3. A continuous extent, succession, or *whole*, no part of which can be distinguished from neighboring parts except by arbitrary division
4. An uninterrupted succession or flow and coherent *whole*
5. A spoken matter serving to link parts of a program or pattern so that no break occurs.
6. An uninterrupted connection or union
7. The property of a continuous and connected period of time

With respect to God's Eternal Continuum, the definitions identify the successive ages and episodes that precede this world and its populations. Meanings highlight His eternal world's histories and specifies what grew out of peopling His planets with free will agents. It implies the worlds that were, have passed, and those that are to come. Impressively, Continnum language alludes to the generations that inhabited God's otherworldly territories and designate the epic sequences archived in heaven's repositories. Continuum initiatives influence God's actions. They reflect happenings in His eternal ages that forever inspired His cause and effect decisions. Those decisions and the experiences that provoked them steer the predestiny of Adam's seed. Moreover,

Continuum sequences as they are strung together compile His prerecording of humanity so nothing it does catches Him by surprise. Down through the ages, progressively unfolding Scripture comprising God's wisdom expanded the revelations He chose to share with this world and its citizens. In the end, they become His eternal life propositions, what Jesus incarnated and came to offer the earth.

DISCERNING THE CONTINUUM IN SCRIPTURE

As if buried and saved for the truly inquisitive, the one who has to see how things came to be the way they are and understand what to do about them, the Continuum's answers hide beneath the obvious. After years of hearing the same Bible stories and their explanations rehashed and recycled, many of God's people, cry out for something more; something deeper and most of all, something that makes sense. Enter the Continuum's revelation. True to her word, Proverbs' Lady Wisdom waited until the desire became insatiable and dissatisfaction with the status quo, intolerable. Then she graced God's people with yet one more mystery to be unscrolled.[24] She pulls from her vault of secrecy, God's Eternal Continuum, the mystery hidden in plain sight, as is the case with all of the Lord's precious truths. The word *continuum* used this way identifies this generation's, unfolding mysteries because it best fits the Lord's Self-disclosures. Six Scriptures lay out the Almighty's perpetuity and indomitability. In addition to reinforcing His interminability, they roll out His succession of ages. They are:

A. Malachi 3:6 "For I am the Lord, I change not; therefore ye sons of Jacob are not consumed".

B. Isaiah 41:4 "Who hath wrought and done it, calling the generations from the beginning? I, the Lord, the first, and with the last; I am he."

C. Isaiah 46:10 "Declaring the end from the beginning, and from ancient times the things that are not yet done, saying, My counsel shall stand, and I will do all my pleasure."

D. Isaiah 48:3 "I have declared the former things from the beginning; and they went forth out of my mouth, and I shewed them; I did them suddenly, and they came to pass."

E. John 8:44 "Ye are of your father the Devil, and the lusts of your father ye will do. He was a murderer from the beginning, and abode not in the truth be-

---

[24] To open or unfold progressively, as a scroll does.

cause there is no truth in him. When he speaketh a lie, he speaketh of his own: for he is a liar, and the father of it."[25]

F. Hebrews 13:8 "Jesus Christ the same yesterday, and today, and forever". What all of these Scriptures project is, eternity, as God's timeless and infinite world.

To wrap it up, Isaiah 57:15 affirms this. "For thus saith the high and lofty One that inhabiteth eternity, whose name is Holy; I dwell in the high and holy place, with him also that is of a contrite and humble spirit, to revive the spirit of the humble, and to revive the heart of the contrite ones."

As has been shown earlier, the word eternity in Scripture pertains to the Creator's person and His first world, its indescribable past and unending future. It houses the kingdom of God and His incorporeal citizenry's[16] forever existence; see as an example Hebrews 12:22-24. It gives another subtle, yet discernible, reference to a world, and ages, that preexist this one.

"But ye are come unto mount Sion, and unto the city of the living God, the heavenly Jerusalem, and to an innumerable company of angels, to the general assembly and church of the firstborn, which are written in heaven, and to God the Judge of all, and to the spirits of just men made perfect, And to Jesus the mediator of the new covenant, and to the blood of sprinkling, that speaketh better things than that of Abel."

So what eternal properties is the Book of Hebrews unveiling here?

1. *Mount Sion* – God's mighty invincible stronghold in heaven
2. *The City of the Living God* – The Lord's eternal capital[17] city in heaven
3. *The Heavenly Jerusalem* – The actual name of the Lord's capital city, after which earthly Jerusalem is named to indicate its peaceful role in creation; Ezekiel calls it the seat of God's throne
4. *An Innumerable Company of Angels* – The eternal beings that populate the Almighty's eternal worlds and serve Him in various capacities in His lesser ones
5. *The General Assembly of the Firstborn* – The eternal population of heavenly citizens apart from the angelic staff. These are the Son of God's offspring; Thayer calls them the Almighty's universal companionship
6. *The church of the Firstborn* – The perfected counterparts of redeemed saints initially hid in Christ's body until His successful redemption. At Pentecost, their spirits emerged from His being to fuse with their eternal physiques and eventually populate His Messianic kingdom.

---

[25] 1 John 3:8.

7. *The General Assembly Written in Heaven* – The registry of eternal beings created, in heaven and those steadily being born again as the originative or procreated citizens of God's celestial world.

8. To *God the Judge of All* – The Creator who judges everything and everyone according to the standards prescribed in His eternal world, including its citizens' creative intents, and their predetermined effects or outcomes.

9. *The Spirits of Just Men Made Perfect* – The immaterial side of those who inherited the Almighty's eternal life, although they were not born in His world. This would include the redeemed Enoch from the antediluvians and Moses, who saw death, but earned heaven in his lifetime and escaped hell at his death. Includes as well, Elijah who was taken from the earth alive and whisked off to heaven; the Old Covenant saints that died in faith (see Hebrews 11); and lastly, the saints under Moses' Law that rose from the dead with Jesus Christ at His resurrection (Matthew 27:52, 53).

10. To *Jesus, the Mediator of the New Covenant* – The redemptive name of the Son of God appointed to make the way of salvation to those born in the flesh.

11. *The Blood of Sprinkling Better Than That of Abel* – The precursor to Jesus' sacrificial blood, the blood of Abel spilled on the earth by his older brother Cain.[18]

Twelve specific out-of-this-world factors are declared in this Scripture. They reflect the Continuum's eternality, specifically its principal characters. There is: a) God, b) Zion, c) Jerusalem, d) angels, e) Jesus as the firstborn, f) heaven's general assembly, g) the heavenly Ecclesia, h) God as judge, i) the perfected spiritual saints, j) Jesus as eternity's mediator, k) Jesus' saving Blood, l) heaven's record of the first blood to be shed on earth, Abel's. All of those named in this passage beautifully support the Continuum's foundational Scripture, Matthew 1:17.

The epistle to the Hebrews' eternal populace of heaven is verified by Moses in Deuteronomy 33:2 mentioned earlier. It names the company of saints the Lord brought with Him into this world to see to the success of His Exodus Project. This mass of tens of thousands is different from the millions of Jews that followed Moses into the wilderness. Jude 1:14 speaks of this group as a portion of Enoch's prophecy. Other insinuations of this group are in Job 15:15, where it says the Lord's saints wielding power enough to maintain the heavens are not wholly trusted by Him. In Daniel 7:27, a strange phrase appears as the prophet recalls God's words to Him regarding the end of the world. It says "And the kingdom and dominion, and the greatness of the kingdom under the whole heaven, shall be given to the *people* of the saints of the Most High, whose kingdom is an everlasting kingdom, and all dominions shall serve and obey him." There is curious phrasing here that can be easily overlooked by those who scan the text instead of reading it word for word. The phrase is "given to the people of the saints of the Most High". Who are the saints in question and who are their people? The traditional idea is that the people of the Most High are the members of the body of Christ, preceded only by the Israelis. Both groups, because of their unique relationship with the Lord, are called saints in Scripture. So who are their people? If what is written in Deuteronomy 33:2 and Jude 1:14 mean what they say then the verse is replete with implications. The ten thousands that accompanied the Lord to Mount Sinai appear to be the very ones that Enoch[26] prophesied would come with the Lord. Another connected reference is Revelation 19:14. It speaks of the armies of heaven that go into battle with the Lord Jesus when He returns to the earth. A last reference is found in Job 25:2 and 3, "Dominion and fear are with him, he maketh peace in his high places. Is there any number of his armies? And upon whom doth not his light arise?" All of these references reiterate the Continuum's point. The Lord's kingdom rules over all because it predates every other kingdom. His entire supernal realm has a populace, governance, rulers, culture, and communities that antecede everything in this world and its universe. His world lives in irreproachable light. To date, except for the earth every other world is dark and barren. The beings and elements identified in these passages span eternity, earth, and back to eternity. Some of the elements are everlasting and thus have beginnings, many of which caused earthly beginnings. Others are strictly eternal with no beginning in this world or any other, except in God's. This explanation provides a fuller picture of what differentiates the two words, *eternal* and *everlasting* that were explored earlier.

A more pointed example of heaven imposing itself on earth is Melchizedek, the key member of the Continuum's eternal priesthood.[19] He precedes Levi's priesthood that originated under the Law of Moses. The epistle to the Hebrews mentions this king-priest as having no beginning or end, no human or mortal lineage, and not of this world. Despite all of that, he did for a season, occupy the planet serving as God's priest over the law of sin and death caused by the first event. In that capacity, it is said that he preceded Levi's Priesthood. Study Scriptures' treatment of him. Numerous Hebrews' passages discuss a mysterious figure that today would classify as an alien. Him, the Almighty God sent to earth to mediate worldwide sin. His priesthood occupied Salem, what would eventually come to be modern Jerusalem. From the passages, it is apparent that Melchizedek was not a lone priest, but was the head of an

---

[26] Jude 1:4.

entire priestly order. It says Melchizedek had more otherworldly beings with him that occupied the city-state he ruled. He governed a super-race of heavenly beings that served several purposes for the Most High God on earth. They functioned in a royal priestly capacity, in anticipation of God's first covenant humans. These heavenly beings are the prototype of the royal priesthood of believers, Peter describes in his first epistle. Melchizedek, also a king, on earth, it should be said, was only a priest. The title High Priest, however, was reserved for Jesus Christ once He successfully redeemed humanity's souls. Until Abraham converted to the Most High from Babylonianism, Melchizedek as God's eternal and everlasting being mediated eternal and temporal sin on Christ's behalf. As said previously, the Continuum's first event made this necessary. He paved the way for the Levites who once born, would take over the duty under Moses' Law. Adam and Eve's Edenic Transgression caused the Lord to dispatch Melchizedek and his institution to earth. Apparently, he was already tending heaven's altar as a priest outside of it. With earth, having gone the way of his world under the age-old serpent, his services became needed elsewhere, namely on this planet to prepare the way for its redemption. How long Melchizedek was in the world before his encounter with Abraham is unknown. He most likely arrived when the Lord installed the fiery sword-wielding cherubim at Eden's east gate to guard the tree of life. It is reasonable to deduce that God dispatched this heavenly ministrant around the same time or shortly after Adam and Eve's banishment from the garden. That event could well have prompted his role in the Continuum, because earth now needed priestly intervention.

Additionally, from what is read, Melchizedek's life began in Christ's world and considering he was created to be a priest, it would seem he served the Lord Jesus in heaven making him a reliable prototype for the earthly version of his mediatorial services. Relative to the Continuum, Melchizedek is one figure that reinforces how sin and death could not have gotten their start in this world, but in God's. Reviewing Abraham's conquest of the five kings suggests that Melchizedek was an accomplished intergalactic warrior. His heavenly origins indicate he too stood by Christ in His divine battles. That Christ's eternal priestly order is taken from Melchizedek's anchors the Continuum's validity. It concretely establishes His pre-earthly existence, heavenly ministracies, and everlasting duty to mediate spiritual sin before mediating earthly sin. If not, why have Abraham, Isaac, Jacob, and Moses, institute another type of priestliness on earth? Everything Jesus achieved by Calvary reaches back to before He became flesh and extends beyond the days of His flesh on earth. It stands to reason, then that sin, death and the other grounds for the Lord's priesthood, including the slaughter and sacrifice, originated with Him. If Melchizedek existed and served prior to the first event, it no doubt forever altered his celestial ministry by adding to what could have only been a service of offerings and worship, the gruesome task of slaughtering and dismemberment. It is something that he for sure did on earth as a priest considering the grisliness of the era.

From what has been said, and numerous Scriptures, the blighting of the Creator's pristine environment began where He lives, not with the pair He placed in the garden. See Revelation chapter twelve; read also, Ezekiel 28; Isaiah 14; Judges 5:20,[20] and Daniel 10. What makes these facts relevant is that they tie the Continuum to why the new creation saint is an immediate member of Melchizedek's Priesthood. They also say why the Lord must naturalize His converts into heaven's eternal nation and why they are adopted into its family.[27] God's is the only spirit of life in heaven. He is the only spirit that abides in its citizenry. On earth that is not so. In the world, there is the spirit of Adam, the spirit of the fallen angels, and then the spirit of Christ. This explanation says how and why Christianity is not of earthly origin. The Almighty, in begetting His Son Jesus Christ outside of earth and time, deposited His descendants within His first begotten Son before He created the heavens or the earth. Melchizedek's priesthood of human converts, what Peter discloses in 2:9 of his first epistle is the royal priesthood gathered as the chosen generation to make up Christ's holy nation. The tiny earthly prototype that sealed Abraham's Covenant with the Most High has majestically morphed under Christ's regime. Melchizedek's ancient city-state is now global and perpetual because of Calvary and Pentecost. It differs from its scale model in that it is wholly made of regenerated humans who were first born on earth and then born again from heaven above.

A heavenly priesthood qualifies those saved by Christ's blood to be grafted into His divine lineage. The only priesthood that satisfies God's criteria is the eternal priesthood of Melchisedec, its Testament spelling. It began in heaven before sin originated and has been mediating the first event's fallout ever since. To see how this particular thread of the Continuum goes full circle within the New Testament church, look at Revelation 7:9-17. It amplifies Revelation 1:6 and 5:10. Once more, God's Eternal Continuum surfaces, this time in the priesthood. It refers to the priestly order of the eternal and everlasting Melchizedek, who ruled over ancient Salem as its approved priest and sovereign. Once the Most High God converts Abraham, he takes over in some respects, Melchizedek's earthly priesthood, which is why the Lord ordained the cir-

---

[27] See Ephesians 3:15.

cumcision. His induction causes eternity's immortal priest to fade into the background, presumably returning to heaven to continue his supernal service from there. Hebrews 7:8, gives a peculiar clue to what he is doing now. In time, the Lord's promise to Abraham performed and eventually birthed the Levitical Priesthood. This order continues until Jesus Christ incarnates. After He dies, resurrects, and returns on high with His church, He becomes High Priest of Melchizedek's order forever. Thus, Christ and Melchizedek's eternal and earthly destinies jointly forge the priestly portions God's unbroken chain running throughout Scripture. Both men originated in heaven. Both were dispatched to earth, both served as humans, and both returned to heaven to resume greatly expanded versions of their temporal duties.

The Generic Elements of the Continuum

The following unfolds twelve Continuum elements that relate directly to today's Ecclesia, its ministers, and messengers. They distinguish and verify what is of Christ because they reach back to His world. Tying the twelve meanings to Continuum teachings alerts God's guardian servants to whom they are aligning themselves with and counsels them on what is done in harmony with it. That harmony, fixed from before time informs them of what the Lord continues to unfold since the Church was born. Observing the Continuum's gauges, helps contemporary Christian messengers in many ways. Above all else, it reinforces all that Christ established before He became flesh. Making Continuum meanings a part of standard Christian discipleship assures what is uttered, and practiced by His servants today continues to advance God's plan instead of stalling it.

God's Continuum Encases:

What follows relates to Scripture's Continuum. It illustrates its elements in the following phrases from God's word. The brief explanations express how the terms apply to the Continuum to support its purposes and ongoing functions until the end of time. Continuum encasements reflect Scripture's applications and contain its featured Continuum's prophecies, revelations, and Jesus Christ as the Word.

1. **Ages** – *That in the ages to come: Ephesians 2:7*, "That in the ages to come he might shew the exceeding riches of his grace in *his* kindness toward us through Christ Jesus."
2. **Eras** – *Since the beginning of: Matthew 24:21*, "For then shall be great tribulation, such as was not since the beginning of the world to this time, no, nor ever shall be."

3. **Epics** – *Dramatization of Jesus Christ: Romans 16:25*, "Now to him that is of power to establish you according to my gospel, and the preaching of Jesus Christ, according to the revelation of the mystery, which was kept secret since the world began."

4. **Epochs** – *Before the world: 1 Corinthians 2:7*, "But we speak the wisdom of God in a mystery, even the hidden wisdom, which God ordained before the world unto our glory."

5. **Worlds** -- *To come: Hebrews 2:5*, "For unto the angels hath he not put in subjection the world to come, whereof we speak."

6. Generations – *To come or yet to be born: Psalm 102:18*, "This shall be written for the generation to come: and the people which shall be created shall praise the Lord."

7. **Sequences** – *Elijah to come first: Matthew 17:1,.* "And his disciples asked him, saying, why then say the scribes that Elias must first come?"

8. **Progressions** – *Beginning at Moses: Luke 24:27*, "And beginning at Moses and all the prophets, he expounded unto them in all the Scriptures the things concerning himself".

9. **Revelations** – *The Law of Moses, the Prophets, and the Psalms: Luke 24:44*, "And he said unto them, These are the words which I spake unto you, while I was yet with you, that all things must be fulfilled, which were written in the law of Moses, and in the prophets, and in the psalms, concerning me."

10. **Communications** – *By the mouth of all His prophets: Acts 3:21*, "Whom the heaven must receive until the times of restitution of all things, which God hath spoken by the mouth of all his holy prophets since the world began."

11. **Series** - The *Scriptures... testify of me: John 5:39.* "Search the Scriptures; for in them ye think ye have eternal life: and they are they which testify of me."

12. **Events** – *This Jesus hath God raised up... whom I preach to you, is Christ: Acts 2:32, 17:3,* "This Jesus hath God raised up, whereof we all are witnesses. Opening and alleging, that Christ must needs have suffered, and risen again from the dead; and that this Jesus, whom I preach unto you, is Christ."

UNVEILING THE FOURTEEN EVENTS

As said earlier, the Continuum consists of fourteen eternal, spiritual, and earthly events that served the purposes of bringing to this world the Lord Jesus Christ, and after His departure, and the new creation church of Holy Spirit born Christians on the planet. Spirit birth, known as the new birth is unique in that ancient texts specify it as being born from above, born again from God in heaven. As far-fetched as this may sound, it is actually characteristic of the Almighty. Take, for instance, when the Lord created Adam and Eve; so named after the fall. Before He formed them on earth, God created them in His person to spend their first day of life with Him, not on the planet but in heaven.[28] They had not yet received their clay bodies; it came after their first communion with their Maker. The Book of Genesis says the Lord made them on day six and formed them on day eight. The implication is that He enjoyed His first Sabbath with the man and woman on day seven and commanded its perpetual observation for all generations. It is why Jesus says in Mark 2:27 that the Sabbath was made for humans and not humans for the Sabbath. People come before their celebrations or commemoration because they are the basis for them.

AFTER THE LORD GOD CREATES THE MALE AND FEMALE, HIS LIFE CHANGES

The Almighty's new family concludes the spiritual portion of His creative works. The new creatures need to meet and get to know their Maker, which is why He made them before His physical labor on the planet recommences. After His rest and communion with the new species, God gets back to work putting every immaterial thing in its clay body. While getting to know each other, God instills in His humans their origins, His ownership and His engrafted eternity.[29] This example shows that it is not outside of the scope of the Most High's normalcy to create life elsewhere and embody it on earth later; such is the case with the redeemed. They were created and hid in Jesus eons ago; deposited in His being before ever there was an earth. He carried the Christian in His being as part of His Person. His incarnation brought God's new creation species with Him into this world to discharge His Messiahship duties. When Jesus returned to God in heaven after rising from the dead, the eternal spirits of those to be saved returned to earth in the Person of the Holy Spirit. What all this has to do with the Continuum is that it is all about Jesus Christ and His inheritance of sanctified souls to populate His eternal kingdom. Time and tradition condensed (and in some cases obscured) the entirety of what God actually accomplished through Jesus on Calvary. Modernists gradually submerged the majesty of what He did under the rubble of institutional religion. In truth, though, everything Scripture--Old and New Testaments—is exclusively about and for the Son of God, the Second Person of the

---

[28] See Genesis 1:26, 27.
[29] Ecclesiastes 3:11, ASV, ISV.

Godhead.[30] Beginning in heaven, and ending there as well, the Continuum unsheathes a series of Creator plotted events He determined would bring His Son's inheritance into existence. Instrumentally, they resolved the sin problem that entered and spoiled His new world when the serpent beguiled Eve in the garden. Many Christians find the Edenic story hard to take, and countless scholars are stumbled by it. The Lord, however, was not blindsided by it and took strategic measures to counteract it all before He created time. Scripture phrases like "beginning in heaven" hint at it. The sin, death, and unbelief commencing in God's world of spiritual creatures carried over to the clay vessels inhabiting this one through the very creature that caused it. Futuristic, ancient, and eternal phrases providing a subtle revelation of the Almighty imply everything pertaining to Him and His celestial creatures was foreordained.[31] The most sagacious of implications intimate how He will produce His predestined cache of human souls to populate His eternal world. Christianity's Continuum tells how He will make it happen using suggestive words like *foreknowledge* and *predestined*. These terms say that nothing catches God by surprise. The developments of His worlds do not stun Him, because He long ago ordained how and where His people would live, how they would perpetuate, how they would leave their worlds to join His, and the processes by which He would redeem the most compatible, and dispose of the incompatible. All of this, the Almighty legislated before undertaking any of His creative, progenitive, or redemptive works.

To remain true to His alpha and omega character and responsibilities, The Lord God saw that His creatures inhabited this world according to a life plan. He prescribed and inscribed what He appointed for them when they were no more than ideas in His mind. He prearranged the way His beings would enter the world, spend their lives, die, and leave their bodies to exit the world. All of it He filed in His heavenly archives. Meticulously, God fashioned everything pertaining to life on earth for humanity's arrival, not because of it. That is why they are the last to be made and deposited on the planet. More precisely, the Lord preresolved it all in His own office in heaven and perfected it in His supernal workshop.[32] Psalm 139:14-18 lays this out beautifully; it says the Lord produces nothing without a prior purpose, a calculated plan, preset responsibilities, and an exit strategy. The details secreted in people's life book are kept in His kingdom's chronicle of souls for their designated generations. Thus, people travel down the Continuum according to what it says about them. They appear in

---

[30] See Colossians 1:16.

[31] 1 Peter 1:20 and Acts 4:28.

[32] See endnotes for clarification of this word.

their eras according to the scripts that predict them. In a nutshell, this is the meaning of destiny. As uncomfortable as it is for some people to accept, the Almighty decided in advance everything about each being He brought into existence, from their looks, lineage, appearance, and proclivities, right down to the very last strand of hair on their heads and the last breath they will take before leaving the planet. His predeterminations encompass every moment people live, including the day-to-day events that occur throughout it. Psalm 102:18 states that God has plans for every generation. For instance, when He gives His Law to Israel, He tells them to record it, to write it down and then faithfully pass it on to their children, successively. As earthbound mortals, they will die, but He will be around to lead their generations into His salvation. In fact, Genesis 15:13 demonstrates this exact thing, along with Acts 7:6. The Lord encoded His entire creation to end up where He ordained and has a massive force of angelic beings to ensure that everything He wrote comes to pass; until this world ends, and thereafter.

Humans go through life living strings of events they think they chose for themselves. If someone told them that it was all worked out before they got here, more than a few of them would be stunned and some of them quite disturbed. Maintaining His Continuum, obligated the Lord to preprogram life happenings and assigned them to ages, generations, families, societies, communities, and leaders. Otherwise, what He already resolved in His realm would replicate itself beyond His control in this one. His foreknowledge and fore-ordainments guarantee His success through the different dispositional aspects of people's makeup. Many passages of Scripture support this truth, giving glimpses of what predates earth that influence God's Eternal Continuum. They show how important writing and recording creature events is to the Lord due to people deciding in their lives what is registered in their spirits. The secret is that the soul and the body have yet to register it on earth. In this world, due to the darkness born in them, people must discover their desires and unearth what it is they believe. Then they must prove how long they can believe it. What God already knows or has written and filed in His realm, though unknowable to everyone else, must be verified by the human will in order to qualify souls for salvation or record their rejection of it. That is what Peter means when he says converts "must believe to the saving of their souls." Thus far, it has been shown how the entire Continuum's life cycles span eternity, earth and time, and back to the endless eternity. What happened in heaven before time bears heavily on what happens on earth in a given era. Synergistically, and synchronically, the two reconnect both worlds so all that what was lost to earth may be redeemed by Christ's blood.

THREE SPANS OF TIME

In effect, the Continuum embraces three spans of time. What Matthew 1:17 is based upon highlights the most decisive ones, which is why generational influences open the New Testament.[33] The passage announces three distinct spans of time, each marked by a major event affecting their generation: a) Abraham-David, b) David-Babylon, and c) Babylon-Christ. All three provide distinct mile markers in God's royal chronology that generationally log the major milestones in His redemptive plan. A plan that primarily constitutes the inheritance He determined to give His first begotten Son, and that the Son, to prove Himself and learn how to rule and preserve His inheritance, was required to accomplish in order to possess it.[34] This perspective cohesively unshrouds the ultimate outcome of God's elegantly portrayed redemption project, namely the genesis of the new creation that constitutes Jesus' royal offspring. That holy nation of kings and priests the New Testament ascribes to those redeemed in Christ. The three markers allude to a complicated strategy that remediates the sin that in God's world and earth's generations. What is often overlooked in traditional and popular teachings is how it all rests on His first begotten Son. Not just the Jesus who ministered on earth for three and a half years, but also the eternal Yahweh that ruled Israel for centuries, and before that, all of eternity. He manifests to the world as God, incognito. Jesus manifests to Israel in the form of a lowly carpenter's Son, subversively setting it for a complete takeover. Many of the clues to Jesus being Yahweh are in John's Gospel and it is no wonder that they are. John clearly affected Jesus in an intensely profound way. The Savior's unconcealed, special regard for the man caused the rest of the apostles to dub him as The Messiah's closest friend, so to speak.[35] John, as The Messiah's closest friend became privy to His eternal life in ways the other apostles were not. The fact that John received the Savior's most comprehensive disclosure, His end time Apocalypse, substantiates this truth. Look at some of the clues John gives to Jesus' heavenly identity: John 1:10, 11 *"He was in the world, and the world was made by him, and the world knew him not. He came unto his own, and his own received him not."* Jesus came as Creator, a revelation Isaiah says only God's covenant people knew at the time.[36] He showed up to His own people, and they did not hear Him because He was unrecognizable to their popular faith. When challenged about His actu-

---

33 Human arrangement notwithstanding, the genealogy of Christ is necessary to establish His identity, His lineage, and His deity as the Son of Israel's God.

34 Hebrews 5:8.

35 What the apostles whom Jesus loved means.

36 See Isaiah 43:10; 46:9.

al age and identity in John 8:58, Jesus boasted of being older than Abraham, Israel's progenitor, and having existed before the patriarch came into being. In addition to reinforcing His oneness with His Father, Israel's God, Jesus further indicates His eternal existence and collaboration with the Almighty. John reports it this way, *"But Jesus answered them, 'My Father has been working until now, and I, too, am working'."*[37] With this passage, John 8:49 agrees.

To continue enlarging upon The Messiah's prior life and identity, 1 Peter 1:10 adds, "Even the prophets, who prophesied about the grace that was to be yours, carefully researched, and investigated this salvation. They tried to find out what era or specific time the Spirit of The Messiah in them kept referring to when he predicted the sufferings of The Messiah and the glories that would follow. It was revealed to them that they were not serving themselves but you concerning the things that have now been announced to you by those who brought you the good news through the Holy Spirit sent from heaven. These are things that even the angels desire to look into." ISV. The most explicit New Testament passage relative to this discussion is 1 Corinthians 10. There Paul, the rabbi of rabbis, makes a startling revelation regarding Christ's pre-carnate identity as Yahweh. Here is the entire passage that divulges His position as Israel's Sovereign:

> "Moreover, brethren, I would not that ye should be ignorant, that all our fathers were under the cloud, and all passed through the sea; And were all baptized to Moses in the cloud and in the sea; And all ate the same spiritual food; And all drank the same spiritual drink: (for they drank of that spiritual Rock that followed them: and that Rock was **Christ**.) But with many of them God was not well pleased: for they were overthrown in the wilderness. Now these things were our examples, to the intent we should not lust after evil things, as they also lusted. Neither be ye idolaters, as were some of them: as it is written, the people sat down to eat and drink, and rose up to play. Neither let us commit lewdness, as some of them committed, and fell in one day three and twenty thousand. Neither let us tempt Christ, as some of them also tempted, and were destroyed by serpents. Neither murmur ye, as some of them also murmured, and were destroyed by the destroyer." [38]

In support of this Continuum teaching, no passage of Scripture better makes the point. The rock that gave Israel water at Meribah was Jesus, alive, just not human; but God, the very Yahweh of Sinai. The very one who commissioned Moses to deliver His people from Egyptian bondage.

---

37 ISV.
38 1 Corinthians 10:1-9.

Another Old Testament incident is recalled in the passage. The Baalpeor incident is quoted. *"The children sat down to eat, and rose up to play"*, recalled from Numbers 25:1-4.[39] Other examples are Galatians 3:8; Acts 2:25-31; John 1:18; and Philippians 2:5-8. Lastly, there is Jesus' appearance to Abraham in Mamre. In Genesis 18:2, He physically appears accompanied by two angels to transact some grave worldly business. He is securing His covenant with Abraham, impregnating Sarah with Isaac, and destroying Sodom and Gomorrah on His divine visit to earth. With John 1:18 saying that no one has ever seen God at any time and Abraham still recognizes Him as his Lord, it is easy to see that who appeared to him is Jesus, before taking on His Yahweh or Messiah personas in the Continuum.

---

39 Refer Psalm 106:28; Hosea 9:10.

[6]

Summarizing The 14 Events

This chapter summarizes the actual 14 events that fold into the Continuum, along with what made them worthy of its inclusion. Extensive detail of their importance and magnitude to the Continuum is discussed throughout the teaching. Here, the goal is to encapsulate their value to it. As stated earlier, the Scripture premise that most props up the Continuum is Matthew 1:17. It reads *"So all the generations from Abraham to David are fourteen generations. And from David until the carrying away into Babylon, fourteen generations. And from the carrying away into Babylon until Christ, fourteen generations."* [40] Extensive exploration of these generations dominates this chapter. This book teaches a great deal about them. The primary purpose is to disclose what Matthew's Gospel has in mind. The chapter investigates how early Israel registered and enumerated its citizens, and the many conflicting conclusions that challenge their authenticity. However, when it comes to the Scriptures overall, their Author, His motives, and methods take precedence over all.

While it is reasonable to assess God's word in the context of the Jews alone, doing so must be tempered with the realization that an outside force constantly acting on them shaped and influenced their thinking and culture. That external authority sketched their world and carved its place among the nations. The Lord, as that outside force, has been legislating their consciousness and conduct from the time He delivered them from Egyptian bondage until their seventy-year exile. He also maneu-

---

40 KJV

vered their life every day, whether they knew or appreciated it or not while in their captive land. Yes, it is true, the obvious answers are more explainable, but ease of explanation does not manifest the sum of revelations to be acquired. Besides this, over-humanizing the Lord, to make Him congruent with the limitations and vulnerabilities of human beings is a mistake that causes those endeavoring to know Him to arrive at erroneous conclusions. It must be remembered that the Old and New Testament genealogies were to track more than the Jewish nation. On the surface, it appears that they had no other purpose. In truth, the aim was infinitely more sublime. Tracing Israel's genealogies had a higher purpose as seen in their registries' beginnings and endings. The records so meticulously kept were important to trace the lineage of The Messiah as He traveled down the line from seed to seed to get into the world. The beginning of His journey was Adam. The end of His journey was Joseph and Mary. Identifying the sperm that housed Him and carried Him from God's being into Mary and Joseph's family was crucial because Adam's descendants had split between himself and Cain. After his judgment, Cain begot an opposing nation that emulated his father's community. Cain was banished by God from his father's community that evidently still basked under the Most High's glory. When he ventured out, he started a kingdom. With no other model to follow, Cain imitated his father's world, even giving some of his sons the same names. It was all he knew. None of it mattered because the Lord God long ago promised the serpent; that old red Dragon who is Satan and God's adversary, a certain woman would give birth to a seed more powerful than all his combined. That seed or male would crush the rule that he had just deceptively wrested from Adam.

The seed of the woman would, the prophecy says, have its own vulnerabilities; because, although it would be powerful enough to destroy the dark potentate's dominion, its place on earth would make it vulnerable to his backlash. Thus, the serpent would bruise its heel. That heel was figurative of The Messiah's Ecclesia, the ultimate center of His earthly rule. Having to walk in the flesh in a planet darkened by Satan's curses made the serpent's head crusher susceptible to his snake bites from time to time. The two, for a season would be unable to avoid each other. God's promise to produce such an offspring would have clearly spoken to Satan inhabiting the serpent's body differently than it did to Adam and his wife. Immediately, it told him how to procreate. Secondly, it convinced him that he had the ability to thwart the prophecy if he got his family into the world first, which he did. The Devil somehow deduced that impregnating the woman would short circuit God's word and populate the earth with his seed first. Pervertedly, that occurred in Genesis 6 when the sons of God reproduced with the daughters of men. Above that, it is also why Adam's firstborn was of the wicked one.[41] As it happened, the Lord anticipated his stratagem and used it to His advantage. Romans chapter 5 recalls it. The Lord let Adam fulfill the serpent's dark agenda and used his lineage to manifest the Christ. He left the heavy work of populating planet to the serpent, whose offspring would be clearly detected from Jesus' when the time came.

Today, the Devil's head crusher is the Lord Jesus Chris. His vulnerable side is His church on earth, to explain the heel bruising part. One of the several definitions for the feet in Scripture is "the basis of power, or rule." Thus, the Church's power and authority in the earth would be susceptible to the serpent's venomous bites, which give the Lord's vow in Matthew 16:19 more poignancy. The gates of hell, Jesus vows, would not prevail against His church. Although throughout its earth walk there would be occasions when its power would be contested and suppressed, the greatest promise is that The Messiah's church at large, universal, and perpetual will triumph in the end. For the record, the gates of hell are laws, governments, armies, prophecies, rulers, ambassadors, judges, communities, and the merchants of the world. The church on earth must in the face of these, learn to empower and position itself to acquire, conquer, and dominate every sphere of human life on earth. It must learn to capture and maintain that power if it wants to enjoy all that the blood of Jesus purchased for it. A good persuasive start is comprehending the fourteen events that make up God's Eternal Continuum.

THE 14 EVENTS IN A NUTSHELL

1. **The Great War in Heaven:** This event is the single one that started it all, which is why it begins the Continuum's fourteen episodes. The heavens were peaceful, orderly, and pristine. At first, its citizens lived life the way the Lord God originally ordained. Every member of His society tirelessly fulfilled the reasons He created him or her. Life was happy for them, until a specially anointed cherub's iniquitous heart moved him to disrupt it all. Not content with the power, prosperity, and privilege he had as Lucifer, this creature felt he deserved better and mounted a full-scale war to get it. Evil thoughts and malicious actions brought about a name change, as he went from being eternity's Daystar to the Old Red Dragon. The name change further brought with it an altered state of existence and a completely downgraded purpose and po-

---

41 See Matthew 13:19, 38 and 1 John 3:12.

sition in creation. He was once a friend, and now an adversary; initially a citizen, now an outcast; once a collaborator, but is now a corrupter. Whether or not the cherub expected the sweeping alterations and mutations his actions brought about is debatable. However, Lucifer's name change, in God's wisdom, says it all. No longer a member of the folds, he nonetheless remains useful for future divine tasks. The Almighty re-employed His first major problem as a calculated solution, and deployed the former covering cherub as the sinister sifter of His creation.

The Dragon's selfish ambition changed everything, and inseminated eternity and its worlds with things it had never experienced before; that is, rebellion, sin, death, war, crime and injustice, to name a few. His rebellion pervasively infected the whole of creation and terrorized its residents. The war, covered in Revelation 12, ignited many things. It triggered the chain of events that evicted Satan forever from heaven's high places, and set in motion the reasons the Son of God would come to earth and die at his hands. That Great War staged the Edenic contest that necessitates humanity's compulsory new birth in return for eternal life. Including this event in the fourteen is significant, it makes a profound comforting statement. The Great War in Heaven, aside from impressing upon every generation of humanity that there is a hereafter, also reveals there is a before. Jesus revisits this world in His glorified state to let the earth know He is alive and His Passion has restored Him to His world's reign. In John's Apocalypse, He discloses how things got to be the way they are on earth. Neither Jesus Himself, nor this world's sin problem was caused by humankind, but by His immortal creatures. Including the Great War in heaven's backstory in His portrayal of the apocalypse is shrewd, because the Lord wants those who come to Him from the world of sin and death to know that without a doubt He is able to save them. He will win His contest with this world because He has won it before and will succeed over and over again. Way before ever the earth was created; the Lord Jesus saved His world and the others. His account of the War in Heaven says the redeemed can rest in hope because their Messiah is not just the carpenter that walked the earth for nearly thirty-four years, ministering for three and a half of them before being murdered. Rather, He is the eternal Son of God who has been active in His Father's creation since before all things, and before all time, ceaselessly warring, ruling, and defending. What all of this says to earth's successive generations is that when one hears the Devil is defeated, one now knows that Calvary is not his first defeat. According to Revelation 12:12, 13 in particular, he has suffered crushing blows from God's Son and His armies before, to explain Christ's comments in Luke 10:18. Jesus further demonstrates His uncontested triumph over this creature in Matthew 8:29; Mark 5:7; and Luke 8:28. Collectively, these show the Devil's Calvary defeat is at the very least his second one. At the time of Jesus' revelation, he will be defeated at least three more times. One, when he faces off with Jesus after His death. Two when he is imprisoned in hell for a thousand years, and three, when his deceptory purposes are finally fulfilled. After completing his doomsday tasks, the Devil is condemned to the lake of fire forever. It seems from these remarks that he has been a worthy opponent for God and humanity, because he is always the chief antithetic instrument used by the Most High.

2. **The Garden of Eden:** The creation of man and woman on the earth appears to reawaken the dormant ambition and deviousness in the serpent imprisoned there. These exact emotions are what got him thrown out of eternity. By the time they are created, his dark aspirations have become his permanent character. Still, the prospect of regaining some of his former glory and re-accessing the Most High's worlds seemed doable, especially now that God has replenished the earth and placed a new species there. Watching the rebuilding of the earth from the outside, the idea took hold and became an objective when the fallen angel saw the Lord God's treatment of, and response to, the man and the woman in the garden. Replaying the same tactics used in heaven, the serpent sets out to repeat history and draw Adam and the woman into his doom. His ploy works and wins him control of the earth once more. But this time his success is calculatedly anticipated. Tactically, the Almighty surrenders the earth and Adam's seed to the serpent to do the grueling work of populating, building, (replenishing), guarding and governing it for His Son. Adam is packed with human sperm that must find their way from his loins into the woman's body, and predestinately, into the world. There are trillions and trillions of them that were darkened by the very sin and death pronounced upon the serpent before he was banished from God's world. As a result, they too are doomed to die. It is what the Lord God meant when He told Adam that he would die the instant he ate from the tree of the knowledge of good and evil. God could declare this outcome, not so much as a decree, but more so as a consequence of disobeying Him and replacing Him with a fallen

angel who has deified himself. Adam's demise and dethronement were inevitable and he should have heeded the warning. The spiritually dead serpent, the Lord already knows, has taken over the tree. Death is in the serpent, although the tree he inhabits is merely the game piece that determines who wins Adam's seed. Which god will reproduce himself on the earth, Creator or creature? It takes millennia for the Devil to realize that he was duped a the eternal part of humanity was safely tucked away in heaven's securest vault, Christ's being. Remembering the dragon's heavenly revolt, God deliberately surrenders it to him. What He hopes in doing so is that Adam believes his Maker enough to avoid the renegade creature's curse. The punishment imposed upon the serpent for attempting to overthrow His Creator's rule and world. Adam does not, and so inaugurates the Continuum's next cycle, on earth.

3. **Abraham's Covenant:** This event is crucial because it initiates God's creation wide recovery plan. Earth's subjection to the law of sin and death began with humans, as 1 Corinthians 15 says, and has to be rectified by (or through) people, as well. The antediluvian flood is over, the earth is replenished, and repopulation is in full swing. The time has come for the next phase of the Most High's elaborate redemption plans. Reversing His heavenly replenishment method in this world, the Lord starts with flesh and blood instead of eternal spirits to recover His preordained portion of lost humanity. Their eternal spirits safely stashed away in His first begotten Son's being, leaves their souls to be distributed as Adam's seed. Abraham joins a long list of souls to get the Son of God into the flesh. The Most High chose him because he proved to be the most faithful and obedient candidate for His goals. Appreciably impressed with Abraham's response to Him, the Most High promises Israel's patriarch that He will multiply his seed to cover the earth. When He made this promise, Abraham was childless and quite old, and both he and his wife were barren. Considering the concubine customs of the period in which he lived, it is logical to assume that Abraham for sure had intimate relations with other women over the years. Yet the Lord affirms that he impregnated none of them. In addition, Sarah, in offering him her maid Hagar to impregnate, further suggests this. Conclusively, it seems that since he had no children, he was as impotent as his wife was infertile, until the Most High blessed him. Why else would he be convinced that one born in his house would be his heir?

Unmoved by all of this, the Almighty God tells Abraham that all the nations of the earth will be blessed through him. No doubt, His words stun the man, but being a former Babylonian prophet, the Most High God was probably no stranger to him. Add to that his father Terah's apparent conversion to the Almighty motivated Abraham and his wife to leave Ur of Chaldea, and their acquaintance with one another becomes assumable. The ulterior dynamics between them suggests God's prophecy fell on good ground. Pleased with his faith response to His prophecy, and with Abraham himself, the Lord also promises to make the man heir of the world through his seed.[42] His faith provides the catalyst the Lord needs to redeem the lost and reclaim the world surrendered to darkness in Eden, way back at its foundation.

4. **The Ten Plagues:** When the Almighty visited Abraham to make His promises to him, He told him that his descendants would be enslaved for 400 years. At the end of that time, after they multiplied extensively in Egypt, the Lord would return to redeem His people from the house of their bondage. To do so, God had to face off with their captor, Egypt's Pharaoh, who saw himself as a God. He was not at all interested in releasing his slave labor. To inspire him to do so, God drew him into a contest that was to prove which of the two reigning monarchs turned out to be the Almighty. The spoils of the war between them were the children of Israel. To deliver His people, the Most High God levied[43] ten assaults against Pharaoh's realm to prove his power. Called the Ten Plagues, those assaults ended up demolishing his kingdom and rendering him too shattered to hold onto his captives. Israel leaves Egypt under the mighty hand of her covenant God and the leadership of Moses, who was once Egypt's heir apparent.

5. **Moses' Exodus:** After devastating Egypt and destroying its rulers, the Lord through Moses, marched Abraham's seed right out of Egypt to become His theocratic nation. To see that Moses succeeded in his commission, the Lord endued His prophet with unprecedented powers and signs that he used systematically to, topple Pharaoh's kingdom. By the time the tenth plague began, death, the people and their leaders were begging their king to let God's people go. Unable to defeat Moses' God, Pharaoh reversed his earlier position and hurried Yahweh's people out of his demolished land. Egypt was weakened, by its contest with the Most High and so no one in the country was able or dared

---

42 Romans 4:13.

43 To start or wage (war).

to hinder Israel's exodus. God Almighty delivered the Jews to worship their God in the wilderness. Once He freed Israel from its bondage, Jehovah began grooming the tribes to become an independent, yet theocratic, state. The first thing He wanted them to understand was that He had not freed them for their own sake or purposes, but for His. He had promised their patriarch Abraham that they would become a world power and the Lord their God was not about to break that promise. Israel was to become His own peculiar treasure and Yahweh, as their God, in turn, would fulfill His promise to Abraham, Isaac, and Jacob through them. Repeatedly, the Lord reminds the world that what He does, began with Abraham, who so pleased Him that He seeks to reward him through his seed forever. For the sake of their progenitor, God takes exceptional care of His new kingdom and their children, choosing them as the vehicle that brings His precious eternal Son into the world.

6. **Moses' Law**: As with any good leader, organizing an acquired mass of souls so that they survive and grow into a mighty nation is primary. Other priorities include teaching them how to succeed, how to secure themselves, and how to prosper in their land. These are what the holy God wanted for His people when He delivered them from their Egyptian bondage. His first order of business was to instruct them in His ways and outline the conditions under which He would bless them and ensure their perpetuity. Motivated by His top priorities, as Israel's God, He proceeds to tell them how they would stay alive and grow into the nation He planned for them to become. The first thing He does is to settle them, to establish His law for them. This was first because lawlessness breeds the anarchy that eventually corrupts and ultimately destroys a community. Festering sin, left unchecked, assures its objects will self-destruct and that, the Most High was not going to let happen to His beloved nation before it could even stand on its own two feet. To this end, God gave Moses the Ten Commandments at Sinai, after spending forty days and nights on the mountaintop with him. At the same time, God gave Moses, now his lawgiver, the rest of the constituents of His brand new earthly kingdom. From worship to warfare, God engrafted and empowered Moses with the wisdom and foresight to institute all it took for His people to thrive away from Egypt and evolve into a mighty nation. The maneuver was significant because Moses, as their deliverer had no desire for God's new nation to reinstitute the Egyptians' government in their new world, despite it being all they knew. Quickly, to impress upon them that His world would not be like theirs,

the Lord imposed His everlasting law on them. Bringing it down from heaven Himself, Yahweh, as He would come to be known by them etched His commands in stone on the side of the mountain He had made the seat of His government. The Lord's full impartations to Moses enabled him to establish a government, regulate family and community life, found the Levitical Priesthood, generate an economy, and build an army. God's law framed their constitution for future divine legislation so the generations to come would not offend their Lord and thereby forfeit their nationhood and divine privileges. For his tasks, the Almighty gave Moses exceptional endowments to execute all He ordained under His watchful eye. Moses in setting up God's government became the Most High's first prime minister over His new nation. His being made such set the prophetic in the realm of national government and as the lawgiver; Moses fits the classification of a shaliach, an Old Testament type of apostle. Israel served Yahweh as their king for a great while before they demanded to go from a theocracy to a monarchy. The king that housed the Son of God in his loins was David.

7. **David's Kingship**: With the Law of Moses' in place and the Levitical Priesthood inaugurated as a result of it, life for the freed slaves settled down. The priesthood was crucial to the new nation's survival, as placating the Lord was a major part of its obligations. With God as their sitting king, human administration of His government to this end fell to them. Under their Theocrat's auspices, Moses ordained citizenship laws for Israel and scrupulously enforced them until his death. After him, the judges took over for decades until it was time for the twelve tribes to become a kingdom. At the close of the judgeship era, Samuel commenced the prophets' official rule and inaugurated Israel's first and second kings. The political climate under judgeship so deteriorated the fabric of the land that it forced the Lord to furlough His Mosaic priesthood, or at least substantial parts of it when the Philistines captured the Ark of God as a war spoil. They took it when they attacked His land and God permitted it to avenge Eli and his sons' crimes against Him and His priesthood.

In the course of time, rule of the nation passed to the kings where it remained until Nebuchadnezzar deported them to Babylon. Saul, Israel's first king proved a dismal failure to the Lord. He bucked against His theocracy and seemed to resent subjecting his throne to Yahweh's. The first king also diverted the main of the nation's resources to his and his sons' private inurement. That is, to their personal benefit and advantage as Samuel prophesied he would. He abused his nation, his position, and his God who tolerated his maltreatment for nearly two decades, while He got a man after His own heart ready to reign in his place. That man was David, the son of Jesse to whom the Lord shifted Saul's dynasty so that His eternal Son Jesus Christ could enter the world through a royal line. Jesus, traveled down His nation's Jewish lineage to spring out of the Tribe of Judah as God promised David He would in 2 Samuel Chapter 7. David was a better king to Yahweh than Saul was, despite two distinct clashes between them that cost David greatly. The first clash is the abuse of power he used to have Uriah, the husband of a woman with whom he committed adultery and subsequently impregnated, killed. The second clash is when he foolishly ordered a national census against the Lord's wishes. Both events brought grave consequences upon David, with the first offense being somewhat mitigated by the birth of Solomon who succeeded him on the throne. David's place and purpose in the Continuum was to provide the human seed the King of kings needed to enter the earth as royalty. It is how The Messiah received His divine right to rule as an earthly King. David's dynasty was marked for perpetuity because his genealogy was granted the privilege of procreating eternity's Sovereign. Following Solomon, David's successor numerous kings ruled, and be spoiled, God's precious land until He could no longer stand it. When His long-suffering was exhausted, He deported them to Babylon, which miraculously turned out to be the saving of the nations.

8. **Israel's Captivity**: Centuries of up and down struggles between Yahweh, and Israel ended with a ruthless warrior king named Nebuchadnezzar deporting the entire nation to Babylon. His conquest of Israel transported its whole population from their land. The event activated the downside of the Mosaic covenant and its foretold judgments took effect. The nation's catastrophe occurred, according to the Lord's word to His people. He reiterated the warning for ages through the mouths of His prophets. Yet, Israel's persistent disobedience to Moses' Law and its abuse of His priests and prophets was ceaseless. As a result, God could not hold back their punishment any longer and authorized a super power to destroy them.[44] The Lord appointed Nebuchadnezzar to invade, plunder, and desolate His beloved land. He also allowed him to take

---

44 Refer to Deuteronomy 32:30; 2 Kings 24:2, 3; 2 Chronicles 36:21, 22; Jeremiah 21:6; 22:8-10; Jeremiah 22:30; 27:5-22; 28; 29, 30 (30:9).

back to his country Babylon, thousands of captives of the children of Israel. The shocking event went as the Lord promised. He told His people through Moses their first esteemed prophet that if they bespoiled[45] His beloved land, He would retaliate by evicting them from it. He even had them swear to obey Him, repeatedly signing renewal scrolls and etching their vow on rocks, all to no avail. When He had exhausted every medial measure, Yahweh performed His word and permitted Nebuchadnezzar to carry off most of His nation. He took all those that did not die in combat or as casualties of war, except those the Lord kept alive to inhabit the desolated land. God's land was to rest seventy years and after that, it would be re-inhabited. Daniel was the prophet that discovered Jeremiah and the other prophet's words to this effect. Their prophecies told him when it was time for Yahweh's people to return home. When their divine sentence was up, again true to His word, the Lord began to move on the hearts of their captor kings, their exile citizens, and rulers to restore His people to their homeland. The captivity is in the Continuum because it shows that the Lord's involvement in His people's lives did not end with their deportation. While in exile, He still held them to their covenant, raised up priests and prophets, and taking advantage of the situation, inducted the Gentiles into His redemptive vision. When He converted Abraham, the Lord promised that all nations would be blessed in him. The prophecy saw its beginnings in Egypt, although there the people largely stayed within their twelve tribes. However, when Nebuchadnezzar took them under his reign, that unity was shattered and he dispersed them throughout his realm as he saw fit, fulfilling perhaps ingloriously, the Lord's word to bless the nations through them.

9. **Israel's Return Home**: When the seventy years in captivity were fulfilled, the Lord began to put it in the heart of certain leaders of His people to return home. To legitimize their doing so, He activated a provision in His word that prophesied He would use a king yet to be born to free His people and send them back to Israel. Had He not done so, they would have been punished severely for attempting to leave their captor's empire. The books of Ezra and Nehemiah record God's performance of these promises beautifully. The prophesied king's name is Cyrus and both Isaiah and Jeremiah foretell his birth, rise to the throne, and susceptibility to Israel's God and His people. Through a series of protracted divine events, the Lord ushered His people out

---

45 Polluted.

of the land of their captivity once more. Only this time it was not by plagues as with Egypt, this exodus came through favor. He put it in the king's heart, to sympathize with His people's desire to restore their religion in their homeland, a territory that Cyrus apparently dominated as part of his realm. What better way to have a devastated region brought back to life than to send the people who once lived there back home to restore it? Cyrus accommodated Nehemiah's yearning to resettle his fellow citizens in their homeland. True to the Lord's word, he was moved with compassion because Nehemiah was quite distressed by the Lord's burden put on him. Above that, the king honored his request because Nehemiah had been an exemplary servant who was unaccustomed to emotionality in his presence. Cyrus' appreciation of Nehemiah's excellent service motivated him to help the man's cause to the point of financing a good bit of it out of his national and royal treasuries. He also used his authority to assure his safety and that of those who went with him. King Cyrus issued royal decrees forbidding anyone in his dominion to impede Nehemiah and his pilgrims' progress or to do them harm because of it. The reason this event qualifies for the Continuum is obvious. The captivity is over and God's people are returning home as He prophesied. Now the Messianic part of the plan can begin.

10. **Jesus Christ's Incarnation**: As the Continuum trudges on for God's people and the world, His redemptive purpose for them finally arrives. The nation of Israel is, as Revelation 12 narrates, to be The Messiah's womb. At last, the time comes and the promised Messianic King of the Jews is to be born. God breaks His centuries' long prophetic silence with John the Baptist, Jesus' cousin being born six months before Him. True to His pattern, He does so with the ancient prophets' writings. To restart His Continuum, the Most High sends the angel Gabriel, first to Zacharias the priest and six months later to the Virgin Mary. God fully activates Malachi and Isaiah's prophecies. John the Baptist, the messenger to go before the Lord's face, is conceived and shortly thereafter, the virgin who shall bear God's Son Emanuel is impregnated. The angel helps the priest locate the prophecy foretelling the son to be born to him in Israel's ancient scrolls. Amazingly, Zacharias and his son are found in Scripture's Continuum as a result. It is also time to impregnate the virgin, so the angel Gabriel makes his way to where she is to tell her the good news. She is to be the mother of the promised Messiah. Of all the women in Israel, then and before her, she alone is chosen and honored to be Yahweh's highly fa-

vored woman. Her virgin womb is to be blessed and commemorated forever. Verifying that she is indeed the one, Mary questions Gabriel on how she will get pregnant. In doing so, she unwittingly affirms her virginity. The angel lets her know that she is the virgin the Prophet Isaiah wrote about ages ago and tells her how she will be inseminated with the Christ Child. Gabriel says the Lord will overshadow her and His Holy Spirit will deposit the seed of The Messiah directly in her womb. From that moment onward, he lets her know, she becomes the mother of God's first begotten Son. In an instant, her reason for living is revealed. Mary learns that she is the woman Isaiah prophesied would conceive the seed to crush the serpent's head. Here the word is one that the Almighty Himself prophesied way back in the Garden of Eden. That is how long the Continuum has been in effect. Immediately after her conception, Mary retreats from the scene and stays with Elizabeth for her first trimester. Elizabeth as a priest's wife knows what is going on with her and her cousin Mary. She knows that it is according to the Scriptures she has heard, read all her life. Luke narrates what happens between them when Mary enters Elizabeth's presence. John the Baptist, already in Elizabeth's womb leaps for joy at the angel's words coming to pass. What Gabriel had prophesied about John before Elizabeth conceived him, "he shall be filled with the Holy Ghost from His mother's womb", happens as embryonic Jesus baptizes Elizabeth's six-month old fetus. It is remarkable, especially when one realizes that, approximately thirty years later, John the Baptist gets to return the favor. It almost goes without saying why this event is included in the Continuum. It is the one that literally set off the series of chain reactions that brings the Son of God into the world and births His church about three decades later.

11. **Jesus Christ's Crucifixion**: Regardless of whoever did or did not grasp it, Jesus never lost sight of His incarnation destiny. He left His throne in glory for one reason and one reason only, to give His life as a ransom for the souls of His lost humanity. All that He did, everything He said, was to see that two things happened: One is that He got on Calvary's cross and died, and two is that His crucifixion landed Him where the real battlefield was, in hell. Unbeknownst to His followers, hell is where God really sent Him. As He waited for the feast day that His Father scheduled in heaven for His crucifixion, Jesus gathered His apostles, preached the gospel of the kingdom, and manifested Himself as Israel's Messiah. He confirmed His identity by working signs and miracles that the people understood only the Son of David would do among

them. On that fateful Passover week, the Lamb of God indeed was slain. Although, to His onlookers He died as a criminal cursed by God, in reality His death outfitted Him for the battle of the ages, at least in this creation. It equipped Him to enter the realm of the dead to retrieve all those souls Adam condemned to Satan's prison. As far as those He had spent the last three and a half years readying for this very moment were concerned, Jesus was just fulfilling the Scriptures. Although at the time, they did not really understand the scope of His obligation to the Old Testament's prophecies. To the holy angels who watched it all unfold, their Lord suffered the necessary horror that would set aright eons of dysfunctions in God's worlds. The powers of darkness on the other hand, were delusionally happy, utterly misinterpreting the events unfolding before them.

The night before He dies, the Lord Jesus reminds His apostles that what is about to come upon Him is His Father's, and their God's, will. It is all according to the word of the prophets that foresaw and prophesied His life, death, and resurrection. Still quite unconvinced about what He said until it happened, the apostles and disciples could not believe Jesus would be taken from them as viciously as He described. None of His followers could accept it until His enemies arrested Him in Gethsemane late at night. His ordeal took place, according to God's predetermined will; His torment was real and cruel. The authorities beat Jesus all night, illegally tried and convicted Him, and sentenced Him to a speedy death. Since His execution is taking place on a High Holy season, His accusers deny Him the normal due process of law. The rulers want His proceedings and subsequent murder over with before celebrating their annual Passover. But none of it surprises Jesus because He is the Continuum and the words of the prophets concerning Him are being fulfilled. If He does not die, He cannot rise. If He does not rise from the dead, He cannot recover the thousands upon thousands of lost souls confined to the Devil's abyss. If He is not betrayed, He cannot be killed because as God incarnate, He is deathless. Everything happening to Him has to occur for the Father's plan to work. Jesus has to meet the Devil on His own turf. They must fight it out for the Lord to retrieve the keys to hell and the grave; evidently what the dragon stole when he left The Messiah's world. Jesus must take from His arch enemy his life-destroying and soul-slaughtering weapons. If He does not, all of the doomed souls remanded there at death will be lost to Him forever. That is what He preached, in spite of most of His audience failing to comprehend it. In parables, the Savior unveiled the plan for three and a half years and still when God's predeterminations took hold of Him His successors were caught off guard. The Continuum nonetheless made provision for the confrontation the two powers must have, so everyone involved must forge ahead until all is fulfilled because, as Jesus said more than once, what they witnessed was according to what is written concerning Him.

12. **Jesus Christ's Resurrection**: If His apostles and followers found it difficult to believe that the celebrated Son of Man was unlawfully seized, unjustly tried, convicted on trumped up charges, and killed as a result, His word about coming back to them from the grave had to be even more incredulous. Appearing to two of them on the road while they were still bemoaning His crucifixion, Jesus once more tries to tell them that it was all written beforehand, and they should have expected His return, not bewail His death. The Messiah's confidence in His Father's word and power shows and holds fast throughout His crucifixion. Jesus is so convinced that He will be back to earth in three days that He tells His apostles where to meet Him when He rose from the dead. In spite of His never lying to them, not once, exaggerating His position or deceiving them with lying signs and wonders, the Lord's disciples still could not quite take His predictions as truth. He told them He would rise again and afterwards the way to eternal life would be open to them. No matter how they took it, Jesus' faith in His Father's plan persisted and at the end of the three days, He rose from the dead just as He said He would. Not only did He rise from the dead, but dozens of saints that had been justified by Moses' Law rose from the dead along with Him. Their resurrection said that not only would God bring His beloved first begotten back to life, but also that His finished work enabled the resurrection of countless others. God raising Jesus from the dead may appear as an act of bias, but raising a bunch of the old saints that were perhaps long forgotten makes a different statement. The act reinforced the prospects of eternal life and the Godhead's power to accomplish it in those that believed. When Jesus rose from the dead, He broke the power of the law of sin and death. With that, He defeats the Devil's ability to enslave humanity, and phenomenally the Gentiles can now become heirs of Christ and participate in Israel's Commonwealth. This is all possible because of the Almighty's stupendous, yet purposefully concealed resurrection power. Clearly, the resurrection goes to the heart of the Continuum. If Jesus is still in the grave, then every account of His life is moot. Paul says it best in 1 Corin-

thians 15:13-19, "If the dead do not rise", he says, then preachers of the gospel and its resurrection power "are above all men most miserable." The entire hope of the Christian rests on the Savior's precarnate, incarnate, and eternal existence. If none of this is true, then from where did the very mention of the word Christian, the mere idea of a Christian church, and the institution called Christianity come? To utter any one of them is to verify Jesus' testimony. It is to confirm the Scripture's entire account of the Son of God becoming flesh, sojourning on earth, dying on the cross, and rising from the dead for the salvation of all humanity.

13. **Jesus Christ's Ascension:** Once Jesus satisfied His Father's resurrection requirements by pouring His blood on the altar, leading captivity captive, and sitting down on God's right hand, He was thus free to resume traversing back and forth between all worlds. Not just as the Son of God, but also as the Son of Man. His Calvary triumph gave Him all authority in heaven and on earth. So for more than a month, He pops in and out of the planet, wrapping up the details that would beget His church. Although the Church is not yet born, the resurrected Jesus reinstates the apostles to their office. The death of Jesus of Nazareth that closed out Moses' Law also vacated their Mosaic commissions. Being the promised propitiation for all human sin and defeating death and hell in the grave, there was on God's part no more need for it. Jesus' demise vacated their Israeli commission and left the apostles with nothing more to do. He as their heavenly Sender for all intents and purposes was gone and nothing was in place to keep their commission going. With the Man from Galilee gone, His apostles no longer had anywhere to preach. They were left with nothing else to do but go back to what they were doing before He came. Jesus on the other hand, had other plans that their disbelief in His resurrection had kept them ignorant of until He returned. Now that He has come back to life, and in order for them to carry out His Great Commission, they must be reactivated as His eternal apostles. Only in this commission, they were not just apostles to the nation of Israel under Moses' Law, but apostles to the whole wide world under the law of grace. The Risen Christ, God's Lamb, and Jesus the Lion of Judah merges to become all creation's only appointed, Monarch and Messiah. It makes Him King of the Jews and Sovereign of all worlds. Because He was dead and is now alive, their post Calvary apostleship does not come from an earthly institution, but from heaven itself, just as His did. They are now eternity's apostles, which is what The Messiah

tried to tell them when He promised they would sit on twelve thrones judging Israel's twelve tribe in His regeneration. As the eternal Christ, Jesus says in John 17:2, He is free to save whom He wills and to appoint them to any position in the afterlife He deems appropriate.

14. **The Church's First Pentecost**: To finalize His preparation of the apostles to preach His gospel and break the barrier separating Jews from the Greeks, the Risen Lord holds forty days of classes to finish their training. The expanded trainings further enlighten them on His work and their office, and primes them to be His witnesses. They spend the forty days and nights learning from Him the things pertaining to the kingdom of God. When their final face-to-face training ends, He tells them to tarry—wait—in Jerusalem to be endued with power from on high. The Holy Spirit who was there training them alongside Jesus, would return to earth to take His place as soon as the Christ arrived back in heaven. Until then, they were to wait until He got home to receive their next and most powerful dispensation. It would invest them with all they needed to spread His word and birth His church. So the apostles and others, a total of 120 souls, waited in the upper room for the blessed event. This spiritual number equates to ten souls per each of Israel's twelve tribes, just as the apostles represented one tribe each. After His final briefing, Jesus steps onto a cloud and is lifted out of their sight. At the appointed time, true to His word, the Savior pours out of His Spirit on the 120 in the upper room. The Holy Spirit's baptism, the one the Almighty intended all along, manifested in other tongues and fire. What John the Baptist said Jesus would do when He came, occurred. The Holy Ghost baptized Christ's disciples, all 120, in the upper room with fire. And John the Baptist was not the only prophet who saw this event back in time; the prophet Joel was the first to get the vision. He foretold the outpouring of God's Spirit on all flesh, and divulged what would happen to the world when it did. As the disciples were speaking in other tongues, the Holy Spirit amplified their voices loud enough for all of those in Jerusalem to observe the Feast of Pentecost to hear. Each one of them hears in their native tongue, what the upper room 120 utters prophetically. As they did, the Holy Spirit interpreted what is said in their individual languages. For the apostles and His constant disciples, all of those years of long nights and days of training they had received at The Messiah's feet paid off. His outpouring revealed them to the world, His and ours as His accredited apostles and trustworthy sent ones. Fully educated, they now completely understood, fi-

nally, what was He was trying to get them to grasp all long. They ceased following Moses' Law and became the firstfruits of the Lord's foreordained Ecclesia. At that moment, Peter acts on the Lord's appointment of him as the rock upon which His church would be built and stands up to explain to everyone what is happening. Drawing on the prophets, yet again, he tells how the Holy Spirit just birthed the Almighty's spirit filled church. Imagine how stunning it was to see what the Lord had been telling them in secret unfold publicly and dramatically. From trying to fathom what He was talking about all those years that they followed Him under Moses' Law to seeing with their own eyes, the Holy Spirit's outpouring touch those who perhaps never heard of Jesus or hardly ever took Him seriously. The apostle's amazement must have stupefied them for ages as they lived out what their Messiah had done, beginning with going from Yahweh to Jesus The Messiah to dying and rising from the grave. Witnessing the prophecies concerning Him fulfilled to the letter and picking up the torch of the kingdom, Peter opens his mouth and preaches the first gospel sermon since Jesus left. God's plan worked. The apostles took their place, the message of the kingdom took off, and the Lord Jesus Christ converted thousands of souls for His kingdom and continues to do so all the way up to today.

SOLIDIFYING THE FOURTEEN EVENTS

The preceding fourteen events, encapsulate the unbroken chain of Divine Initiatives that successfully materialized the Second Person of the Godhead. Jesus Christ, the Almighty's first begotten Son came to earth in the flesh by way of predestined events and the prophecies that predicted them. His Messianic arrival was not the way He historically appeared to Israel. In the past, He often manifested through some phenomenon like fire, smoke, lightning, or other spectacular apparition. To identify with human sin and to eradicate it from the people's soul. God's Son became a little lower than the angels to die, and go to hell. His human form was to get Him into hell to recover those Adam lost in His eternal life. Refer to Acts 2:25-35; this passage regards Jesus. It is brought forward from David's writings. He records how he foresaw the Lord and prophesied about Him in the eighth Psalm; see 8:5. Paul, later in his letter to the Hebrews acknowledges the prophecy's fulfillment in 2:9. Furthermore, in Psalm 22:22, David predicts Jesus' response to His own death experience and its resultant outcome. God's second king foretells how Jesus will beget family members after His own kind that He can acknowledge as the Godhead's progeny in the great congregation. What is Jesus Christ's congregation? Because identity is the key to destiny, the Lord's congregation is identified as:

1. The congregation of the Lord -- Micah 2:5.
2. The congregation of Israel -- Exodus 12:3 and 20 other times.
3. The congregation of the righteous -- Psalm 1:5.
4. The congregation of the mighty -- Psalm 82:1.
5. The congregation of the saints -- Psalm 89:5.
6. The assembly of the elders -- Psalm 107:32.
7. The assembly of the people of God -- Judges 20:2.
8. The assembly of the saints -- Psalm 98:7.
9. The assembly of the upright -- Psalm 111:1.

Two other references are worth mentioning here. One is Isaiah 14:13, where the fallen star Lucifer, son of the morning or Daystar vows in his heart to exalt his throne to be like the Most High. The other is Hebrews 12:22 that disclose the general assembly that apparently existed in heaven before the birth of the Savior's Ecclesia. It seems that the Ecclesia as God's elect, has always, and today continues to reside there, to reinforce the reality of its eternal origins.

The Continuum, Predestination, and God's Elect

Jesus' future climaxes heavenly His past. His present materializes that past for those beyond His world. With morality being the last of His life cycles, see Colossians 1:15-18, He long ago set aside a portion of those born on earth to birth anew into His kingdom. He does so to enable them to inherit and enjoy His eternal life. That is what He means when He refers to God's elect. The Lord does not make decisions about people's eternality at their birth or death. He resolved their afterlife inheritance before He created the world (or entered it). He is merely waiting to confirm who in His portion wants to join Him there. Those who take issue with this are confused because popular teachings on His plan of redemption tend to focus exclusively on the earth and its inhabitants. The Scriptures, however, do not. They show that the gospel of Jesus Christ encompasses all of creation. New Testament phrases such as "chosen in Him before the foundation of the world" refer to His elect. They indicate His foreknowledge of the people who will or will not choose Him. When it comes to salvation, the only decision humans on earth get to make is to accept Christ or not. It is their only choice. Rejecting the Savior is innate to humankind because of how people enter the world. Therefore, in reality, their only decision is whether to receive Jesus' salvation, not to refuse Him. Rejecting Him comes natural to those born of Adam, since all of his seeds begin life doomed to die, being born under the law of sin and death. The spirit of this world precludes humanity from God's life and inherently compels it to resent Him as their Maker. The two inspire people to reject His redemption without cause. He answers their rejection with the call to be saved. In the end, it is left up to each person to accept the Lord on earth. While the Almighty knows personally, who will receive and prize His salvation and who will not, those who do not share His omniscience must discover and declare it for themselves in this world because human sin and death originated on earth and not in God where humanity got its start. If the Genesis creation account is to be taken at face value, then its beginning with the command, "let there be light" is significant. God's creative decrees did not start with "let there be earth" but with "let there be light". The earth, verse 1 says, already existed. It reports that the waters and the darkness already covered the planet. What the Genesis account actually pictures, is the Lord's renovation of the earth. It narrates He is repopulating and replenishing it, not that He started from scratch. Discerning what is taking place in chapter 1 and comparing it to what is happening in chapter 2 is important. Chapter 2 looks as if the Lord is duplicating His efforts. He has just said, "let there be" which should have done the job. However, here He seems to be repeating chapter 1 creation on the planet.

As it happens, the lengthy string of commands that God has just uttered schematized earth's renovated infrastructure, while He was yet outside the globe. The rest of His recreation required Him to get down into the dirt and hand make everything He decreed from His heavenly station. He seems to be redundant in chapter 2, but that is not the case. His spiritual creation must be adapted to His physical world. So He gives all that He spoke into existence a body, which says He did not step on this planet until it was renovated. When He descends into it, He brings with Him the male and female that He has just created and communed with outside the earth. The Lord remains on the planet to form the self-generating bodies they will live in until they leave it. While He sculpts their clay vessels, the male and female remain nestled within Him. When the first human body is complete, He breathes the man out of Himself in his new world. Indicating, as He does so that humanity's spirits and souls are not indigenous to the earth, but to His being, inferring why they are accountable to His immortal laws but answerable to them on earth. It is because the earth's after life emerged from God's eternal life.

The Lord holds on to the woman a little longer while He acquaints the man with his world and his duties concerning it. To show the collaborative nature of their relationship, God forms the bodies of every creature that He spoke into existence and gives Adam the privilege of naming them based on his first response to each one. After this project is over, Adam notices he has no comparable mate and somehow conveys to the Lord that He is lonely because of it. Despite their closeness, Adam notices that there is a difference between him and his God and longs for one more like himself. The Lord, having anticipated this, goes to work to embody the last of His hands on creation, the woman, and presents her to Adam. Finally, the massive venture is finished. The earth is renovated, its new inhabitants are all deposited there, and the world's latest guardians are installed and instructed. All that is left to do is to observe them and wait out their confirmation. On whose side will they stand? Will the man and his woman stay in the light with their Maker, or will they instead choose the darkness that once covered the face of the deep; are they aware the consequences of either one? It does not take long before the decision is made. Once it is the Almighty's predestiny plan to get humanity back into Christ and Him into their world to make it so goes into effect.

Predestination is somewhat like a planned celebration for someone who suspects it may take place, but is unsure it will, even though it is customary. The sponsor does not forego the event just because the celebrant knows about it and the celebrant does not refuse to meet the conditions of the event because the secret got out. The parties' foreknowledge of the planned event does not nullify its validity or provide grounds for canceling the plans. That everyone knows in advance that the celebration will take place and how the celebrant will act when he or she arrives is just foreknowledge, everyone else involved has to live it out and so too must those born on earth out the afterlife decisions that God, the party planner knows in advance. How God brought the human race into being is why the earth must bear witness to what the Most High knew before it began. A person deciding for or against Christ has other witnesses besides The Messiah to attest to their righteousness or sin. A mighty cloud of spiritual and earthly witnesses must agree on a departing soul's chosen destination. Think about Nebuchadnezzar's watchers or the angels that kept not their first estate. When it comes to souls departing this world, spiritually speaking, there are the angels who guard and observe people throughout life and the demons who tempt them to forego eternal life and die in their sins. There is also the heavenly cloud of witnesses that Scripture announces observe earth's events, and the saints who make up the Lord's elect. All of these beings testify to a person's decision to choose and serve the real Jesus Christ, and none of them is innately privy to the Most High's omniscience.

With nothing in this world obviously transpiring to prove God's inward knowledge, it is hard for those looking on the outside to trust His conclusion or to know if He will do the same with them should the occasion arise. Knowing what a person is capable of and acting on that knowledge before it is shows itself deprives others from the privilege of feeling one way and deciding another. People need the opportunity to agree with God, to celebrate His good judgment and buy into His salvation in this world. By the time, they get to His it is too late, because the legal system to judge them changes. Human onlookers cannot bear witness to what the Lord knows is true, and for the Lord it is always about a public witness to His truth, because He sees witnessing as legitimate. When it comes to endorsing what happens on earth, for God, the Holy Spirit is His most credible witness. Alongside Him, the angels are seen as credible testifiers. In addition to them is the Church, the righteous and even creation itself as stewards of His invisible creatures are all witnesses. Paul says in Romans 2 regarding this that the human conscience is an immediate witness to people's righteousness. He says it accuses or excuses their behavior and conduct before the Lord. It judges their motivations. Predestination has never been just about what God foreknows, it depends on the public testimony a person garners in the flesh regarding His righteousness. Living for God is an individual matter that must be recorded in heaven and on earth. It is imprudent to presume upon His foreknowledge and deduce that what He knows voids exhibited human responsibilities to Him once they enter their clay bodies. That is fatalistic and the Lord definitely condemns it. What God as Creator knows in His Spirit has little bearing on what He needs His creatures to manifest in their worlds, because that is where one person affected by another can bear witness. The predestined piece enters with God's standards and eternal life criteria. They characterize what He wants to live with forever in His world and what He will refuse entrance to it. Those who comply, as with the country one wishes to migrate to, will inherit His free gift of eternal life. Those who do not, verify they are unworthy of it.

Consider the following analogy to make the point. A nation receives numerous immigrants from other lands and graciously allows them entrance into its country. Those that request to live there permanently may be granted temporary permission to do so, providing they meet its citizenship conditions. The conditions may involve training, conformance, or something similar. Whatever the case, the understanding is that the person will be treated as a citizen in the making and granted certain privileges, as long as he or she works to become a genuine citizen. While working toward the conditions, all is well and remains so up to the day everything must be proved. The prov-

ing process determines if the petitioner lived up to his or her side of the arrangement. If so, formalities officially make the temporary resident a permanent citizen. If
not, the petition is denied, no matter how long or hard the person worked for it. If
along the way criminality or other violations enter, the agreement is immediately nullified, and the petitioner is deported to his or her homeland. This is a small illustration of what it is to enter God's world. Thus, all of creations onlookers must judge
God's fidelity to His creation on the merits of their eyewitness testimony of how a
soul entreats God's redemption offer and conforms to it in the world.

GOD'S ELECT

God's elect are so classified because they prove consistently that He is their choice
and His way of life is their preference. In Scripture, the word *elect* relates to God's
heavenly populations more than twenty times. Its three Old Testament references are
in the Book of Isaiah. See endnotes on Isaiah 42:1-4[21]; 45:4[22] and 65:22.[23] The first passage clearly looks to The Messiah and Israel's restoration as assigned to Cyrus, the
king that authorized it. Daniel's prophecy foretells it. The remaining Isaiah references record the Lord's thoughts about Jacob and Israel respectively, His chosen people and covenant nation. Isaiah 65:9 alludes to His identity and shifts the elect's
emphasis back to The Messiah who comes out of Judah. Elsewhere, He is of Davidic
lineage, the line of Yahweh's approved kings. His everlastingness is implied; He will
inherit the Lord's mountains, figurative of governments to rule through His eternal
elect. The Hebrew translator in this context settled on the word *bachiyr* to identify the
Lord's elect. It speaks to the chosen of God that are appointed to eternal life, after being tried and found excellent enough to join His other excellent ones. Eklektos on the
other hand, is the Greek word for it. It identifies God's elect as His favorites. The
apostles and other Scripture writers understood an authority figure's favorite to be
preselected because they are the best of the best of their kind and the highest in their
class. They are chosen because they meet the authority's pre-established often well
circulated criteria. The Messiah's seeds, fit this category. Those to populate His age
are the most preeminent of Christians, as verified by His Father. Consequently, these
believers manifest the choicest of God's handiwork. They are in the regeneration, appointed to live forever and entrusted with His eternal kingdom's hidden treasures
and powers. God is fiercely passionate about, and protective of His elect. Their making it into His world is so critical to Him that it motivates Him to:

1. Shorten the days of earth's trials and tribulations so His elect is saved -- Matthew 24:22.

2. Insulate His elect from prophetic deceptions -- Matthew 24:24.

3. Protect His elect from false Christs -- Mark 13:22.

4. Specially mark and secure His elect for His angels' end time harvests -- Mark 13:27.

5. Avenge injustices against His elect when they cry out to Him -- Luke 18:7.

6. Vindicate His elect when false accusers rise against them -- Romans 8:33.

7. Qualify His elect to embody His proclivities and sensitivities -- Colossians 3:12.

8. Outfit His elect to be recognized by God and Christ as part of their heavenly entourage with their elect angels -- 1 Timothy 5:21.

9. Upgrade His elect to enter Jesus Christ's salvation and eternal glory -- 2 Timothy 2:10.

10. Capacitate His elect to acknowledge God's truth -- Titus 1:1.

11. Publicize His elect throughout His realms so they are recognized as God's foreknown and foreordained offspring -- 1 Peter 1:2.

12. Condition His elect to be sanctified by His Holy Spirit and Jesus Christ's blood -- 1 Peter 1:2.

13. Specially enhance His elect to believe in Jesus Christ as Zion's chief cornerstone without confusion -- 1 Peter 2:6.

14. Predispose His elect to be shepherded by His chosen ministers who have known the truth -- 2 John 1:1 and 2 John 1:13.

God has reserved special providences for His elect that He conceals from unbelievers. He gives them a different measure of grace that exceeds the natural charisma given to all His creatures. What the Lord reserves and dispenses to His elect comes from the Redeemer's Messianic storages to sanctify them from sin, empower them to live His kind and stature of life, and cause them to triumph in the face of the same harshness endured by Jesus of Nazareth. These details relate to the Continuum, because they were revealed not only to the prophets that verbalized Christ's coming, but also to David and the Messianic seeds coming through his line. While simultaneously in heaven on His throne and on earth in David's sperm, Jesus personally crafted His own physiology, fashioned the days He would live on earth, and schematized His return to heaven. He did these things all the while He traveled down David's genealogy.[24] In short, in preparing for His incarnation, the Savior did for Himself and His earthly mission what He did for every other being He made. He sculpted His flesh, assembled His own soul, selected His preferred genetic lineage, and scripted the days He would walk the earth. He synchronized His preparations to coincide with the day prescheduled for Him to die. Meticulously, the Lord mapped out His death and His resurrection and ascension in the process and notified every generation preceding His arrival on earth of it all through prophecy. To reiterate, here is another reason is why John's Apocalypse says the testimony of Jesus Christ is the spirit of prophecy.

Since the Godhead chose David's lineage to dispatch their Redeemer to earth, Jesus enters the planet with a good part of his human progenitor gene pool. As if to assure His kingly purposes and accomplishments were well publicized, Christ in His precarnate state prophesied significant pieces of them to David by His Holy Spirit. It is unclear from what David wrote how much he realized about The Messiah to come from his body or how much he felt his writings related to his present experience at the time. It does seem, however, from Peter's use of his prophecies in his first sermon that David may have had more than cursory insight into the person he was actually writing about in his psalms.[25] For sure, Nathan's prophecy to David in Samuel's second book suggests he well understood that Jesus was to be among his future offspring. The wording implies David knew full well that he was chosen by the Lord to beget His incarnated Son in the distant future.

The Continuum and the Law of Sin and Death

The Lord Jesus humbled Himself to manifest to the world as the Son of Man, a classification that eternity applies to all Adam's doomed offspring[46]. Human fathers' doom affects them because Adam's disobedience made all his children mortal. Seen in the death, disease, and aging born into humans, mortality guarantees people return to the earth from whence they came when they die. To assure that they do, the Lord God cursed the ground after Satan successfully entered Adam's being. Genesis 3:17 records that this curse took place after God condemned the serpent and the woman it seduced to betray Him. He did so because there is nothing more pervasive on the planet than the ground. It is the source of everything that is, whether animal, vegetable, or mineral. Everything created or invented comes first from the dirt. When a person or thing's life force departs, its material side returns to the earth to be reused. The earth's recycling enforces the law of sin and death so everything in the world remains subject to it. To legislate earth's life and death cycle, God's wisdom could not be more brilliant. Whatever the ground produces passes the curse on unbiasedly un-

---

46 1 Corinthians 15:22.

til the earth is no more, and no one can escape it. That single curse proved to be the most efficient way for the Almighty to let nature take its course and sustain the life and death cycle that grips the planet. New life enters the world and death ushers departed souls out of it. When the Most High said to Adam the ground was cursed for his sake, He had the far-reaching effects of Adam's transgression in view. Simply feeding himself and his family eventually brought this once mighty being to a screeching halt. The Lord knew full well this would happen, because He had imposed the very same death on the fallen cherub Lucifer that Adam had just authorized to fuse with him and his wife's genetics. As dead as his new god was before he entered him is how dead Adam and his family would be from then on, until something happened to interrupt it. Read Romans 5:14, 17 to appreciate why humans' physical bodies deteriorate over time or die when fatal blows drive the life out of them. Their souls, upon leaving their bodies, meet the same fate that befell the Devil and his angels when they sinned in heaven and on earth. Like their spiritual and natural predecessors, humans, too, will be banished to the abyss of hell. Or, as in the case of Lazarus and the rich man in Luke chapter 16, hell's fires should they fail to receive the law of the spirit of life in Christ Jesus in place of the law of sin and death at work in them.

[7]

Abraham, Lazarus and the Rich Man: In Hell Together

Romans 4:13 shows the Almighty designated Abraham to be "heir of the world". When He decreed this destiny upon the man, it was outside of Moses' Law. Abraham and his promise happened long before Moses time. The patriarch received it when he was not a Jew, yet, but a Babylonian, which is why Babylon's inclusion in the Continuum is crucial. The Jewish nation the Lord ordained to flesh out the prophecy had yet to be born. This is deliberate on God's part, because although He wanted a nation, He did not want that nation to be comprised of a single human lineage. He wanted, as Acts 15:14-18 says, a kingdom inhabited by all nations having one distinguishing feature that meant everything to Him. Why? The answer is because that is how the Almighty and His Son began. Both originated with everything they would ever make integral to, and coming from within themselves with Jesus inheriting His produce from His Father. Here is yet another unique factor that sets Christ and His Father apart from all other deities. They want all nations, not just a single lineage, unlike the many single race religions on the planet. John comments on this distinctive in 1:12, 13 of his gospel. Hence, God's chosen nation was to be born with the same nature as His first begotten Son Jesus Christ. It would share one spirit diversified in many ways. Jesus' Father incarnated Him to reproduce its predestined earthly offspring and thereby coalesce them with the Godhead. Notice in the following passages how the Continuum shows up:

- Acts 15:15 – "And to this agree the words of the prophets; as it is written".

- Acts 15:16 – "After this I will return, and will build again the tabernacle of David, which is fallen down; and I will build again the ruins thereof, and I will set it up".
- Acts 15:18 – "Known unto God are all his works from the beginning of the world[26]".

All of the above Scripture teaches that at the present time in everyone's present life, the Lord actively works to manifest His promise to fulfill what He spoke by the mouth of His prophets from the foundation of the world. Thus, what the prophets embedded in the Continuum modern prophets are qualified to corroborate when they are authentic and faithful. Here is why modern prophets get lost. They attempt to use the predictive sides of their prophetic faculties, minus the words that founded and validated their ministries. Misunderstanding what the prophets of old meant to, and did for, God, they fall into Balaam's delusions by giving prophetic credence to any spiritual voice they hear. Without the Continuum to anchor their otherwise lofty spirits, prophets fall prey to divination because they lack the filtering mechanisms Scripture provides. Contemporary prophets can be convinced the Bible is outdated and therefore irrelevant for their times, because they do not know how it came to be and what makes it timeless. This attitude sentences many of them to minister disconnected from what the Almighty has done since before the world began, and will continue to do until its end.

In respect to the Savior's earthly advents, interestingly, His promise to return is intriguing since it is not the first time He utters it. In Genesis 18:10, He says, "... I will certainly return unto thee according to the time of life; and, lo, Sarah thy wife shall have a son..." His use of the word return indicates an appointment to resume something He started earlier. God scheduled Sarah's son Isaac in His book of earthly families.[47] Given the age of his parents at the time of his conception, Isaac should not have entered the world, but God had decreed his birth long before time began. The child is eternally written in the destinies of the Almighty, Abraham, and Sarah because his life paves the way for the advent of God's Son. Isaac's appearance on earth was already on the books in God's Continuum, and nothing was going to impede his pre-scheduled arrival on earth. So the Lord announces that He will come again to Abraham and Sarah to ensure His project's success personally. The sentiment repeats itself in verse 14, "Is anything too hard for the Lord? At the time appointed I will return unto thee, according to the time of life, and Sarah shall have a son." To bolster

---

47 Refer to Isaiah 41:4.

their confidence and cause them to rely peacefully on His word, the Lord reminds Abraham that He has already begun the surreptitious workings of what He prophesied He would do. Now all that remains is to materialize the prophecy in its physical form.

An additional example of the Continuum and the Lord's superintendence over it is Romans 15:16. There Paul aligns his entire apostleship to the Gentiles with the Lord's Continuum. In doing so, he demonstrates his knowledge of its existence and his responsibility to adapt all of his ministracies to what fulfills God's word. See Colossians 1:25 and 26 and contrast them with Galatians 1:1, 1:15 and 16 which all agree. Collectively, these passages convey the Bible's enforcement of God's Continuum, and explain why in God's mind, human and earthly chronologies are less relevant to world events than His performance of His word. Isaiah 55:11 declares it cannot return to Him void. Prophecy then embodies the Creator's utterances. This includes those that are embedded in the world's orders and happenings until the words materialize and take on their predestined function in their time. Only when that occurs can the heavenly messenger dispatched with the message return to God's throne to report that everything performed as He decreed. The Isaiah 55:11 reference strongly suggests that a type of simultaneous and synchronous action takes place between God's world and this one.

SYNCHRONICITY VS. SIMULTANEITY IN THE CONTINUUM

This Continuum discussion would be incomplete without addressing the popular usage of the word synchronicity, used to define two or more events occurring at once and together. In contrast to its popular applications is the word simultaneity. This term is closer to what the Lord Jesus had in mind when He prayed what has come to be known as the Lord's Prayer. In Matthew 6:10 and Luke 11:2, the Lord discloses a greatly concealed truth about how heaven works on earth. Often people are accustomed to hearing how heaven and earth work together. What is not as commonly understood is how heaven imposes itself on earth. (See the referenced passages of Scripture in the footnotes.[48]) Today, synchronicity is taught as being the term to express spiritual and natural things happening at once, due to higher causes acting upon lower ones. This idea is of course not new and it is accounted for in the Continuum. The Lord Jesus says in the above references "thy will be done on earth as

---

48 Deuteronomy 32:39; Daniel 4:17, 25, 32; 1 Samuel 2:6; Psalm 103:19; Psalm 115:3; Job 10:7; Isaiah 43:13;

it is in heaven." The phrase "as it is in heaven" reveals the simultaneity of a continuum.

Simultaneity comes from the words *simultaneous* and *instantaneous*. Put together they form the single word simultaneity. The term originally meant to show how heaven's initiatives compel the earth to manifest them on cue. Heaven's eternity entwined itself throughout earth's real time. Jesus personally set all that the Godhead ordained in motion when He entered the planet. He commenced His end time program by announcing His kingdom was coming to earth. Once He did, God's predetermined will sovereignly began to impose His escatalogical programs on the earth. Christ's manifestation started outwardly working what the Almighty wrote ahead of time. Apocalyptic prophecy encoded throughout creation went to work achieving His foreordained purposes. Providentially, He long ago designated each element and agency's duties and responsibilities. After that He appointed their respective eras, seasons, generations, and events. Availing Himself of His laws of simultaneity and synchronicity, God released His coding to act on the planet as scheduled. Prior to Jesus, the Holy Spirit, and the Church, all of this was done by angels as the Old Testament shows. Today they have the potent reinforcements of the full Godhead's muscle on-site in the person of the Holy Spirit, and the immediacy of Christ's body on earth to expedite their efforts. His Messianic shift inaugurated the Church age that marked God's new day.

Simultaneity was not absent in the Old Testament era, but barriers to its efficacies prevented it from performing as instantaneously or as pervasively. The Lord Jesus' removal of the princes of this age and His replacement of them with the Holy Spirit and His Ecclesia accelerated the pedestrian simultaneity of the old world. It provoked Him to declare Matthew 11:12, 13.

> "And from the days of John the Baptist until now the kingdom of heaven suffereth violence, and the violent take it by force. For all the prophets and the law prophesied until John." KJV

> "From the days of John the Baptist until the present, the kingdom from heaven has been forcefully advancing, and violent people have been attacking it, because the Law and all the Prophets prophesied up to the time of John." ISV

God's supernal kingdom was secure in heaven until the end time phase of the Continuum began. From the moment that the Angel Gabriel broke through to impregnate Elizabeth and Mary, all that changed. At Christ's birth, hosts of angels flood the sky to announce and celebrate His mission to earth. At the same time, God's heretofore concealed kingdom was migrating to the planet to serve His Son and later His Ecclesia. Based on the Lord's words, it is clear that He is announcing the kingdom of heaven was doing something different. It was extending itself into the earth realm and opening its vaults to every spiritual and physical being that understands its reserves. Jesus apparently sees the event as unavoidable, but necessary. He warns His present and future family that their God made their kingdom accessible to all intelligent creatures willing to fight for control of it. Although it belongs to them, to enjoy and keep it, the children of light will have to fight for it. The reality of this is a concern to Jesus so He warns His people against taking their access or station in His heavenly kingdom for granted, or assuming its spirituality has no worth or impact in the material world. To a lesser extent, the kingdom of heaven is the new Eden where the serpent and humanity merged and multiplied. Both sides now war for its powers and treasures. Before the Church's first Pentecost, Jesus says it was all predictive. He says the law and the prophets prophesied the coming kingdom and its tremendous powers. Once John the Baptist was born, all of that changed and now the kingdom is replacing the Old Testament's Mosaic Law and its prophecies to marry the earth to its Maker forever.

Simultaneity and Synchronicity -- A Comparison

The word simultaneity also defines existing, occurring, or operating at the same time. That is, as concurrent episodic events. As said previously, the word's formation contains the joint implications of the terms <u>instantaneous</u> with the Latin root *simul*, to mean at the same time, together. Simultaneity applies to simultaneous (same time) movements, actions, and operations happening in a precise space of time, in the exact instance, often in two different places. The term was coined to connect the words *instantaneous* and *spontaneous* to reveal an event occurring in two places at the "same time, in the same moment." The words denote the sameness (not similarity) of their actions in effect. For example, to understand the word better think of simulcasting. Usage Example: Scientists are now beginning to solve the mystery of this feat of simultaneity.[27]

Other Ways of Looking at Simultaneity

Here are a few other ways to look at simultaneity and its relationship to the Continuum.

1. Existing and so happening or done at the same time; operating concurrently; extended to take place at the same time in more than one place or in addition to more than one thing together.

2. Simultaneity is two events happening at the same time within a single frame of reference. The *simul* prefix speaks to the similarity or better yet the simulation of one thing that is or comes from another.

3. Simultaneity is simulation plus *instanteousness* joining *temporality* and *distance* to identify something occurring in one place at the same time is occurring in another at the same moment of time the same way.

4. Simultaneity distinguishes itself from synchronicity by multiplying its event innumerably without losing any of its qualities or elements.

5. In contrast to the word *synchronicity*, simultaneity is the experience of two or more events that may be seen as causally unrelated or unlikely to occur together but by chance as a single experience, as a distinct happening that occurred together in a meaningful manner. All of the actions and elements that contributed to the cause inherently triggered its duplication in a distant place at the same time. Thus, what existed to fuel the cause likewise exists to operate its repetition. Think about Jesus' words, "thy will be done on earth as it is in heaven."

6. Simultaneity was understood by early Bible scholars to explain the Almighty's sovereign cause and effect involvement in His creation's affairs and events, which is how the word supports the Continuum's teachings. More precisely, simultaneity identifies His heavenly triggers encoded in earth's creation, igniting and executing a preordained action in the same instant that He scheduled it to actuate spiritually in His world. In effect, God's preordainments ignite something in heaven that executes it on earth in the very same moment.

7. Simultaneous is a single event that happens at the same time in different places, whereas synchronous implies two separate events that occur at once irrespective of distance. Two things can be synced to occur at once, but not necessarily be simultaneous because the event can be instantaneous and not synced, they can cascade due to different causes. For example, a simultaneous broadcast can be spread abroad while a synchronous one is merely broadcasting at the same time. Distance is essential to simultaneity, but is insignificant to synchronicity. For example, two different televisions can be timed to start and stop at once or even change channels to show the same

program. However, the word *simultaneous* comes in when the same game is broadcasted to different televisions at one time from a single originating source. Another reason the event cannot be called synchronized is because different time zones mean the simulcast has a different schedule in each location.

SIMULTANEITY IN JESUS' PRAYER

Simultaneity shows up and best explains itself, as described above, through Jesus' prayer class, in the following passages of Scripture: Matthew 6:10 and Luke 11:2 *"And he said unto them, When ye pray, say, Our Father which art in heaven, Hallowed be thy name. Thy kingdom come. Thy will be done, as in heaven, so in earth."* Matthew's version says, *"As it is in heaven." Luke phrases it a little differently; his version reads, "As in heaven, so in earth."* Matthew's version could convey the idea of God's will, acting or performing on earth exactly as it is in heaven at the same time. Luke on the other hand, implies that as God's will is done in heaven, so let it be done the same way (and at the same time) it performs on earth. Therefore, according to Jesus, *as it is in heaven*, means human prayer is heard and answered at the same time in both places; in heaven and on earth at once. Some angels that accompanied Him will be stationed throughout the planet to attend His church, as Hebrews 1:14 suggests. Jesus' word choices imply the synthesizing of the two places with the single event that is taking place between them, prayer, and answered prayer, to permit a joint transaction that causes one to benefit the other. Why and how will this be? The kingdom of God that departed the earth after the Edenic Transgression is returning to earth, bringing with it an immediate audience with God and faster answers to prayer. But there is more.

MORE SCRIPTURE SIMULTANEITY EXAMPLES ARE:

1. 2 Corinthians 5:19 "To wit, that God was in Christ, reconciling the world unto himself, not imputing their trespasses unto them; and hath committed unto us the word of reconciliation."

2. John 5:19, 20 " Then Jesus answered and said to them, Truly, truly, I say to you, The Son can do nothing of Himself but what He sees the Father do. For whatever things He does these also the Son does likewise. For the Father loves the Son and shows Him all the things that He Himself does. Moreover, He will show Him greater works than these, so that you may marvel.

3. 1 Timothy 3:16 "And without controversy great is the mystery of godliness: God was manifested in the flesh, justified in the Spirit, seen by angels,

preached among nations, believed on in the world, and received up into glo-ry."

4. 1 John 5:7 "For there are three that bear witness in heaven: the Father, the Word, and the Holy Spirit, and these three are one. " And there are three that bear witness on the earth: the Spirit, and the water, and the blood; and the three are into the one."

5. Matthew 17:5 "While he yet spoke, behold, a bright cloud overshadowed them. And behold a voice out of the cloud which said, this is My beloved Son in whom I am well pleased, hear Him."

6. Mark 16:20 "And going out, they proclaimed everywhere, the Lord working with them and confirming the Word by miraculous signs following. Amen."

7. John 5:17 "But Jesus answered them, My Father works until now, and I work".

SYNCHRONICITY IN CONTRAST

In comparison to simultaneity, synchronic[49] events reveal an underlying pattern... Jung coined the word to describe what he called "temporally coincident occurrences of acausal (without cause) events."[50] Synchronicity appears to focus on the coincident and is more slanted toward the result of simultaneity because the latter, simultaneity, includes the *preexistence* of the events themselves along with the operations that manifest them. *Simul* prefixed to the word *simulated* classifies their two occurrences behaving as one the same way in two different places. Hence, the main difference between the two terms appears to be unrelated mechanics versus a deliberate outworking of the unseen in the realm of the seen, by way of extraordinarily real and operating dynamics. Two synchronic Scripture examples are Acts 10:44 and Matthew 3:16, 17.

1. The first synchronous Scripture example is Acts 10:44 "While Peter yet spake these words, the Holy Ghost fell on all them which heard the word". The Holy Ghost fell on all those present in the room all at once, but He affected none of the people around them. It is partially the same as when He fell on those in the upper room where the 120 were baptized at once. However, synchronicity gave way to simultaneity when they began to speak in other tongues and everyone in the vicinity heard them in their own language.

---

49 Online Etymological Dictionary.
50 Online dictionary sources.

2. Another example is when Jesus in Mary's womb baptized John in Elizabeth's womb when Mary spoke. Neither mother received the Holy Spirit's baptism even though each one carrying the babies inside them did.

3. The second Scripture example is Matthew 3:16, 17 "And Jesus, when He had been baptized, went up immediately out of the water. And lo, the heavens were opened to Him, and He saw the Spirit of God descending like a dove and lighting upon Him. And lo, a voice from Heaven, saying, this is My beloved Son, in whom I am well pleased." While everyone in the proximity of the Lord's baptism heard His Father's voice, it nonetheless remained between those who were together in one place. No reports of people hearing what the Almighty said were made outside of their gathering at the water. Although one version of the account says, some heard intelligent words and others merely heard thunder.

Maintaining the integrity of the Continuum means to undertake overt actions to keep it intact. Those sent by the Lord today to speak His truth, to preach His Gospel, and lead others to Christ must take deliberate steps to learn what was done, and has gone, before them to adapt their present methods to what the Continuum has already approved. As easy as it may sound, doing so takes hours of study, years of training and proving and above all else, a heart determined to do it God's way. Upholding the Lord often sounds simpler than it is because it begins with caring about what He is, all that He has done, everything He is presently doing and will do. All of it comes from studying His word with His mindset and a strong sense of His duties and responsibilities to the worlds and creatures He has made. Anything less will cause one to dismantle His Continuum.

DISMANTLING THE CONTINUUM

The aggressive, age-old campaign to dismantle God's Continuum found its zenith in the decision to divide the Bible into testaments. While doing so better organized and defined its purposes, the effect on the Christian down the line is today cause for grave concern. Dividing the testaments in two makes it far too tempting for believers to pick and choose what they want to learn about God and His truth and reject what they resent or disapprove. Theologically, dividing the two testaments too easily entices Christians to favor the division they prefer and dismiss the other as superfluous or spurious depending on their view of it. Moreover, having a New Testament-only Bible deprives Christian converts of the other half of the story. It ends up creating gaps that expose them to heresy and error. New Testament-only Scriptures may celebrate Jesus and His victory, which they should do, but isolating it from the Old Testament prophecies and the promises that foretold Him does little to explain The Messiah's heavenly, royal, or national roots. Apart from the Old Testament, people scarcely understand Jesus' human lineage, beyond Luke and Matthew's Messianic genealogy that numerous readers skip as too tedious to be important.

Scripture's veiled references to the prominent figures that most contributed to getting Jesus from heaven to earth is not unveiled by either testament alone. As a result, the complete history and destiny of God's Son are sketchy at best. It is debatable whether these outcomes were intentional; perhaps they are just the aftermath of shortsightedness. Whatever the motive, the outcome is troubling as New Testament-only Christians smugly spurn the Old and vice versa. The drawback is that one-testament-only readers fail to append fully their knowledge and faith to the Continuum, because they lack considerable links to it. The result is they handicap and splinter their revelations. New or Old Testament-only students of Scripture are at a loss to explain how the Almighty and Abraham bonded, the premises for Sarah's aged motherhood, Moses and the Exodus, or to appreciate the characters mentioned in Hebrews chapter eleven. Additionally, how Peter arrived at his revelation of the Church's royal priestly status in 1 Peter 2:9 is found in the Old Testament books of Genesis, Leviticus and the Psalms. What makes the Church Jesus' Christ's eternal nation, the book of Exodus explains. Woefully deprived of God's big picture, one testament-only Christians have no basis for understanding God's promissory events. For instance, countless saints have never heard of Melchizedek and others cannot confirm if revelatory teachings of the Christ are correct, let alone how they authenticate the true Jesus. Christians confining themselves to one testament pursue their faith on only half of the story--another consequence, and there are more. An additional effect is that New Testament-only Christians, because of their disconnection from the rest of the Bible, tend to despise prophets and prophecy and dismiss apostleship as a defunct office. While some single-testament readers may appreciate end time eschatology, they still cannot truly conceptualize how God will bring His word to pass, because they are uninformed on what happened before time and since the world began. For these insights, one needs the Bible's entire 66 books of episodes that open in the Old Testament.

Many believers today are unstable because they only know excerpted portions of God's Scripture. These are the souls that concerned Paul and motivated him to use strong admonitory words against wrangling them in his epistles. Fragmented truth and cherry-picked doctrine unsettled his converts back then, and both continue to destabilize the contemporary Christian. Uncertainty surfaces when believers encounter challenges to their faith that make them unsure of Jesus Christ, who He is, and what makes Him the only way to God Almighty. Whenever part of the story is missing, believers question if there is a heaven or hell; and sadly, they shrink back from their faith, terrified of the costs of contending for it. In these instances, many saints muse that He just may not be real or alive. Reconnecting them with the Continuum and instructing them in its unbroken chain of events is the best way to help the body of Christ today. For that, they must grasp the wisdom of both Testaments. Taking God's children back to Genesis and bringing them all the way through to the Revelation reacquaints them with His ancient wisdoms. It shows them how everything connects and intersects to tie this world to His. Only by apprehending the whole of Scripture, can Jesus' true believers cement their faith in God's history and so appreciate His destiny for them. Strongly locking them into God's Eternal Continuum awakens believers to the Church's corporate purpose and frees them to embrace Jesus Christ's destiny as their own. As it stands today, far too many Christians see their life goals as separate from their afterlife destiny, and both as independent of the Savior's. Depriving them of the entire Bible leaves the Lord's family with no sound way to understand or fulfill His Father's purposes for them in this world or in the hereafter. That is because those who are only taught the New Testament do not know Him in His fullness, making them more vulnerable to falling away[51] from Him because of it. In comparison to these, those who are only taught the Old Testament lack a sense of The Messiah's Davidic majesty, and misconstrue how and why He birthed them anew into the Godhead. It should be said at this point that there are many ways the Bible's two major divisions helped the Church comprehend God's writings. However, teaching His people to view them isolatedly only works to dismantle His Continuum in their eyes, it reduces their ability to divide it rightly in study and lifestyle. In the end, they are at a disadvantage to protect themselves from heresy and doctrinal error.

Potent, sometimes imperceptible antics disconnect God's people from His Continuum. Deliberately or not, numerous devices can subtly dismantle it. For starters, Continuum Dismantlers resort to sketchy Scripture narratives, incomplete doctrine, inaccurate anecdotes, personalized storytelling, false witnessing, and subjectivized testimonials. To these can be added incongruent sermons, misapplied Scripture ex-

---

51 Apostatizing.

amples, and spiritual and doctrinal hybridization. When all the <u>separators</u> work together, the links in its chain sever. Once the Continuum's chain links break, its severed parts make errant continuums out of its strands. This paves the way for strange doctrines, beliefs, and worships, to come from slivers of ambiguous truths and the knowledge gaps they create. As things go along, those gaps get filled with whatever makes sense to the messenger conveying them and are believed by whoever agrees with the messenger. Vary this scenario enough times and before long Bible learners cease to discern God's truth from His adversaries' lies. Over time, converts fail to recognize the word of the Lord from the wisdom of this world. These reasons are why the Holy Spirit impels His people throughout Scripture to learn His truth thoroughly, and walk in circumspectly it after learning it. To this end, He designated where to find His truth and explained how His children could sidestep the seductions of Satan's lie. God's truth, as Scripture and His Continuum show, is more than a concept, a thought, or a philosophy. It is a person, the person of Jesus Christ that John's Gospel identifies as the Word of God that became flesh. Today, He is His church's "Word Incarnate".

The Almighty, as Creator and Keeper of the Continuum, shrewdly determined to engraft His word in living vessels. He deposited it first in heaven with His celestial beings and then on earth within clay people. The primary repository of His mind, will, providences, and ordainments was His first begotten Son. That established the pattern of the living God instilling Himself within living beings. Creature embodiment has always been His ideal means of idio-transmission.[28] He never intended for any part of His personal self or privacies to be bound to inanimate objects like scrolls, stones, or paper, which is why He is so resistant to being imaged on manmade objects. From the very outset of His divine communications, the Lord envisioned embedding His heart and soul into those of the creatures He made. As with any intelligent Creator, He archetyped[52] a model that would serve as His supreme prototype of the human He discovered to be most compatible with Him. That archetypal[29] rendering provides the blueprint for every species the Maker conceived in some way. It is composed entirely of everything He ever thought, said, dreamed, hoped, willed, and performed and weaved throughout that perfect One the Creator calls His first begotten Son. Born directly from His very Being,[53] God's first begotten became His

---

52 (Wiktionary The Free Dictionary). ((American Heritage® Dictionary of the English Language, Fourth Edition).)

53 That is, His Godhead's genetic stock that is normally reserved for those to share their essence and existence verbatim that was closed off and vaulted after its third member came into being.

only approved representation of His Godhead and thus the sole progenitor used to reproduce after its own kind. Yahweh, as He is named for Israel and Jesus (or Joshua), as He is given to the Church is made eternally and carnally after the Maker's own image and likeness, spirit, soul, and body. [54] God's[55] exemplary model made the perfect template because He never has to be taught His Father's word, since He is His first generation offspring. Everything that makes the Lord God what He is, makes Jesus Christ, His Seed, all that He is. In word, will, and essence, they are one and the same. Jesus fully personifies the Almighty and so never has to be instructed in His way of life. He is, what He does and does what He is, which makes Him His Father's Logos. In concept, consciousness, and conscience, they are inseparably one. The Son does not have to be disciplined in the Maker's truth, because that truth is what His Father is and not only what His Maker believes.[56] Jesus is intrinsically made up of God's truth, and therefore, contextualizes[30] the Almighty as only one born directly from Him could.

Christ's type of humanity is the only one the Almighty deems flawless enough to reproduce infinitely throughout all of His worlds. Romans 8:29 says it this way, *"For whom he did foreknow, he also did predestinate to be conformed to the image of his Son, that he might be the firstborn among many brethren."* Hebrews 7:23-26 clarifies it in this manner, *"And they truly were many priests, because they were not allowed to continue because of death; but He, because He continues forever, has an unchangeable priesthood. Therefore, He is able also to save to the uttermost those who come unto God by Him, since He ever lives to make intercession for them. For such a high priest became us, who is holy, harmless, undefiled, separate from sinners and made higher than the heavens."* The phrase "made higher than the heavens" is interesting in that Thayer's Greek definitions identify it as the word "ginomai". He defines it as "to become, i.e. to come into existence, and begin to be, to receive being." The idea of the word *ginomai* is "to become by or through events or happenings being brought to pass: To arise from nonexistence and appear on the world stage. It includes making one's way into history; to be made and finished." Lastly, it connotes "miracles wrought to make, or trigger, what did once not exist but as a result of exerting power comes into being".

To guarantee He remains unconquerable, the Most High enforces His Continuum. Although He does so contending with interminable conflicts, His continuity has

---

54 Hebrews 1:3.
55 Luke 2:49.
56 Refer to John 14:6.

wended its way through countless generations and revolts already. From Adam's command not to eat from the tree of the knowledge of good and evil, to Noah's Ark, Abraham's circumcision, and Moses' Exodus and Law, the Most High has waged war with His Continuum's opposers. Working through Samuel's prophetics, David's kingship, Jesus's incarnation, the Apostles' Great Commission, and the reign of the Christian church, the Lord God personally (and agentially),[57] throughout all ages pressed on with His Continuum. At every milestone or obstacle, the Savior uncovers what they ignore or suppress. He revives what is killed, and reconnects what is severed to keep His Continuum intact for the next generation. Relentlessly fighting all resistance and facing off with every revolutionary convinced that He is outdated and displaceable; The Messiah exposes and combats destructive movements that seek to undermine or subvert His power. Zealous for His word and protective of His truth, the Lord vigilantly surveils His church and kingdom for counterfeits, imposters, and corrupt agents distorting or weakening the Continuum's unity that He aggressively guards. Disjointed, conflicting, and irrational variations of Scripture are routed out and their messengers disciplined or replaced. With ages of defenses behind Him, God knows the end of such tactics. They are to marginalize and shipwreck people's faith in His Bible, to build a case for disputing and undermining everything Christ and Christianity.

New Testament Not Discredited

None of the preceding discussion is to denigrate the New Testament, because it is vital to the Church's faith. What this is saying is that the Almighty's dealings with humanity and His journey with them did not begin with the Church's composition. They began, not with the gospels or the epistles that close out the Bible's formative periods, but with the prophets above all, and other prominent figures in earthly history. To be truly converted to the whole Godhead and its way of life, Christians must be baptized in the whole word of God, including its every counsel, mystery, revelation, and prophecy. The testimonies, statutes, and ordinances of life that pit the Almighty's superiority against the ruin and destruction of the world must be clearly taught in order to discipline His people in His righteousness.

---

[57] From agential, "of or relating to an agent or agency, agentive." Defines the purposes and functions connected to a representative, one who acts on behalf of other persons or organizations.

THE PRINCIPAL CHARACTERS OF THE CONTINUUM

The Lord's Continuum encompasses several foremost paragons celebrated in Scripture as His faithful messengers. Named the principal characters of the Continuum, this book notes twenty-five of its most prominent ministers. These include the most effective or catalytic of them all. Many of those figures were the prophets. Jesus notes the prophets as a collective. With them are the psalmists, the kings, and priests that contributed to the Lord's unbroken chain of events. God's Continuum, as the Lord Jesus says in Luke 24:44, Acts 24:14, and Acts 28:23, also encases the Psalms, which are largely prophetic due to their predictive, historical, and devotional narratives.

To the surprise of many New Testament-only readers, the Lord Jesus personally canonized in the New Testament the Law of Moses, despite many Protestant scholars today claiming it is obsolete. However, the largest contributors to God's Continuum are the prophets who advance it from Genesis to Revelation, almost without interruption. The Savior's earthly ministry largely rested on the prophecies of the Old Testament prophets and those that predate it. Consequently, this work has shown why and how the prophets are the principal characters of the Continuum. For sure, there are other instrumental characters, but these people's ministry involvement in the Lord's unwinding Continuum most decisively advanced His plan. One character that did not make the list that is nonetheless crucial to the Continuum is the Devil. Read about his Continuum roles and responsibilities in the next chapter.

[8]

The Devil As A Principal Character In The Continuum

The one constantly appearing and unlikely essential character in the Continuum is the Devil. His unsuccessful bid for power in heaven, way back before earth's time instigated its inception. The Devil's perversion of heaven's glory and his corruption of its righteousness caused the Continuum to emerge, and be threaded throughout eternity. His perpetuity is why it passes on to the earth and God's other worlds. [58] Revelation chapter 12, reports on this creature's part in the Continuum's ever-unfolding dramas. The Apocalypse tells how he ignited God's need for salvation and gave rise to the Continuum's predestined cast of characters throughout the ages. No single verse in Scripture more comprehensively unveils the rationale of the Almighty's salvation plan or more summarizes the Continuum than this one. Replete with innuendoes, justifications, sublimity, and revelations, it speaks to the tough questions regarding the whys and how's of life on earth and the big deal about Jesus Christ. Connecting it to Luke 10:18, effectively solidifies its timeline in the Godhead's eternal chronology. Jesus, after He comes to earth, says to the seventy He sends out in His name to spread His word that He "beheld Satan as lightning fall from heaven." By the time He reveals this pre-earth fact, Satan's fall was old news in His world. That means before the Son of God encountered him in the wilderness after John's baptism, Satan had long since been exiled from his heavenly home, which is why Isaiah 27:1's[31] promise exists. What could Jesus mean by His recollection except that long before He came to earth, the war that banished the Devil from the Al-

---

58 Enfold into this wisdom, Isaiah 14:12-14 and Ezekiel 28:13-19.

mighty's celestial worlds was won by His kingdom? Thus, the sin problem Satan brought to earth was, for them, long settled.

To reinforce this truth, Revelation 12:3 indicates Lucifer,[59] the anointed cherub had already mutated into the great red dragon and his revolt against the Most High's holy kingdom was resoundingly squelched. This was the case despite his having taken one third of the stars—a metaphor for angels—from its ranks and casting them down to earth.[32] It discloses how and why he came to be on the planet when the Lord renovated and replenished it for Adam and Eve. Previous discussions reveal how earth was Satan's prison. At the appropriate time, the Creator set out to reuse the planet and renovate it for His next population. The Devil, already confined there has watched God recreate it and waited for Him to set Adam in the garden. After He did, Satan just went about doing what he has always done. He went to work on regaining some dominion. He tempted and accused, incited, and seduced the man to surrender his world to him. In doing so, he recouped some of what he had lost long ago that caused the earth to languish in its vacuum.[60] Rarely when people read this account, do they ask where the serpent got the brass to seduce the man and his wife. Also not often asked, is why the Lord responded with such vehemence when He so severely judged a seemingly helpless animal. God reacted bitterly to Satan, the Devil inhabiting the serpent that was hijacking Adam and his wife's souls from Him. Revelation 12:7 further elucidates the otherwise murky development by divulging their previous experiences with each other. It says there was war in heaven. Michael, the Almighty's archangel fought against the dragon. Notice his identity; he is a dragon, not a cherub or archangel, but a dragon. This creature, along with his angels fought against the Lord's armies. His angelic forces are the one-third of the stars he drew away with his tail.[61] Not only did the dragon and his angels lose the war, but afterward the Christ evicts them from heaven and its hallowed celestial territories forever as a result.[62] The defeat no doubt was a crushing blow because so much was at stake.

Revelation 12:9 further says the Lord cast out the Great Dragon. Scripture gives other epithets[33] for the dragon as well. He is that old serpent, called the Devil and Satan, who deceives the whole world. God cast him down to earth along with his angels when he was still one of its residents. Here is how and why he was in the garden to

---

59 What he is called in Ezekiel 28 and Isaiah 14.

60 Isaiah 14:17.

61 His military and prophetic horde.

62 Compare with Luke 19:27.

tempt Adam and his wife; he was there because he already inhabited the earth realm from the time his failed coup sentenced him to the planet. Until the Lord renovated the physical earth, it was his spiritual penitentiary, *his* hell so to speak. Perhaps that is why hell and its fires are pictured as being located in the heart of the earth, especially when the Lord Jesus says, it was created for the Devil and his angels. In order to perform his seductive sifting tasks with the latest species, the Lord releases the Devil on what would be called today, a work release. Revelation implies He will do so again after the thousand years are up. Hell, according to Deuteronomy 32:22, existed back in time. Peter's second epistle, infers it predates the renovated earth because the Almighty imprisoned angels there before He restored it, 2:4. Revelation 9:14 says that there are four criminal angels bound in the bottom of the Euphrates; 9:16 of the same book further adds they are not alone. It describes a horde of hybrid demonic beings there with them, awaiting the Lord's last days' maneuvers. Clearly, when he lost his power bid, the Lord drastically altered the Devil's being to prevent him from using his former state to reenter their world. Despite the earth' surface being a dark watery vacuum, God sentenced Satan to it and apparently dispossessed him of the ability to leave. This world, as his prison, was a watery abyss on top and a raging inferno at the core. Both served the Lord's purposes well when He condemned this arch criminal to it. More immaterial than material, earth's realm made the ideal prison until God returned to the planet to say "let there be light". The garden where the Adam's contest took place was apparently the most delightful place on earth. The remainder of the restoration was evidently barren waiting for Adam and his godly seed to develop it. The garden, it could be surmised, was to be his home, his safe haven where he returned to rest and refresh periodically during his building projects. Had he not succumbed to the serpent's temptation, he would have had a perfect paradise, the meaning of Eden, to dwell in for ages while he and his family outfitted and repopulated the rest of the planet. From the way the story is told, hell on earth is not necessarily just a metaphor. From what Scripture suggests, it is here and was active when the Lord renovated the earth. It seems that what is now called earth's magnetic core, could have metaphorically housed foolish spirits that thought they could overturn their Maker. God dissolved the vacuum and relocated or encased hell to free the earth to be used again as a dwelling place for another creation. Since it was made before time and is built to be everlasting, hell is as much a valid part of the Continuum as heaven.

HELL IN THE CONTINUUM

Hell is an everlasting doom because the Almighty damned it. It constitutes the most devastating of His *eternalities*. Matthew 25:41 in saying the Lord prepared hell's fiery sentences for the Devil and his angels, pictures it as an otherworldly penitentiary awaiting whatever humans refuse Jesus Christ. To assure that the effects of rejecting Him when acted out are never free to spoil creation again, God created a place for His rejectors to live out their carnate choices without corrupting His other worlds. The Lord pitched a place outside of His glorious abode to restrain the rebel spirits of His kingdom who rose up against Him. That place has been adapted to incarcerate dead human souls along with the dead, celestial ones it was made to detain. There are many arguments about hell, for or against it, because people cannot justify its cruelty and so see its finality as unjust. The *endless chance* mentality of some religions makes the idea of a once and for all sentences of doom impossible to take. Irrationally, they have no problem trumpeting a once and for all paradise for the righteous, just with an interminable hell for the ungodly. Christians, on the other hand, are not left with any such delusions because their faith's Founder took great pains to describe hell, explain its permanence, and warn His family to fight against going there. Hell is hot, brutal, and dark. By default, it is dark because the Lord situated it as distantly from His homeland as possible because His is the only kingdom with its own self-generating light.

Outside the Godhead, there is no light, life, or power. The Lord made hell dark by depriving it of its own sun, moon, and the other luminaries inherent to the earth, as well as His very emissions. That is how deeply He buried it in the earth realm. Light belongs only to God's world and those He extends Himself to. When He withdraws the light of His eternal world, the only thing left is darkness that is not merely light-less, but also energy-less and therefore powerless. Spiritual darkness is devoid of innovative materials or ingenuity, so the idea that all sorts of inventions can be created to mitigate hell's suffering is pure nonsense. The absence of material resources makes creating anything worthwhile there impossible. Without the Lord's light and life, hell's gloom and doom leaves nothing to harness to answer the sufferings and deprivations it contains. Everything that makes for life, liberty, and prosperity stays where the Godhead resides or supplies. The Lord is not supplying hell with anything that enlivens those He condemns to it, not even a useful body. Only those destined to live forever with the Lord Jesus receives a new body to equip them for immortal living. Those condemned to hell remain without one.

The Holy Spirit is creation's omni-diffuser.[63] He embodies God and Jesus to disperse what is corporately shared between them throughout creation. The Lord's Spirit is the power source and preserver of everything containing His life. Jesus is the Almighty's embodied light source and life force. He lights up heaven and illuminates this world, which is why He keeps declaring Himself to be the light of it. However, as is widely accepted, the Lord does not light the whole universe or its solar systems. In spite of the trillions of stars out there and the immense energy they throw off, the universe remains dark and cold to suggest what makes it habitable or creatable resides somewhere else or within something else. Unless one discovers and taps into what that is, this world and His world, are the only places to enjoy God's light and energy. A good rationale for this, is the darkness lets earth know that He has a dark side, a side that He purposely denies His light, warmth, and virility. The Lord let space remain a dark vacuous cosmos to illustrate how real hell is and to demonstrate that no matter how many utopian or valhallan stories are spun, leaving this planet plunges one into that darkness. It is foolhardy to think there is any light in the underworld beneath the earth if it is obvious that the universe is deprived of it. Besides, seeing the other planets languishing under dark watery, gaseous, or frozen abysses proves the beginning of the Genesis story, "the earth was (indeed) void and darkness was upon the face of the deep".

What is it that caused hell; the spirit world's penitentiary to be created is the former Daystar's[64] rejection of his God's rule and his subsequent military revolt against His Maker. Elements of the story are scattered throughout Scripture and when pieced together, they explain the first of the Fourteen Events Continuum. All of it culminates in the incarnation, crucifixion, resurrection and crowning of Jesus Christ. What is often left out of this traditional string is the word incarceration. The Son of God was incarnated in hell too, for three days and nights. The Creator episodic spearheaded events deliberately to reproduce Himself in human form. However, before everything that makes this present age what it is began, there was a spiritual detainment site for rebel angels and other unclean forces in God's kingdom that was captured and incarcerated for criminalizing His world. Down through the ages, it took on many names and today its latest one is hell, but its identification is the same. A place where light-and-life-deprived spirits abide, hell's residents have only impotent power sources because their Maker's heavens are forever off limits to them. Hell's light is dim and its

---

63 It comes from the word diffuse that means to pour out, to spread anything such as light, water, sound waves, or fragrances. Includes gases and other nonsolid substance.

64 Isaiah 14:12; 2 Peter 1:19; Revelation 2:28; 22:16.

climate visually and environmentally dark because the only light available to its occupants is the light of darkness Jesus warns against in Luke 11:35. Beneath hell's dark stratum, is the lake of fire awaiting those subject to Christ's final judgment. The eternally sentenced under Moses' Law are in the fire because they rejected The Law's means of eternal preservation, which was then Abraham's bosom. Christ emptied this region when He left hell. The rich man's indifference to Lazarus sent him straight to the lake of fire because, as Abraham's answer revealed to him, he rejected The Law of Moses and the prophets. Today, those banished to hell sleep in its dark regions until the full plan of redemption has been executed and The Messiah's judicial lake of fire proceedings begins. Those in that world subsist on whatever residual gloom leftover in their beings at the point of their death. Generating only dead static light, hell's climate that goes from gloomy gray to pitch black is all they have to energize their world, which is remarkable since the Lord describes it as an infinitely raging inferno. Long ago stripped of their initial luminescence, hell's intended residents lived out a bleak eternity without any hope of tapping into the Creator to reenergize themselves, their celestial privileges being forever revoked. From these revelations, emerges an interesting implication. If hell was prepared for the Devil and his angels as the Lord Jesus asserts, does it too predate earth? Traditional theology and philosophy, portray it as commencing in the fall of mankind. If that is so, then it has little place in the Continuum and may or may not be real. But if it indeed functioned as a spiritual penitentiary prior to this world, then hell is an otherworldly institution that has been jailing rebel spirits since the Great War in Heaven. Another spiritual group sent there are the angels that left their first estate. Since then, human beings have gone there. Both disclosures imply God created humanity subject to an everlasting divine judgment and celestial penal system. Humanity was created after a means of disposing of their sin was already well in place. Way before the Godhead said, "Let us make man..." earth's residents were subject to heaven's super advanced justice system.

Before His mortal judgment code, the Most High's eternally dispensed afterlife prescriptions were a long time in effect. Hell is no more a joking matter to God than criminality and judgment are in this world because it is as everlasting as God Himself. When people see the Almighty as a ruling being and not just a venerated icon, the reality of Him requiring a means to adjudicate spiritual crimes against His creation makes more sense. Accepting that He has a world, actually numerous worlds, to govern and trillions upon trillions of freewill creatures to regulate, makes His penitential hell take on a very logical, and embraceable significance. From what Christ says, hell goes back to the Continuum's earliest days either before its first event, perhaps in anticipation of it, or not long after what motivated it. Thus, it would seem from the Lord's gospel teachings that hell has been holding His world's criminals a long while before this world began and since. Consequently, assuming He somehow had a change of heart and decided to tolerate crime under the Church's dispensation is ludicrous. For Him to do so is to mock the cross and compel Himself to release every being already imprisoned there. Unquestionably, hell as Christ discusses it was never about humanity. It started out strictly being about His angels and the spiritual citizens of His world. After the effects of Adam's rebellion, this everlasting institution became a practical solution to human crimes as well. All of this is more than probable, it is likely as one of the New Testament words for judgment is the Greek 'krima' from which comes the English crime. It is possible that earthly rulers and judges wanted to differentiate God's moral law from the world's legal terminology, applying the word sin to human immorality and the word crime as earthly villainy. In God's judgments, no such conflicting distinctions are made. In His system, the word sin may be the shorter of the two terms, but it is the most comprehensive one because it encompasses all deviations from His holiness. Look what Scripture records as the first group to occupy hell. Jude, one of the Lord's brothers identifies them:

> "And those angels not having kept their first place, but having deserted their dwelling-place, He has kept in everlasting chains under darkness for the judgment of a great Day." Jude 1:6.

Peter supports this in his second epistle: "For if God spared not the angels that sinned, but cast them down to hell, and delivered them into chains of darkness, to be reserved unto judgment." 2 Peter 2:4.

Scripture portrays, of the antediluvian[65] generation, only Enoch escaped hell. Under the Mosaic Covenant, Moses[66] and Elijah[67] escaped hell while every other person to die on earth went there after death. They both appear with Christ on the mountain of Transfiguration[68] before His crucifixion and not as escapees from hell granted a one-day pass. Moses and Elijah visit Jesus on earth as two of the *"spirits of just men made perfect"* mentioned in Hebrews 12:23. Jude 1:9 says that Michael, the archangel, and the Devil argued about Moses' body after he died to keep the Devil from taking God's mighty prophet to hell. Elijah, the book of Kings says, was raptured to heaven in a

---

65 Pre-flood.
66 See Jude 1:9.
67 2 Kings 2:11.
68 Matthew 17:3; Luke 9:30.

chariot of fire. All references show hell has a long history that the Lord Jesus discusses openly and repeatedly. Several of His discourses, about fifteen in all, record Him addressing the subject. Two verses in Acts chapter two mention hell as the place where even the Savior Himself went after dying on the cross, according to David's words in Psalm 16:10. Prophetically, they show that hell existed back then for those condemned by Moses' Law. Also, despite the Lord Jesus as Yahweh banishing souls to hell when He ruled as God on high, David foretells that God's Son Himself was destined to go to hell in the distant future.

It is no wonder Jesus in vivid detail, describes hell. He has more than enough knowledge of it to say what it is, how it works, why it exists, and what it awaits. Given the explicitness of His descriptions and His certainty about who was in hell, how they got there, and what made them deserving of it, the Savior indicates that in His precarnate reign, He divinely sentenced the angels and the humans confined there already. In Luke 16, quoted above, He shows the extent of His firsthand knowledge of the subject, which is how He could depict it so graphically during His earthly visit. Messianically, Jesus strongly advises against treating hell as purely metaphorical. He bluntly talks of the invisible beings, fallen angels, and disobedient humans imprisoned there. His familiarity with the circumstances surrounding their arrest and banishment urges Him to warn present and future generations to avoid it at all costs. As the world's appointed Savior, His impending Calvary Passion promises He would make it possible for them to do so. Presenting hell as a long-standing institution that reached back to His sovereign days and forward to His interminable monarchy, Jesus explains that hell is as endless as anything else His world commenced and extended into this one. Amazingly, His intimate knowledge of hell did not deter Him from agreeing to die the death of the cross to go there Himself, fully aware of what awaited His obedience. That decision made His sacrifice even more magnanimous since He, unlike Adam's seed, was not compulsively surrendering to some unimaginable fate that He only heard about but never encountered. Never confused about His mission, Jesus declared more than once that He came to earth to die and to give His life as a ransom for the souls lost to sin and death. He planned long before earth to spend three days and nights in a place that He had created for the criminals and fugitives of His world. By the time He incarnated, He had imprisoned (presumably) millions of spirits and more than a few humans there, and had been doing so for ages. Yet, Christ's deep love for His creation moved Him to taste death as God in human flesh, as fully as those He condemned to die and suffer in hell forever. As the incarnated

Son of God, Jesus volunteered to experience firsthand what His clay vessels lived and feared on earth for eons. His sentiments are voiced in Hebrews 2:14, 18:

> *"Since then the children have partaken of flesh and blood, He also Himself likewise partook of the same; that through death He might destroy him who had the power of death (that is, the Devil), and deliver those who through fear of death were all their lifetime subject to bondage. For truly He did not take the nature of angels, but He took hold of the seed of Abraham. Therefore in all things it behooved him to be made like His brothers, that He might be a merciful and faithful high priest in things pertaining to God, to make propitiation for the sins of His people. For in that He Himself has suffered, having been tempted, He is able to rescue those who are being tempted."*

The previous discussion was interjected to connect hell's everlastingness to God's Eternal Continuum. It also shows how, and why, hell was created, which amplify the Devil's role in the Continuum and illustrates the ways it began with him. Returning now to the book of Revelation's record of his heavenly defeat in the Great War in Heaven, it is helpful to revisit the Devil's banishment.

SATAN'S BANISHMENT, HEAVEN'S EXULTATION

Revelation 12:10 reports Satan's defeat brought huge relief to the residents of God's supernal worlds. They had violently wrestled with this vicious creature for some time. His expulsion is cause for joy and celebration. He is forever barred from their world, no matter how free he is to traverse the terrestrial realms. Their victory was not just wrought by Michael and his angels', but verse 10 says God and Christ's power defeated and captured the dragon. Again, the Apocalypse identifies the Second Person of the Godhead as integral to the Almighty's eternal kingdom. It says He did not become Jesus Christ when He took on flesh and entered this world. Jesus was always God, the Word, and from this reference, Messiah long before He did so. This line of thinking can easily be traced in the Continuum. Before the Christ—God's Anointed One—donned flesh, He seized for God's kingdom a tremendous victory in heaven. Verse 11 on this issue is puzzling because John phrases it as if the crucifixion of the Lamb, the shedding of the Son of God's blood, has already happened; giving the impression that John is looking back to Christ's on the cross, or prophesying about some future time. But, is he? Which is it? Could it be that Jesus' election to become this world's Christ is secondary to His Messianic work in heaven, the way Melchizedek's was on earth? It would seem so, since the text says that they (heaven's hosts) overcame him, the dragon, who is the Devil by the blood of the Lamb and the word of their testimony. He was clearly a literal threat to their citizenry because their martyrs loved not their lives to the death. Scripture readers' traditional conflict with these implications lies in humans' beliefs regarding life in heaven. The prevailing belief is that there is no death there, so how is Jesus the Lamb slaughtered and for whom is He killed? After all, it is only on earth that people die, right? Are not the angels—all angels—immortal and therefore invulnerable? Jesus' earthly slaughter purged creation of its sin problem, but clearly some sort of life cessation occurred during and throughout heaven's war. From this text, it would seem so.

If one reads Isaiah 14:12-20 supernally and prophetically, one discerns its clues. It records the Lord telling on the Devil, how he lost his status as Lucifer, the son of the morning, or morning star. According to the rest of the passage and its counterpart in Ezekiel 28, his success has deceived him. Evil ambition has gripped him, making him dissatisfied with his cherubic station and colony. He has higher ambitions that will only be gratified when he is shoulder to shoulder with the Almighty and all the angels are subject to him. He has yet to get the words out of his heart before the Almighty hears and reacts to them. Iniquity is found, discovered, in him and so a deceived heart has turned him aside. Now nothing will stop him from accomplishing his sinful imaginations. Aggressive reactions to imagined threats bore deeply into the cherub's heart and moved him to try to overthrow the kingdom of light to make all of its citizens, captive to his menacing command. God knows him better than he knows himself; he is a terrible ruler—actual or probable. The dominions that he craves end up destroyed under his hand and its cities as devastated as the ones he has already ravaged. His record is abominable and the victims of his previous crimes know it. If and when he comes to power again, it is unlikely that things will be any different. He imprisons his citizens so they never revolt against him. Those he leaves free he debilitates through addictions, to make them incapable of resisting his dominance. Enslaved to his machinations, they obey him mindlessly until it kills them.

The Most High sees His delusions of grandeur for what they are, but those he empowered under him realize too late that he is unable to deliver on what he promises. At his defeat, they go to their doom, and when the appointed time comes, the dragon will also. The prophets Isaiah and Ezekiel record that when he shows up in their abysses, his casualties are only marginally surprised by his coming. When they served under him, he was not that impressive a leader. Although, they did not anticipate the desolation of his rule until he ruined their kingdoms. They know why he joins them in hell, because in reality he is no better than they were when they reigned on earth. Now he is their equal, and they taunt him cruelly for his failure and their losses. The account is generally purported to refer to a human ruler, but how can the insertion of "Lucifer, son of the morning" be explained any other way?

Returning to Revelation chapter 12 and examining its language in light of the preceding paragraph suggests that somewhere in the eternal world the Devil had a rule and a population. When he did, Scripture implies he killed his citizens. Recalling how Jesus labeled him a murderer from the beginning, this is not so hard to believe that those he murdered lived in a world outside this one. The next verse fortifies the suggestion. There are lives in heaven and previous world's civilization that suffered miserably when this creature was in power there. Revelation 12:12 says this,

> "Therefore rejoice, ye heavens, and ye that dwell in them. Woe to the inhabiters of the earth and of the sea! For the Devil is come down unto you, having great wrath, because he knoweth that he hath, but a short time."

Obviously, from these words, humans have much more to learn about God's earlier creations and their worlds than is known today. This text seems to imply that at a time when the earth's clay people did not exist, the occupants of heaven struggled with the catastrophic fallout caused by the cherub that decided to become a dragon. Lucifer, the first morning star, determined to become Satan, their adversary and accuser. Evidently, the situation was as grave for them back then as it is for the earth today. Perhaps it is more so because the struggle to overthrow him here has yet to happen. Here is why Hebrews 2:16 says Jesus did not take on Himself the nature of angels. He had already delivered heaven's hosts from their nemesis, as Revelation 12:12 recounts. He delivered His citizens so completely that the Devil was cast out of their world and down to this one. So there was no need for Him to embody angels to redeem them. As their God, Christ the Lion, Lamb, etc., The Messiah had long ago wrought their victory; now it was time to do the same for humans on earth. His next task as the Creator's Son was to set humanity free from the fallen cherub's wickedness.

THE EFFECT OF HEAVEN'S GREAT WAR

The war in heaven succeeded in delivering those who were dying a kind of death in God's world. Jesus' words in Matthew 24:31 and Mark 13:27 seem to convey this. They intimate that the Lord has elect beings in the heavens and the seas. Given what Peter and Jude say about the angels that sinned in or from heaven, alluded to in Genesis 6:2, 4, the likelihood of this being true is more than plausible. It is highly feasible, considering Revelation 12's comment about those who dwell on earth, and in the seas, that death like everything else physical did not get its start on this earth. Yes, as hard as it is for a mortal to grasp, some semblance of mortality originated in God's world and loss of life in some form or another happened there. Somehow, the dragon found the key to separating his fellow citizens from their Creator's life force, and seeing as his most constant tactic was accusation; it appears he managed to do so somewhat legitimately. No doubt, he invented a corrupt justice system to do so. If there was no death there, then why write Revelation 12:7, John 8:44, and Luke 10:18 at all? Until the dragon lost his battle with the Christ, Michael, and his angels, he appears to have roamed and ruined their world unchecked.[69]

Once the heavenly battle was over, casting out the dragon liberated all of heaven and allowed peace to return to their lives; thus, "rejoice ye heavens". The devil that so grievously tormented them and devastated their societies is now permanently expatriated to the earth and contained in hell. As exuberant as they are for themselves, they know what lies ahead, in the earth, and they mourn and lament over it, because it is now to experience what they endured for ages. The destructive, murderous dragon is resuming his authority in their world and its inhabitants are about to endure the brutal horrors they have just abolished. Jesus' foreknowledge is not merely predictive when it comes to the dragon; His words are reminiscent of what His world suffered under this arrogant being that well deserves His testimony in John 8:44, although it is directed at the dragon's children. *"Ye are of your father the Devil, and the lusts of your father ye will do. He was a murderer from the beginning, and abode not in the truth, because there is no truth in him. When he speaketh a lie, he speaketh of his own: for he is a liar, and the father of it."* Look at The Messiah's assessment of the Devil: A) He is a murderer: Whom did he murder in heaven and how did he do it? B) His murders go back to the beginning: What beginning does He mean? C) He abode not in the truth because there is no truth in him. D) When he speaks a lie, he speaks of his own creation, for he is a liar. Satan introduced untruth, contradictions, and contrariness to the Almighty's conversations and cultures. E) He is the father of lies. By reinventing himself, he concocted his own persona to be the complete antithesis of his Maker. All of this, he does celestially, presumably before God made the earth or this world, and their consequences were resolved back then too. The Godhead was well equipped for Calvary because it settled these creational issues long before the Son of God incarnated. From

---

69 Perhaps this is why when Jesus appeared on earth He struck terror in the hearts of the demons He encountered. They met His power before and knew that whenever He appeared they would be evicted.

these revelations, it is plain to see how the Continuum indisputably reinforces its worth and work here.

The heavens have rid themselves of the dragon and his destructions. The earth now has him, but only after the Lamb's slaughter, bringing out another strange point. If Jesus said on earth, He already saw Satan fall as lightning, the timing of Revelation 12's recount has to be precarnate and not post ascension as might be assumed. Else, the story is distorted. Consequently, it must be taken at face value that when Jesus and the Devil met each other in the wilderness, this world was the one at stake. Although His world too, would be once and for all purged from the serpent's sin, which is why He had to take His shed blood back to heaven to purge its altar, Hebrews 9:22-26. Having to pour out His blood on heaven's altar says that heaven was as, if not more, infected by Satan's villainy as the earth. If it were just a matter of earth's sin, then an earthly sacrifice would be enough; in fact, Abel's death would have sufficed. That being true, Revelation 5:6 is better explained; the Lamb still wears the scars of its slaughter. Nonetheless, He is celebrated for overcoming the dragon and his emissaries of sin and death in all the Creator's worlds, see again Colossians 1:20. The Lamb is the eternal King David that Samuel promised Israel's second king would come from his body. David knew, per Psalm 16:8 and affirmed by Acts 2:25, 31, that his lineage housed the Christ, Israel's Messiah, and everlasting King. Once more, the Continuum is upheld because it extends into the tribe of Judah and David's genealogy. The Lion of Judah is the Lamb of God, and the Lamb of God is the Lion of Judah. Both fuses to rule the world as promised to earthly King David. To do so, the Christ has to recover it, restore it, and repopulate it with beings after His own kind. To make Him earth's King, God has to give Jesus kindred, something the new birth accomplishes in all those that believe in Him. All these reasons make the Devil useful to the Continuum. He is as useful to it as its other characters, because it will not (cannot) stop until he is forever cast out of the world the way he was cast out of the heavens.

Although he is not as obvious in the Old Testament, Satan's works from the Garden of Eden to Malachi show up from time to time. Appearing almost silent since Eden, Scripture captures him in 1 Chronicles 21:1 where he tempts David to count Israel for selfish reasons. Job seems to hold the most Old Testament references to him. Psalm 109:6 has David authorizing Satan to antagonize those who reward evil for good and hatred for love. His judgment is that those guilty of such are to be ruled by the wicked in return for the wickedness that they commit. David feels quite strongly about this because he follows his edict up with a call for harsh judgments on the unjust and unanswered prayer. This decree comes from the king that so pleased Yahweh that He brought His first begotten Son through his family line. David's Psalms condemn the cruel to a short life span, career displacement, fatherless homes, and widowed wives. He decrees that such a person's child suffers the Cain's fate. They are destined to be vagabonds wandering from place to place begging for food. While it is tempting to think that David is just being vengefully superstitious, his 109th Psalm verse 8 challenges that response. "Let his days be few and let another take his office." The Holy Spirit brings forward this passage to Peter when it is time to replace Judas. Remaining in the Continuum to fill the apostles' vacancy, he draws on the Psalms the Savior already canonized.[34] It is apparent from this comparison that the Lord Jesus in David prophetically inspired his writings. That is how he as Christ's progenitor foresees The Messiah, coming to and leaving the earth. It is further how he could predict the means by which the Lord would do so.

The Christ as Yahweh, established His apostleship, for the sake of His kingdom and church way before time. This passage is as prophetic and replete with futuristic thinking as Psalm 16, used by Peter in the book of Acts. David's temporal authority is eternal and reaches all the way into the future. Although his words originate in his life during his reign, he knows root of the wickedness he confronts with them. The corrupt spiritual agents behind them cannot die so their destructions will never cease. Zechariah 3:1 and 2 reveal that Satan stands to oppose every new minister the Lord appoints, especially His prime ministers. Before that Leviticus 17:7 says that Israel, before it settled on the Lord's land, sacrificed to devils, something they learned to do while in Egyptian bondage. Deuteronomy 32:17 bears this out. There, it implies that the devils masqueraded as gods that arrived on earth or popped up from it regularly as new spiritual powers. In 2 Chronicles 11:15, Jeroboam creates a demonically staffed religious order for the devils he engages to replace Yahweh's worship. He wants to keep Israel from abandoning him for its divinely mandated annual pilgrimage to Jerusalem.

The last Old Testament Continuum reference on this subject is in Psalm 106:37. It records Israel's human sacrifice of her sons and daughters to devils. These are all included to show the Devil's antiquity and the Lord's ongoing struggles with him. Such longevity cannot help but carve this menacing force's place in His Continuum. Isaiah 26:21 says Yahweh will punish the inhabitants of the earth. Isaiah 27:1 extends His judgment to Leviathan, the piercing serpent, and the dragon in the sea. If it were not for Revelation chapters 12, 13, 16, and 20, Isaiah' mentioning the dragon would be dismissable. But they show the dragon as a key figure in the Lord's last days' eschatology. The Dragon fuels false prophecy, is fiendishly deified, and produces false prophets. Revelation 20:2 specifically calls heaven's cherub turned serpent the Devil and Satan for the second time. Revelation chapter 12 before then bluntly identifies him as such and frankly says he got his start in heaven and not on earth and his first assault was on celestial and not terrestrial beings. As dominant Continuum figures, Scripture's long line of prophets, says much about this antagonist of the Lord Jesus Christ and His angels. By the time the New Testament era arrives, all prophets foretelling Him voice familiar sentiments and predictions concerning this destructive creature. He in turn is well acquainted with them and the Lord's feelings about his dark career. Jesus includes many eschatological statements in His discourses. He paints vivid pictures of the state of the world immediately before and when He returns to collect His church. The Savior adds another measurement that foretokens His imminent advent. It is the days of Noah.

THE DAYS OF NOAH

The teaching that best illustrates the world conditions at His return embraces Noah. Hebrews 11:7 pictures him for us. It says that *"By faith Noah, being warned of God of things not seen as yet, moved with fear, prepared an ark to the saving of his house; by the which he condemned the world, and became heir of the righteousness which is by faith."* The Scriptures below reveal much about what the Lord will meet when He comes back to the earth in the last days. Noah, who is very integral to the Continuum, resurfaces as a God approved world figure. He is commemorated by the Lord for his response to the Almighty's case against his generation. Jesus draws on those days to portray several important things. The first is that the Lord changes not; what angered and grieved Him back then and moved Him to destroy the world will vex Him until the end of time. The second is that He has reacted against sin severely in the past and is poised to do so again at the appointed time. The third is that humanity cannot help but repeat history, its Maker's, and its own. The fourth is in the same way that consumption with its own way of life shut down humanity's spiritual insights, once more at the end of the Gentile and His church age on earth, His deadly judgments will again be blindsided because they are caught up in life as usual. Review His end time teachings in the following passages.

    a. "But as the days of Noah were, so shall also the coming of the Son of man be. For as in the days that were before the flood they were eating and drinking, marrying and giving in marriage, until the day that Noah entered into the ark, And knew not until the flood came, and took them all away; so shall also the coming of the Son of man be." Matthew 24:37-39.

b. "And as it was in the days of Noah, so shall it be also in the days of the Son of man. They did eat, they drank, they married wives, they were given in marriage, until the day that Noah entered into the ark, and the flood came, and destroyed them all." Luke 17:26, 27.

c. "Likewise also as it was in the days of Lot; they did eat, they drank, they bought, they sold, they planted, they builded; But the same day that Lot went out of Sodom it rained fire and brimstone from heaven, and destroyed them all. Even thus shall it be in the day when the Son of man is revealed." Luke 17:28, 29.

d. "Which sometime were disobedient, when once the longsuffering of God waited in the days of Noah, while the ark was a preparing, wherein few, that is, eight souls were saved by water. 1 Peter 3:20

e. "And spared not the old world, but saved Noah the eighth person, a preacher of righteousness, bringing in the flood upon the world of the ungodly." 2 Peter 2:5

The phrases offer clues to the era that brings Jesus back to earth to collect His own.

a) Eating, drinking and marrying dominate the age. In today's vernacular, global preoccupation with food and drink refers to partying.

b) Marriage as the Lord sees it here speaks to dating and mating and implies swapping mates as well. Whatever the case, marrying seems to be another obsessive global preoccupation.

c) Noah's preparations caught their attention, but failed to do more than raise their eyebrows and perhaps court their scorn and mockery.

d) Lot's day adds more to the picture: They too were consumed with surfeiting, eating, and drinking. Fleshly pleasures and pursuits occupied their minds and time.

e) They too were marrying and giving in marriage, only theirs was same sex marriages.

f) They were also consumed with buying and selling, making money.

g) They were consumed with business and enterprise, peddling lust, greed, and indulgence.

h) They were consumed with building and expansion, domination.

The above descriptions sound a great deal like today, and the conditions noted promise to intensify until the majority of the world lives according to a single lifestyle. A lifestyle that is utterly absorbed in human pleasures and accomplishments.

Noah and Lot's days may have been long ago, but they were still speaking when Jesus recalled them. To advance heaven's timeline, Jesus as the Great Prophet that revived Moses' mantle instructs His world of the future, using the Continuum's past, a past that He pulled forward from God's world to this one. His true believers respond to God's history and destiny the way Noah and Lot's families did. They adapt their human beliefs and conduct to those of the world that brought everything into existence to become compatible with it. People seeking to live with the Lord forever understand by faith that He requires human converts to behave the way His eternal citizens already do. Curiously, in his recall of Noah's days, Peter hints at entirely different worlds as if the flood and heaven's fire changed more than earth's landscape. The implication is that it changed time and maybe reset the earth's astronomical clock as well. All of that notwithstanding, the Continuum informs, warns, and as far as the faithful are concerned, reforms. The next chapter tells how the Old Testament prophets operated the Continuum until Jesus and the apostles arrived on the scene.

[9]

Precarnate Jesus And The Old Testament Prophets

More than 88 times the New Testament refers to the prophets. Jesus being taken for one substantiates their testimonies of Him; see Matthew 2:23. Matthew 5:17 and 7:12 pair the prophets with the Law, something that happens repeatedly throughout the New Testament writings. Matthew 11:13 links the Law with the prophets in reverse, to say they and the Law prophesied Jesus' coming, and they did so until John the Baptist. From his manifestation until Jesus' ascension, it became all about the kingdom. One can deduce from this that the Law refers to the Ten Commandments, the Levitical Ordinances, and the Pentateuch.[70] Matthew 13:17 is a precursor to Peter's revelation in 1 Peter 1:10-12. In the Matthew reference, Jesus remarks on how many prophets and righteous people desired to peer into His futuristic life on earth but could not. The epistle further says they were shut out of it because although they received it prophetically, its revelations were scheduled for later in the future long after their deaths.[71] God did not need them expounding on it, under Moses' dispensation as if it was for their times and not the future. Matthew 16:14 gets even more specific by naming certain prophets that foreran Jesus' coming. It names John the Baptist, who by then was executed, Elias (Elijah), Jeremias (Jeremiah) and the rest of the prophets. Matthew 22:40 makes an additional declaration about God's

---

70 This idea begs further exploration.
71 See also Luke 10:24.

prophets. To the Lord, the prophets and the Law are interdependent and equally underpin Scripture's first and second greatest commandments. According to Jesus, the first is to love the Lord with all one has and is, and upon mastering that, the second becomes possible; to love one's neighbor as oneself.

Additionally, Matthew 23:29 (and later Luke 11:47) records Jesus chiding His antagonists for their tradition of murdering prophets and righteous people. He does so because, appallingly, they routinely celebrate the tombs of the prophets that their foreparents slaughtered, which Jesus finds despicable. Nevertheless, in spite of their historically tragic ending, and considering He is about to die as a prophet Himself to close out Moses' age, the Lord prophesies that He will continue to send prophets into the world in Matthew 23:34, notwithstanding his disgust at His nation's obsession with destroying them. Nearing the end of His time on earth and looking into the face of the horrible death He must suffer, the Lord Jesus in Matthew 26:56, resigns Himself to His destiny knowing that it is because the Scriptures of the prophets must be fulfilled. Moving onto Mark, it opens with the words of the prophets. Mark 1:2 recalls Malachi 3:1, the prophet that foretold the revival of prophecy when The Messiah appeared. Moses' predicted that the prophet would be like himself; see Deuteronomy 8:15. Mark 6:15 echoes Matthew 16:14, as does Mark 8:28.[72] Luke 1:70 gives the reason for Zechariah's miraculous impregnation of his aged wife Elizabeth. It is to restart and advance Yahweh's Continuum. God decreed it by the mouth of His holy prophets, who have spoken for Him *since the world began.*[73] Luke 6:23 records the Lord warning and exhorting His future prophets. Some will be killed, and others reviled, but whichever it is they are to rejoice because their fate confirms their high calling and vindicates the prophets that have gone before them. Luke 11:49 reinforces this, but identifies the prophets' and the apostles' actual sender. It is the wisdom of God, which goes along with Isaiah 11:1-5. Jesus reiterates that becoming His prophet can potentially prove as deadly to them as it did for Abel, the very first prophet, and Zacharias[74] who wrapped up the Old Testament prophet's age. John the Baptist reopened the office. Jesus tells them He like Abel, Zechariah, and all the slaughtered messengers since their deaths, will be sacrificed. The reason is because of His words. Luke 13:28 has Jesus, foretelling the eternal inheritance of His slaughtered prophets. They will join Abraham, Isaac, and Jacob in the kingdom of God. Not long after though, He laments again over Jerusalem's compulsion to rid itself of Yahweh's prophets, repeat-

---

72 And Luke 9:8 and 19.

73 Continuum language.

74 Refer to 2 Chronicles 36:15-16.

ing the Law and the prophets governed Israel until His arrival despite His chronic resistance. Upon completing His mission, prophet dominance ends and gives way to His own eternal kingdom. Luke 16:29 in reinforcing the Continuum, reaches all the way to hell itself, because until Jesus opened the way of salvation, even His most faithful prophets went there.[75] He recites the account of the rich man who, after ignoring Lazarus' suffering at his gate for years, lands in hell for his callousness to the poor. His indifference was a direct violation of God's commands. Jesus recalls the incident because of the bosom of Abraham that received Lazarus when he left this world. As Abraham too was a prophet; first to Babylon and lastly for the Almighty, he escapes hell's fires. Converting the Most High God redeems him from his Babylonian heritage's eternal damnation.

Sentenced to hell for his cruelty, the rich man realizes that its judgment is not only real but also permanent. In its flames, he understands he is there because he snubbed poor Lazarus in his agony. Wishing to spare his brothers who are still on earth his doom, he appeals to Abraham, who is in a cozier part of hell. The once rich and powerful man asks his nation's patriarch to send one of those abiding with him back to earth to warn them of how serious and severe hell truly is. The account recalls that Abraham refused and responded with this; *"Abraham saith unto him, they have Moses and the prophets; let them hear them. And he said, nay, father Abraham: but if one went unto them from the dead, they will repent. And he said unto him, if they hear not Moses and the prophets, neither will they be persuaded, though one rose from the dead."* The patriarch's words are prophetic and pragmatic at once. He alludes to the death of the coming Messiah that he knows, according to Galatians 3:8 is approaching, and at the same time reveals his knowledge of the powers of unbelief. The supernatural or mystical are not enough to persuade those determined to resist God's truth to abandon their ways and views. No matter how spectacular the warning against doing something, people will do what their heart wills them to do. Such is the case with the rich man's brothers. They are no more willing to behave any better than he did, even if they witnessed someone rising from the dead. In fact, the tenor of Abraham's words implies they will be tripped up by what was available to the rich man before his death: the Law of Moses and the words of the prophets. Both failed to convince him of hell's reality or severity, and if his brothers land there, it is because they likewise refused to heed them.

---

75 Noah, Abraham, Samuel, David to name a few.

Notice though how Abraham, who died ages before Moses knows what is happening on earth. He knows the Law governing his seed and the prophets that birthed and governs their nation. Both tell Abraham that the Almighty kept His promise to him. He indeed multiplied his seed as the sand on the seashore and the stars of the sky. Furthermore, the patriarch not only knows Moses, who is not in hell with him, nor was alive when Abraham lived, but he knows the prophets that perpetuated Moses' office too. Abraham somehow knows their words are the final determining factor in who goes to the fire and who awaits The Messiah in his underworld haven. He knows full well that by faith, those who heed Moses and the prophets will escape the rich man's fate. Abraham understands not only how the pre-mosaic generation escapes hell, but how those under Moses' Law avoids it as well. How does he know? Perhaps a clue may be found in 1 Samuel 28:10-19.

In support of this revelation, there is Hebrews 11:24-26 that says Moses left Egypt, severed his family ties with its Pharaoh and adopted mother, and rejoined his fellow citizens in captivity. He did it because he had a visitation from the invisible Christ, who showed him the rewards of forsaking all and following Him. This almost incidental truth correlates with what is said above about Abraham and further expands the Continuum's Principal Characters. Here is the crucial question: How is it that back in time, when Jesus The Messiah had yet to be expected in this world, did Moses happen to see Him and be persuaded by His visit to give up everything sitting on Egypt's throne had to offer him to resume being a Jew? The language of these passages clearly states that Moses saw Christ, the invisible one like David did in Acts 2:22-36. Moses has a similar encounter with the precarnate Christ. He recalls Jesus' earthly appearances as Yahweh before Peter's sermon on the Church's first Pentecost as stated in Psalm 16:8. Luke records Jesus as subtly revealing Himself as having always existed when He asks the question about David and Himself being his descendant. In Luke 20:41--44, Jesus asks, "*How can people say that The Messiah is David's son? Because David himself in the book of Psalms says, 'The Lord told my Lord, "Sit at my right hand, until I make your enemies a footstool for your feet"'. So David calls him 'Lord.' then how can he be his son?*" Luke's narrative reiterates Matthew's in 22:42-45: "*What do you think about The Messiah? Whose son is he?" They told him, "David's". He asked them, "then how can David <u>by the Spirit</u> call him 'Lord' when he says, the Lord told my Lord, "Sit at my right hand, until I put your enemies under your feet".'? If David*[76] *calls him 'Lord', how can he be his son?*"[77] Jesus, in

---

76 David as the king would never call his sons by an equal or greater title.

77 Luke version goes a bit further by adding to the Lord's subtly in that a) the Lord is God, the Lord God is speaking to is Jesus, and the Spirit is the medium through whom He is speaking.

this example, draws forth the second Psalm that He spoke to David when he was alive and when He as the Christ was his future offspring. The Lord's Messianic duties were yet a ways down the line when David received and penned this prophecy. All of these examples exemplify the precarnate state of Jesus Christ as He unfolds His gospels. They show numerous historical figures encountered, and had a relationship with Him before His appearance in human form. In fact, the Lord immortalized Abraham as His friend, and Moses as one He wished to continue working with long after he died. What is most impressive about all this is how the Son of God as Yahweh personally empowered all of these paragons of faith to conquer on His behalf in their respective ages. The references also reinforce Jesus as God's Son having a pre-existent life and career that interposed itself throughout creation's human affairs. It is as if He has always functioned as the Almighty's Prime Minister, handling everything that must be done in all His worlds since their beginning. Daniel 7:13, fortifies this truth. Daniel *"Saw in the night visions, and, behold, one like the Son of man came with the clouds of heaven, and came to the Ancient of days, and they brought him near before him."*

Continuing in this vein is Luke 18:31. It has Jesus, heading to Israel's capital city to meet His fate. Again, He shows no surprise and minimal sorrow over what lies ahead for Him, because it is according to what the prophets wrote about Him when He became the Son of Man. Unlike His followers, Christ's world understands why their God joined the ranks of the mortals to die. After His ordeal and resurrection from the grave, Jesus reprimands His apostles for not expecting His return. Their sketchy faith disbelieved all He said to the end. Not stopping at recalling what He told them while He was still with them, Jesus wants them to know how to prove His Messiahship to pass His whole story on to others correctly. He says to them in Luke 24:25, 26, *"O fools, and slow of heart to believe all that the prophets have spoken: Ought not Christ to have suffered these things, and to enter into his glory?"* He speaks about Himself as the object of their prophetic writings as if what He has just undergone somehow altered His identity. Instead of "Ought not **I** have suffered...?" Jesus says, "Ought not **Christ** to have suffered..." What is written in the next verse further certifies the Continuum's record, *"And beginning at Moses and all the prophets, he expounded unto them in all the Scriptures the things concerning Himself"*. (Luke 24:27). Going all the way back to Moses and through all the prophets that spoke of Him, the Lord Jesus reiterates where they can find all truth concerning Him and His dominion over the earth when He sits on His throne in heaven. In Luke 24:44-47, He does it again because it is important to Jesus that His followers look nowhere else for truths concerning Him but to the Old Testament's prophets. Which prophets would that be? Those He deliberately named when He was with them on earth and those whose words He used or referred to in His teachings. Jesus leaves His apostles with incontrovertible signposts to His success. He tells them that they can trust every prophet He called by name or whose words He quoted in His office for accurate truths concerning Him. With that information, they could establish His church, authenticate His doctrine, and fend off heresy assured that they were obeying the real God's teachings. As long as they stayed with the prophets the Lord Jesus affirmed, they would be safe.

Moving on to John, the pattern continues, as Philip recognizes Jesus from Moses' Law as "that Prophet", and the one the prophets said "would be called a Nazarene." Andrew identifies Jesus after His baptism as the Messias, John 1:41. Philip also found Nathanael and persuaded him to meet Jesus with these words: *"We have found him of whom Moses, in the law and the prophets did write, Jesus the son of Joseph of Nazareth."* All through His ministry, Christ proves He is not winging it. He is not working in the blind, but is following a carefully devised plan that has been unfolding since the Almighty told Eve in Genesis 3:15 that she would bring forth a seed that would bring down the serpent's kingdom. In Isaiah 54:13, the Lord quotes John 6:45 to tell His disciples who could and could not ask Him to be their Savior. Isaiah says, *"And all thy children shall be taught of the Lord; and great shall be the peace of thy children."*[78] Locating His actions in Scripture for them so that they are not to just take His word for it, He recites Scripture for their ears and their time. Letting them know that, to come to God, they must go through His only begotten Son. So the Savior says, *"Everyone therefore that hath heard, and hath learned of the Father, cometh unto me"*. If anyone wants to come to the true and living God, long before Jesus arrived the Godhead established that he or she has to come through Him. The entire chapter majestically lays out point for point, why Jesus is The Messiah, what He came to earth to do, that He is not innately a citizen of the planet but an alien to it.[79] These and a host of other truths He teaches as if His country should have known them. And they would have, had their teachers done their jobs well. A good illustration of the faultiness of Israel's teachers is noted in Ezekiel 36:24-27. There the prophet is prophesying the new birth that Jesus later uses to explain to Nicodemus as the way into the kingdom of God (See John 3:5). Additionally, in debating with His contenders, in relation to Himself, Jesus refers to Abraham and the prophets. Essentially, He says that His Father, in John 8:52 and 53, appointed them to witness Him.

---

78 KJV
79 John 8:23; 18:36.

Staying with the path that His prophets laid for Him in the Continuum, Jesus for this sake of all His worlds, duly complies with it. He sets up its next stage of fulfillment, the book of Acts. There the Holy Spirit takes over by revisiting the Psalms. Appearing first in Acts 1:16 with the Holy Spirit speaking to David, Peter directs their testimony to the Psalms that Jesus has sovereignly canonized for them. He pulls from Zechariah 11:13's fulfillment, a reference that addresses the void that Judas' dying created in their apostleship. They must, encouraged by the Holy Spirit, replace him. The Scripture the Lord brought to Peter's mind to quote was, *"Now this man purchased a field with the reward of iniquity, and falling headlong he burst asunder in the midst, and all his bowels gushed out."* Zechariah uttered it back in time this way, *"And the Lord said to me, "Throw it to the potter"--the handsome price at which they valued me! So I took the thirty pieces of silver and threw them to the potter at the house of the Lord."* Here is the rest of the story. When Judas, who had betrayed his Messiah, saw that Jesus was condemned, he was seized with remorse and attempted to return the thirty pieces of silver to the chief priests and the elders that paid him to betray the Lord. Matthew 27:3, *"So Judas threw the money into the temple and left. Then he went away and hanged himself."*[80] Peter witnessed this prophecy's fulfillment. Competently trained by Jesus' advanced classes, he saw the Scriptures more pragmatically. He discerned from the Spirit's recall of this particular passage that the prophets foretold Judas' betrayal of the Christ and his suicide long before any of them was born. They just did not know it until then. Other passages that enlightened Peter on God's mind for them includes Psalm 41:9; John 13:18; Psalm 69:22, 25; and Psalm 109:8. All of these passages told Peter what to do to advance the Lord's campaign. The last reference remembers the Holy Ghost speaking to David about the Christ's coming passion. Next is Acts 3:8, where God's foreknowledge and foreordainment in ages past determined what would happen to His Son when He sent Him into the world, *"But those things, which God <u>before</u> had shewed by the mouth of all his prophets, that Christ should suffer, he hath so fulfilled."* Verse 21 of the same chapter rephrases the same thought but adds, *"... all His holy prophets since the world began"*. Verses 22-24 narrow it down a bit by naming the prophets that participated in the Continuum. Referring to Samuel (one of the prophets), Moses words in Deuteronomy 18:5 are recalled. Both Samuel and those that followed him prophesied things concerning The Messiah. This chronology underscores how Jesus Christ expects His successive prophets to reiterate the same subject matter and theme He brought to earth. He fully expects His contemporary prophets to fall in line with His ancient ones.

---

80 Matthew 27:5.

Peter's Pentecost audience as Abraham's seed is the offspring of the long line of prophets that prophetically orchestrated The Messiah's arrival, suffering, and death. To remind them of it, he rehearses the Lord's promise to their progenitor: *"And in thy seed shall all the kindreds (nations) of the earth be blessed"*. Stephen picks up on his technique and uses it himself when he confronts the synagogue of the freedmen, or the Libertines. From Acts 6:8 to 7:53 he recounts in abbreviated form his nation's entire history and God's issues with them. He quotes the Law, the prophets, and other Scriptures to show His people how displeased Yahweh is with them and how wickedly they have treated their covenant God. Acts 7:42 and 43 captures him drawing on the words of the prophets again; this time He pulls from Amos' prophecy (See Amos 5:25). New Testament, Stephen chastens his audience for their predecessors' despicable treatment of Yahweh's prophets, what Jesus vehemently denounced during His earthly ministry. In preaching to the Gentiles, Peter passes on what he learned from the Lord. He says in Acts 10:43 that all the prophets give witness to Jesus, who is now their Savior. In Acts 13:16-48, Paul delivers a meticulous discourse to the Gentiles on the order of the one Stephen preached to the Libertines, with one difference. Paul's version is global while Stephen's was national. Still, Paul too is persecuted by the Jews for his sermon. The Lord, however spares His life. His inflammatory speech from Acts 15:15, attaches itself to the Continuum through the following passage:

> "And to this agree the words of the prophets; as it is written, after this I will return, and will build again the tabernacle of David, which is fallen down; and I will build again the ruins thereof, and I will set it up: That the residue of men might seek after the Lord, and all the Gentiles, upon whom my name is called, saith the Lord, who doeth all these things."

This quotation looks back to Amos 9:11 that resonates Isaiah 45:21. Paul continues the apostles' practice of linking everything preached and taught to the prophets that foretold the whole event leading up to Jesus' and now his ministry. Here is what he says in Acts 24:14: *"But this I confess unto thee, that after the way which they call heresy, so worship I the God of my fathers, believing all things which are written in the law and in the prophets."* The Way that chafed so many people of their day, despite their Jewish heritage as partakers of Abraham's covenant and Moses' law is not a sermon but a person: the Lord Jesus Christ. The Way, as more of a person than a path causes people to stumble the most. Paul continues his argument in Acts 26:22 where he asserts that what he is preaching is what Moses and the prophets said would come to pass. He preached Jesus' suffering; His resurrection from the dead; His illumination of the world's evil; and His grafting of the Gentiles among His redeemed. Agrippa is cornered by Paul who asks him a question that should not have been rhetorical, though Agrippa responds as if it is. Paul's powerful arguments come from the prophets and Agrippa, as the temple's leader, should have believed it. Instead, his only response is not that Paul is wrong, but that he just is not willing (or ready) to stop being a Mosaic Jew to accept Jesus Christ and become a Christian. Nearing the end of the book of Acts, Paul (in 28:23) gets an opportunity to teach Jesus. His fundamental source is the Law of Moses and the prophets. Faithfully, he shows his listeners that Jesus is in the very Old Testament Scriptures they listen to every week. As he does so, he simultaneously composes Jesus' Messianic and ecclesial theology. In his salutation to the Romans, the Apostle Paul makes a most bewildering statement about himself as an apostle of Jesus Christ and the gospel he conscientiously preaches. Paul declares God separated him from his mother's womb to be the Lamb's apostle to spread His gospel to the Gentiles. Subliminally, both are according to God's promise made *beforehand* by the mouth of His prophets in the Holy Scriptures. Prior to his birth and since the gospel is eternal, before the foundation of the world, and Paul himself, apostleship was foreordained by Israel's God. In Romans 3:21, Paul advances his premises by adding that righteousness is not some vague moralistic concept, but a derivement of Moses' law and the prophets. If this is all sounding redundant, it is because it is just that constant throughout God's word, which is why prophets function as the brain and prophecy the major vein of the Continuum.

The Continuum presses on with Paul naming another prophet in Scripture, Elias (Elijah) in Romans 11:3. Also in Romans, 16:25, 26, the Continuum is reflected in the gospel Paul preaches. He said he received it by revelation of the Lord's *mystery kept secret since the world began*. Paul notes that God's prophets recorded it in their earthly Scriptures and progressively revealed the mystery. This passage goes well with what he wrote about Abraham, who received the gospel before he died. The very gospel revealed to the prophets, Peter says, came from the Spirit of <u>Christ who was in them at the time</u>. Ephesians 3:5, reinforce the assertion that the Spirit of Christ was in the prophets who foretold His coming, even though they did not know what they wrote, or to whom they were writing their prophecies. What these disclosures accomplish is substantiation of the Apostle John's statement that, *"the testimony of Jesus is the spirit of prophecy"*. A statement that he rephrases from his gospel in John 5:39: The Scriptures *"testify of Jesus"* to say why only His testimony is what the Godhead approves as the genuine "spirit of prophecy." Hebrews 11:1 however, says it outright. In the past, before the coming of His Son, God spoke to His people through the prophets. The end of the chapter includes them in the faith chronicles that epitomize their fidelity to God.

James' epistle uses the prophets as an example to encourage the Lord's family to have patience in tribulation and suffering. They too were retaliated against for their faith, as the saints of his congregations were, but remained faithful to the Lord to finish their courses with His praise.

First Peter 1:10, referred to more than once, stresses how the prophets foretold a salvation that neither they nor the angels transmitting[81] it had any real insight into when they were writing. In 3:2 of his second epistle, he exhorts his believers to heed the words of the prophets that were *before* them, and presumably those that were among them, then. He wants their words ever in the forefront of their minds to guide them. Revelation 10:7 indirectly reminisces Ephesians 3:5 when it says *"But in the days of the voice of the seventh angel, when he shall begin to sound, the mystery of God should be finished, as he hath declared to his servants the prophets"*. From before time began until now, the mystery of God has been unfurling generationally through the mouths of God's prophets. At the end of time, when the Lord winds down His entire earthly ministry, He remembers them and credits them with being the primary source of His secret plans and dealings with humanity. Their faithfulness helped Him succeed in a venture that began before they were made. For this reason, the Almighty never forgets His prophets, or those that have mutilated them because of Him. Revelation 16:6 says as much and includes God's vowed recompense for the suffering of all of His saints. End time Babylon is to be destroyed for assassinating His prophets.

When the Almighty downs the whorish city Babylon the Great, the world's sorrow over its destruction is eclipsed only by heaven's greater exultation over its destruction. They are free, their enemy is cast down to earth, and the holy apostles and prophets that suffered mercilessly at the hands of both are neither dead nor in hell. They are alive and well forever with the Lord, who urges them to rejoice with the rest of eternity over His last days' triumph over evil and death. His judgment on the city is as much to avenge His brutalized messengers, as it is to end sin's earthly reign. The Apocalypse records how God plans to vindicate His prophets and retaliate against the world for shedding their blood. His vengeance reaches back to Abel all the way up to Zechariah, who is the last one to be born and killed for His righteousness under the Old Testament. That vindication extends to God's New Testament Prophets as well. Revelation 22:6 ends this trail with the Almighty declaring Himself to be the Lord God of the holy prophets. He wants them to, like Abraham, believe that even after they are long gone His finished doomsday campaign will vindicate them. Yahweh's long de-

---

parted murdered prophets are to realize that His targeted assaults on the planet settle the score with the unbelievers that destroyed them because of His truth. Against this tragic backdrop, Abraham from the grave knows Moses' Law ruled his promised descendants along with the prophets that followed him. The Law and the prophets together kept the Most High's Continuum moving forward. The patriarch's answer to the rich man burning in hell's flames witnessed first-hand what transpired on the earth, in much the same way Samuel knew, after Saul tricked the witch of Endor into performing the séance that called forth his spirit. God's fiercely loyal prophet was summoned from its underworld abode to prophesy the future. Like Abraham, Samuel knew that Saul and his sons would soon join him in the grave. The prophetic references used so far under this heading speak to the prophets, plural. Below the word prophet, singular is discussed.

SPECIFIC PROPHETS REMEMBERED IN THE CONTINUUM

The Messiah interprets Daniel's 9:26-27; 11:31 and 12:11 prophecies. His revelations penetrate because as the Savior, He has been accurately revealing things only someone from the past could know. In Matthew 27:9-10, the Lord personally credits words to Jeremiah that the Old Testament ascribe to another prophet. *"Then was fulfilled that which was spoken by Jeremy the prophet, saying, And they took the thirty pieces of silver, the price of him that was valued, whom they of the children of Israel did value; And gave them for the potter's field, as the Lord appointed me."* However, the Scriptures as compiled today register Zechariah[82] as speaking these words. No doubt, as with other prophecies, the Lord repeated Himself to several prophets to assure His words made it into the earth's record. It is highly probable that Jeremiah's version got lost, because Jesus would not have erred in something so significant. The conflict is somewhat as it is with Luke, who received the words of his gospel from the apostles who were eyewitnesses, and his mentor Paul. Jeremiah and Zechariah apparently received the same prophecy for the same purposes. However, Zechariah's version must have been a failsafe to etch the prophecy in the world's record anyway. See Zechariah 11:12-13. Nonetheless, Yahweh incarnate says He delivered the prophecy to Jeremiah. According to Matthew chapter, Jesus came to set many records straight.

The following examples further speak to why Jesus claims in this passage that He gave a word to Jeremiah, who ancient Hebrew writers recognize first in the Book of the Prophets. Perhaps that is why Jeremiah's word appears in Zechariah's prophecy. A

---

82 See Zechariah 11:12, 13.

similar thing happens to Jeremiah regarding Cyrus. In 2 Chronicles 36:21, a reiteration of Ezra 1:1-3, Jeremiah is credited with prophesying a word that involves Cyrus the king. Yet, none of his writings actually mention the man the way Isaiah does. Still, when the time comes for the Jews to return to their homeland, Jeremiah and not Isaiah are remembered as the prophet who foretold it. Jeremiah prophesied for a long time. It is not beyond the realm of possibility that only fragments of his words were found. So, Isaiah calls Cyrus by name, foretells his military prowess, rise to power, and ascension to the throne. Yet when the Lord stirs this king to restore His people to their homeland, Jeremiah's words are recalled. Although the mass deportation and the decades of exile for sure lost some of Jeremiah's prophecies on earth, the Lord nonetheless remembered and fulfilled them. Multiple prophets and versions of the prophecy are necessary for God because anything can happen to forestall a word He needs to fulfill. Therefore, Zechariah's utterance of Jeremiah's words may have landed in his book, but Jesus sets the record straight when He comes to earth. He says He first, or directly, gave the prophecy to Jeremiah, implying perhaps that Zechariah got it second hand. If Jesus is who He says He is and came to His people as the exact Lord, they worshipped over the centuries, then His recollections must be taken as correct.

Other comparisons enlarge upon the prophetic references given so far to identify the prophets specifically named as contributors to the Lord's incarnation and thereby His Continuum. These references show it is essential for modern prophets to know their predecessors and the prophecies they spoke because all Christian prophets should align with those Scripture memorializes and exalt their words above their own in their times. Such is the case in Matthew 1:22. It recounts how Joseph and Mary became The Messiah's earthly parents. *"Now all this was done, that it might be fulfilled which was spoken of the Lord by the prophet, saying, behold, a virgin shall be with child, and shall bring forth a son, and they shall call his name Emmanuel, which being interpreted is, God with us"*. The prophet quoted here is Isaiah.[35] In Matthew 12:17-20, Isaiah's prophecy is repeated, while Jesus in 12:39 of his gospel draws on Old Testament Jonah to rebuke their unbelief.[83] Matthew 16:4 also recognizes the prophet Jonah, and the words of Zechariah 9:9 are revived in Matthew 21:4. Haggai 2:9 and Isaiah 56:7 both find fulfillment in Matthew 21:13. Aside from these, look also into Psalm 78:2-3. It explains the Lord's teaching methods. When He comes to earth, He chooses to speak almost exclusively to His audiences in parables. Continuum-wise, His words announce secrets that heaven has concealed from the foundation of the world. God's founding revelations go all the way back to everybody's beginning to the only prophet that Scripture

---

83 Jonah 1:17.

recalls from that period, Abel. Indicating by this that the secrets The Messiah unseals or those spoken in His name must be those from his ministry forward. Aside from the very prophecies He spoke to Adam, his wife and the serpent. This is especially true when one realizes that Abel and Enoch are two of the three antediluvian prophets' Scripture names. Noah is the third.

Besides, what has been said, there are other immutable facts that should be unveiled concerning Jesus Christ as the Old Testament Yahweh.[84] As said elsewhere, Jesus' arrival in Israel in a human body was not the first time the Lord visited His land or appeared to His people. He shows up to Abraham in Genesis 18 and appeared to the seventy elders in Exodus 24:7 on the mountain top, clad in brilliant sapphire. He shows up to Ezekiel in Babylon, and there are other occasions that He manifests on earth before His incarnation. These incidences are recalled because Micah says His (Christ's) goings forth have been from of old.[85] Jesus even stated in John 8:56 that pre-Mosaic Abraham rejoiced to see His day. In the Old Testament, He said He appeared to Solomon three times, and David in his Psalms said he foresaw the Lord always before His face. Lastly, on this point, John's Gospel says the world was made by Him, and without Him nothing was made that was made. While the people of His day lacked the illumination to discern His character and nature, the modern saint, especially commentators and theologians are without excuse. The New Testament does its job of decoding for future converts to Jesus Christ, the mysteries of the Old Testament Prophecies well. However, reading one without the other causes the seed not to reveal its fruit and the fruit not to identify its seed.

Addressing Scripture Gaps and Inconsistencies

What has been laid out above, speaks to why Jesus states that He gave a prophecy to Jeremiah that today only appears in Zechariah. Taking the eternal Lord as He is, means accepting The Messiah's memory is infallible. After all, as the all-wise God, He would surely know what He said to whom. Many plausible explanations can be given for this and other Bible discrepancies. For instance, it is highly probable that a prophet heard the message and kept it to himself, or shared it with a personal friend or colleague. It is common knowledge that the Scriptures held today are but fragments of all that was ever written about the Lord in Israel. If, for instance, the Lord merely voiced His word to a prophet privately who did not write what he heard, but only

---

84 See 1 Corinthians chapter 10:4; 1 Peter 1:11; Luke 4:4; Psalm 2:2; Revelation 12:10.
85 Micah 5:2.

spoke it aloud, there would be no written record of it. In all likelihood, Jeremiah's version of the prophecy was misplaced or still buried. The same is possible for all of the named messengers in Scripture whose works are no longer available. In the case of Jeremiah, this is unlikely in view of 2 Chronicles 36:21 and Ezra 1:1-3. That his prophecy is recalled more than a century later, suggests there was a written record of it somewhere to guide future prophets' declaration of Israel's time of liberation. Daniel is one such for instance. It seems quite a few of Jeremiah's words got lost down through the years. Daniel stumbled upon those that were still obtainable to announce the time of his people's return to their homeland. Although, he searched all the prophets' writings, he found the end of the exile period in Jeremiah's scroll.

For sure, there are many statements in the Bible attributed to writers whose works are not available today, making them, in all likelihood, inaccessible to God's scribes when they were compiling the Bible. To say that Jesus, the very God, erred in memory or that the historical accounts He drew on were figments of His imagination undermines His godhood and casts dangerous aspersions on Him as God's Word incarnate. Such is not the way of His family or ministers; it is a device of His enemies seeking to abolish His authority in the Church and to obliterate His esteem in the world. If the Lord said, a particular prophet prophesied a passage, then he is the one who did. The Savior went to great lengths to name whom He prophesied what words to in the Old Testament because He had to rectify ages of error that had accumulated in His records. He also sought to clue His future messengers and teachers on what was and was not Him speaking. The Lord's sermon in Matthew chapter 5 seems to say as much. A repetitive phrase makes the point, "You have heard it was said, but I say…" The Lord's words and tone suggest He is correcting error and setting His prophetic record aright. His need to do so goes to the security of His Continuum. Jesus uses His earthly visit to seize the opportunity to repair its breaches and keep its immutability intact.

These are but a few reasons why not everything that is written by individuals referenced in Scripture is available in modern times. Consequently, Christian leaders and teachers should be wary of declaring something as errant, nonexistent, or mislabeled exclusively on the grounds of what has come down to today's church as the Holy Bible.

OTHER OLD TO NEW TESTAMENT PROPHECY CONNECTIONS

Mark 13:14 recalls Daniel's prophecy. Luke 1:76 alludes to Isaiah 40:3, as does Luke 3:4. The famous, "spirit of the Lord is upon me" passage in Isaiah 61 is used by the Savior in Luke 4:17-19. Elijah's stupendous ministry, Luke 4:27 recalls along with the prophet Jonah and the Ninevites, Scripture mentions the Queen of Sheba who visited Solomon. Moving forward to John's gospel, he opens with John the Baptist's identity that reminded the people of age old Elijah. They thought perhaps the ancient prophet had returned from the dead as John the Baptist, and, considering how the record says he left the planet, they were not completely irrational in this notion. Strangely, their response to Jesus repeats itself to suggest that in some manner the people of His day did not find it unusual for the ancient prophets to reappear to them from time to time. John 1:21 indicates just such an occasion. John the Baptist identifies himself as the manifestation of the special messenger that Malachi prophesied would prepare the way for The Messiah's arrival. Because John's ministry so mirrored Elijah's with the exception perhaps of the former prophet's mind boggling miracles, the people question John's denials and ask him repeatedly if he is Elijah. Luke seems to be of this conviction because he records Zacharias, saying such about his son John the Baptist before his conception in Elizabeth's womb. John 6:14 concordantly invokes Deuteronomy 8:15 to confirm Jesus as the Prophet Moses predicted would arise from among them that was just like him. The affirming revelation resurfaces in John 7:40, again drawing on Isaiah 53.

Acts 2:16 in response to the Pentecost outpouring draws on the prophet Joel. In Joel 2:28-32, precisely what the upper room saints were experiencing happened just as he said it would. Those in the street were not overlooked in the glorious moment for they all heard, in their own native tongue, the wonderful works of God. Acts 2:30 remembers David's prophetic reign and Samuel's words to him that the fruit of his loins that he later learned to be the Christ, would be raised up to sit on his throne. Thus, The Messiah is King of kings because He comes from David's kingly line. Some of Israel knew this because they addressed Jesus as the Son of David. Matthew 1:1 recognizes Him as such. His foster father Joseph is from David's line as is Mary His mother. Matthew 9:27 acknowledges Jesus as David's Son. His phenomenal feats make Him that laudable because His followers credited His miraculous acts to His Davidic genealogy, see Matthew 12:3. Jesus is petitioned for healing in Matthew 15:22 and 29:30, 31 on account of this. Recognizing Him as Scripture's prophesied Son of David, jubilant crowds bless the Savior in Matthew 21:9 and 15. The Lord in the course of His ministry often quizzes His antagonists about His true genealogy. He repeats such a quiz in Matthew 22:42. Mark and Luke's gospel record His continued response to the challenges to His identity the same way. The key to the Christ's preeminence is David. He is the promised seed in Isaiah 22:15-14 who is realized in Revelation 3:7 as the one Isaiah had in mind. The New Testament calls Jesus, David, about fifty-eight times. The last one is in Revelation 22:16. It has Him declaring Himself to be the root and the offspring of David. Correlating with the question Jesus asked His followers regarding Him being David's Son, this passage eternally engraves the point in all worlds. Jesus is David's God, but David is the Lord's father. Both men, though eons apart, end up being one another's offspring.

Acts 2:30; 3:23 and 7:37 all quote Moses' Deuteronomy 18 prophecy. Stephen uses Isaiah 66:1 and 2 in arguments with the Libertines. As if this method of meeting Israel's God is universal, Candace, the Queen Ethiopians' eunuch asks Philip to help him understand Isaiah's prophecy concerning the Christ in chapter 53. Being perhaps a product of the Queen of Sheba's visit to Solomon, their faith is what he knew. It paved the way for the man to receive Jesus Christ and take His salvation to His nation. This is found in Acts 8:28-30. Samuel is recalled by Paul in Acts 13:20 when he referenced Isaiah 6:9-10 to close out the book of the Act's contribution to the Continuum. Next, a prophet who did not serve the Lord, but nonetheless contributed to the Continuum.

BALAAM, AN IMPORTANT CONTINUUM PROPHET

In the same way the Devil is instrumental to God's Eternal Continuum so too was one of his most impressive prophets, Balaam. This pre-mosaic prophet shows up in Numbers 22 when the children of Israel were fresh out of Egypt. News of their triumph over their captive nation traveled fast and by the time they began to march across the desert led by the Lord God, their reputation was widespread. What He did to free them was unparalleled. A mob of slaves, it was circulated, rose up and destroyed their slave nation and departed the land with much of its wealth. All of the surrounding nations were terrified as fear for their lives and their lands gripped them at the very thought of the Hebrews approaching their territories. It sent them into a panic. Rulers of all the nations in the region scrambled to protect their people and their kingdoms. The king of Moab was just one of those kings, except he was not relying solely on his army. He figured out that more than weapons of war were used to bring down the Egyptians by paying attention to the string of natural disasters that dethroned the long-standing world power. Moab's king decided along with the Midians[86] they were not about to suffer the same fate. Since it was exclusively divine power that warred for Israel, then he would take his cue from their battle and draw on a little divine intervention of his own. So King Balak of Moab sought out Balaam, who was then the most powerful prophet in the region.

Balaam was everybody's prophet and sold his services for a handsome diviner's fee. There was no deity in the area that did not use Balaam's formidable abilities. It is told in Numbers 22:6 that whoever Balaam blessed was blessed and whomever he cursed was cursed. Evidently, over the many years of his prophetics, Balaam built an unassailable reputation for getting the job done. He had become an apparent undefeatable weapon in the hands of many kings of the day. For certain, Balak trusted him to assassinate the neo-nation of Israel before it grew big enough to destroy Moab. The very least he wanted was to have them driven out of his land. The account begins with Balaam being approached by Moab's messengers with a request for his services. Israel's latest conquest was the Amorites, which, added to their Egyptian victory, made any sight of them worthy of stark terror. After meeting with the elders of his land and a few allies, namely the Midians, it was decided that Israel was to be stopped and Balaam was the man to do it. His Chaldean[87] expertise would certainly take on Israel's God and prevent Him and His people from invading Moab and Midian. When the messengers, really ambassadors, wanted Balaam to weaken Israel spiritually enough for the Moabites to defeat them in battle, they sweetened the deal with what the King James calls "the rewards of divination".

Balaam did not jump at the offer right away. He instead pretended to seek the Lord to gain His permission to take the job. His reaction is strange since he was widely known as anyone's prophet. Something about this assignment red flagged him, so Balaam tells the king's messengers to lodge with him for the night while he slept to receive an answer from the Lord in a vision. The prophet's response is peculiar as several things stand out in the account. Numbers 22:9 says God came to Balaam in the night, presumably in a night vision. Behaving as if unaware of the purpose of the men's visit, God asks Balaam what the men wanted and why they visited him. Balaam tells the reason for their visit, pretending to not know the people that came out of Is-

---

86 Continuum tidbit: Moses came from Midian to carry out the Exodus. His former countrymen are now partnering with Moab to destroy Moses' nation.

87 According to Thayer, Balaam was a native of Pethor a city in Mesopotamia. Easton says his name means, "Lord of the people; foreigner or glutton".

rael. Exaggerating their size, as anyone gripped by fear is inclined to do, Balak claimed God's people covered the entire face of the earth. Of course in reality it is not true, but perhaps as far as their world went, it was the case. God responds to Balaam by refusing him permission to take the job. He tells Balaam not to go with the messengers, and not to curse the people because they are blessed. Upon waking, Balaam informs Balak's men that he cannot go with them to curse Israel. Balak is troubled and not about to take no for an answer, so he sends higher-ranking messengers to persuade Balaam to work for him and ups the ante in the process. Now, in addition to the customary diviner's fee, Balak promises to promote Balaam and to reward him with anything he wanted if he would only come and curse God's people for him. The extremely tempting offer weakens Balaam's resolve. His response becomes more tentative as he announces that he can only go as far as God will allow him to go and no further. Yet, in Numbers 22:20 he again invites them to stay with him for the night while he seeks God a second time. The Lord's first answer to him is not enough, so he wants to try again. Maybe the Lord changed His mind. God appears to give in to Balaam and permits him to go with the messengers. Now His instruction is to go and when he goes, to be prepared to speak only what God says, nothing more. Balaam is excited because he believes he can make the money, win the king's favor, and advance higher in life. It is a good deal, so he thinks. Balaam saddles his donkey and elatedly gets on the road with Moab's messengers to perform Balak's will. Here is where it all gets stranger still. The Lord, after releasing Balaam to go with Balak's messengers seems to have another change of heart afterwards. He angrily seeks to kill the man as he heads out to earn his pay.

This incident is somewhat like when the Lord sought to kill Moses along the way because he neglected to circumcise his sons. Moses' wife did not want her sons cut, but after watching the life draining out of her husband in a strange inn, she concedes to save His life. These quirks of the Lord's make Him appear fickle and indecisive and without appreciating His character and commitment to His words' fulfillment, one is left with that impression. But in Moses' case, God was dealing with his unconscious hypocrisy. Think of it, he was headed into battle with Egypt to release the Lord's people from bondage without bringing his own sons into the nation's covenant. His wife's aversion to the circumcision suggests he sought to placate her, to indulge her wishes. Moses imagined he could quiet her and do the job at the same time, and deal with their conflict later. A similar situation exists between God and Balaam. That Balaam petitioned God to go and work for Balak after He strictly forbade him at first indicates that other rebellions and disobedient notions rested in Balaam's heart. To make sure this evidently powerful prophet did not curse His people and cause spiritual unrest, hindrances, and setback among them, the Lord showed Balaam that he would kill him if he disobeyed him. Balaam's greed had taken over by then and as Peter says, drove him mad. Enticed by Moab's riches and promise of prestige consumed Balaam and rendered him senseless. He would do anything not to miss the opportunity to ingratiate himself with the terrified king. God was even more determined, and moved to impress upon Balaam that he was still His prophet and that he could and would do to him whatever He wanted. As it happened, the Lord convinced Balaam that He would do whatever it took not to have His plans for Israel frustrated or His glory on their behalf nullified. Meanwhile, in a frantic haste to bring in his exorbitant wages, Balaam's avarice blocks his normally keen spiritual sight. Obsessive preoccupation with his good fortune prevented him from seeing the angel standing in front of him poised to take his life. The tenor of the account indicates that Balaam was accustomed to seeing visible and invisible creatures. His donkey on the other hand did see him and was properly afraid. She refused to sidestep or plow into the angel.

Balaam, angered by the delay took it out on the animal by hitting her three times. Finally, the animal spoke to him in his own tongue and challenged his abuse. To pierce the blindness on his eyes and mind, she appealed to his common sense to snap him out of it. The reason her voice was amplified was to cause Balaam to hear the Lord's voice and to heed His will. The donkey chided him for not seeing her resistance to his commands as abnormal and asked him if she had ever done that before as long as he owned her. When he answered his animal, the Lord opened Balaam's eyes to see the angel poised to strike him dead. The realization of how close he had come to losing his life brought Balaam to his knees and laid him prostrate before the Lord. The angel questions Balaam's unusual abuse of his animal, implying it was unjustified. Balaam's way is perverse and worthy of death, but he is given a simple rebuke instead. The angel tells Balaam that the donkey he treated so badly actually swerved to save his life. Otherwise, he is told, the angel would have killed him on God's behalf. God has a further use of him, so he is spared. Balaam admits to his momentary insanity and offers to abandon the project and return home if God is that set against his plans. Numbers 22:35 has the angel telling Balaam to continue with the assignment, but to beware of saying anything other than what God put in his mouth. The object lesson is over and God's will for His brand new nation is secure. The great prophet known to have power to establish or destroy kingdoms will be rendered powerless against Israel. Balak, unaware of all that has just taken place, is excited to see Balaam has come to help him and assures him the wealth and honor he promised is guaranteed. All the prophet has to do to earn it is to get rid of these terrifying people threatening his land's security and stability. Balaam is still reeling from his near death experience with God's angel. So he reminds Balak that he can do no more than God will allow him to do, no matter how much money and prestige are on the table. Balak thinks he understands and urges Balaam get to work. Balaam presses on with the job and attempts to get God to change His mind again. After all, He did forbid him to take the job at first. He changed His mind then and let him go and serve Balak in the end. Yes, there was that nasty bit with the angel, which was frightening, but it is all over now.

Balaam engages in the rituals known to empower his word and accomplish his will. He performs the customary seven spiritual protocols of the day: seven altars are built and seven oxen and rams are slaughtered to petition some deity to curse Israel. Every altar was used in the sacrifice. Balaam then goes to the high places to seek God to learn what He wanted the prophet to say. Does this sound confusing? It should, because Balaam is conflicted. He hopes a stronger deity will override the Almighty's decree, or that the sacrifices may change the Lord's mind. Secretly, he imagines that he just might earn his fee after all. Being without His own nation and thus His personal prophet, the Most High has been availing Himself of Balaam's prophetics for years. Throughout that time, he was for all intents and purposes, the Almighty's prophet, although he hired himself out to other deities for extra money on the side. Their working relationship continues as the entire account implies, but unknown to Balaam, it is their final project. God meets Balaam in the high place in response to the offerings. When He does, the prophet tells Him how he has met the requirements of the prophecy he seeks. God responds accordingly, by putting a word in Balaam's mouth and sending him to Balak to declare it.

The gist of the word is that although Balak called for Balaam to curse Moab's enemies, God has blessed them. He delivers his prophecy parabolically. These people are different from all the nations because they belong to the Most High God, and they are not reckoned among them at all. God's future for His new nation is fixed and blessed, and Balaam pronounces it to Balak's displeasure. The king surmises that where he set Balaam up to work is the reason why the prophet ended up blessing what he hired him to curse. So he moves the prophet, his helpers, and the ritual's sacrificial emblems to another location. Balaam defends his actions by reminding Balak that he told him in advance that he could only say what God put in his mouth. The first process is repeated and God sends Balaam to Balak again with another parable. The stakes rise as Balaam now realizes his insufficiency in the face of God's will. God is not like his other divine contacts, and although He indulged Balaam for years, the Israeli assignment is a different situation entirely. God's word is on the line and His will is immutable and is not about to let His enterprise fail. Balaam also learns something else during the ordeal. He learns God is utterly devoted to Israel and begins to call them Jacob. Balaam's enchantments, and divination are powerless against the predestiny the Most High appointed for His chosen people. More and more of the Lord's vision for His young nation emerges as Balaam continues to peer into the Almighty's world. Balak is frustrated as his purposes are thwarted. He tells Balaam to neither curse nor bless the people because he is not helping the matter at all.

However, desperate Balak repeats the procedure one last time. Seven more altars are built, the rams and bullocks are slain, and offered for Balaam to go God one last time. Both he and Balak have yet to get the message: God is pleased with Israel and is not about to allow anything to harm them. They both understand that they are dealing with a new aspect of God, whose reputation is unfolding afresh to them now. The two men recognize that they are clashing with His will but still hold out hope that He can be persuaded by Balaam's historically potent mantle. They press God to abandon Israel and defend Moab instead. It does not work, but the prophet has a real epiphany in the process. He finally sees that although what he is doing angers Balak, it pleases the Lord. The experience seems to be a new one for Balaam as God's presence on him enlightens him in ways that have never happened before. This time Balaam meets another side of God; the side that does not need, nor desires enchantments, divination, and such to respond. He moves by His own will and speaks when He gets ready. Balaam, now fully surrenders to God in a way that is uncustomary for him. In fact, the wording of the text changes a bit. In whatever ways the Lord met and communicated with Balaam in the past, and however He put His words in the prophet's mouth previously, their last encounter is unlike any of these. Numbers 24:2 says, *"The Spirit of God came upon"* Balaam. He had more than an apparition; he had a literal induction into God's mind and feelings regarding Israel. Mysteriously, he discovers his prophetic eyes are really awakened and his spiritual channels are wide open, something else that had never happened to him before. Balaam until that moment had never had such depth of prophetic penetration before from any of the deities he worked with prophetically. But Israel's God is different and Balaam finally discovers personally how and why. The Lord lays Israel's history, destiny, and future bare before the prophet for hire to declare it all exactly the way God wants. Balak is furious and angrily dismisses Balaam from his presence. He lets the prophet know that he could have been wealthy and prominent had he just ignored the Lord and did what he was paid to do. God cost Balaam and Balak bitterly let him know it. Balaam has resigned himself to his loss, at least for the time being, and gives the king one last prophecy on the house so to speak. He advises the king of Moab of Israel's future and the futility of continuing to try to subvert it. Balaam prefaces his final parable with three statements that distinguish his service as a mercenary prophet from the excellence of being momentarily, the Lord's Spirit-endowed one. His eyes are wide open. That is, his prophetic or spiritual eye; the prophetic eye that sees God vividly as only few others can. His ears are likewise open and he hears God distinctly as well. These two events are topped by one more thing; Balaam has entered God's knowledge. He now knows things that were previously hidden from him because of his worldly prophetic station. He knows them because he is brought into the Almighty's sphere where knowledge and clarity are abundant and unobstructed. Gripped by the sight and overwhelmed by what he sees, the greedy prophet prophesies the end of all of the reigning nations existing then and Israel's rise to a world power because of the lion of Judah's scepter. Afterwards, he returns home saturated with the Spirit of God and out of favor with the king, who no doubt spread his failure abroad. The incident most likely cost Balaam his prophetic career, or seriously damaged it, when other kings heard how he lost his power to decree a nation's rise and fall, which could be why he worked to redeem himself in Moab's eyes at Baalpeor.[88]

BALAAM'S SIGNIFICANCE TO THE CONTINUUM

So why is Balaam included and what has he to do with the Continuum? The answer is prophecy. Balaam was a very potent prophet in the region. He was well known by royalty and all of the other powers of the land. God, who created and ordained Balaam to be His prophet, was forced to share him with every other divine being spiritualizing the ancient world. However, now some very dramatic changes are taking place. The first is the Lord's birth of His very own nation. All of those in existence, then belonged to and served other gods. Israel will be His alone. Second, it ends the unimpeded reign of false prophetics. Balaam, whose mantle was uncontested till then discerned his star falling as the mighty prophet Moses took his place in the Almighty's service. True to His pattern, the Lord lets Balaam meet his replacement. Moses will now handle all of the Most High's spiritual transactions and settle His new nation as well. He will also defend Israel and protect them from the otherworldly assaults of

---

88 See Numbers 25.

nations who cannot defeat the Balaams of the age. Israel would have Moses, who was so much more than a prophet, and so well able to fend off the spiritual onslaughts of the demons and devils ruling the planet back then. That God already had Israel's future mapped out is witnessed in Balaam's ability to see all the way down into its destiny. He saw the incarnation and dominion of God's Son Jesus Christ, who would destroy all of the nations that existed to antagonize their Maker. Elements of Balaam's prophecy echoed Enoch's words and those of other prophets before him, like Abraham. Balaam does recover himself and seeks to earn his diviner's fee later by seducing Israel to provoke God's ire against His beloved nation. From that *time* forward, Balaam and God tussle until the money hungry prophet's death.

The incident between Balaam and Israel is recalled in Deuteronomy, Joshua, Nehemiah, and Micah. In the New Testament, Balaam is held up as an example of prophetic greed, waywardness, and unrighteousness before God. See 2 Peter 2:15. In Jude 1:11 Balaam is paired with Cain back in the world's foundation, and again remembered for his greed and betrayal. The last time he is mentioned is by the Lord Jesus. In the Book of Revelation, Balaam is remembered for false doctrine. When he returned to Balak to recoup his lost wages and prestige, he taught Moab how to seduce Israel. Using his vast knowledge of spirituality and demonism, he taught them how to court idols and engage in ritual sex practices that he knew would expose them to God's judgment. Numbers 31:15 says, *"Behold, these caused the children of Israel, through the counsel of Balaam, to commit trespass against the Lord in the matter of Peor, and there was a plague among the congregation of the Lord"*. The Continuum connection is established by precedence and pattern. The Lord uses prophets constantly to bring His words to pass. Balaam, although he was a money hungry, divinatory sorcerer, was still used by God as a prophet. His authority over Balaam is seen in the man's Moabite job assignment. That Scripture refers to him repeatedly indicates that Balaam was responsible to God until Moses. After the Moabite incident, the Lord's prophets come exclusively from His own nation. The Old Testament does not report that God ever resorted to another nation's prophet again. In fact, in Jeremiah 2:8, the Lord condemns Israel's prophets for prophesying by Baal to evade His law and subvert His commands. Their doing so, in His mind, is equivalent to theocratic treason. Subversive prophecy relentlessly haunted the Lord and His people down through the centuries. It proved to be His nation's demise and ironically the reason He restores them. Unless one fully understands the Continuum, differentiating true from false prophecy is virtually impossible. The Lord, however, was never so deceived. In Matthew 7:22, Jesus says that many will prophesy in His name, and still never have been known by Him or acknowledged as His. While false prophets figure prominently in the Continuum, God entrusts the fulfillment His word is largely to His own messengers and ministers. The next chapter tells how the Continuum finds its way into the Gospel of Jesus Christ.

[10]

The Continuum And The Gospel

The New Testament refers to the gospel repeatedly. Peculiarly, this chapter reveals the gospel is as old as the world, if not as old as the Great War in Heaven. It reaches back to Eden and God's promise concerning the seed of the woman. Galatians 3:8 reveals that God preached it to Abraham. He could do so because the Continuum was set in motion before the Garden of Eden. Its many mentions make it vitally important to God and His Continuum. Insofar as the gospel goes, two Scriptures firmly establish its life cycle and perpetuity, Romans 16:25 and Galatians 3:8. Paul in Romans identifies his preaching as being according to the gospel that had been kept secret since the world began. The believer seeking and learning Christ today subsists on mere slivers of all that God has ever said on earth because only fragments made it into the Scriptures. In reality, the gospel is primordial, despite its shrinkage over the years since the Lord first released it on the planet. Primordial naturally brings in the antediluvian prophets Abel or Enoch, and perhaps Seth. Noah, being the first pre and antediluvian prophet could also be included. In any case, only bits of Enoch and Noah's words are available to the typical Christian today, their possible seclusion in some hidden vault notwithstanding. Luke 3:37; Hebrews 11:5 and Jude 14 all mention Enoch. Jude says he is the seventh from Adam and that he prophesied the coming of the Lord with tens of thousands of His saints. Back then, God's plan of redemption at work in the earth was public knowledge, and although the world as Enoch knew it would be no more, his ministry—what earned him the high honor of not seeing death, came from his telling and prophesying the Almighty's truth to his evil generation.

God's chosen prophets' writings, those of Abel and Enoch, were no doubt preserved by Noah in the ark. Enoch's prophecy is pointedly adventist in nature, something perhaps none of those alive at the time understood. Peter's words in 2 Peter 3:6 have Jude's flavor when he uses the phrase, "the world that then was" in his admonishment to the doubters in his congregations. That the flood was well known then is seen in his statement:

> "For this they are willingly ignorant of, that by the word of God the heavens were <u>of old</u>, and the earth standing out of the water and in the water: Whereby the world that <u>then was</u>, being overflowed with water, perished: But <u>the heavens and the earth, which are now</u>, by the same word are kept in store, reserved unto fire against the day of judgment and perdition of ungodly men." 2 Peter 3:5-7. KJV

Peter's comments suggest he is well aware that God has had several versions of the heavens and the earth. He knows why the Lord removes and restores them and uses that knowledge to prove that future judgment is pending. Peter says there was a world that is no more. There were once heavens that fell under the Almighty's judgment. The heavens and earth that exist today are not those, but are different ones under threat of the same fate. Peter's language, like Jude's words display a rich understanding of God's ongoing eternity-to-eternity dealings with the creatures He made. They also, unlike many modern preachers, present the gospel's fullness. They teach its beginning and end, cause and effect, initiatives and outcomes. The Continuum has many outlets and numerous mediums through which to operate and manifest.

THE GOSPEL

In establishing the continuity and universality of the Continuum, the gospel the Lord said must be preached in all the earth has to be addressed. Researching Scripture shows it is made up of over twenty strands. The gospel, really the Almighty's good news or glad tidings, appears more than a hundred times in the New Testament's twenty-seven books. Theoretically, it averages out to be about four mentions per book. The original understanding is that the word "gospel" is translative of the Greek term *euaggelion*. It is a combination of its word for good *"eu"* an angel *"Aggelos"*. Together they reveal another impressive, but consistent truth about the Continuum. As with everything the Lord does on earth, it all starts with His angels, and the gospel is no different. The reason angels are at the heart of the gospel is because they are the nearest he Lord, and so are the first ones to receive anything He wants to do. Angels are messengers—which is why the gospel's meanings terms rest heavily on them. The gospel, like the law, began with the communications of angels.[89] Throughout history, God's and humanity's, angels have been the Most High's first point of contact. Their first mention is the cherubim, He placed in East Eden. In fact, the seducer in the tree was once an angel. More precisely, Lucifer was once a cherub—which makes it an interesting fact that cherubim kept him from re-entering the garden. In addition to speaking for Him in the world, angels from eternity to eternity function as the Lord's custodians, warriors, and initiators of all the Creator's ventures. When the Savior entered the planet, angels announced His arrival and guided those He chose to the babe's location. They warned others when His life was in jeopardy; and when Jesus was baptized and driven into the wilderness, it was angels that ministered to Him. Furthermore, they continued to do so throughout the Lord's earthly service. When the Church was born for the apostles to establish, angels were dispatched for them too. These interminable beings have watched over God's word to perform them, consistently advancing His kingdom. Thus, it is logical to view them as the Continuum's major supporting characters exceeded only by the Godhead. Without them, the gospel could never have been delivered and sustained in the earth. Angels were and continue to be the Lord's first messengers delivering His communications to the world, most notably His prophecies and the gospel. So what is the gospel exactly?

THE GOSPEL DEFINED & DEPICTED

The New Testament gospel is so much more than a collection of narratives or circulated letters made into a sacred book. It goes beyond a compilation of spiritual writings. The gospels are the messages that Christ and His apostles proclaimed and propagated throughout their world. They are what His apostles later used to found and ground His church. The gospel of the kingdom begins and ends with prophecy, specifically prophecy about a coming world king that will never be dethroned. Beginning with the woman to birth the seed of the serpent's defeat, they end with the Holy Spirit and Christ's bride saying come in Revelation 22:17. Between the two prophetic periods is Jesus, their leading man. Replacing the fallen Lucifer (star of the morning), Jesus, the root, and offspring of David becomes the bright and morning star. Jesus' epithets speak to governing the world's thrones[36] and the Devil's rebel stars' that were surrendered by Adam in his Edenic Contest with the serpent. Isaiah 14:12 elaborates on this. The gospels and the epistles proclaim who won creation back as the Church's

---

89 Hebrews 2:2; Judges 2:1-5; Judges 5:23; 6:11, 12 and numerous other passages of Scripture.

infancy blossomed into a full-blown kingdom. Jesus, the eternal King David took back, and over, ruling all the stars (Read Luke 4:5-12 and Revelation 11:15).

Curiously, as with Eve and Mary, the woman's Continuum roles runs throughout Scripture. Its narratives close with two females' dominions in Christ's history. There is the one that menacingly mimics The Messiah's kingdom and the one that is married to Him; the Ecclesia built upon the foundation of the apostles and prophets. The first woman is the Babylonian Whore; the last is the celebrated bride of Christ, His new creation church. The Continuum's earthly compilation gels with Abraham, who begot sons and daughters from three women: Hagar, Sarah, and Keturah. Of the three only Sarah's child was the son of promise. Why? The answer is that Isaac was of the progenic[37] line that brought the Christ into this world. Abraham's lineage embodies the Son of God who passes His genetics on to David's line. In His incarnation, Jesus lands on earth as the Lion of Judah traveling from heaven by being inseminated in the womb of a woman. Isaiah's prophesied virgin, ordained to bear Emmanuel, "God with us", centuries' later fulfills the Lord God's words to the serpent about the woman's seed to bruise his head. The prophecy goes in motion to depose the Devil's deceitfully captured earthly reign. A series of ages-long divine maneuvers brought the world Mary, the mother of Jesus Christ. This feat is the heart and soul of the gospels. Take away the virgin birth of the Son of God and there is no good news, no eternal hope, and no offspring begotten by and for the Godhead.

THE GOSPEL AS GOD'S SPELL

The word "gospel", is of Anglo-Saxon origin and specifically means *God's spell*. It reflects the word of God delivered to the world by Jesus Christ His Son disseminated globally after His departure by His servants. The term *gospel* sums up the message, meanings, methods, and ministry of carrying the Almighty's good news. With that said, how the gospel started out being perceived as a good spell should be discussed. It is because of its uplifting powers and effects. The God whose word is the essence of all power condescended to decree blessings, privileges, and life to a species that He had previously doomed to curses and death. Briefly, these constitute the affluences of His mercy and grace that are bestowed in Jesus Christ. To separate the use of the word spell, as it is traditionally understood from its godless magical contexts, one must remember that the word *spell* fits many other settings. It is unfortunate that its connotations in the Church are strictly negative. Thus, it is understandable why use of the word *news*[38] replaced it. It is equally understandable why the word spell was chosen to characterize it. The word spell goes outside of the potion/hexing purveyors of the dark arts practice. It started out just meaning words or news, or report. Simplistically, the word spell initially just meant talk. Thus, to spell is to engage in the process of forming words from letters, or describing imagery from symbols for communicative purposes. The etymology of the word means to *name the letters of*,[90] *to tell; to speak, declare, and publish; to talk, tell, say aloud, and recite.* In addition, the word *spell* expansively means to write or say the letters of a word read letter by letter. As first recorded in 1940 in American English, spell meant to speak something out by explaining it step-by-step. Refer to Etymology Online Dictionary.

Generic Definitions of the Word Spell

Look at the word spell's basic definitions below and you will see how it was thought useful to Christ's gospel. The word spell, setting aside its magical and superstitious distortions defines:

1. Composing letters to form words or words to articulate thoughts
2. Signifying what is named or written in an order that causes letters to compose a word or part of a word
3. Forming words by means of letters orally or in writing, especially with the proper letters
4. Explicitly explaining something to prevent comprehension or behavioral mistakes
5. Gaining knowledge or learning the meaning of anything by studying it
6. Spelling out the sense of an author by fortifying, profiling, or representing a work in all its parts
7. Spelling out a verse in the Bible
8. Telling; relating; teaching or a saying or tale, or giving a speech by expressing its meaning

The reason for the extensive definitions above is the root meaning of the word gospel that fundamentally means "God's Spell". Explaining why this is the case required understanding the word spell outside of its superstitious and magical contexts. When severed from its popularized occultic meanings, the word spell is a harmless term that academically identifies the process of combining letters into words.

Applying it in this sense to the Greek *evangelion* for God's good message is now understandable. In this respect, what gives the gospel, God's Spell, its weighty influence is its communication of the Godhead proper. The gospel's power, as the Apostle Paul

---

90 For instance an alphabet, or a term.

understood it, was the precise reason why, everything the Almighty does, succeeds. He is all-powerful because no word of God is devoid of power. The gospel falls right in with His habitual success as His power source working in earth to benefit humanity. It conforms to His Logos as salvation's intelligence and to His Rhema as its verbiage. The gospel as the four chronologies of the Lord's life, imparts His doctrines, preaching, proclaiming, and teaching. It also issues His commands and judgments. Notice how these all concur with the definition of the word spell. In respect to the Continuum, the prophets of old and those in the Christian church had for their official mantleship, the redemptive gift of discerning spirits—among other ecclesial faculties. Their duty was to inspect the words people spoke in the name of the gospel to check them for the introduction of pseudo-inspired sermons and writings that sought to discredit the Lord's truth. These were all seen as attempts to derail the faith of those who trusted in it. This duty the apostles and the early prophets carried out effectively as Paul shows when he rebukes the Galatians for beginning in the spirit and trying to perfect their Christianity in the flesh. He often in like manner, exhorted his readers to learn the gospel and trust the emerging word of God only after it proved to comply with what had already been written and established by those that came before him, the other apostles, and the Old Testament prophets.

The Witness of the Gospels

After more than two thousand years, the gospels remain the most powerful proof of Christ's life and ministry. They continue to amaze their eras with mutual coherence, although none was personally penned by Jesus Christ, Christianity's Founder. Persuaded eyewitnesses and converts scribed His life and ministry and noised them abroad. These eyewitnesses broadcasted the news throughout the world for Christ after He was gone. Jesus deliberately committed nothing He did to writing, because He said that if He bore witness of Himself, His witness would be untrue. He said this, not because He would lie or exaggerate His accomplishments, but because He wanted His works to speak for Him. He entrusted His accounts to eyewitnesses, the most objective authenticators of His ministry. Besides, His three and a half years' ministry left little time to chronicle His exploits and complete His mission together. Instead, He left it to observers and experiencers of His Presence on earth, via the Holy Spirit, to testify impartially of the genuineness of His word and its power. Those impressed by their encounters with Him in the flesh, along with those laborers who would be later filled with His spirit, could say for themselves how the Christ transformed their lives.

Jesus was leaving the planet and with Him all the accouterments that facilitated His ministry.[91] The Holy Spirit was coming to take His place and carry out the remainder of the commission He entrusted to His apostles. As His invisible and pervasive Self, the Holy Spirit would perform the very same acts and feats that He did, from within converted human vessels. God's Spirit would persuade them of His supremacy and incite them to give the strongest testimony of His work. Another reason the Lord did not write His own story to leave behind is because He wanted it in people's hearts and souls, not just in their heads and hands. Had He done so, they would have only circulated His writings and not His power; and the Savior wanted both spread throughout the world. Leaving the writing for others to compose and compile freed Him to work out His commission through them. For Christ, it was more effective and enduring because the Christian church is the preeminent, undeniable sign, and certification of The Messiah's earthly visit. It perpetually boasts of His Calvary success (Read His words in John 16:7-16). Prior to His appearance, there was no talk of Christian, born again believers, or the Church of Jesus Christ. At the time, the old Atheno-Greco-Roman deities had ruled the world up to then, with some lingering ancient gods that found their way into His modern world. Insofar as His Ecclesia was concerned, setting aside its eternal existence that Hebrews 12 proclaims, the only earthly version belonged to the civilians of the Atheno-Roman world. When Christ said that He would build His Ecclesia..., He envisioned His heavenly prototype making its way to earth after He returned home. So He says to His disciples, "It is more expedient for you that I go away..." John 16:7.

Today, Christianity dominates the world's spiritual and religious-scape to prove the lowly carpenter from Galilee indeed achieved what He came to earth to do. He shifted the world from its plethora of doomed gods that were hostile to humanity to the one true God, His Father in heaven. The goal of Jesus' brief work was never merely to captivate people with His spectacularity. He was not sent to entertain or perpetuate an already flawed system. He came, as the psalmist foretold, according to the Almighty's Continuum. David the Psalmists says of his future seed, in Psalm 40:7-11, "*Then said I, Lo, I am come; in the roll (volume) of the book it is written of me: I delight to do thy will, O my God; yea, thy law is within my heart. I have proclaimed glad tidings of righteousness in the great assembly; Lo, I will not refrain my lips, O Jehovah, thou knowest. I have not hid thy righteousness within my heart; I have declared thy faithfulness and thy salvation; I have not concealed thy loving kindness and thy truth from the great assembly. Withhold not thou thy tender*

---

91 Review Luke 22:35-37.

mercies from me, O Jehovah; Let thy loving kindness and thy truth continually preserve me.[39] The prophecy is fulfilled in Hebrews 10:7. Enabling clay vessels to execute the perfect will of God is the whole reason for the Savior's incarnate work on earth. He became flesh to offset and ultimately do away with human frailty and failures. Pay attention to the wording of verse five of the Hebrews 10 reference. The message is that the ages of dead animal carcasses are said to have accomplished little to placate an angry God or to atone for humanity's genetic sin. So the Lord prepared the only sacrifice acceptable enough to expunge it; a sacrifice fit for a king and a body fit for the Prince of life to enter the world. The two passages, one written by David, and the other illuminated by Paul in Hebrews show how the Most High did both.

The gospel, though cloudy in its unfolding generations is nonetheless preached throughout the entire Bible. Its revelations are left up to each generation's era to ferret out. Here is what Isaiah 53:8 has in mind: God's gospel message, His good news is what His apostles take to their own and the Gentile's world. Philip uses it to enlighten the Ethiopian Eunuch in Acts 8:33 for him to take eternal salvation back to his homeland. The generation of Jesus Christ that Isaiah sees ages ago is what He brought within Himself to earth. It is the spirits of those souls that fell into sin through Adam. That Christ generation traveled with Him to hell, rose in Him from the grave, partook of His new birth when He came alive from the dead, and ascended on high with Him to His Father's altar. After inspecting His sacrificial Lamb's work, the Almighty approved Christ's seed as fully acceptable to convert to their eternal image and likeness. With His approval, the new creation was dispatched to earth again. This time it was within, the Holy Spirit who delivered eternal life to those chosen before the foundation of the world. For their sake, Jesus took upon Himself flesh, a human form to reproduce Himself infinitely (and verbatim) in this world until its end.

WHY JESUS HAD TO BECOME FLESH

The Messiah's duty when He donned flesh was to gather the souls His Father had long ago primed for eternal life and hidden in Adam. It is what He means by John 6:44, 45. For these reasons and numerous others, Jesus left the writing of His memoirs to those that carried on His work. Wisely as the Living Word of God, Christ understands the strength His testimony would take on when witnessed and corroborated by others, He trusted His disciples to establish His faith throughout the Church age. Their changed lives and cultures would demonstrate the veracity of His Father's testimony of Him as the Faithful and True Witness. The Savior garners His witnesses, one by one after He has accomplished Ezekiel 36:24-27 in each one of them. That is the Lord's prophecy of the new birth that the Savior decodes in John 3:3-8 and depicts in Ephesians 4:24. In short, the Lord has not allowed just anyone impressed by Him and His message to be His witness. He only entrusts the honor, and responsibility to those who have been born again from above and are filled with His Holy Spirit.[92]. Only those walking and talking with Him inside them can really say with powerful eyewitness conviction that He lives, reigns, and is coming again. This is what witnessing the gospel means.

Jesus chose to let His disciples witness Him because, practically speaking, the likelihood of people hearing a person bearing witness of him or herself courts rejection. Customarily people label self-witnessers as prejudiced and self-serving when they do. People often criticize self-witnessers and treat them warily. Typically, the spoken or unspoken sentiment is everybody tends to exaggerate their own successes. Others feel that some people coyly downplay them, which is also not a full measure of truth. Not willing to cost His Father and His mission a single soul, the Savior proves that the only credible self-witness a person can have is to be seen as well as heard in action. It is why Jesus referred others to His signs and miracles during His earthly ministry. He, in doing so, defers to His Father as His most credible witness (See John 5:36-39). He chose to let those affected by His ministry tell His story for Him because people trust second and third party accounts and personal testimonies more. He exemplifies this with the woman at the well, the apostles after Pentecost, and Paul under the power of the Holy Spirit. All of these real time accounts of The Messiah's personal works continue His mission all the way up to today without His being physically present.

Seated at the right hand of the Majesty on High, Jesus now performs supernally what He once carried out personally on earth. How does He do it? By inhabiting people by His Holy Spirit. That is how He vests humans with the same power that He possessed to do the greater works that He prophesied. The best and most enduring, and up to date, witnesses of what Jesus does throughout humanity's generations can only come from His converts and contemporary ministers. Today, He is in heaven, glorified and not visible to the naked eye, and His voice inaudible to the uncircumcised ear. No matter how much He wants to speak for Himself, without the Holy Spirit, the typical human cannot hear Him. In addition, most of them that do hear Him are without the heart or ear to hear Him as He intends. As a result, they are unable to rightly judge or

---

92 1 John 5:6-8.

act on what He says. The redemption and conversion process must be completed first. Only then can Christ's witnesses' testimony in their times assure His eternal and ancient works never die but continue and fit the age in which they are proclaimed. Simultaneous witnesses, what the writers of the gospels are, work with the kingdom of heaven in their worlds and guarantee that every people group and sphere of life has the opportunity to hear and witness their testimony of Christ's ministry directly. They accomplish this by the Holy Spirit within them. Thus, the Scriptures, though vital for corroboration, are also meant to continue unfolding and triggering their manifestations until the end of time. Unquestionably, the gospels present the most powerful proof of the Savior's perpetuity and His Continuum. Being timeless in origin, they fit each age's temporal and eternal needs perfectly.

Astoundingly the gospels provide the mutual coherency of writings composed by the Founder of Christianity's eyewitnesses and not by the Savior directly, although He watches over it personally. After the fact, encounterers[93] experiencing Him and His fruit in their lifetime give marvelously agreeing accounts of miraculous works and revelations unheard of before by any other religion or deity. Supported by organized presentment of His system of spiritual development and the transformations that come from it, the doctrines of Christ and God overtake arcane faiths to capture God's ordained converts to make them steadfast citizens of His kingdom. The Lord's so persuaded His converts that their testifying in turn change other's lives, and produce remarkable resilience in the face of the fiery trials that arose because of Him. Christ's true witnesses are undaunted by the opposition, and gladly lay down their lives for the Savior who shows Himself to them alive and in power.

ALL FOUR GOSPELS TELL THE SAME STORY

Although the individual gospels differ in language, detail, and emphases, they manage to tell the same story years and locations apart from each other. This fact alone attests, they are not simply annals or biographies of a charismatic minister's impactful move. Rather, they put forth the Lord's records: memoirs adapted to various providences of the Christian life. Their contiguous narration is compiled chronologically to lay out Christ's life, death, and resurrection. Brought into complete mutuality by the Holy Spirit, the four different aspects of His earthly mission complement one another's view of The Messiah's journey, faith, and conquests. These views, as well as the many other prophecies that foretold His ordeal, describe how Christ triumphed in the

---

93 Collins English Dictionary.

face of heinous opposition and died to fulfill Genesis 3:15. Uniquely, the gospels convey God's manifold wisdom[94] with the Holy Spirit fostering the Almighty's new familial relations with His divine offspring. They instruct the believer on how to migrate from the kingdom of men to the brilliantly radiant kingdom of Christ. Each gospel distinctly characterizes the Continuum's progression climaxing with John, who portrays the Son of God's divinity in contrast to the others emphases on His humanity. Comprehensively they portray Him from four distinct—yet cohesive—vantage points. Various perspectives of Jesus include Jesus, Israel's Messiah-King, Jesus the lowly hard working servant, Jesus the Son of Man—the God who became flesh, and Jesus the eternal Son of God. The gospels capture Him in all of His roles in heaven and on earth. Many see them as four different gospels, but in truth, they are not. They are modern newscasts: four distinct angles of the Savior's earthly work. They may vary in days and repeat themselves as He repeated His sermons; but in the end, they are more harmonious than they are discordant.

The Holy Spirit allows Christ's gospels to be seen as a cohesive, and fundamentally uniform, whole to be taken as one fourfold narration. As the Godhead's agent on earth, He recollected The Messiah's entire earthly ordeal adding a generous sprinkling of heavenly truths to give the four intelligent agents His story from their individual life paths. Each gospel writer reports from his personality, temperaments, and life experience. They tell the Lord Jesus' history from their individual characters and circumstances. Because of their station in the community, these reporters deliver their synopses to their readers in a way they could hear and respond to best. Overall, the gospels providentially feed the Church's universal and individual purposes throughout all ages. The four men reported on Jesus' lifetime as rabbinically unlearned correspondents, who managed to remain thoroughly congruent despite time and space (First Corinthians 14:37; 1 Corinthians 12:10 and 1 John 4:1 shed further light). The Holy Spirit's supervision of handpicked writers resolves any seeming discrepancies found among them. Scholars who take a purely intellectual approach to exegeting Scripture lock themselves out of its hidden revelations to settle for mere surface information instead. Treating Scripture exegeses as no more than a forensic[40] exercise sets the stage for their strictly argumentative response. The effect is to isolate the Scriptures from the Holy Spirit and the Person of the Lord Jesus Christ. Doing so is to say that their Author is dead. That He never rose from the dead. That He had no part in or knowledge of their compilation or narration. The Lord Jesus antici-

---

94 Ephesians 3:10.

pated this inborn penchant of man and sent the Holy Spirit to oversee His words and their doctrination of His church. Here again, the Continuum comes to the fore. The writers of Scripture did not just rely on the Old Testament scrolls for their accounts; they were holy men that moved as Peter says, by the Holy Spirit. Jesus' presence within them edited their works, guided their decisions, and appended their texts to what He had already released and has been releasing, to the earth.[95] Unlike other religions that trace their sacred texts' sources to their founders and no more (except for perhaps the appearance of an angel, Jesus' surpasses them by spanning heaven and earth). He diffuses Himself throughout all creation to be present everywhere personally watching over everything He set in motion. The Spirit filled Christian knows this deep within and responds to the Bible differently from those whose light is darkness and whose wisdom are derived from and confined to this world. The Christian reads God's word under the Holy Spirit's control, knowing that He rectifies any unlikely errors throughout His revelatory processes. He or she knows that Jesus is alive. He is God and is the same Almighty that created the world, orchestrated and superintends their faith. Non-Christian scholars limited their probe of the Scriptures to what they see in print. His true converts have a deeply penetrative experience with God that enhances how they see the gospels, which makes the whole Bible resonate with them differently.

CHRISTIANS' CINEMATIC EXPERIENCE WITH SCRIPTURE

An apostolic and prophetic student of Scripture enjoys what is tantamount to a cinematic[41] experience when engaging with the word of God. Sight and sound classically portray the Lord's word to them in dreams, visions, trances, or some sort of mental imagery. These are transmitted to this world from His archival remembrances. The transmission is streamed by the Holy Spirit who at the same time enlivens God's word to His family. Also, the visualization is strongly attended to by inward unction supplied by the Lord's Spirit as well. That fact alone explains why believers' faith is empowered and advanced and the unbeliever is incensed or bored with the Scriptures that so gratify the saint. To the Christian, the gospels make perfect sense and answer more questions than they engender. For the unbeliever, it is the other way around. Often they are an irritant to their carnality, appearing outdated, irrelevant, and too spectacular to pertain to anything as somber as the afterlife. Saints, on the other hand, see them as inspiration that moves them to more diligent search.

---

95 Cross-reference Revelation 1:19.

The discord outsiders see in the gospels is a result of the Lord restricting them from piercing the veil that harmonizes the Scriptures and increases His children's faith. Thus, His offspring look to connect with the common thread that they know is Jesus Christ, their Messiah and the eternal God of all creation. That thread tells them that they are indeed in the family and now privy to its mysteries, its ciphers, and the commonwealth that enriches and empowers His heavenly and earthly family. These are how believers can cherish the gospels' harmony and vindicate their superficial fragmentariness. Constant contact with the Godhead ceaselessly fills in the blanks for them to complete their Lord's history. It corrects their perceptions, upgrades their pneuma intelligence, and *celestializes*[42] the human language used to explain His work and word. For these reasons, true believers do not label Scripture's gaps, overlaps, or variations as discrepancies. They know what the Lord instructed His writers to insert is there waiting for His Spirit's revelation to clarify it for them. Believers' trust in the Lord's omniness tells them that what Jesus left out of His word is deliberate. They understand that the King aims to reveal to every reader personally the nuances of His truth as it pertains to each of His children individually. He does this so His family relies on His insights and not their own understanding. This approach is standardized to drive them Him so He can help them grasp His Scripture's application to their individual lives and particular situations.

The Gospels' Global Reach

Jesus is the Sovereign of creation, which is the whole point of His coming to the planet. The whole world was lost to Him and His Father when Adam surrendered his dominion in the garden. His salvation furthermore reached all the way back to His homeland where the serpent's first revolution began.[43] Since all His creation was lost, His redemption needed to extend to the whole world, which it does.[44] The gospel record, then had to address every group or type of human aliveness during his or her composition and those to be born. Remember, the Old Testament prophets said that what they foretold was for the generations to come: generations that the Most High already had in His book of life.[45] The gospels, composed throughout the latter half of the first century, are to be commended for their recognition of four races or classes of people groups, representing the four phases of human thought at the time.

The then known and populated world fell into four distinct nations and cultural groups: The Jew, the Roman, the Greek, and the Christian. Therefore, the gospels as they were created address them severally, to assure universal depiction of the Risen Lord. They help His truth appeal to and be understood by the Jewish mind with its centuries old practice of the Law of Moses; to the Roman's divinely saturated mind that exuded a highly imperial perspective of kingdom, law, and culture; to the Greek mind's god-man persuasions, and the Christian's eternal identity as offspring of the Godhead. Matthew's Gospel speaks to the Jew and depicts Jesus as Israel's promised Messiah-King. Mark articulates Jesus' labor, conquests, and eternal grip on His world and this one, portraying Him as the Sovereign who humbled Himself to serve His subjects. Luke's gospel slants more toward the Greek with their love of wisdom and obsession with the divine world, contrasting Christ's divinity, and righteous rule with the wicked frailties and flaws of the deities they venerated. John's gospel lets the Christian know what happens to him or her when Jesus becomes their Savior and why it is the most wonderful thing in any world. He stresses the Son of God's precarnate, incarnate, and post-carnate excellencies and how these may be passed on to the Christian. The afterlife and Jesus' power over it dominates John's accounts.

The Gospel's Evangelium

The evangelium, God's good message of joy instructs all people in His ways and how to inherit eternal life. They are particularly vital to His covenant people because they are the source and sustenance of their eternal redemption. Detailing what is foretold by the Old Testament prophets, their writings show unwavering commitment to the Almighty's Continuum. The Lord's messages are captured by each gospel writer differently to present His birth, life, actions, death, resurrection, and ascension compositely. They narrate how the Pentecost outpouring that birthed His church magnified Jesus and highlight His doctrines, God's grace, and mediatory work. He stands between His Father and His fallen humanity apostolically, prophetically, redemptively, and judicially. Anticipating the distortions and deceptions to come after He left, aimed at diverting His disciples and church from His truth, and given His history with the serpent and his minions, Jesus tells His family before He ascends, where they could find credible truths to propagate His gospel. Luke keenly latches on to the Lord's subtlety concerning the prophets and prophecies that foretold His Messianic advent. He rehearses His passion and judging from the unmistakable clues the Lord constantly gives, taps into how Jesus changed the world. The passage that makes it clearest of all is Luke 16:16, *"The law and the prophets were until John: since that time the kingdom of God is preached, and <u>every</u> man presseth into it."*

As previously addressed, the most peculiar fact about the gospels is how God embedded them in the Law and the Prophets. Because He did, they have been around since before the Christ's incarnation. His Yahwehic ministrations as Israel's covenant God, and Moses' Law all show semblances of what came down to the New Testament as the kingdom's gospel. Galatians 3:8 says their message reaches all the way back to Abraham. Enoch and Noah's prophecies about the Lord returning to the world say they got their start before him. The Savior's recall of Abel's death sets the prophets and their prophecies further back than Melchizedek's earthly priesthood. The angel aligning his prophetic ministry with John's and his fellow prophets takes it back further still. The celestial being's words indicate that the gospel indeed originated in heaven. Notwithstanding, the most prolific precarnate prophecy in Scripture has to be the Book of Isaiah with its numerous allusions to The Messiah and His salvation. It is replete with prophecies of the future, even if they are coded for spirit filled messengers to decipher down the line.

The Gospels and the Law of Sin and Death

Insofar as the Bible goes, the Law of Moses is the most comprehensive model of divine pre-resolve available on earth. Second to it are the Gospel of Jesus Christ and His kingdom with its perpetual liberties and final judgments. In respect to the gospels, grace and mercy preempt the rigidity of Moses' Law. Where the Law stressed blessings and curses pertaining to a long life on earth, the Gospel of Jesus Christ communicates resolutions that impart and ensure eternal life over eternal death. Although it should be pointed out that, the gospels too, have their own pledge of blessings and curses. In contrast to Moses' Law, it is more severe as its curses are irremediable, and so enact the ultimate irrevocable judgment, the fiery furnace. Being eternal, there is no way to reverse the gospel's judgments. Their provisions contain no hope and are devoid of any afterlife appeals or pardons, such as what the Law held for those that died in Abraham and Moses' hope. The gospel's pre-solutions are final because of the finality of Jesus' death and resurrection. Meaning by this that spiritual death is unalterable, which is why it is the second death and physical death is the first. As far as dying went back then, from Adam to Christ all the earth went to hell when they died with the exception of a highly select few. This was so because the divine nature the Creator's righteousness, His Spirit's consciousness and empowerment were lacking and without them, those who exited the flesh had no way to arrive and thrive in heaven. Adam lost this equipment in the garden, but the Savior returned it to selected humans.

To reverse the effects of the fatal decision that caused the sin problem, God created a new species of humans that would be predisposed to His nature and affined to heaven's immaculate environment when the time came. The prototype of that species had to precede earth's existence, and be exempt from Adam's sin nature and its consequences to be qualified. This was necessary because Satan's nature spiritually reproduced itself in all who were born to Adam. To sidestep these absolutes, God's new race of humans required a sinless progenitor not subject to Adam's curse. The most suitable ancestor had to be willing to suffer the vulnerabilities of the curse to succeed in the plan. His success would enable true life to pass on to those that meet the criteria for the kind of life the Almighty and His family live. In addition, the way that life was passed on had to bypass normal reproduction since that is how Adam's fallen nature reproduces the Devil in his progeny. Also, since the first sin in creation came by a free will act, to ensure those receiving eternal life really want it and will be godly custodians of it, candidates are forced to ask for and comply with other requirements to obtain it. Moreover, the ideal progenitor had to initiate His life-giving program, not on earth, but in hell to release the souls bound to it. Of course, such a father had to come from outside this world and He did, which further magnifies Jesus' incarnation.

All of the above demonstrates how the gospels and their grace surpassed the Law of Moses. Under his Law, there was some possibility of afterlife redemption for those who died fulfilling it. This is because the way of eternal life was reserved for Jesus Christ and He had not yet opened it. As a result, the Law's highest earthly reward was merely long life, along with good health material riches. Jesus Christ's reward, on the other hand, is eternal life; and there is a big difference. Departing this world back then was not the immortal fate, it became under Christ. Under Jesus, afterlife judgments are permanent because He, as the only acceptable sacrifice for human sin, by His death opened the way for the righteous to escape hell and ascend into heaven. Before Him, those who died in Moses could expect a coming Messiah. Those who die under Jesus' reign today without His forgiveness can expect nothing more than eternal damnation. There is no second, third, fourth or infinitum Jesus to incarnate, crucify, or resurrect to catch those thinking they fell through eternity's cracks. He did that once and for all. He never has to repeat it because His first time was perfect enough to be His last time. Insightfully, the gospel's message of grace and hope delivers more than what Moses' law or Abraham's faith did. The two supersede Yahweh's long life promise, by delivering eternal life instead. Meaning by this that the redeemed of Jesus Christ has not just been vindicated; His converts are imparted the very life force of the eternal world and granted entry into the ranks of its citizens. Since the life Jesus imparts is the Godhead's literal life, it is as irreversible as death itself with one major caveat. Once endowed with the celestial world's life force, and admitted into its kingdom, there is no returning to the earthly form or its hope without calamitous judgments. The reasons for Christ's severe apostasy penalties are because once the Lord imparts eternal life into a person he or she is upgraded to the very immortality that the Savior and the members of His kingdom possess. Those counted worthy of Christ's eternal life can no longer live the way, earthbound mortals live, sanctification, and maturation processes notwithstanding. Eternally alive spirits are not to crave or practice what God condemned for earthly beings. That is what got Jude's angels that abandoned their first estate in trouble. The way hell was meant for the Devil and his angels, but now incarcerates humans, is how eternal life and perverting Christ's immortality likewise, passes on their condemnations to new creation humans.

ONE LAW FOR IMMORTALS & ANOTHER LAW FOR MORTALS

The flood of enlightenment and wisdom that accompany the Almighty's life force prohibits eternal creatures from engaging in earth's doomed cultures and customs, and for good reason. The cross and Christ's shed blood are efficacious for mortal souls that have never fallen. These redemptive instruments are not designed to redeem angels or other celestials that left their first estate with full knowledge of what they were leaving behind. Unknown to some Christians, salvation makes those very supernal changes in Jesus' converts and the consequences of risking His eternal blessing irreparable. In contrast to immortal judgments, earth's judgments on mortal sin pale in comparison, review Hebrews 6:4-8. This outcome is also what Hebrews 10:26 has in mind.

Here is why the Lord reacts so harshly when the blood of His Son is trampled underfoot by His saved ones. In the same way that Jesus did not take on the nature of angels to provide them with eternal life because they left the best there is for less, so it is with the Christian's everlasting soul. It is incapable of being redeemed again after being transformed into His very nature. No longer mortal and not redeemed to die, the Lord's judgment on Christians transformed into His eternal beings is the same as it is for the angels that sinned. Believers ought to know that the angels, Satan included, began where God is and not on earth. For aeons, they lived in His world. In His righteous judgment, those that fell into mortal sin did not forfeit a hope; they forfeited their home and country. They rejected their Maker for reasons of their own. Showing the Lord's capacity for pre-resolving how humans treat Him and His irrevocable judgments on them as a result. The wages of sin is death and the eternal life gift of God comes with no backup plan or recovery cycle. The reason people die is the result of the Creator's condemnations. As productive as His word of life is, equally potent are His death commands. They reverse His life giving forces and turn them off. When this happens, His words begin to kill instead of replicate. The way that the angels that fell from heaven chose to leave the best to wallow in the worst, so it is with the human that goes back into sin. This answers why Jesus did not redeem the angels to give them a second chance at eternal life. Simply speaking, they started out as beings of eternity already indwelt by its life. The angels that sinned did not need to be given another chance because they were not deceived into sinning, nor were they devoid of the intelligence and insight to foresee the aftermath of their action. With this said, Scripture clearly states that there is no atonement or remission of intentional sin, so angels' willful disobedience to God's eternal law provided for no recovery plan because the very influences that convinced them to try once could not be erased. They would only attempt to have their way again later.

God, due to His eternal existence does not view sin as humans do. People see their sin as superficial errors amounting to no more than invisible or disappearing ink that fades in time. In God's world, that is not the case and everything a person does, celestial or terrestrial, imprints it. To Him they are blights and stains that mar the soul. The soul, considered a garment, is stained in the way that earthly stains sully natural materials. It does not matter if sin's moral side effects, immediately experienced or not, are discerned by humans. As far as the Almighty is concerned, every soul garment's stain must be expunged. The solution He provided to purge the soul of its sinful stains is the blood of Christ, steeped with the word of God. Hence, the washing and regenerative powers of God's word. To avert such spiritual crises, the Lord sends His messengers to teach people about their salvation and to paint the picture of its benefits and detriments as predetermined by Him. Every effort is made to see His converts are not duped into risking their eternal life on something they knew nothing about and yet are vulnerable to. God's faithful messengers teach that death, for a natural man who dies in faith under Abraham and Moses may not have been final, spiritually speaking, but under Christ today it is. Now that He has paid the price for humanity's sin to ransom them from the power of its doom all the rules are changed. Humans that die under Jesus, who has authority over all flesh, do not get another chance. Their doom is irremediable because Jesus is not going to hell a second time. He went there once to retrieve those who meant to do well, but lacked the power and volition to do things His way. The new birth has eliminated and forever taken away that excuse by imparting to the penitent God's divine nature, His Holy Spirit, and His word of truth. The Almighty's eternal world, subsists on and employs all of these resources to stay alive and remain perpetual for its societies. Thus, the basis for law and judgment, and grace and mercy; and it says how the gospels supersede Moses' Law. As the next chapter shows, immortals are citizens of God's eternal kingdom and are subject to the laws governing the spirit of life in Christ Jesus. Those refusing to exit the laws of sin and death are subject to the penalties and doom attached to Moses' Law. Here is why, Jesus says the kingdom of God is within the redeemed. Whether His converts fully know His laws intellectually or not, they nonetheless govern them, because salvation inscribes them in the heart, and embeds them in the head of the redeemed.

[11]

The Kingdom of God

The kingdom of God differs from the kingdom of heaven in that heaven is a place and God is a Person. The Lord's extension of Himself by His Spirit to inhabit the beings He saves comprises and extends the kingdom because He is a King who lives within those He accepts into His family. The kingdom of heaven is the incorporeal dwelling place of all Spirit indwelt beings the Lord blesses with His life. The distinction is important because the kingdom of God like the word eternal, has no beginning and no end. Since the Lord would have pre-existed His abode, it is logical to assume that the kingdom of heaven is everlasting. It is also penetrable, as the Lord Jesus reveals in Matthew 11. His kingdom is, by virtue of His title, a theocracy. Petitions and permissions more than demands and threats move the King, and that is but one major difference between kings and presidents. The saint seeking to spend eternity with Jesus Christ should know and appreciate Jesus as King, not an elected official. The rules for elected officials do not apply to Him, in much the same way public service does not impart all of the prerogatives of royalty. Jesus was made King by God Almighty. It is a vital fact that this book reiterates repeatedly.

Unlike earthly monarchs, The Messiah does not rely on public opinion, agreement, or sentiment to secure His position. God made His rule eternal and His subjects' attitudes cannot annul it. Jesus reigns forever, period. That is why natural disasters and other absolutes like death and aging continue, despite humanity's bitter resentment of them. Each one of them serves His sovereign purposes that are only overturned by Him. In addition, Jesus as the Old Testament Yahweh has been ruling and leading this planet since it began, besides His otherworldly reigns. He is not auditioning for eventual kingship here, nor is He a novice prince, hoping to bring His afterlife promises somehow to pass in the end. He is sure He will bring the righteous into His eternal world. The entirety of Scripture says He is not winging it, but working according to a preordained plan that has been in effect for ages and will play out for ages to come. It is with infinite experience and expertise that the Lion of Judah incarnated to go from being Yahweh to Joshua, and came to earth to induct yet another planet and its populace into His impervious kingdom. He did it according to Scripture mysteries concerning Him that He revealed to His apostles and prophets. Along with the implementable wisdom that is innate to their mantles, the Savior carries everything out through them. Such realities are intrinsic to their offices and show why they must discharge their posts consistent with the word of God. For the reasons given so far, the protocols of the elected officer do not matter when one is preparing a soul for eternity.

Jesus as a King is a divine not a public official, and His redeemed are entering a world that has existed, reigned and been governed by Him forever. John 17:1-5 says it this way: *"Jesus said these things; then, lifting his eyes to heaven, he said, Father, the time has now come; give glory to your Son, so that the Son may give glory to you: Even as you gave him authority over all flesh, to give eternal life to all those whom you have given to him. And this is eternal life: to have knowledge of you, the only true God, and of him whom you have sent, even Jesus Christ. I have given you glory on the earth, having done all the work which you gave me to do. And now, Father, let me have glory with you, even that glory which I had with you before the world was"*. Jesus shows in this passage that He has a vivid recollection of His eternal life with God the Father in heaven. He knows He reigned as God and King and that He was in power before this world ever existed. The Literal Translation of the Holy Bible says it this way: *"And now Father, glorify Me with Yourself, with the glory which I had with You before the existence of the world"*. The International Standard Version of the Bible reads, *"So now, Father, glorify me in your presence with the glory I had with you before the world existed"*. Jesus is revealed throughout the New Testament as the Lord God Eternal ruling and reigning over creation long before He made the world. This is alluded to in Proverbs chapter 8. This truth makes His incarnation – the setting aside of His godhood to take the form of humankind more magnanimous. That God became a man is benevolent, but to go so far as to leave immortality to become mortal and consent to die is tremendous. Jesus' submission to God the Father means He set aside His sovereignty, ceased to be Yahweh, Israel's covenant God, divested Himself of His Creator deathlessness, and consented to being regarded and treated as a mortal, all the way to the cross. Because He was King of kings before He came to earth, veneration as Israel's King almost goes without saying. Receiving His inheritance demanded nothing less than going from undying sovereign to one doomed to die. It has also been His goal to return earth to heaven's dominion and to pass on His deathlessness to all born of Adam that believe in Him.

Jesus' eternal plans for His family are that they dwell with and serve Him in a kingdom. That is why Christians are identified by Peter as God's royal priesthood. His statement goes to the Lord blending His divine offspring's royal and ministerial destinies into one heritage. It is how John could identify the redeemed as a nation of kings and priests in the Apocalypse. Continuum-wise, this idea first appears in Exodus 19:6. Therefore, it is important for ministers, to teach obedience to this world's leaders while not neglecting their duty to prepare the saint for eternal life in Christ's ever-existing kingdom. Teaching God's redeemed how to be democratic Christians is just not enough to prepare them for eternity. They must know how to survive under Jesus' kingship here to thrive as one of His under rulers there.

When believers say they have or need the mind of Christ, they typically mean His humility, meekness, love, and morality. Hardly ever do they mean His subservience to His Father, His submission to the Almighty's Sovereignty, or His mentality as a King Himself. Rarely, do such thoughts enter the religious mind bent on restricting Christ to being no more than a Savior and Shepherd, and perhaps a Divine Parent. Ecclesiastes 8:4 refutes this by saying, *"Where the word of a king is there is power"*. A king's word in action is seen under the monarchical age. Ancient monarchies, and even the few that still exist today in essence, all understood that a king's word was powerful, and it was law. No matter how just or unjust, compassionate or cruel, or even how wise or foolish, no one dared contest a king's word. It was etched in community, culture, and consciousness that to do so was to imperil one's own life and risk it on the king's wrath. Much of that sentiment is lost in today's largely democratic climate, but in God's world, the rule remains the same; where the word of a king is revered and is:

- Supremely backed by great power – by the longevity of their kingdom or the direct delegation from the god of the land
- Authoritative – Potent enough to compel obedience, submission, and fear
- A powerful command – Incapable of being ignored without severe consequences
- Absolute authority – Needs no permission to speak, act, or enforce commands with indomitable action
- Full of power – Able to be wielded without resistance, competition, or restraint

The very substance of a king's person is itself the essence of power, exuded in the monarch's person, word, staff, and so forth. Such personified power answers to no one in the realm and is released with a mere nod, or less. The less part is when the sovereign's staff is so familiar with his or her will and desires that, a simple look releases the power that authorizes them to act. Jesus is a Sovereign of sovereigns who did not discover what it is to rule supreme when He ascended on high. His precarnate reign was inherited and delegated as the Father's first begotten Son. The second Psalm and Psalm 89:27-29 speak about King David in forever terms. It refers to a king more enduring than Israel's second king David. Add these to Psalm 45 and numerous other passages and the king in question, is the Son of God who is now absorbing another world into His reign. These all say why the differences between the royal and elected ruler should be well learned by God's people. It will prepare them to submit to Jesus' uncontested sovereignty and to reign with Him as a royal priesthood when they leave this world. To teach God's redeemed to be good democratic Christians is just not enough to prepare them for eternity. Depriving them of true eternal life education forebodes their disappointment with Christ when they enter His realm. It will make it very difficult for them to submit to a monarch that can never be opposed or countermanded. Worldly teachings that promote human liberties and citizens' inherent right to influence their government may serve this realm as well, but they are virtually nonexistent in God's world. Perhaps that is why so many believers dread Jesus' kingship and sovereignty.

WHY JESUS' KINGSHIP IS DREADED

Today's modern Bible translations work aggressively to scrub away any blot of royalty and its weightiness in the Scriptures' wordings. They do so because of the negative connotation monarchies earned in ancient and medieval times. When fear of oppression is the case, any taint of sole person governance is squelched. Even now, many advanced societies, yet reel from the abuses of the godless sovereigns of their past. That sentiment is bred in modern Christians' consciousness through schools, business, and entertainment. The downside of kingship is circulated to assure people fear coming under a lone ruler and prefer to have a plurality of governors ruling them to balance autocratic extremes. As long as the earth and its world systems remain, this could be sage wisdom. However, one of its Christian shortcomings is the subtle undermining of the kingdom reign of Jesus Christ. The endless negativity spewed by His antagonist's labor to overshadow the world where Jesus rules. If His ministers fail to separate the Lord Jesus' world from this one, the subtle effect is to frighten believers out of reverencing, and so pursuing, His kingship and thereby trusting His sovereignty. Stringent efforts go into breeding fear of having to live with Him in His world forever in the hearts of His saints as anything more than a Shepherd and Savior. Teaching the world to despise monarchs and all they represent unsettles believers' eternal hope, and motivates them to cling to life on earth. Far too many Christians today, struggle to hang on to the world and its ways for the sake of exaggerated or imagined freedoms. History shows there is justification for these attitudes, looking back to when medieval citizens fought brutally for their independence. Once freed from the tyranny of their monarchs and their kingdoms, they evidently vowed never to be subject to them again. That vow shows up in every stratum and psyche of many societies. What instigated their revolt also led to modernity's aversion to royals and monarchies. Over time, it mushroomed into an institutional stronghold with theology and culture allying to ensure its permanence. People, once free of monarchs and kingdoms, began to cherish their supposed liberation from oppression and independent free will agency. Cultural philosophies passed that conviction onto succeeding generations. By now, the fear has become a tradition as Christians like the rest of humanity agree they are independent agents in the world and in the nations to which they belong. In many countries, citizens are convinced their liberty is the single most important thing and believe it is only assured by not being under a king. That cannot equip them for their eternal destiny.

Subconsciously, this persuasion crept into the Church world and undid the very hope the Lord gave His life to impart to those who believe in Him. The prevailing supposition is that a democratic system is safer and more amenable to human liberties than a monarchy. Perhaps in this world that is true, and necessary, but in Christ's it is not. There He is the Great King, the Good Shepherd, the Loving, and Merciful God. He is Paul's Immortal King to His eternal citizens where those are not just words, nor their positions empty figurehead terms. Kingship is the very essence of Christ's Person and so the nature His kingdom. From what has been said so far, it is apparent that people believe strange things about their future with the Lord, most of which is not entirely or substantively true. Moreover, what many of them imagine about heaven, in contrast to earthly governments, is likewise inaccurate.

THE SUPERLATIVENESS OF JESUS' MONARCHY

In the preceding discussion, a case was made for reconsidering one's position on monarchies in eternity when it comes to the Lord Jesus Christ. Here, the reason the saint need not fear His reign is discussed. It aims to inspire people to sanctify the Lord in their hearts and hallow His extravagant kingdom plan for them. Remembering that natural Israel is a nation and not a church is essential to grasping and rightly dividing the Lord's truth on this subject. It is indispensable for and interpreting the sentiments of the prophets' Scriptures and their conception of Him as their permanent King. They were not appealing to a congregation and its membership when they penned their words, but a nation of theocratic citizens. That mindset apostles and prophets innately possess and cultivate as His representatives. How God thinks, His right to rule and command His people, and His vision for the creation He made with His own hands are never soft peddled by these two officers. They do not shun His deep truths to downplay His authority or misrepresent His righteousness by limiting their messages to His love alone. Faithful ministers know and treat the Lord as a whole person, more whole and balanced than any human. Thus, they have no problem accepting and exercising His authority when needed and know the wisdom of delegating responsibility with corresponding authority to empower true leadership. Paul understood this well as 2 Corinthians 10:8 shows. The meaning of this, that the shortfall and the frailties of human nature should not be imposed on the Savior's eternal kingdom and its righteousness. To reverse the trend, what people think Jesus' world is and how it runs needs a complete overhaul. Relative to this, Isaiah 55:11 says God's thoughts are not humanity's thoughts and His ways are not humanity's ways.

The Almighty's lofty view of life makes His thoughts and ways higher than anything a human can surmise. His exaltedness means that it is virtually impossible to conceive of His world with its grandeur and sublimity in pathetic earthly terms. No matter how drab this world's dark agents, paints it, God's eternity and its glories are far too majestic for anyone on earth to imagine, let alone depict accurately. Therefore, a kingdom paradigm shift is needed. That means the Christian psyches, archetypes, and the epitomes of present and future generations must be reformed and molded to view the Lord and His world as He does. It is the only way His rich Scripture promises may be desired and embraced by His people. However, the means by which He ordained this to happen is through His Continuum. An unfettered bond with Him and His unbroken episodic chain creates the best converts and servants of His truths. But it only prospers when His people are holy, humble, and loyal.

THE SOUL OF A KING

The soul contains the heart, the mind, and the will. In talking about kingship, one must remember that sovereign leaders are so from the core of their very beings. They have highly peculiar mentalities concerning their purpose in life that empowers their role in the lives of others. Kings are acutely aware of what actually rests on their shoulders. Winning is uppermost in their minds because the consequence of losing is that they cease to rule or reign, so they are natural fighters to assure their permanence. This teaching is important for all those who are fond of declaring that the members of Christ's body and His new creation church are kings and priests. It is to reshape their perception of what that means, and disclose what lies ahead for them as divine royal offspring. It is also to demonstrate how they should conduct themselves wisely in this world as God's representatives, which is the way David did, in order to rule in the next. This advice is worth taking because Scripture says saints that fail to suffer with Jesus forfeit reigning with Him.

The reality is many of those celebrating their royal priesthood status in Christ and appropriating what they believe are the prerogatives of their position must make serious adjustments in their attitudes. They must upgrade their behaviors, motivations, and perspectives significantly. Kings have an enviable sense of self. Something within tells them that they exist for reasons most other souls cannot fathom. They are strong willed, focused, and dutiful, if for no other reason than they want to remain in power. Monarchs are concerned about their dominions, committed to their populaces, and zealous about their realm's prosperity. Above all, royalty is resolute about the perpetuity of what they found and leave behind. These attitudes are foreign to the democratic mind, but they are the ones the Savior was born into. Jesus did not become a king on earth, but rather in heaven. His kingdom was not just this tiny planet but takes in the infinite vastness of all His Father's worlds. Reading between the lines of His discourses in Scripture reveals a determined, focused, resolute man with no identity crises and a keen awareness of His destiny and purposes. Jesus stays on task; remains vigilant; and lives acutely aware that He is what He is. He never loses sight of what He brings to the world and all that is at stake for Him and His dominion. Jesus ceaselessly pursued the establishment of His kingdom, the overthrow of His enemies, preparation for His eternal takeover of the planet, and thorough consecration and indoctrination of His future citizens. Very few claimants or aspirants to Revelation 1:6 and 5:10 exhibit this magnitude of devotion and absorption with why they were born, and born again, but the Savior never lets it go. His past prefixed Him, John 13:3;

His present inspired Him, John 4:34; and His future guided and drove Him, Mathew 19:28; 25:31, and Luke 18:8. Nothing staring Him in the face moved Him away from His identity and destiny, but rather defined Him and ultimately exalted Him. What endangers the Christian's inheritance is a misconception, and worldly perception of eternity. The believer that only wants to see Jesus in the roles he or she can manage and indulge presents a problem because as Paul says, when He appears He will not be known (or treated) as He was when He departed this world. See 2 Corinthians 5:16.

Jesus as a King is foremost concerned about and protective of His kingdom. As John's account of His war in heaven shows, He is fierce about defending and guarding it and those, whose lives and prosperity He holds in His hands. Unfortunately, His church feels He is only concerned about shepherding it, and cannot imagine Him, having the heart, soul, and steely will of a Monarch with much to defend and recover. Yet His words in John 6:39 make this very point. The Lord of glory, despite how humble and loving He is, has a massive burden on His shoulders that exceeds this world and extends to its successive generations. Hebrews calls it a far greater weight of glory. The Messiah cannot afford to get locked in time because the souls to come will be disinherited if He does not move forward to meet them when they arrive. He cannot afford to trivialize any portion of His duties because He has a very determined adversary waiting for Him to slack up so he can pounce on His birthright. He has to superintend the entire life span of everything He and His Father created, otherwise their creature hood would idly waste away, their gifts and talents failing to justify their remaining on the planet. Most importantly, Jesus as creation's Sovereign must secure the destinies and eternal rewards of all who come to Him until the end of the age.

Think about what kind of mental preoccupation a person with such weight on his shoulders would have to carry every day. What day or time would such a leader pick to rest and relax or what duty or responsibility could he safely shirk, and how about the job itself? What daily routine and ongoing function would one so heavily charged have to maneuver day by day to remain conscientious? These are the thoughts the average Christian would never consider when it comes to their personal Lord and Savior Jesus Christ. The church at large shudders, almost as much as His enemies do, at the prospect of His having all power in heaven and earth. Reading about it devotionally is uplifting; living with what it means and requires of them is terrifying. Most believers do not know what Jesus' dominion means, and others hope that it is not as supreme as it sounds. Although it is fun to sing "He's Got the Whole World in His Hands", living with the implications of that reality is scary for the world, and for His church until they need Him to flex His muscles on their behalf. Somehow, the Ecclesia misreads its duty to keep what is entrusted to it, feeling that putting it at risk or losing it altogether is acceptable since Jesus' possessions are really not theirs but His. They poke fun at much of what He does to secure His eternal kingdom and criticize the most common protections as fanatical or religious. The Savior does not share this view. A great example of His protective side is seen in the Lord's stationing the cherubim to guard the way to the Garden of Eden. The cherubim were stationed at the east end as if other points of entry did not exist or were not in jeopardy. The flaming sword was specifically situated to prevent access to the tree of life. This example shows the Lord's zealous protection of His eternal world's treasures and His terrestrial world's provisions. His sovereign act kept Adam and the serpent out of the garden that both had access to prior to his fall. What the account says about Him is that guardianship, security, and defense are important to the Lord; evidently more important to Him than it appears to be to His church. It would be, since He had to evict the dragon and his angels from His world, send them to this one, and watch him and his angels destroy it generation after generation. The Lord's concerns were well warranted as the Devil is ever attempting to regain his former glory. In the garden, he tried to do so through the Lord's approval of Adam. He figured that once he entered Adam's soul, he could use his privileges to reenter the Most High God's spiritual domains. His plan backfired, and his attempts at becoming eternity's number one monarch are thwarted. His calculations apparently failed to accept the severity of his punishment and its diminishment of his abilities. The Lord evidently stripped him of his formidable powers to keep him imprisoned. Abandoning His celestial duties and station for his private ambitions changed the fallen cherub's nature, reduced stature and potency, and revoked his liberties. By defrocking him, the Almighty withdraws all of the resources that once served his Maker's purposes and allowed the old dragon to depreciate in order to rule those he enslaved to sin and death as their father.

THE KINGDOM OF GOD

Scripture makes reference to the word kingdom more than 300 times. Aside from the fact that the era in which it was being lived out was predominantly monarchical, there is the question of why the Lord chose that era. The answer has more to do with the composition of His kingdom than the idea of His being stuck in a particular period in history. The word kingdom simply expresses the dominion of a king. Kings back in time were considered to be the offspring, usually the firstborn, of the deity that founded or territorialized a particular land. Generally speaking, their relationship to the deity was thought of as kinship, thus the word king to designate the offspring of a divine being. Many cultures held to this view, as it wended its way back to Adam's relationship with the Almighty His Creator. The kingdoms were established for several reasons. One of them was to manifest a particular divine being in the flesh. That is to beget offspring for it. Abraham and the Lord demonstrate this as Deuteronomy 32 reports. Another reason was to materialize the nature, stature, superiority, and majesty of the deity in human forms and culture. Over time, with the multiplication of both, an added goal became guardianship. What was created, produced, and populated was endangered when other powers, seen and unseen, entered a land, and saw its wealth. Their desire to take what they wanted, paved the way for warfare and militarism for the monarch of the land to defend his or her people and their possessions. Essentially, that is the fundamental of kingship and it got its start from heaven and not earth, which is why the divine beings predate the human being. That motif basically lies at the heart of everything on earth, no matter how advanced or sophisticated it is.

In God and Christ's mind, God's kingdom, kingship, and priesthood, find their zenith in the new creation. It is well understood and articulated by Peter in his first epistle. In the spirit of the Continuum, he brings it forward from Exodus 19:6 that says *"And ye shall be unto me a kingdom of priests, and an holy nation. These are the words which thou shalt speak unto the children of Israel."* Obviously, through his close relationship with Jesus Christ, Peter as His lead apostle grasped The Messiah's mind and mission on this matter. He is a King and Divine and desires offspring to manifest Himself and populate His kingdom. That is how it all began, and according to John's Apocalypse, it is how it will all end. Enter then, the holy nation spoken of in 1 Peter 2:9 *"But ye are a chosen generation, a royal priesthood, an holy nation, a peculiar people; that ye should shew forth the praises of him who hath called you out of darkness into his marvellous light."* Paul says in Ephesians chapter 4 that God's entire family in heaven and earth is named after Jesus Christ, making that family as much royal as it is holy. The only way to assure that He gets what He wants to acquire His holy royal offspring, the Lord must beget them, which He did with the new birth that defines redemption and salvation. Conversion to the Godhead, is how Peter in his second epistle says it happens. John his apostleship colleague agrees with this according to John 1:11 and 12 and 3:5-16. Paul the latecomer to the office reinforces it in 2 Corinthians 5:17-18. Condensing the heretofore extremely diverse barriers that once separated humanity into groups, clans or races, Paul brings it all down to one thing: in Christ or out. So he says that anyone that does not have His Spirit, the Spirit of Christ, Scripture says are none of

His. The progeny of a king founds a monarch's kingdom. Those not born directly from the king's lineage may receive the opportunity to enter the family through adoption. That is how the Lord adopted those engrafted into His, and Christ's, family line. With no legal system in place to accomplish the adoption through human court proceedings, the Lord as Judge of all simply completes the transaction through the new birth. He converts from within those who would be naturalized to Him and His Father's lineage.

The new birth genetically alters the human born into Adam's line by removing the old spirit and heart and replacing it with the very same one the Godhead possesses. The process that happens faster than light strips the person's spirit of all its death and imparts eternal life in its place. From that moment onward, the convert is legitimate and genetically God's child, not just technologically but genealogically as well. With a new breed of people to host and house, the necessity of a kingdom emerges. Thus, the kingdom of God and its importance have been sifting its generations of citizens since before Moses' Law. For instance, some of its named heirs are Abel, Enoch, Noah, Abraham, Isaac, Jacob, Samuel, and the holy prophets, naturally David the king all the way to Jesus' generation that began with the saints that resurrected from the dead with Him.[96] From the time the Holy Spirit took residence on the planet in place of Jesus; the kingdom that He had preached began to populate itself through the apostles' words and those of His newly born Ecclesia. Following are some of the aspects or dimensions of the kingdom as presented in the New Testament. They represent its residents, works, word, and overall sphere of existence. More than 120 times, the word kingdom surfaces in the New Testament. Here are some Scriptures related examples to make the point.

What Constitutes the Kingdom of God

What is listed on the next chart enables the student of Scripture and the inquisitive saint pursuing heaven to recognize what is or is not the genuine kingdom of God (and heaven). To grasp its enormity and benefit from its content, one must perceive what the kingdom of God is and how it came to be on earth. Other chapters discuss God—the Person's kingdom, in contrast to the kingdom of heaven—His place of residence. In a word, the kingdom of heaven is His abode. The kingdom of God in comparison applies to the Person of God and constitutes His Presence indwelling and

---

96 The author is aware of the conflicts about the term Godhead. However, the term encapsulates God as divine, the generative deity and the head of all that exists.

empowering those that receive Jesus Christ as Savior. This is in addition to the innumerable masses that have occupied His world long before time or earth began. They too are considered the people of God, His saints and therefore citizens of God's kingdom. What this says is that anything God makes, He inhabits to seal it as His own in this world and every other one He made. Regarding those born from above in Christ, they became residents of God's kingdom when they were born as offspring of His divine seed through The Messiah's blood. That blood blends Almighty God's divine bloodline with the blood that made David's descendants of royal descent. The entire event elevates those who come to God through Him to the status of divine progenies as a result.

The poor in spirit are in the kingdom	The comforted mournful are in the kingdom
The meek of the earth are in the kingdom	Righteousness' hungry and thirsty are in the kingdom
The merciful are in the kingdom	The pure in heart are in the kingdom
The peace making children of God are in the kingdom	They persecuted for Christ's sake are in the kingdom
Those persecuted for righteousness sake are in the kingdom	The reviled and abused for Christ's sake are in the kingdom
Persecuted and abused the prophets of Jesus Christ are in the kingdom	Preachers of Jesus Christ are in the kingdom
Christ's violently forceful takers are in the kingdom	Receivers of God's mysteries are in the kingdom
Genuine hearers of God's word are in the kingdom	Keepers of the commandments who do and teach them are in the kingdom
Extreme righteousness is in the kingdom	Power and glory are in the kingdom
Those who put the kingdom first are there	All doers of Jesus' Father's will are in the kingdom
Abraham, Isaac, and Jacob are in the kingdom	Adopted heirs of God are in the kingdom
Healing and deliverance are in the kingdom	The fruitful in Christ are in His kingdom
Seeders of Christ's truth are in His kingdom	The good seeds of the world are children of Christ's kingdom
The righteous in Jesus Christ are in	God's treasures are in His kingdom

His Father's kingdom

The pearls of wisdom are in the kingdom

The well instructed scribes are in the kingdom

The keys of heaven's authority are in the kingdom

Those of childlike faith and humility are in Christ's kingdom

The merciful and forgiving are in the kingdom

The resolutely moral are in the kingdom

The despised in the world that are in Christ are in the kingdom

The fruitful nation is in the kingdom

The faithful steward is in the kingdom

Those who revere its King are in the kingdom

The faithfully well prepared are in the kingdom

The diligent and industrious are in the kingdom

The Christ conscious and obedient is in the kingdom

The martyred are in the kingdom

The steadfast and committed are in the kingdom

The flock of God is in the kingdom

That which offends is in the kingdom

The productive and profitable are in the kingdom

The born again (from above) are in the kingdom

Sufferers in the tribulation are in the kingdom

Jesus, Moses' Law, and the prophets are in the kingdom of God

The kingdom of God concerns Jesus Christ

The kingdom of God is in word and power

The kingdom of God is God's dear Son

The kingdom of God is righteousness, peace, and joy in the Holy Ghost

Jesus Not Like or One of the Angels

Jesus Christ is God the Father's first begotten Son. That means He was given life in ways the angels and other celestial creatures were not. He was born and not formed, to make it easier to see the difference between the two. As such, He came into being as a King. As God's first offspring, He inherited His first monarchical title by birth. His additional titles, signified by His many crowns were earned in other ways. When the Almighty brought siblings for Jesus into existence by the very same means He used to take Jesus out of His being, they too qualified as royalty. This cannot be too much of a stretch to believe since everything on earth emerges from something else that lived before it. Thus, the way God became the Father of the Lord Jesus Christ is by birth and not by handcraft, making Jesus *sperm made* and not *handmade*. The way the Lord God makes Himself Christians' Father is by the new birth. He begets them anew to upgrade Adam's descendants from His handcraft to literal offspring. Discussed elsewhere, this distinction clarifies how the believer in Jesus Christ is born of the Spirit of God, further shedding light on Romans 8:9 and 1 Peter 1:11. The new birth makes a Christian the very same way Jesus was made as the first begotten. To be precise He was born in heaven by the Almighty to be the Almighty, He appears as, to John in the Revelation. God breathed Me out of His being by the Holy Spirit, what He tells Nicodemus in John chapter 3. The Almighty keeps to the pattern by begetting His Messiah's human form on earth the same way. To put Him into flesh, He simply breathes Jesus' sperm into Mary's womb. These hands-free actions are the way the Almighty responds procreatively[46] to all those that come to Him for His Son's salvation. Deific reproductive processes transform Jesus Christ's converts into God's divine progeny. Since God is Spirit and inhabits all He creates, the question is in what way and to what degree does He do so? In the case of the Christians He indwells, His entire substance inhabits them parentally to naturalize people as God's kingdom on earth. Peter calls it, being made partakers of God's divine nature in his second epistle. Thus, when one uses the phrase kingdom of God, one is stressing what the Self-Existent Being that brought all that is out of nothing reproduced after His own kind. Thoroughly discussing the kingdom of God establishes what it is made up of and what its seekers must do to enter and remain there. God as the first King bestowed kingship next on His firstborn Son, who in turn joined Him in creating and giving life to everything else that exists today. Populating their worlds started with personally crafting and animating (and automating) every life form they envisioned and housed within their Beings. God is a living God so all that He creates lives as well in different levels and with varying degrees of His power. To create and populate, the Godhead had to generate every resource, material, energy, and supply to begin the grander work of creature building. Scattered throughout Scripture are inklings of this truth. Self-generation, first begotten, joint expansion, and extension together commenced what is today the kingdom of God. However, before there could be a place, a heaven, there had to be a person, God, who created His dwelling place. To rule His creation He had to envision and determine how everything would happen to pass on to His kingdom, a thriving existence. Every bit of information contained in His Holy Scripture His Son legitimized as Yahweh first for Israel through Moses and when He appeared on earth as Jesus Christ for the Church.

[12]

Jesus Christ Canonized The Scriptures

In Luke 24:44, Jesus personally declares that His prophets delivered the Old Testament Scriptures to the world. The Apostle Paul reasserts it in Acts 24:14 and 28:23 to ensure future Scripture readers knew where to find John 14:6's Jesus Christ and His message. Before His incarnation, it was the Law and the Prophets. Later Jesus Himself added the Psalms. Following the pattern laid down for them by the writers and upholders of Moses' Law (see John 12:34), Christ's apostles took strong measures to ensure that His worshippers did not get lost in the predictable muddle of confusion meant to discredit The Messiah's word and thereby His faith. Opposers of God's truth attack its spiritualities to confound His believers with endless harangues about gaps and inconsistencies. What they refuse to accept is that the New Testament is a synoptic narrative of all that Jesus <u>began</u> to do and teach, and later what His Spirit accomplished on His behalf in the Church. There is no way a person with His exalted dignity could be captured fully in writing, from the three and a half years that He ministered on earth. John says that if one tried, the world could not contain the books written about His brief but staggering earthly exploits. As it stands today, countless people still write books about Jesus, who remains the world's most popular enigmatic figure. Anticipating this, He perceptively preached about His resistors and the effects of His truths on the faithful and the unbelieving. His most extensive exposés on this subject are found in His parable of the sower that sowed the Word found in all three gospels about a seed sower sowing the word. The parable allegorically casts Jesus as the sower and the seed as the word He came to earth to spread.

THE HOLY SPIRIT AND THE CONTINUUM

Treating the tide of impostors pretending to be Him as an inevitable consequence of His success, Jesus corrals His divine communications in one place, what is today accepted as the Holy Bible. Later, Paul, imitating the Savior, did the same thing. Streamlining the vastness of what He has said and has been saying for ages, the Lord confined the gist of what He would communicate to His world to the Scriptures that He entrusted to the prophets and the Levites stewarding His nation. After His Son defeated and evicted the gods of this world, the Most High God transferred the charge of His truths to Christ's Ecclesia for three reasons. First, the Holy Spirit once localized in Israel returned from heaven, where He accompanied Jesus after obsoleting Moses' Law. He is now on the planet to protect the world and no longer just a single nation. Second, the Holy Spirit, as the Almighty's eternal guardian of truth in this world, abides on earth not only in the atmosphere but also within those redeemed by the Lamb's blood. Thus, He serves as a custodial witness to how Jesus' message is handled and disseminated throughout the generations. Third, the Holy Spirit functions as heaven's immigration services and customs Agent on earth. He meticulously inspects the fruit of God's word preached to examine its effects and outcomes in the lives of those it touches. To this end, He facilitates the new birth, sanctifies the saved, and transforms God's elect into Christ's image and likeness. Beyond that, He secures the Church, confirms its ministers, fortifies its hedge, and carries out the Godhead's reclamation of the souls He pre-appointed to eternal life.

What makes the Holy Spirit heaven's one and only indisputable witness is that He is God. That status also makes Him a reliable superintendent of God's covenants. His validity as an authentic firsthand witness comes from His having been around since forever, which is more than long enough to know everything that happened before the earth, how it affects its ages, and how it will all end. The Apostle John recognizes this about God's Spirit and noted it in his first epistle when he publicizes The Messiah's most trustworthy witnesses. There he names the Word,[47] Water (also representing God's word), the blood of the Lamb, and the Holy Spirit dwells in the redeemed. In essence, regardless of the roles they fill individually, jointly creation's most scrutable[48] witnesses are the Godhead itself in all His manifestations. The Lord's Triune witnesses reveal that He trusts nothing He made to bear witness to Him because everything is a product (or byproduct) of Him and not Himself. He alone is true while His handiwork, however superior, can be subject to error that would lend itself to fallacy. In short, God trusts no one but Himself to tell the whole truth about Himself.[49] It does not matter that He does it through handpicked ministers and messengers. As God's authenticator on earth, and within humans, the Holy Spirit through all of the measures discussed watches over His eternal and temporal works. His chief verifier is of course the word of God, the letter and the person. For continuity sake, what humans need, the Lord composed and compiled His divine communications for all generations to know how His will is consistently done on earth as it is in heaven. The Holy Spirit, along with the entire Godhead, is intricately involved in the Continuum portrayed in Scripture because it is their vision, their project, and their wisdom at work.

God's Scripture based Continuum propels His purposes forward until the end, despite the Bible's formative years coming to a close. As an archival and revelational instrument, it contains the immediate accounts, prophetic or experienced, of how the sources it names unanimously depict Jesus Christ's incarnation and redemption as Israel's and the world's promised Messiah. The Scriptures capture His passion on the cross, His resurrection, ascension and His resultant church. Hence, the Continuum that God obliges all ministers to advance, serves as the Church's and its converts' most reliable guide. They refute what modern ministers have come to believe about Christianity, that there is no set way to preach Christ's gospel because there is no guide to determine what it actually says and means. The Continuum disproves this notion. It instead unveils its structure, so Christ's ministers do not have to make anything up as they go along. He did this because John 2:25 says, *"He knew what was in man."* The Lord Jesus left nothing concerning His truth, up to the flesh, or chance. In fact, to protect the Continuum from their effects, the Apostle Paul and the others preached against the flesh more than they did anything else. They, unitedly held that the flesh profits nothing because in it dwells no good thing. According to them, the best way to honor God is to stay within His Continuum. Another way to honor God is to appreciate His command of a powerful force of angelic beings charged with seeing that His word and work continue and thrive on earth. Of course, the highest way to honor God is to cooperate with His best witness, the Holy Spirit.

Alongside the Holy Spirit, the angels' part in God's Continuum is celebrated because neither ages nor dies. God's celestial ministers, more than any human being best maintain and administrate His covenants and government generation after generation. The same cannot be said for people because they get sick, age, and eventually die. When a person dies and leaves his or her work undone, replacements must carry the unfinished work forward. Under the best of circumstances, an originator's continuity is difficult to maintain when a work changes hands, even when the successor and predecessor fully agreed on it. No matter how strong the respect the two may have for each other, fundamental differences and life experiences can mean they innately think differently, which may not show up until the successor is promoted. The moment God's replacements find themselves empowered to make things happen, pet visions and cherished dreams can surface to remaps an organization's course. This is because diverse life paths lead people to approach their worlds from varied perspectives, causing replacements to assume a work with their own visions at heart. Some replacements perpetuate their founder's vision and others take the occasion to fulfill their own, but neither group replicates the founder's vision verbatim. It is common for those entrusted with the resources to change what a founder or predecessor had in mind to do so, thereby breaking an organization's continuity chain. When this very human scenario transfers to God's Continuum, a string of severing events breaches its unity and veers it away from the Holy Spirit and His celestial agents. Whenever the Continuum's inimitable actions are jeopardized, heaven steps in to cordon off self-willed successors' effects so their countermands do not disrupt the Continuum's timeline and derail His scheduled events. Charged with this responsibility, God's Spirit has some definite ways to prevent crises to His Continuum. Starting with sermons preached and the doctrines taught, He reacts in different ways to ensure the Trinity's pre-designated outcomes.

Divine influences ensure everything associated with the Continuum perfectly align to guarantee heaven's will is done on earth at the right time and under Creator engineered circumstances. Spiritual maneuvers in the backdrop of human life routinely assure the Continuum ceaselessly does its job. Should its integrity be compromised, God's built-in Continuum Protectants release pre-decreed countermeasures so things go as He planned. Sometimes astute people sense His interventions and others miss it altogether. Either way the Lord watches over His word and work to perform them according to the big picture He has in mind and does not surrender His goals to the human imperfections known to snarl His plans. Even they are all accounted for in the Continuum to compel all things to work together for God's good in heaven and humanity's redemption on earth. Continuum duties are what the Holy Spirit orders and delegates to God's spiritual and ecclesial ministers. He begins with the angels, His spiritual ministers, because they are the only ones who can precisely carry out God's will from beginning to end. Bridging the supernal and the natural, they in turn pass His orders and delegations on to the humans they supervise in the world according to their respective gifts and calling. The Lord's angelic forces have served Him from the beginning and witnessed firsthand in their world what earth lives through every day. They, for these reasons, share His mind and heart for humanity and recognize its incompatibility with their supernal world and its citizenry. The angels that refused to sin agree with the results He is going after and the type of fruit He aims to produce.

All of this is to say that God never left full responsibility for His eternal plans and programs up to humans; He merely uses them as the Holy Spirit's subsidiaries in conjunction with or beneath the angels. God's unchanging realm succeeds because of its deathless agents and agencies. They are what He relies upon to ensure that His Continuum is not breached. The Lord authorizes His angels to protect, perfect, and correct whatever people disrupt in His Continuum for all the reasons given, and most significantly because they will outlive them. The greatest example of this is found in the words that open Jesus' class on prayer. Traditionally known as the Lord's Prayer, Jesus prays, *"thy kingdom come and thy will be done on earth as it is in heaven"*. Those principalities and powers in heavenly places ensure the Lord's will is done on earth, as they know it to be carried out in heaven. Recall the angel that struck Herod dead when he perverted the gospel,[97] and the ones that released the apostles from false imprisonment. Both angels were authorized to secure Jesus' venture, going so far as to prevent or abort human antics that threaten to impede. In light of all that has been said about His world preexisting this one, God's words should ring out differently now. With renewed understanding, muse on Christ's statement for a moment, *"Thy will be done on earth as it is in heaven."* What could that mean but that the earth's collective creation is bringing it into something the heavens have been undergoing and executing long before it? God intends earth to copy its Maker's world exactly, manifesting it governmentally, judicially, culturally, and politically in every regard. It was never His intent that it manifests the darkness more than the light, as most people think. His vision conveys the Bible, its world, and ministers are eons ahead of this one, not lagging archaically behind it as is so often taught.

Faulty assumptions cause church leaders to lower the bar on everything God, seeing their sheep as God's underlings instead of as His beloved progeny. Buying into Satan's propaganda, weak-minded and weak-willed leaders agree with him that the Bible is old fashion, Christianity is outdated, and God is out of touch. Their beliefs keep the saved gripped in such delusions because they have not read or truly understood God's word regarding His worlds. If they did, they would know that sin, disparaging the Almighty's ways and laws, and disdaining His truth and holiness, are not new. Such criticisms go all the way back to before the Continuum's first event. They fomented Heaven's Great War. Unenlightened thinkers confuse antiquity with eternity and assume earth's primitivity outmoded God's eternality, concluding earth's antiquity is God's only era. Seeing earth as the first to be created and heaven afterward is a

---

97 Acts 12:22, 23.

fantasy that deceives people into believing what they think sin is, is in fact all that it is. In reality, sin is as old as the dragon that lost his bid for heaven's sovereignty. It is as dated as the serpent that preyed on Adam in the garden, as redundant as the fallen angels that stalked Israel, and as imitative as the false christs ruthlessly plundering the Lamb's church. The Bible provides this information to tell the world that Jesus did not bring it a new or untraceable religion, nor did He create a never done before salvation plan. Throughout His ministry discourses, when challenged on His doctrine the Savior steadfastly asserted that His word came from the very Scriptures, they heard every Sabbath that recounted Moses' Law, the Prophets, and the Psalms. Consequently, Jesus reproved them for not recognizing their cherished scrolls when they came from His mouth. Without hesitation, their Messiah, let them know that it was not just His message that they disagreed with but Himself, the prophesied stumbling stone that proved to be their rock of offense. His personification as the eternal David is what they took issue with more than the foreignness of His teachings. In spite of their claims to look for their Messianic David's return, they were not prepared to believe he reappeared on earth in the flesh, and as a lowly carpenter no less.

The King David they expected was an eminent monarch who would forever deliver them from the Romans. A lone straggler, that only preached and exposed their sins was not what they had in mind, and His nation's rulers let Him know it at every turn. Jesus' chosen manifestation was their real obstacle and He exposed it whenever they entered His Presence. His fellow citizens, though they looked for their Messianic David, preferred perpetually waiting for him rather than dealing with who stood before them. Accepting Jesus of Nazareth as the promised Messiah required them to change their ways and yield their faith to a carpenter. The Scriptures that foretold His coming commanded them to follow The Messiah when He came and surrender to His lead. None of this, were they prepared to do because it meant they had to decrease and allow Him to increase. With ages long reputations riding on the institution built around His ultimate arrival, precious few of them were willing to accept Jesus' nativity or to corroborate His identity in their times. Doing so would repeat John the Baptist's reaction when he encountered Him; their earthly preeminence would have to give way to His heavenly Messiahship. Painfully, Jesus incarnating as promised nullified their religious functions and ended their Messianic waiting game. That would leave them with nothing else to do but to fade into the background. Recognizing Jesus as The Messiah implied the prominence they derived from exhorting God's people to pray, sacrifice, and yearn for their Messiah would end, along with all of the corresponding dignities and economies. As a political and religious defense, the rulers of the people concluded Jesus was better off dead than worshiped as their God. That was how the esteemed Rabbi Gamaliel persuaded them to eliminate their problem. In brief, this is the crux of the Savior's conflict with His world, and His world's conflict with Him.

Though He proved Himself as Israel's eternal King David, most of His contemporaries steadfastly resisted Him because of what His Presence would cost them. On this ground, Jesus exposed their true selves and motives because He always referred to the Scriptures of the prophets that foretold His coming to convict them of their deceit. This He did repeatedly, although He knew it was futile. Knowing their custom of shunning His Father's prophets, Jesus counted on their habitual reaction to His truth. He knew in their contempt for Him and His Father's way they would, as usual connive to destroy Him as an unwanted prophet. Jesus was certain their envy, fear, and resentment would crucify Him to remove Him as a threat. Unbeknownst to them, God had planned it that way, counting on their customary enmity to destroy His sacrificial Lamb. After all, how else was He going to get the Son of God out of the flesh and into hell where the real contest waited? Along the way though, they constantly disputed His doctrine, disparaged His nativity, and invalidated His lineage, cruelly undermining His purpose at every turn. The plan was working. These things His contemporaries did even with His stupefying works and unprecedented word that perfectly aligned with the Scriptures they claimed to revere. The reason their hypocrisy was predictable is that God knew how in love they were with the ceremonies that celebrated waiting for their Messiah. However, obsession with Moses' religious system kept them from recognizing the fulfillment of His word. All of these signs and tokens say the manifested Christ fulfilled every prophecy pertaining to Him in the wake of His children's[98] steadfast opposition to Him. At the appointed time, they would slaughter their God and King, what He and His Father wanted all along. Any sermon or teaching determined to remain true to the letter and the spirit of the Lord's word will revolve around or weave these truths throughout it. Discussion in the next chapter comes under the heading of Divine Communications, what prophecy actually is.

---

98 John 8:49.

[13]

Christ's Kingdom's Divine Communications Media

Divine Communications Media is an all-encompassing term that embodies the different ways the Most High God speaks to the world through His people. It embraces all prophecy, mysteries, revelations, doctrines, visions, and dreams transmitted from God to His messengers. Collectively, they publish His thoughts and will. Aside from the trances and face-to-face apparitions used to talk to His people, God's communications are primarily spoken, which justifies His unending need for divine communicants, especially the prophets. That is, except for His visions and dreams. The Holy Spirit is the medium of all of the conversations the Most High has with humans. That is, when He does not send angels to speak for Him. These are why the New Testament contains so many references to the Spirit, spiritual, and similar or related terms.

The word "spirit" shows up in Scripture more than 450 times and nearly 575 verses discuss the immaterial and celestial sides of the Maker's creation. Without question, the word spirit is the most difficult one to define on earth. While there are many synonyms for it, none of them accurately conveys the idea of the spirit world initiated and developed by the Creator, His Son, and the Holy Ghost. To populate their world, the Godhead created celestial citizens; angels, ministering spirits, seraphim, and cherubim. With them, He made the twenty-four elders, living creatures, demons, and numerous other beings innately invisible to the human eye. Just about every world religion's sacred text acknowledges a superseding world ruling this one. In doing so, they too agree that there is a world pre-existing[99] this one. God's world, heaven's, pre-existence substantiates the Continuum on so many fronts. In the end, it alone accredits its teachings and demands acknowledgment, and obeisance, from God's subordinate worlds. Its pre-primordial status means God's world has eons of experience, degrees of expertise, ages of successful governance and limitless innovations that transcend everything His subordinate realms can imagine. Long before the earth, the Most High perfected His supernal territories' flaws and inferiorities to secure later worlds' foundation. He personally certified His truths before affixing them to His Continuum and imposing them on His creatures down the line. Consequently, His tried and true word authenticates what He today verifies and approves as suitable for earth and its inhabitants. That pre-earth authentication is what this world calls foreknowledge.

The Lord's foreknowledge rests in heaven's experiences, which He filed away in its incontrovertible archives. Hebrews 12:22-24 undeniably declares that the earth is way down its Maker's creation chain, as do countless other passages. Ages of living and wrestling with the citizens of His eternity, watching their behavior, conduct, manifestations, and character taught the Lord well what makes for life and what makes for death. The health and stability of a civilization and the strengths and deteriorations of a nation are all quite clear to the Most High, and have been for endless ages. For example, take the accounts of the angels that left their first estate. The Lord's handling of their defection enhanced His timeless wisdom to equip Him well to contend with rebel humans and the vicious spirits that exploit them. Scripture says that He imprisoned rebel angels under the earth for final judgment. Perhaps that is why Jesus spoke so frankly about the hellish prison God made for the Devil and his angels. God's experiences with His heavenly creation are why the psalmist writes, *"The Words of Jehovah are pure words, like silver tried in a furnace of earth, purified seven times."* These truths further answer the proverbial question people ask about how the Lord knows everything; how He foreordained and predetermined everything for His creaturehood before time began. The Godhead has lived forever and was neither idle nor impotent during its kingdom's lifetime. The three live as one, created lives, observed their handiwork, and addressed the issues that arose from their created beings. Over the ages, the Almighty recorded every iota of what transpired in His world to reuse it all with the worlds and civilizations He planned to create. Excerpts from His notes and

---

99 This means to exist beforehand; to exist in a previous state; to exist prior to something or someone else; to precede; exist beforehand or prior to a certain point in time. To antedate; to precede; to exist earlier or before. To have existed before something else, to exist before the current activity commenced.

chronicles became this world's prophecies and revelations. With the spiritual cast of characters remaining unchanged, as far as God is concerned, it was a foregone conclusion that what is to be on earth has for Him and His world, already been.

Planning, something innate to every intelligent leader and enlightened society is not an earthly or human innovation. Along with recording everything that took place in His world, especially its citizens as they lived their lives, the Lord also planned how things would, and would not go there, or here. He did not write these down passively as an indifferent or unaffected observer. No, as Creator, He actively wrote what He observed, corrected, planned, and programmed in is handiwork. Extensive forethought went into what He ordained it to crave and subsist on and the ways it would self-perpetuate what He initiated. What God wrote for all of His creatures, He endowed them with the capacities to become or perform according to His will for them. Being more technologically advanced than this world, He imprinted, none of His vital information on inanimate objects like paper or stone, the way this physical world must. He left that up to this world's scribers to do. He furthermore did not use temporal implements to record it. The Lord embedded His will and purposes directly into everything He brought to life. Once He committed His will to the beings to be born or created, a means of enlightening and instructing them arose. The Maker endowed all His creatures with some semblance of His intelligence for living their lives. Additionally, His sovereignty encoded in each creature, the ability to discover who and what they are, the drive to know what they are to do in life, and in the highest of His creaturehood, the yearning to learn why He created them. All of these passions substantiate God and humanity's need for His Divine Communications. Heavens' accumulated excerpts make up the Christian Bible, even though it contains spiritual and natural subject matter. Its spiritual content forms the prophecies uttered by His messengers throughout the ages. The natural accounts narrate how heaven interfaced and interacted with the earth. The decision to include both come from the Lord's eternal archives and makes them divine communications.

God's heavenly library is vast and pertains to the myriad of societies occupying all His worlds. Relative to His creative aims and the lives He envisioned, the Lord deposited His wisdom in the physical world to encode its subliminal replication of His own. The selections He chose to compile the sacred texts summarize heaven's control over this world. What He released to mortals are but tiny excerpts of His voluminous atemporal[100] works. The divine library's fragments detached and deposited in the earth

---

100 Independent of time; timeless. Unaffected by time; timeless; permanent or unchanging.

typify His world's administration of earth. They are how He guides the planet's inhabitants throughout its generations. Any comprehensiveness displayed is due to their originally serving a vast and more advanced society than this one. As extracts of God's infinite government, earth's scaled down version targets issues emerging from a lesser civilization, a less complex one. God modified Adam's variation of His eternal codes for a species ordained to die, and be replaced by a higher order. The patterns Moses received on the mountain for instance and the models Jesus brought to earth to build His church are both extracts from God's never ending world. Revelation 12 shows the Almighty and His Christ have extensive dateless histories that experienced every possible connivance, His future worlds could concoct. They long ago completed the test cases for this planet, and any others, and recorded their outcomes future insight, guidance, and government. What earth and its diverse worlds are living are but decelerated, and downgraded replicates of what God and Christ already mastered. After assessing and approving what His world manifested, from His sphere, God legislated His divine solutions for the rest of their handiwork. This is how Genesis could declare what He did during the six days that He created the earth was good. From a human perspective, there appeared to be nothing to evaluate His creative works by, but in light of His eternal expertise, what came forth from His word fit preternity's design. Review how it reads in light of what has just been said. At the end of every creative act in Genesis, God says everything He created was good. From light to humanity, in His eyes, it was all good.

Seven times the Creator judged the quality of His work by declaring that it was good with the seventh time adding that it was very good. How could He make such assessments except He had a preexisting model and standard by which to measure it? If the earth was without form and void, where would that standard have come from in the first place? The answer has to be from another world, His world and establishes that the earth was not the beginning of His created works nor was mankind. Before ever the first word was spoken, divine blueprints and procedures guided every creative word's work and approved what materialized from God's mouth.

THE MESSIAH'S ETERNAL KINGDOM & ITS RECORDS

In the ways The Messiah is vital to God's Continuum, so too are His interminable kingdom and its citizens. His dominion precedes the rest of creation and extends His rule and reign to the rest of His worlds. Jesus' Godhead status compelled Him to construct a prerecorded model to operate and regulate everything that happens here on earth. To keep Himself in control of all creation, the Lord timed its utilities beforehand and pre-appointed its operations according to His will. He prepared this world's facilities outside of time, in His world, and preprogrammed them all to work by seminally embedding in it His foreknowledge, wisdom, and technologies. A cagey tactic maneuvers every being to, compulsively choose His options. Since in His world, there are no incidents and no accidents, then nothing that happens on earth is incidental or accidental. When it comes to the Almighty and His sovereignty, it should be accepted that whatever occurs on earth, regardless of how phenomenal or far-fetched it is, first took place in the Creator's world. That is the premise of the Continuum's teachings. If every possibility or potentiality did not originate with the Lord Most High, then the "omni" attributes ascribed to God and Christ are mythical at best and erroneous at the least. If they are actually not the Alpha and Omega, if Jesus is not the first and the last, the beginning and the ending of everything that was, is, and will be then where did Christianity come from and what made it survive and dominate so long? If they are not the Creators of any world, then they certainly could never have initiated what happens in this one, or verify if there are any others beyond this vast empty universe. If that is the case, the Lord, His Christ, and the Spirit are out of touch with what takes place in heaven and on earth and are woefully incapable of addressing their issues. It also means they are covertly misleadingly accountable to a power above them. If any of this is true, these circumstances mean mortal humans enter this planet hopeless and helpless, propelled by and for nothing. However, if on the other hand, the opposite is indeed true, then God scrupulously calculated, prearranged, and deliberately automated everything that was, is, and will ever be. His sovereign expertise painstakingly decided all that is to be up to the end of this age and beyond. The numerous books, records, and registries the Scriptures almost casually mention encompass the heavens and the earth. Biblical references to them indicate that there is a plan and a Master Planner who had determined how life began and will end and begin again. There is no way to belong to the Lord Jesus Christ, to be a part of His body and not realize the two most fundamental things about Him. First, that He is a King, a King over every king in God's creation and its only Sovereign Monarch. Second, that His is a kingdom and not just an everlasting organization or a mere organism, but an indomitable world that can never be destroyed. Daniel saw and declared it this way, as did other prophets. They received their revelations from the Lord's ageless archives that are still being unveiled as life on the planet forges ahead.

ETERNITY'S BOOKS & RECORDS LOGGED IN THE CONTINUUM

The purpose of the following information is to uncover the Lord's up to the second recordkeeping systems. It supports the fact that nothing is new under the sun and that God is intimately aware of every aspect of His kingdom, its inhabitants and doings. It has already been established that the Lord's world is a kingdom, one that has conquered and outlasted its enemies from time immemorial. To govern it, He wrote books for every situation that according to the Bible make up a significant part of His Eternal Continuum. The books that Scripture talks about are references, revelations, records, and registries. They are also plans, destinies, judgments, testimonies, and of course laws. Beyond these, heaven's books include the history; current and future events of everything the Lord made, and document His own past, present and future with His creation. The Godhead registered every life it created and regardless of each one's nature, all was entered in its books. The Lord's books are where prophecy comes from and how He stays ahead of His handiwork. Remember, He is outside of time, which is how He remains ahead of it, and not time bound. In keeping with His pattern, God continually required Israel to write everything it lived, lost, won, conquered, and captured. His commanding them to do so mirrors His own method of tracking what goes on in His worlds. Scripture identifies numerous books that show the King of glory takes nothing for granted, but predetermined, crafted, and engineered everything to take place on earth long beforehand. The Bible names 60 specific types of books that the Lord originated and continues to apply to the earth and its inhabitants. The books provide insight into what is contained in His archives relating to the earth. The types of books He names further clarify the Continuum's revelations and how the Lord honors, and keeps to His revealed word, using their writings to guide His generations. As heavenly data, the Lord's books contain His church's unfolding record, even if prognostically.[50] A final note about prophecy has to do with when God issues a new word, particularly one that is legislative in context. Scripture notes, occasions when He invokes heaven and earth to witness what He prophecies or decrees as if their testimonies are the most enduring chronicle of His interventions. Why would He do something so seemingly inane unless they are occupied. Summoning them as witnesses reveal His reliances on unseen forces, dispersed throughout creation for supervisory, preventative or rescue purposes, to record what He says.[51]

VISIONS & THE CONTINUUM

Any discussion of the Lord's divine communications would be incomplete if it did not address the rich visions He gives. Ordinary visions are mental or spiritual depictions of an otherwise immaterial object or event. They generate images in people's minds based on what they believe or desire, understand or want to achieve. Visions as mental images form the most fertile part of the thought life. People visualize what they think, know, recall, or conjure. Visions fall into two main types: natural or human, spiritual or supernal. Natural visions are what ordinary people cast in their minds. Supernatural visions are those that come from outside the human realm and are otherworldly. Supernal visions are beyond this world too, but they are decidedly celestial and divine, not just otherworldly or ethereally inspired. While often more silent than prophetic utterances, visions serve well as vital communication vehicles for getting the Most High's thoughts from His mind to human heads and hearts. Prophecies often come by way of visions or at the least; they are so generated within the prophet. These must be interpreted before they can be uttered intelligently. Visionary elements include foresight: to see beforehand; insight: to see into or beneath the surface; imaging to draw mental pictures, and manifestations: a spiritual being projecting images in the mind. Visions can be experienced asleep or awake and the more powerful ones can *entrance* the visionary. That is, they bring the one having the vision into a trance.

Scripture mentions visions more than 100 times. Often they are paired with or enfolded in dreams, which are mentioned more than 95 times. Both are essential media of divine communications and effective tools of human insight. God uses visions and dreams because, pictures are more universally understood than words. Words require interpretation while visions mainly rely on instruction and description. The one having the vision simply needs to know where the sight fits and how to use it. The Almighty God introduced Himself to Abram in a vision. Numbers 12 says the Lord makes Himself known to prophets in a vision and speaks to them in dreams. Job 4:13 says that night visions are how the Almighty generally speaks to all people, to confirm that everyone has the capacity to dream and/or envision. For example, in a dream, God rebuked Abimelech for taking Sarah from Abraham to place her in his harem. To validate Job's comment, the Lord warned Laban in a dream not to continue to defraud Jacob, who experienced his most profound encounter with his father's God in a vision transported by a dream. Numbers 24:4 says the Almighty, for the first time, drew Balaam, a mercenary prophet into visions to receive revelations he had never before received from the lesser gods he served. However, the word trance better defines Balaam's visionary experience because it was quite dramatic. Iddo, David's seer alongside Nathan the king's chief prophet received his divine messages in visions. Nathan on the other hand received his prophecies verbally.

Ezekiel likewise received his divine communications from God through visions. The Lord appeared to him with His heavenly entourage in a vision and caught the prophet up to Him through them as well. God used Ezekiel to prophesy away from Babylon by catching him up in a vision. Furthermore, hardly anyone in Christian prophetics today does not know about Issachar's sons who had understanding of times and seasons. No doubt, much of their information came by way of dreams and visions to make their divine communications expertise as practical as it was spiritual, which earned them much acclaim. God's most notable visioning prophets include the Major Prophets Isaiah and Daniel. Others include Zechariah, Obadiah, and Nahum among the minor ones. Like Iddo, Scripture distinguishes Zechariah the prophet as a visionary—a chozeh--prophet who understood visions, dreams and could ably interpret them. The Lord's dream and vision motif continue all the way up to Matthew's Gospel where Jesus' true Father protects His Son by guiding His adopted father Joseph through dreams. Acts chapters 9 and 10 say the Lord by His Holy Spirit continues to convey His thoughts and issue nonverbal instructions through dreams and visions. Paul's conversion, Ananias' ministry to Paul, Cornelius and the angel that visited him, Peter's dispatch to Cornelius, and Paul's Macedonian call were all through visions and dreams.

Dreamers, like visionaries, have keen sight faculties that transcend their natural organs to peer into the world behind this one. They are also astute interpreters that translate into human language what they see with their spiritual eye. To break through humanity's inherent dullness and blindness about Him, God speaks in different ways as Hebrews 11 says, to mirror Job 4:13. He uses them so that the literate and illiterate can hear and speak for him to their respective groups. He also uses visual communications to break through all human boundaries to enable the closed and open minded, those that know Him and those who do not know Him to hear from their Maker at pivotal times in their lives. To promote these ends, the Lord constructed prophets that hear His voice in ways others do not, or prophets to see Him and His world more than they hear Him. Seer is the name for the latter group and it indicates how they most often receive the word of the Lord. To avail Himself of their faculties,

God depicts what He wants to say to seers more than He voices it because their vision faculties spiritually supersede their auditory ones. The major visions of the Bible are:

Scripture's 46 Major Facts About Its Recorded Visions

Genesis15:1	God's Visionary (Depicted) Word To Abram.
Numbers 12:6	God's Disclosure Of Visions Being The Main Way He Acquaints His Prophets With Himself.
Numbers 24:4, 16	Balaam Receives Visions From The Most High For The First Time.
1 Samuel 3:1	The Lord's Infrequent Visions To His People Before Samuel's Ministry.
1 Samuel 3:15	God Introduces Himself To Samuel In A Vision.
2 Samuel 7:17	God Sends A Prophecy Through Nathan To David By Way Of A Vision.
2 Chronicles 32:32	God Communicates With Isaiah Through Visions.
Job 20:8; 33:15	Visions Are A Frequent Means Of Divine Communications.
Psalm 89:19	God Speaks To The Godly In Visions.
Proverbs 29:18	Visions From God Restrain People.
Isaiah 21:2	Visions Are Sometimes Grievous.
Isaiah 22:1	Visions Sometimes Appear As Burdens.
Isaiah 29:7	Visions Often Travel In Dreams.
Jeremiah 14:14	Visions Can Be Lying.
Jeremiah 23:16	Visions Can Be Conjured In The Heart.
Lamentations 2:9	God Can Withhold Visions From His Prophets.
Ezekiel 7:13	Visions Can Pertain To The Entire Multitude.
Ezekiel 7:26	Visions Are Often Sought By Prophets.
Ezekiel 8:4	The God Of Israel Appears In A Vision.
Ezekiel 11:24	God's Spirit Transports People In Visions.
Ezekiel 12:23	Every Vision's Words Have Appointed Times To Manifest.
Ezekiel 12:24	Visions Can Be Vain.
Ezekiel 12:27	Visions Can Prophesy Things Afar Off.
Ezekiel 13:7	Vain Visions Facilitate Lying Divination.
Daniel 2:19	God Reveals His Secrets In Vision.
Daniel 7:2	The Spirit World Shows Itself In A Vision.

Daniel 8:16	Sometimes Angels Reveal Visions.
Daniel 9:24	Visions And The Prophets Are Treated As Synonymous.
Daniel 10:1	Visions Can Be Concentrated In Certain Prophets.
Daniel 10:16	Visions, Though Immaterial, Can Cause Physical Sensations.
Daniel 11:4	Visions Must Be Physically Or Materially Established.
Obadiah 1:1	This Prophet's Words Came Primarily Through Vision.
Micah 3:6	The Lord Punishes Prophets By Depriving Them Of His Visions.
Nahum 1:1	Nahum Is A Prophet Of Visions.
Habakkuk 2:2	Habakkuk Is A Prophet Of Visions.
Zechariah 13:4	Many Prophets Must Prophesy Through Vision.
Luke 24:23	Angels Appear In Visions.
Acts 9:10	The Lord Instructs And Guides Through Visions.
Acts 9:12	God Prepares The Way For His Interventions And Instructions Through Visions.
Acts 10:19; 16:9; 18:19	The Apostles Too Are Instructed Through Visions.
Acts 26:19	God Summons Ministers With Visions.
2 Chronicles 9:29	Many Divine Messengers Receive Visions.
2 Chronicles 26:5; Daniel 1:17	Prophets Can Specialize In Interpreting Visions.
Ezekiel 8:3	God Transports Prophets In Visions.
Hosea 12:10	Visions And Dreams Are The Staples Of Prophets' Ministries.
Joel 2:28; Acts 2:17	Visions And Dreams Are Staples Of The New Creation Church.

Understanding visions and dreams aids appreciation of their importance to God's Eternal Continuum. It shows how those with little to no spiritual aptitude or awakening can still hear from God and connect what He says today to what is encased in it. Scripture further says on this subject that God uses angels to transmit dreams and visions, and to interpret them, once more reinforcing their vital role in the Continuum.

THE CONTINUUM AS A GUARD

The Continuum exists and continues to guard God's purposes and carry out His will because of what the preceding lists relate about Him. His words are not just His thoughts sounded aloud. They are how He <u>does everything</u>. The spoken word is also how the Lord empowers His handiwork to behave according to His will. The charts at the end, cover all of the areas God's divine communications address and demonstrate how He, through the Continuum, connects other worlds to His own. They also explain how continuity, consistency, and contiguity all unite to facilitate His perpetual rule of all creation. Continuum messengers should respect the numerous branches of God's kingdom and actively stir up His people's faith in them. They can only do this when Continuum knowledge and persuasive communications congeals to impart its sage wisdom. However, there is one more kingdom worth mentioning because it is instrumental to the Continuum. It is the Beast's Kingdom mentioned in John's Apocalypse. Revealing it is integral to the mysteries that the Lord steadily unveiled to earth since before the world began, as its redemptive elements. His absolute end time eschatology of the world to dispose of its sin is the reasons Christ brought John into His apocalypse in the first place. Like the Devil, since they are intrinsically one and the same, the beast and his false prophet justify God's Continuum. The dissatisfactions that sparked the Great War in Heaven, discussed already, started it all. Down through the ages, Satan's banishment and his seduction of one third of the angels to sin with him propel it forward. They are the constant driving its momentum. Each generation born into sin; the globe caught in the grip of its law and death, and God's merciful determination to save the souls implanted in His Son before the foundation of the world all depend on the Continuum to see His plan through to the end. The Continuum is so deeply entrenched in the Almighty's future that Jesus already knows the rewards that He holds in store for those who endure to the end. He can promise this because Isaiah's prophecy says that He calls the end from the beginning. What could such a statement mean, but that God is pursuing the outcomes that have nothing to do with what His creatures believe to be His objectives? God envisions from His outcomes and then objectively plots the courses and offsets their complications to guarantee they come to pass.

[14]

God's Mysteries

The word mystery befits this study because God's Eternal Continuum is filled with them. If it held no mysteries, then the Continuum itself could not exist, because nothing futuristic would be contained within it, and the future is all a mystery. God's mysteries, as Paul uses the term, emphasizes the secret arts, trades, ministries, and practices that characterize Christianity and separate it from other religions and their gods'. A mystery is a hidden purpose or counsel reserved for specially selected trustees and confidantes. God hides His mysteries from the godly to prevent their indiscretion; from the ungodly to condemn their sin and contain their deception; from leaders wishing to deform His government, and from special servants that demonstrate the inability to protect His privacy enough to be trusted with His confidences. His mysteries, particularly the most profound ones are reserved for His proven confidantes. Enoch, Abraham, Moses, Joshua, Elijah, Jesus' three closest apostles, and Paul are Bible figures who fit this description. Enoch walked with God so closely that he could no longer stay on the planet and God could no longer bear to leave him here. God calls Abraham His friend because he took up the Most High's causes and carried out His wishes to the letter. The Lord rebuked Aaron and Miriam about Moses with whom He spoke face-to-face. Joshua entered the tabernacle at a young age and did not come out until it was time for him to succeed Moses. Elijah was so close to the Lord that he did not see death at all. Peter, James, and John were privy to the Savior's divine form and the eternality of Moses and Elijah. These are just a few examples of people who so pleased the Lord that He wanted more than a duty bound relationship with them. An enhanced affection inspired the release of His hidden mysteries to them. From the Lord's perspective, what is a mystery?

The Latin word for <u>mystery</u> is *mysterium* that come from the Greek *mysterion* (usually in the plural, the word mystery). The word as the Bible and its writers understood it fundamentally defined a secret rite or doctrine unveiled to an initiate. It comes from the roots of *myein*. It means "to close, shut" or "kept hidden", except for the eyes of initiates who earn the privilege of seeing, learning, and handling a closed society's sacred rite. The word *mystery* further and most surprisingly means handcraft, trade, or art. Originally, an alteration of *the Ministerium*, the Latin word for ministry, a mystery refers to a secret knowledge or rite that equips and appoints to a private office that grants access to its professional practitioners. In this context, it identifies the specialized arts and praxes that operate them. From the Online Etymology Dictionary, a mystery earlily[101] meant a service, occupation, office, and ministry. That is, prior to the Church excessively spiritualizing everything pertaining to it, this is what was intended. Before then, a mystery had as much to do with actions, as it did with the theories that directed them. To conceal something as mysterious was back in time to confine its arts and practices along with its wisdom and knowledge. Thus, the word mystery was often treated as synonymous with the word ministry because at the time, the mental and manual were viewed as mutually inclusive of each other. Take, as a for instance James' epistolic insight in 1:22-25. There he links knowing with doing in James 2:20 and 26:

> "But be ye doers of the word, and not hearers only, deceiving your own selves. For if any be a hearer of the word, and not a doer, he is like unto a man beholding his natural face in a glass: For he beholdeth himself, goeth his way, and straightway forgetteth what manner of man he was. But whoso looketh into the perfect law of liberty, and continueth therein, he being not a forgetful hearer, but a doer of the work, this man shall be blessed in his deed."

Clearly, James has a strong grasp of the correlation between what one knows and what one does with that knowledge. He makes a similar connection in James 2:17. These two verses say, *"faith without works is dead."* Ministry then is a major objective of mysteries; at least that is how it is in God's mind. He sees no profit in pure philosophical knowledge because He is a doer and His words are His *manifesters* and performers. His wisdom answers why the Ephesians 4:11 ministers are to manifest their ministries practically, with Paul designating the "equipping of the saints for the work of the ministry" as their end goal. Way before time, God hid the Church's ministries,

---

101 Earlily means at or near the beginning of a period of time or course of events or before the usual or expected time. Vocabulary.com.

giftings, and operations in Christ. He only divulged a small portion of them when He appeared to Israel. Prior to this, in Psalm 68:18 He spoke of human gifts in veiled terms when in public. Deuteronomy 29:29 speaks to the wisdom of God's secrecy that underscores His kingdom's ecclesial ministries. As much as the Continuum contains and guards theological and doctrinal as well as revelatory information, it also guarded the Church's mystery and ministry link. Spiritual gifts are supernal and temporal from those of the earth because The Messiah's needs are different and are hidden until the Holy Spirit discloses them. They are concealed pending the person's call to enter God's service. Until then, "The secret things belong to Jehovah our God, but the revealed things belong to us and to our sons forever, so that we may do all the words of this Law".

A mystery, *mysterium* its original, further defines mastery. Judges 20:18 exemplify it in this context. The Lord names the tribe of Judah as the one to lead the war effort only when His army is ready to fight it. Until then, He conceals a particular servant's role in the strategy, from everyone. Another example is 1 Samuel 14:3 that describe Jonathan's skills that qualified him for what he is to undertake. Both examples reveal God's mysteries as intellectual though confidential information. They explain His classified agency service's intelligence. In this respect, think of the high-level positions in some organizations that restrict complex and sensitive or volatile information to those best qualified to handle it. That is, those who can properly and safely use it to their entity's advantage. Prudently revealed information, strengthens the secrecy connection between a mystery and ministry. The Savior employs mysteries as part of His commission. They exhibit His sovereign omniscience of His people's varying stages of readiness to be used by Him in any way. He foreknows who can do what because He deposited their capabilities in them before conception. Knowing the endowments He gave each person guides His knowledge of their makeup and determines how He communicates with them. For example, Jesus speaks in parables to the masses because He knows their spiritual and fidelity limitations. As enthusiastic as they may be about what He says, the masses He knows are not in any way awakened to what He came to do. They cannot comprehend or execute what He has in mind for them to do with His profound wisdoms. To guard His mysteries, He reserves His clearest explanations for His apostles and those on par with them. On earth, when He was alone with them, He trusted them with His majesty and instructed them personally in His pre-ascension class. As the Risen Lord, Jesus gave the remaining eleven apostles specialized training on the kingdom of God, the most pervasive of all His mysteries and the backbone of God's Eternal Continuum. Furthermore, He educated the eleven *before* appointing Matthias to replace Judas in His commission as if the deepest mysteries shared with the originals are not to be unveiled to His newest apostle.

The secrets Jesus brought to earth with Him and those He shares by His Holy Spirit in the future include how His church will live, learn, and work for Him. These mysteries were then, and still today, remain guarded for the select few who consider Him and His destiny as precious as His world does. Safety and profitability are why He preserves His profoundest revelations for a chosen few in any generation. The Savior knows what His powers and wisdom can do for His people and against His efforts in the hands of the unscrupulous. Due to contending with the adversaries of His truth, since before antiquity, the Godhead would rather His church grope for truth than for His powerful wisdoms to fall into the hands of the wrong messengers. To safeguard His most detrimental knowledges from Satan, God would just as soon bury His deepest spiritualities and leave His people to languish in ignorance for decades, than risk His complex endeavors being distorted and diverted to those who hate Him. History shows He has opted to do so again and again throughout the ages. God's judiciousness deems the success of His everlasting campaign more crucial to His worlds than He does sensationalizing His body with pointless revelation. To secure His operations, He cordons off His spiritual wisdom to the naïve, so they do not frustrate His most sensitive ventures. He also does it to avoid reckless dissemination of His plans that can hinder His actions, or premature publication of volatile intelligence. To prevent both potential crises, the Lord shrewdly enshrouds what He does in a mystery to hide it from those who would impede His visions. Examine some of the areas of wisdom and knowledge the Bible classifies as mysteries and imagine the vulnerabilities the Lord has to cover to further His platform.

It has been shown previously that the word mystery has a two-pronged definition. It defines God's spiritual and ministerial secrets and the best way to use them in His church. His word says He hid each mystery for its appointed time in earth's history. To access His secrets on earth contemporaneously, the Lord buried His secrets as resources in human vessels. Hidden talents are the buried treasure the Lord stashed in the clay vessels that Paul mentions in Corinthians. Every dispensation of mysteries the Lord has been assigned to the generation to give Him the most profit from them.[102] He does this to assure His people derive the greatest benefit from His heavenly blessings and to garner for Himself the greatest reward from His spiritual and

---

102 Consider Jesus' parable of the talents and the mina.

natural deposits as possible. What He hid way back in the foundation of the world, Jesus unlocked when He came to earth. It is what His Isaiah 53:8 generation enjoys. The Holy Spirit brought heaven's powers to earth with Him. Eternal energy, mobility, and light all enable His predestined generations' productive use of His Creator bestowments. The technological era, as planned spreads His wisdom wider and faster than any other age before it.

Throughout Scripture, it is shown that the Most High earmarks future generations for His kingdom's special providences. Jesus brought those providences to earth within Himself as part of His plan to defeat and evict Satan's regime from this world. As His prophets foretold, God's far-reaching salvation converts the penitent to His eternal life and redeems His chosen ones from among the Jews and the Gentiles. Study the Continuum's Mystery table for the Bible's generalized mysteries to identify them for those who would uphold His Continuum. Examining the list carefully suggests the right ministry training and education programs the Lord needs to finish His work on earth. Most programs today limit themselves to the Church and forget that Christ is King of kings over the whole earth and not just the Great Shepherd of the Flock. His global dominion means more diverse readiness programs are needed to equip His saints to go into all the world and truly disciple the nations. Along with eternity's mysteries is their hiding places or packaging, the secrets. God's mysteries are protected by the secrets that have been kept hidden since the foundation of the world, for such a time as this.

GOD'S SECRETS

The word *secret* refers to what is private, isolated, and exclusive. It defines what is not for the public because it is personal property. Along with weaving His mysteries throughout the Continuum, the Lord also submerged in them His secrets. Sometimes these two are synonymous, and at other times, they are quite different from each other. For instance, a secret may not be a mystery to the one who knows it as a lone individual with knowledge of it. Mysteries tend to belong to a group and are only secret to the uninitiated. Mysteries may hold secrets, but not all secrets are a mystery, although they too can be mysteries that are just treated differently. It is usually a group, organization, or field's proprietary knowledge, veiled because it is more complex than that which is open to the public. A mystery can also be a classified secret that is a simple code, a single piece of information, or a private matter. Secrets can be classified and yet not be mysterious to those authorized to know them. A collection of secrets can be the mysterious body of knowledge a closed community or secret society embraces as its way of life. It holds the key to the principles, and practices it believes protects and benefits it. Another thing to know about a mystery is that it contains more than hidden knowledge for knowledge's sake.

Mysterious knowledge has working components attached to it. They include practices, habits, customs, behaviors, and protocols as well as principles. In ancient times, mysteries included the trade secrets and the how to's of a business, group or venture. Divine secrets are mysteries kept for immortals, God's celestial beings, that a normal human has to earn (or win) the right to access or learn. Paul's account of his visit to heaven and its aftermath buffeting meant to subdue his pride is of this sort. His divine encounter is why he calls what happened to him and what he heard as unlawful. Isaiah's visit to God's altar and other such biblical accounts are examples of the divine mysteries of the Lord's word that He elects, to share with worthy humans. What makes them secret is the mysteries are always outside humans' sphere, its natural understanding and intelligences. The chart lists some divine secrets to be found in the Scriptures. It portrays the secret side of mysteries as the Lord characterizes them in His Scriptures.

THE REVELATIONS OF GOD

Another aspect of the Lord's Continuum worth highlighting is its manifold revelations. Ephesians says they are what He gives to His apostles and prophets to disseminate throughout the world. One Ephesians passage implies a revelation is a spirit. More precisely, they are what the Holy Spirit releases to disclose portions of heaven's knowledge of Jesus Christ God's Son. The same epistle, has Paul saying he received his knowledge of God's mysteries by revelation. Lastly, along this vein is the Apostle John's entire apocalypse. It is called in English, the Revelation of Jesus Christ the Son of God. Apocalypse is one English term for the word revelation. John's revelation of Jesus Christ is a meticulous yet a broad panorama of all God's ages and works. It emphasizes Jesus Christ because of His supreme place in Creator God's life. Jesus as His first begotten fills every progenic role an offspring can fill for His omnipotent Father. The Almighty's narrative depicts Him as His warrior, commander of his hosts, co-creator, slaughtered sacrifice, and redeeming ruler of his worlds. These are but a few of the roles the Lord Jesus filled for His Father in heaven before taking upon Himself flesh. Without His Holy Spirit to unveil His eternal record of service to the Most High however, none of it could be known. It would be a secret in God's world and a mystery to this one. That is why understanding the applied meaning of the word *revelation* is necessary. There is just no other way without the spirit of revelation and knowledge for a human to discover what took place before this world, or what is constantly transpiring behind it today. Earth is slow, its rotations are plodding. Its movements are largely pedestrian, still greatly dependent upon the wheel. All of this is to say that peering outside itself is difficult because viewing beyond its galaxies is prevented. Additionally, when God speaks His words and will to His prophets, He is revealing some aspect of His impenetrable mind and Creator experience to them.

For a rich appreciation of the Lord's revelations, most people want to know where they come from and how He transmits them from heaven to earth. For starters, divine revelations are not abstract ramblings from the Godhead. They are genuine divulgences of concrete information from its eternal archives. Meaning by this that, God's secrets and mystery revelations are not vain conjurations but are truth disclosures from His heavenly library. When God shares His thoughts with His world, He is as much recalling His past experiences with His creation as He is enlightening them on what is transpiring at the time of the communication. Past, present or future, the Lord unlocks a mystery to reveal His knowledge of what is to come. Mysteries are a significant arm of His foreknowledge. It is why previous sections give so much attention to the books He wrote and the records He filed over the ages of His existence. Basically, these explanations define the core meanings of the word revelation. Simply put, it is an uncovered truth of something that need only be unveiled to circulate as public knowledge. All that Scripture conveys about its revelations portrays them as realities the Lord unveils, or unseals, at His discretion. No one answers it better than the Son of God. Jesus announces, and reveals Himself and His Father at will, to whomever they will, whenever He deems it prudent to do so. Paul later says that the Lord reveals His Son in His saints. These and other truths are what the Almighty reveals when He so desires. In the Old Testament, the Lord usually pairs His revelations with His secrets. He does this particularly when He reveals His secrets to His prophets.[103] The church's single instrument of divine revelation is the Holy Spirit, whom Jesus says takes what is His as Messiah and shows it to His family.

The Continuum's revelations cover the hidden secrets about Jesus Christ, what the human heart conceals, God and His strengths, God's wrath, and righteous judgments. Other revelatory mysteries include the Lord's impartation of faith to His saints, His dispensations to His apostles and prophets, and Paul's mysterious gospel

---

103 Amos 3:7-10.

of Jesus Christ. In addition to these, there are the revelatory mysteries of Jesus' appearing with His angels, sin's iniquities, and the mysteries that reveal the wicked creatures in God's kingdom. Besides them, there is the mystery of God's salvation, Old Testament prophecies and, the saints' eternal glory with the Savior. As has been shown, mysteries go hand in hand with Christian ministries. In addition to God's mysteries, secrets, and revelations, the Continuum houses their collective repository, the doctrines of God.

THE DOCTRINES OF GOD

God's Doctrines are among the primary substances of the Continuum's teachings. They set the standard for truth and lies, authenticity and heresy. The Lord Jesus' doctrine was effective because it remained true to His Father's eternal premises. He and His apostles did more with God's truths than preach them. They reasoned with their opposers and seekers and allayed people's fears over their salvation and relationship with God. Messianic doctrine answered enigmatic questions, solved life's thorny issues, and increased people's understanding of God as their heavenly Father. Jesus made Him real, feelable, and desirable. He ignited a fervent interest in the Almighty that His nation had not felt for decades. They pursued Him because He made His Father make sense to them, which created a voracious appetite in them to learn more about Him, His world, their future. The outcome of His teaching is what sound doctrine produces. Those who hold to it grow in every regard. Conversely, when these qualities are absent in a believer, it is because sound doctrine such as that which makes for good sense, better yet God sense, is lacking.

Throughout the New Testament, God's recurring admonishment is that His doctrine is sound. Paul exhorts Timothy and Titus to assess what they and others teach according to His definition of the word. For instance, when it comes to Moses' Law, Paul tells Timothy that God never meant His Law for the righteous[104] but for all those predisposed to sin, ungodliness, rebellion, idolatry, and infidelity to Him. Unlike modern Christian teachers, he knew that the conflict people had with God's law, lay in their own character flaws and not in its inherent righteousness, or rigidity. Paul's words say that if it were not for destructive behaviors, the world would not need laws.[105] What is his answer to his generation's godlessness? It is sound doctrine consistent with the glorious gospel committed to his trust. In 2 Timothy 4:3, he also explains the

---

104 1 Timothy 1:19.
105 See 1 Timothy 1:8, 10.

real cause of believers' aversion to God's sound doctrine. It is the lusts of their flesh, conditioned by their saturation and fascination, with this world. Paul's use of it resonates with Ezekiel's wisdom in chapter 33 of his prophecy. He follows his comments with a description of the lengths that avoiders of God's truth will go to escape His conviction. He further outlines their chosen method of soothing their discomforts when their wants clash with God's will. People disinclined to God's way of life will ignore and reject his teachers and find doctrinal alternatives to approve their error. When it comes to Titus and Timothy, Paul assigns the Lord's bishops the responsibility of holding fast to His sound doctrine as if this ecclesial authority possesses a peculiar capacity to recognize and defend it.

POPULARITY OF DOCTRINE IN SCRIPTURE

More than 50 times, Scripture accentuates the word *doctrine*, beginning with Moses in Deuteronomy 32:2. Logically, as the nation's first notable prophet Moses is His most likely *doctrinator* because he delivered His people from Egyptian bondage. In the passage referenced, his words blend prophecy, legislation, warning, and instruction. In a lengthy speech that is replete with subtleties and nuance wisdom, Moses coaxes the Lord's people to live their liberated lives as Yahweh commands. In the discourse, he likens his doctrine to a gentle rain. The words Moses says distill as the dew. Using the softest of tones and the tenderest of expressions possible, Moses rehearses God's word to insight the nation in His ways. He hopes they glean from them how to get the best out of their Covenant God to prolong their statehood and its prosperity. Tapping into Yahweh's mind, Moses' teaching instructs His people in His ways. He enfolds his own and their past experiences into it, speaking to them as a parent does to a child about to go out on his own. Doctrines' goal, then, from this example, is to impart God's wisdom to His children so they court His blessings and not His judgments, to their chagrin, and His grief.

Later examples of God's doctrines and His messenger's duty to them include Job, Proverbs, and a long line of prophets. As a case in point, Job's friends' use the term *leqach* for doctrine, Job 11:4. It means instruction, learning delivered by fair speech. The word includes, according to Brown-Driver-Briggs' Hebrews Definitions, the thing taught, subject matter, the teacher's power to persuade and the effects of transforming learners by that persuasion. Taking learners from the unenlightened to the insightful are likewise meant. Proverbs' Lady Wisdom says her laws constitute good doctrine or teaching; what the New Testament calls sound doctrine. In wisdom's case, sage counsel strengthens her instruction and gives wholesome reasons for heeding her laws. Isaiah, on the other hand, uses a different word for a doctrine that underscores its use in news reports, rumors, and announcements. His type of doctrine equates to a public announcement meant to benefit the community. Its teaching elements are not just for learners interested in increasing their knowledge. Instead of preparing its audiences for professional or personal use, Isaiah's[106] doctrine emphasizes public notifications made to curtail misbehaviors and provoke godly obediences. Jeremiah's synonymic choice for the word doctrine is the Hebrew *musar*. He uses the term to zero in on the doctrine's chastisement, reproof, warning, and rebuke, and discipline. The goals of such lessons are correction and restraint. Jeremiah wants to reform God's people to bind them again to their true God. His powerful message seeks to stimulate the conviction that yields repentance. More than prophesying, despite being a prophet, Jeremiah's retraining is stern and borderline severe to goad God's people to return to His ways and will. He knows what they are risking despite their being unable to see it and is fiery because he wants to avert the crises that the Lord has shown him will come upon his nation as a result.

The New Testament primarily uses one word for doctrine, *didache* for the acts of instructing and the instruction itself. This word covers the learner and the teacher to show both bring something worthwhile to the education process. Jesus as God's Word incarnate, doctrination figures prominently in His Christian conversion portfolio. Jesus is the consummate embodiment of His Father's will, thoughts, determinations, and objectives. This He conveys to His followers in the form of doctrine that is called sound because of its therapeutic properties. It heals, restores, and preserves. Look at Luke 13:32 and Matthew 10:1. Sound doctrine, the Lord and His Spirit show are essential for Christian stability and prosperity in this life and the triumph that secures them in the next.

THE AUTHORITY OF GOD'S WORD

Jesus as God's Word personified exhibits His most outstanding quality, apart from His miracles and His teaching. Jesus constantly awed people with His wisdom and authority. When they praised His word for being with authority, it was because they considered it to be sound like their author would use and not a reciter, like their scribes. Jesus' word was so commanding that it disturbed the invisible forces listening to them. Hiding in secret until His truth incited them, the unclean spirits insidi-

---

106 Isaiah 28:9 and 24.

ously lurking in the peoples' souls manifested whenever He spoke. When they did, the Lord Jesus expelled them from their human bodies. The Messiah's word was potent because His doctrine was sound. Its soundness purged all defects, flaws, and contaminants from His teaching that could make His doctrine counterproductive to the hearers. His unyielding faith freed His doctrine of the deviations that cause God's righteousness to break-down in Him and in those who heard Him. Jesus' convictions engendered confidence in Him, and its truth made it logical. It filled His audiences with good judgment and common sense. His, was the error free doctrine because of His allegiance to His Father's prophecy and revelation Continuum. Jesus stayed within the Continuum that He initiated with the prophets that prophesied His manifestation on earth as the Son of Man. These features proved to be the source of His words' power and exemplify why they yielded such extraordinary results. Learning and working within the Lord's Continuum is how to tell if a doctrine is God and Christ's or not. As a rule, Continuum teachings always provoke responses from God's seen and unseen listeners as neither can passively listen to them and do nothing afterward.

A good question to clarify at this point is what makes a doctrine sound? The answer to it is Jesus' words in John 7:16, 17. When asked the question, He answered that His doctrine was not new, but the teachings the Father has been speaking to His people since time began. Thus, sound doctrine is teaching that correlates with all that the Lord revealed from heaven to earth. It intelligently weaves eternal wisdom, articulates God's purposes, and imparts the spiritual substances required for transformation into Christ's image and likeness. God's Eternal Continuum holds the sum of His empowerments and warnings. It lays out God's instructions for godly living, and equips for eternal life. Continuum revelations charge and counsel God's people with His timeless directives to prepare them to exist as immortal beings. The Continuum's mysteries, the doctrines it presents, and the secrets it unfolds all emanate from the ancient prophecies that issued God's promises. Tried and proven over the ages, Continuum doctrines heal and metamorphosize those who receive it. The doctrine arm of the Continuum shows up again in Act 2:42-47 that says Christ's apostles' doctrine sustained the believers and protected those who remained within it.

In Ephesians 4:14, Paul warns his believers against accepting anything he and the named apostles or those that they verified did not preach or teach as God's doctrine. He let them know that there are those who use intellectual knowledge to seduce believers into defecting from Christ. He asserts that it takes maturity to discern these teachers from God's true messengers because their tempting words allure the naïve. Paul gives the Ephesians two standards by which to evaluate their doctrine, God's truth, and God's love and how both manifest Jesus Christ. He told them how to know if truth and love motivate their teachers' instruction. If the result is that they grew up in Christ, showing more of His wisdom, and less of the world they had just left, they can be trusted. Paul's was justified in his concerns. Ephesus was Diana's stronghold, making his misgivings about the purity of the Church's teachings quite justified. The Ephesians were steeped in Diana's lore and titillating tales of her warrior escapades. Born into it, they grew up knowing little else when it came to their religion. That heritage made them more vulnerable to error and heresy, and the gospel's disrepute. To guard God's doctrine, Paul left Timothy in Ephesus to move on to Macedonia. He instructs Timothy to stay loyal to the doctrine he received from his mentor. Timothy is not to listen to fables or get into genealogical debates aimed at unsettling his faith and that of those entrusted to him. Paul urges Timothy to stay with the gospel he received and not try to compete with fantastical tales that engendered endless questions and strife. To be left in charge of Paul's work, Timothy had to prove himself an exemplary student of the Lord's gospel. Paul would have tested his young mentee to ensure he was sound in the Lord's long history with the world and His dealings with Israel. Timothy would have had to be knowledgeable of the Almighty's string of divine revelations steadily communicated to the earth. He would have had to know how they brought Jesus Christ and Christianity to this world.

Teaching, another way to say doctrine, is the second half of the Great Commission in Matthew 28:18-20. Doctrine serves just about every fundamental and transformative purpose a convert to Jesus Christ requires. It should be understood that doctrine affects people differently than preaching does because doctrine penetrates the mind and intellect while preaching pierces the heart and stirs the emotions. Preaching sways the feelings to react, while doctrine guides the will into acting responsibly on it. Sound doctrine always makes its way to the heart to mix with the faith that moves people closer to the Lord. As previous discussions show, prophecy can contain either or both preaching and teaching. The Continuum has specific doctrinal strands and subject matter that support and sustain it. Without the Continuum and quality education in it, God's messengers can unintentionally stumble into false doctrine, being deprived of a gauge to measure a new doctrine's quality. These measures also reveal when or if a teaching steps outside the bounds established truth according to God.

GOD WISDOM AND THE CONTINUUM

Proverbs says, "Wisdom is the principal thing." No other phrase establishes it as the highest among all the virtues better than this one does. The passage well articulates wisdom's importance to the Continuum. Presented as a principality, it fuels all the other virtues. It is to be sought and acquired early to obtain the choicest life has to offer. Wisdom is foundational to all decisions and dealings and that is what makes it more essential. Without wisdom, life stumps people; the unscrupulous take advantage of those devoid of it. Wisdom is the champion's standard that steers responsible people down right paths. It paves the most trustworthy roads to maturity. Unconditionally, Scripture teaches that wisdom is the way to prosper in the world. Wisdom is the bedrock of godly fear and without it; one may bask in God's love, but be out of His good pleasure because of irreverence.

If Wisdom herself says, in Proverbs chapter 4, that she is the principal thing, should not believers be wiser and more subtle and prudent in their dealings than those without it? If these are lacking, James' epistle says to ask for wisdom. Proverbs, on the other hand, says to get wisdom, one must have a germ of it. Solomon, the book's author, knows that without a stalk of wisdom in the heart, people cannot recognize if what they use to guide and guard their life is wise. To increase wisdom takes more than asking or claiming it as if one can snatch and take it. Wisdom requires asking and using it to gain its increases. Along this vein, many saints claim the Lord gave them the gift of wisdom. Aside from Scripture, not mentioning a specific *gift* of wisdom, there are numerous biblical examples of what it means to live abundantly endowed with the Most High's wisdom. The greatest example the Bible has for God's bestowal of wisdom is Solomon. The number one thing to note about his wisdom is that it was for God's advantage. Solomon was set on Israel's throne as David's successor. In his world, there was just no higher position than being king. The young man had some intelligence, no doubt from his father David's teachings, so he knew what he lacked. Core wisdom told him the cost of his naiveté to the millions of people he was to lead. When he asked the Lord for wisdom, it was not just to be smarter, for head games, or parlor tricks. God had a goal for Solomon's wisdom. He was to lead the Lord's people wisely in war and prosperity, and to judge them fairly. Solomon showed he was worthy of being given greater wisdom because he could express to the Lord where he lacked it and what he would do with it should the Lord bestow more of His wisdom upon him. The man's words impressed God and granted Solomon's request because his motives pleased Him.

Upon receiving an unprecedented impartation of wisdom, Solomon went on to achieve otherwise impossible things for the Lord. He used his wisdom to undertake massive ventures for God, and he excelled at them. This example shows that the first thing wisdom does is to promote an individual, or empower those the Lord promotes. Proverbs chapter eight says it bluntly: "by me (wisdom) kings reign". So those claiming to have a more than average amount of wisdom should be in leadership or authority in or out of the Church. They should be installed in a serious position where ordinary human wisdom and knowledge are inadequate. Most believers do not know that wisdom from God is for His predetermined purpose. It is to help the Savior to His rule His realms. God gives His most talented and diligent promotes special senses to do His work, so they advance His visions and bring His purposes to pass. The Lord, different His customary generosity, gives extreme measures of wisdom to those who will give Him the greatest return on His endowment. Jesus said as much in Mark 4:24, 25. God's Wisdom is a prestigious commodity because it catalyzes human potential and attribute. It teaches those who will hear how to master life's mysteries and subtleties. Wisdom says the Lord possessed here at the beginning of His way, long before there were heavens, earth, mountains, and such. Job says the Lord discovered wisdom by searching out unknown things.[107] He investigated and experimented with all that He created to learn the best and the worst of each one. His example is what He expects His creatures to follow to acquire the wisdom they need to achieve in life. Whatever the Lord wants done, He assures its success by imparting His project's wisdom to chosen vessels. Doing so guarantees they succeed in their assignments from Him.

Wisdom is not a superficial adornment, it is not a cosmetic or a prosthesis; it is a power. Wisdom is a powerful reservoir, a resource that gives its possessors a prodigious edge over all else. That is why Scripture reports that everyone the Lord heavily charges with His business affairs He also endows with supra-normal wisdom. As cases in point, take Moses, Samuel, David, Solomon, and the prophets, each one's ministry exploits share this testimony. Christ's apostles and so on are all examples of God's extraordinary wisdom at work. Their testimonies reflect the reasons He gave it to them. Drawing on divine wisdom, they accomplished great things for God that advanced their present and His future. Their inclusion in His word and counsel today confirms that wisdom is not a spiritual trinket, but a dynamic power granted to

---

107 Job 28:20-27.

achieve unprecedented feats in this world for the Almighty. There are nearly ninety most vital wisdoms contained in Scripture that support the Continuum.

[15]

The Prophets' Words

E arlier chapters spoke extensively about the prophets' role in the Continuum to document their value to the Lord and show how their Old Testament writings paved the way for the New Testament. The Lord Jesus, whose testimony is the spirit of prophecy, gives stern admonishments about His prophets there, saying they are to be respected because they keep this world's ear open to God's voice. The Lord wants His prophets warmly cared for because of the uniquely vulnerable status, they hold in His service. The Messiah's position is that the Almighty's regard for His prophets should inspire people's kindness and respect for them. To those who obey, the Lord shows His gratitude materially by releasing His blessings in the believer's life. God further wants His prophets compensated for their service because their mantle release or transfer His wealth from one person to the next. Historically, the Most High used prophets to upgrade and advance His kingdom, to answer why they figure so prominently in His leadership appointments. Jesus also cautions people against shunning His prophets and says they should never be banned because their intercessory capacities are superior to those of the average saint. God wants people to seek His prophets for His answers to their lives and their world because of what the Psalmist wrote about His creatures in Psalm 139. It tells how God formed them in the womb, fashioned their days before they were conceived, and according to Isaiah, pre-assigned their generations from the beginning. Luke, in Acts 17 adds that the Almighty predetermined all human boundaries as well. Insofar as the prophets and prophecy go, both rely, or should rely, on the Continuum that contains the Lord's many writings for His multitudinous creation. Every creature's life and intelligence began with Him so what He wanted a thing to be and to do He wrote down beforehand to manage its existence before it left His being. This enables Him to prophesy their existence ahead of time as He holds all futures in His hands. To activate His words and will for His, God gives His prophets the keys to their predestiny, authorizing them to unlock earth's tomorrows through prophecy. He relies on His prophets to do this, not out of their own hearts and minds, what Ezekiel 13:2 condemns, but because their words come from the Continuum. The Messiah's contemporary prophecy is to come from the voluminous archive of books He wrote on people's lives. Personal and corporate prophecy are to reflect the spirit and the letter of what He has been saying or is accustomed to speaking on a particular matter. Therefore precedence and patterns should shape prophecy and the Continuum should affirm it.

WHY THE PROPHETS

As the prophet Daniel shows, God reveals His secrets to His servants the prophets. Amos Chapter 3 picks up on this truth. When God wants to communicate something to this world, He typically begins with His prophets. This is not to say He confines all of His communications to them because that is not true. However, it is to say that prophets experience God speaking more fluently and directly to them than most other saints. Kingdom and ecclesial divine communications are assigned to the office that began in eternity. This fact is important because it says that spontaneous prophecies that deviate from what the office is appointed and supervised by His angels to do can be refuted by what the Continuum purports. Refer to the chapter on God's Prophetic Angels. It recalls why the Lord begins with His prophets. He does so for two noteworthy reasons. The first is the office's supernal beginning. It originated in His world, not this one. As the chapter explained, the prophet's office functioned in God's world long before He extended it to earth. The second reason is that He designed human prophets to conform to His angelic ones, meaning their design and construction sanctifies them to be especially susceptible to divine communications and to translate them to earth responsibly. These two reasons explain how, and why, the Most High equips human prophets uniquely to serve on His staff. Besides them, the prophets hold a highly confidential position with the Almighty that He proves them for early in their careers and obliges them to throughout it. That unique position predisposes Him to conveying His innermost thoughts and sentiments to them instantaneously. Other reasons He does so include supplying them with the wisdom and insight they need for their spokesperson duties, which heads the list. The Lord divulges more complex and typically, more classified information to the higher trained prophets, He finds worthy of His trust. Scripture says this has been His custom since before time began, a custom that dates back to Abel, the very first prophet, and continues today. As a result, prophets knowingly or not, embody the mysteries of the Lord's tomorrows, as well as receive them in spontaneous transmissions, yet another reason they hold the key to His Eternal Continuum, not to mention how much their office contributed to it. To illustrate, think about Moses receiving the Law and Israel's government on Mount Sinai.

Yahweh called Moses into His service as a prophet, although today earlier Judaic writings count him as a shaliach, the Old Testament version of the apostle. Another example is Joshua who received God's takeover plan from Moses to lead Israel's possession of the Promised Land. A third example is Samuel, who succeeded Eli after his demise. These prominent leaders share one commonality; they are all prophets and their ministries and messages all fell within, and came out of the Continuum. Peter flat out says so in Acts 3:24. These are but a few examples and there are countless others. Such as, the several occasions where Jesus comments on the words and the Scriptures of the prophets that came before Him. More than a dozen New Testament passages reiterate the preponderance of prophecy, God's prophets prerecorded in the Old Testament that concerned Jesus' mission to earth. They set the boundaries of Scripture revelation and doctrine in their times for the Lord's future gospel messengers. Their words, the Savior stresses testify of Him and are the only yardstick by which future doctrines, prophecies, and revelations may be measured. Christ took the time to highlight this because He knew how His enemy would regroup from His Calvary defeat and deploy ungodly powers to regain what he lost to The Messiah's cross. Therefore, to minimize His own losses and setbacks, Jesus took pains to show where legitimate messages from He and His Father could be found. He directs all His ministers to the prophetic writings that spoke of Him and instructs seekers to seek them out under the auspices of His Holy Spirit. The two together, Jesus is confident, will lead His people to and in His truth, and preserve the integrity of His word and wisdom in the process. The superintending charge that He first gave to the prophets in the Old Testament, the Savior after His passion transfers to the apostles of His New Covenant.

TRUE PROPHETS REMAIN IN THE LORD'S CONTINUUM

God's faithful messengers, work within and not outside of the Almighty's prophecy and doctrine Continuum. The Lord Jesus as their Creator knows what is intrinsic to the prophet's makeup. He knows their susceptibility to spirit and soul contamination because of an endowment to reach beyond this world into His. Before all time, as discussion of the Angelic Prophets proves, Jesus embedded His word in select humans to disclose His consciousness and communiqués to earth. Here is God's primary justification for making the testimony of Jesus the spirit of prophecy. Christ supplies every world stratum with prophets as His chief divine communication vehicles. They disperse the prophecies ordained for their generation and educate people in their emergent spiritualities. In doing so, God predetermined heaven's prophecies would foreshadow and pass to the office as its service cutouts. The Old Testament prophetic office reposits ages of the Lord's spoken words before He incarnated. These He implanted into its mantleship before time began to dispense the wisdom and knowledge that would always preserve His messages' consistency and continuity. Human prophets as the Lord's spokespeople are the corporeal side of His celestial institution. Hence, modern prophets must adhere to their predecessors' works, using it to impel and validate their service. Upon entering and discharging the office today, no matter whom they are or what aspect of His divine communications they emphasize as His messengers, every true prophet must affix his or her words to the Lord's continual sayings to secure His Continuum and thereby fulfill His past, present, and future words. Divine communicants committed to the Almighty's truth, seek a corroborator like the Continuum to validate and regulate them and their heavenly utterances.

The Old Testament's prophets laid down the Continuum tracks that back their office the way other institutions, organizations' constitutions, and operational guides do for their representatives. These perform the very same functions for the Lord Jesus' future divine messengers. Nothing in Scripture notes that God expects those entering the prophet's office today to craft their prophecies from their own hearts and minds. In fact, the exact opposite is true. God, no more expects profits to conjure His words on their own beings than a person expects a recording device to think up what to say and record it on its own. People want their recording devices to repeat what they say without making random edits to their communications. Granted, the Lord gives His messengers the latitude to make His thoughts intelligible to their audiences, but He does not authorize them to unsay or undermine His eternal establishment or its intents. God expects His prophets to articulate what He decreed to advance and enforce His Continuum. Their sayings are to affirm and reassert what prophets occupying the office before they did, and said. They are further expected to circulate and clarify the revelations the Lord Jesus dispenses to His apostles in their generations. Together, these underscore how prophets are to use Scripture prophecy to judge and critique the prophets of their age. Based on these requisites and the institution's long-standing advantage to Him, the Lord and prophets form an extraordinary guardianship union that secures the office and its mantle and safeguards His people. That union makes the prophet more accessible by God and ready to communicate His thoughts. Ongoing divine disclosures from this vantage point directly position prophets to stream the prophecy God metes out to them. To equip them to do so, He intellectually trains and corrects them to discern His communications and release only calculated excerpts from His extensive writings as they are led to. This is to say that despite the breadth of information prophets constantly glean from God's Spirit, as the discussion on Balaam shows, they are restricted from 'prophetically dumping' so to speak. The Most High's prophets are obliged to speak, in the moment only what the Savior releases, and only as He instructs.

So constant are the exchanges between God and His prophets that the two dynamics merge and fuse with the minister's everyday life. Over time, the prophet loses track of how much God implants advance words in their souls for them to speak for Him later with only a moment's notice. In this vein, because prophets work for God, they rarely have to engage in extensive petitions and other spiritual machinations to obtain the word of the Lord. They are His official spokespeople. As permanent members of His staff, and not just visitors to His temple for private devotions, prophets quickly retrieve Lord's opinion on various human and world issues because their ongoing interactions keep them in His mind. Being ceaselessly infused with His thoughts and will, often long in advance, fits prophets to declare His word on a matter instantly. Since the prophet's workstation is God's Holy Spirit and His work desk their spirit, closeness with the Godhead brings the vessel swiftly into His judgments and responses. The benefit of Jesus indwelling His New Testament prophets by His Spirit is that it allows Him to keep an uncommon grip on their beings and their mantles. Being stationed within His prophets extemporaneously issues, prophecy, and prophetic projects to them. His prophets as specially outfitted members of His staff receive and process His revealed thoughts swiftly. For such interactions and their corresponding responsibilities, the Almighty potently enhances His prophets' intelligence and other faculties to accustom them to His ways and attune them to His voice. His goal is that His prophets accurately translate His thoughts to others in actionable human terms.

When prophets' complete their training and apprenticeship, He upgrades them to respond to issues on His behalf the way any other head of state or an organization would do. He does not fully authorize or delegate them until they complete their training and demonstrate the requisite maturity, integrity, and accuracy for their office. This is true even if human authorities choose to dispense with these confirmations. The Lord's restraints assure His divine communicants conform to, and indicate their intent to cooperate with His Continuum. Prophetic vessels that prove to be incapable of rightly representing Him, or who fail to safeguard His interests, or who lack the conscientiousness to discharge the office as He created it, God uses exclusively in a gift capacity. He does not trust them with an office because it, as with literal offices, comes furnished with operational and administrative duties and resources that permit the messenger unrestricted access to His spiritual terrains and classified information. Thus, He limits such prophets' awareness and apprehension of His mysteries. Insofar as the Continuum goes in this respect, protecting its sensitive information has ever been a high priority with God that obligates Him to safeguard it using various measures. To cap underdeveloped prophets, the Lord narrows their responsibilities and restricts their authority. Doing so weakens their grasp of His Continuum and forces them to mainly see and prophesy according to this world. While some restrained prophets can easily tap into the supernatural, the Lord's supernal spheres remain largely off limits to them so they cannot pierce them to retrieve spiritual information. While earthly prophecy can be quite fluent with these ministers, the authority, enforcement power, and significant celestial backing approved prophets possess are all conspicuously absent.

The prophets whose words did make it into the Bible can easily be substantiated by its Major or Minor prophets. Their words are clearly registered in God's Eternal Continuum. However, there are some whose works are not, but to give them credit for being part of His staff, the Lord mentions them by name in Scripture, as likely contributors to it. Examples of prophets recognized in scripture include Shemaiah, Nathan, Iddo, Gad, Ahijah, Jehu, Elijah and Elisha, Oded, and Hananiah. The world may have buried their words, but their service to Him evidently proved reliable enough to be remembered as messengers Continuum He relied on to carry out His plans.

WHAT ELSE MAKES PROPHETS UNIQUE

One more reason the Lord relies so heavily on His prophets is the wisdom He profusely saturates them with to act as His agential ministers. By design, prophets' spirits gravitate to and hungrily absorb the Lord's pragmatics because He built them to be malleable to Him. Christ firmly engrafts prophets entering His service into His Continuum, so they expand what He has done and ignite all He will do righteously. For this reason, the duty of remaining in the Continuum immediately suits true prophets entering His ministry because they know their revelations had to get their start from somewhere. When God shows them in scripture what they are perpetuating, and extending, they agreeably commit to carrying on the traditions and practices of their predecessors. They are God's communications and so to broadcast Him, He professionalizes His prophets as kingdom representatives that function according to His eternal works. Drawing from His eternal registries and archives, they undergo years of pruning and training, to sort through competently what He reveals in order to pronounce prudently what He sends them to prophesy. For this work, the prophet is predisposed to capture heavenly information to read aloud to the world everything the Almighty ever spoke, and did, as Creator God. More than training and frequency qualifies them for their assignments. A special construction prefits them for it and authorizes the well-trained ones to be inducted into the Continuum's knowledge and revelations. Once enfolded into it, approved prophets are transformed mentally and emotionally to issue its prophecies on cue. The Lord treats His office holders much the same way as those of any other entity that authorizes credentialed leaders to access its files and records and speak on its behalf. Moreover, His special messengers are enhanced to process divine information on several fronts and in at least two dimensions at once. For service to His Continuum, God gives prophets the cyphers they need to, decode His yet to be revealed hidden truths in their eras, and to reinforce those already publicized by their predecessors. This degree of trust comes neither easily nor early in the prophet's career. Years and more often decades of trial and error determine what messenger should be cleared to receive what level of information to spread as God's voice. For example, not just any messenger could have received John's Apocalypse. What Jesus revealed to John, as a prerecorded depiction of the world behind his own, John was to publish veraciously. The same is true with all of the all-encompassing word the Lord through His prophets committed to Scripture. Moses, Samuel, David, Isaiah, Ezekiel, Jeremiah, and Daniel distinguish themselves as faithful divine communicators by their capacity to verbalize Yahweh's mind clearly and judiciously. For security's sake, over the ages of His messaging the Lord released many things to different messengers to test their fidelity before unveiling His most detrimental information to them. John, history shows, underwent decades of rigorous training, trial, and warfare to prove his allegiance to the Lord Jesus Christ. Amazingly, these all came after he spent three and a half intense years with Him in training, and after that, decades of active service as His apostle. With Patmos in view, it seems all of it was to prime, John to end up on that island for a visit with the glorified Messiah. John was well up in years by the time he received the Revelation and had earned the privilege by withstanding cruel retaliations for his witness and devotion to Jesus Christ.

Being exiled on a prison island was quite brutal for John, but it proved worthwhile in that it certified his trustworthiness. The trust he earned released to John's world what Gabriel's Scripture of truth released to Daniel's and infinitely more. It dramatized what its Maker had in store for it. Jesus revealed a future to John that affected him the way prophets who foresaw The Messiah and His generation to come were affected in their days. In many ways, Christ's revelation made little sense to John at the time, not in its fullness. After all, how could it? All of the elements and features it portrayed, were for the coming eras, not yet known to his age. Light, energy, self-propelled beings and vehicles; angels wielding unearthly power and devils so treacherous they can be counted on to destroy the world could have only been marginally appreciated by John. Yet they all demonstrated how Christ would expel the very evil powers out of the earth that He cast out of heaven after its Great War. What Jesus unveiled for John, come from His Continuum archive. The Savior said He disclosed to John what is, what was, and what is to come recorded and filed away until the appointed time. John sees a stupendous future while confined to the dark, dank island. His Savior and friend chose him to peer into the age that; then was, that existed then, and that which is to come. The Lord ushered him in the Godhead's future eras where electricity, communications, technological marvels, and other wondrous achievements were commonplace. What the apocalypse shows John is Christ's old world, and still it outdid John's world then. The Lord could reveal it to Him because the Revelation had already played out in His world and so was available for John to witness as the world to come. The Lord's Continuum gave the apostle a rare glimpse of what the Godhead had planned, was doing, and would do to bring the world to its predestined end. He lets John know it is so His Father could occupy this planet as the capitol of all worlds forever. Scripture establishes that God routinely shares this sort of revelation with prophets. The closer they remain with Him the more expansive the revelations He shares with them. Other significantly apocalyptic prophets include Moses, Daniel, Zechariah, of course the Lord Jesus and John the Revelator.

[16]

Continuum Prophecy

Continuum prophecy speaks of a distant preprogrammed activity or event scheduled to reproduce itself at a preappointed time in the future. God's goal of advancement makes the Continuum and prophecy indivisible. It has been shown to be the heart and soul of God's Eternal Continuum. The Almighty speaks from outside this world, which means He speaks outside of time and utters events and developments before they happen on earth. Add to this that the Lord's Spirit is in the earth is, in contrast to His carnal Self, and the necessity for Him to do so becomes clear. God must stay ahead of His worlds. He must know in advance what will happen and have resolved it before anyone outside of the Godhead knows about it. His eternal archives that hold His worlds' prophecies prescribe what He saw, logically and how He pragmatically wrapped it up before taking on other creations. Prophecy is archival for God because He wrote them before He began His earthly works. Recording and storing it all in eternity prefixes this world's prophecies and their boundaries, limiting what His earthly messengers can prophesy in His name to what His angelic messengers prophesy. The word for the Most High's preresolved foreknowledge of this world, present and future, is presolve. The Continuum in this respect teems with ages of pre-solutions the Lord eternally applied to all His kingdom to await their scheduled manifestations. The most well-known term for all this is providence.

God's Providence

God's anticipation of how His clay world would go led Him to provide for what He knew it would require to survive long enough to return it to Him. John's Apocalypse demonstrates the Lord's ability to foresee and presolve earth's issues before they happen. Revelation 1:8 has Jesus saying that He is the Alpha and Omega, the starter and finisher of everything, everywhere. The same verse adds that He is the beginning and the ending. Revelation 3:14 supports this with Christ identifying Himself as "the beginning of the creation of God". In designating Himself as such, The Messiah reaches back to what He said in Mark 13:19 where He foretold the world's afflictions to come were His design, and are to be more severe than anything that has ever hit the planet before since the beginning of the creation of God. The tragedies He announces will never be repeated because the disasters planned to address them permanently resolve the world situations that provoked them. Matthew 24:21 reiterates the same thing. The tribulations to come are so horrible that there will be no need for them to reoccur, so the Continuum scheduled them once.

Jesus' recollection of God's creative eras is impeccable. For instance, in John 17:5 He asks His Father to restore His divine glory to what He had with the Almighty before this world was. He shows by His prayer that He always existed and demonstrates it throughout the gospels by recalling events only an alien to this world could know. How does He do it? The record He reads come from those hidden heaven's libraries. Drawing on them again and again, Jesus as their embodied carrier continually remarks on creation's bygone eras. He knows when Satan fell from heaven and what it looked like, why His Father wiped out the antediluvians, the mysteries the Lord holds in store for the future, and how He must die to keep the Continuum's chain unbroken. Mark 10:6 is another example. It shows the Savior's vivid memory of what transpired between heaven and earth before He took upon Himself flesh. In the Mark reference, Jesus establishes that way back in the beginning of God's creation, in this case His creation of humanity, God "made (humanity) male and female."; what Genesis 1:26, 27 records. Jesus can certify it as true because He was part of creation's team. The Genesis account says, "Let Us make man in our image and according to our likeness". The Us in the passage includes Him, what the Scripture references below say.

In the Beginning of the Creation

The passages used for the purposes of this discussion emphasize "in the beginning of the creation". Notice they do not say "in the beginning of the world" but "in the beginning of the creation". Jesus clearly knows the difference because Paul states in Ephesians 3:9 "God created all things by Jesus Christ". He reiterates his revelation in Colossians 1:15-18. His motivations are also why John could write "In the beginning God." A last relevant passage is 2 Peter 3:4 where he reinforces the certainty of the

Almighty's future world judgment. Peter no doubt draws on a history lesson he received from Jesus during his apostleship training. His goal is to tell his followers that their God has (and has had) other worlds He has ruled for ages. To persuade them, Peter recounts pre-flood events only an eyewitness can share. God's worlds he says span both time and space, meaning that some are actual planets and others are former ages. The world Peter is discussing is an age that reaches back to Noah's days, before the flood. It was the time when the sons of God that left their first estate or celestial principalities procreated with the daughters of men. Their rebellion sired a wretched race that tortured Adam's line and frustrated the Lord's plan for his seed. The wickedness they spawned was so pernicious that it gave their offspring cruel unfair advantage over humanity. Their malevolent society forced God to send the flood to destroy it, and they. It was the only way to separate the devils from their mortal bodies. To preserve the human race that He planned to bring His incarnate Son into the world, the Lord God had to extract the godless genetic strain of the fallen angels from Adam's seed. To do so, required killing the bodies the two shared to rescue the human spirit. His solution isolated the renegade devils to imprison them for their sin. Peter in reciting this event wants the saints of his day to accept the prophesied end of this world. The Scripture, John 10:35 says cannot be broken. He subtly demonstrates this truth by quoting from Psalm 82:1. Peter, following His Master's lead, wants his followers to know also that the Lord Jesus is pivotal to that end. God is not prophesying unknown never happened before events. No, it is not like the primordial age when no one had ever heard of rain or water dropping from the sky. This time it is all a matter of record. The world that then was perished, and so too will the one they live in at the appointed time. Paul resorts to Psalm 102:25, 26 to reassert that the Creator programmed the heavens and earth to deteriorate and eventually self-destruct. Refer to Hebrews 1:10-12.

The Creator has destroyed the world before and has already planned how and when He will do it again. In fact, the language of Genesis 1:28 infers He has destroyed it more than once. The Creator tells the male and female He just made to "replenish" the earth. He does not say plenish the earth as if they are its first population; He commands them to replenish it. Yes, plenish is a word from whence comes the word plenty. The Lord repeats the same command to Noah: "be fruitful, multiply, replenish the earth." The destruction He has planned for this age's future though is a little different. This time He appointed a remnant to rescue from His planned disasters. The number of these people is immense, much larger than Noah's eight souls. The masses that He plans to redeem are the new creation saints of the Lord Jesus Christ.

The world's first flood back in Noah's day appears to serve many purposes for God. In addition to its mass annihilation of everything that was destroyed His world, the event also appears to enable Him to observe everything that could happen to humanity. Watching life unfold during this period showed the Lord all that humanity could do to itself and all that Satan could exact (and enact) upon it. As Maker of all things, His witness of these events became a matter of record for His future generations. When the Bible speaks of Scripture, particularly Peter's more sure word of prophecy and Gabriel's Scripture of truth, it refers to the annals of heaven that foresee and prescribe creation's future based on God's eternal past that enables His wisdom. Going back to Solomon's words that there is nothing new under the sun and that which is has already been, recording it all for future occupants of the planet allows all people to trace His truth in action. To continue the before the beginning of God's creation comparison, Jesus establishes in Matthew 24:38 that He was there with His Father way back in the beginning, all of their beginnings. He was part of the world that preceded this one that Lucifer once ruled and the spiritual and earthly creatures that replaced him. One of them is the world that Peter talks about which existed, and was destroyed. He draws on history for signs to God's imminent judgments. The pre-flood world for instance multiplied and perverted marriage; it seems, in an apparently ungodly way. God evidently told them through Noah that their world was about to end, but they ignored him and the signs of their end time until he entered the ark and shut them out. So where did Peter get His facts? From Jesus who got it from all that He lived before coming to earth. What source did both messengers use to utter their prophecies? The answer is the Continuum. That is how Solomon could say with certainty that which is has already been. What Jesus and His Father lived from the Great War in Heaven to the antediluvians to the Roman age to the end of time, all of it is old news to them. However far back in their history their records begin, by the time this world starts and the Lord manifests in the flesh on the planet, everything pertaining to the world and His reasons for entering is settled. Heaven has seen it all, lived it all, and conquered it all. That experience is how it can say immutably that there is only one way for sin to behave and only one way for it to end.

Nothing happening in this world can turn out any different from how it happened and turned out in the Christ's other worlds, especially since He made this one an infinitely lower version of theirs. God uses the same devil with the same sin nature in the world to sift the wheat from the chaff again and again. These two realities are, how and why prophecy exists. They are also why the Law of Moses could never be broken and why all Scriptures must be fulfilled. Prophecy discloses God's mysteries and eternal Scripture's revelations. These are celestial chronicles and not just spontaneous musings from highly stimulated mystics. Uttering them is what distinguishes true prophecy from the false. The Continuum's accounts cannot be falsified, however suppressed, they may be over the ages. Falsified messages are, actually, what the Lord Jesus calls idle words because they have no power beyond their appeal to the deceived hearer. This is one explanation of false prophecy that shows what makes it false. God calls false, anything not filed in His heavenly archives. Such messages fail because the Lord has no obligation to them. Their impotence lies in the fact that words He finds useless are never assigned any of His holy beings to perform. Any false prophecy spoken, the Lord allows His dark powers of deception to manifest false fulfillments. However, the problem with their false prophecy fulfillment has to do with its resources. Being outside the Continuum, they are frail, corruptible, and unenduring. Relying on what the Lord cursed and withdrew His life from; false prophecy's fulfillment effects are temporary because they like their agents are subject to the Almighty's law of sin and death. God persuades prophets on His staff of these things before He entrusts them with the words of His mouth. He drenches them with their realities so what He wants said through them is said His way and on time. Backing His prophets and performing their prophecies is the work of God's Holy Spirit and the holy angels who expose false prophets for what they are and condemn false prophecy for what it is. Christ's holy angels in their guardianship of His Continuum incriminate false prophecies' as precluded from God's Continuum. Their judgments release them from bringing false words to pass. Remember, the angels long ago vowed their allegiance to the Most High and will only harken to the voice of His word and do His bidding. It should be emphasized that the Lord and His angels are going by their plan and not earth's developments.

TESTIFYING OF JESUS

In the Creator's view, the essence of Christian prophecy should be, "the testimony of Jesus Christ". So far, teachings showed Jesus' testimony encompasses His eternal existence, His earthly life, and ministry. In addition, there are Jesus death, resurrection, ascension and His church. All are what God certifies as Christ's testimony. To absorb Jesus' testimony totally and spread it as His faithful witness, one would have to include all aspects of His life as threaded throughout the ancient (and celestial) writings recorded in the Continuum concerning His era as Yahweh.

According to the angel speaking with John in Revelation 22:6, Jesus and His Father share the title "Lord God of the holy prophets". In the same passage, the Risen Lord affirms His equality with Creator God in 22:16. Jesus reiterates the angel's words by saying "I Jesus have sent mine angel to testify unto you these things in the Churches". At the behest of Jesus Christ, an angel brings John Christ's Revelation from heaven. He shows John what they in the Almighty's world have seen and knows for certain will happen. He knows it because He encoded all creation to act (and react) the way its Maker decreed and to self-decompose according to His plan and timeline. The angel's remarks appear to rephrase the other statement concerning The Messiah. John's angel says, the Lord God of the holy prophets sent His angel to show John and God's servants the future. In verse 16, Jesus declares He sent His angel. The inference is that the dispatched angel belongs to both of them, or he is shared by them. The first one seems more accurate, particularly in light of Exodus 23:23 and 32:34. Revisiting Revelation 19:10's perplexing remark, then, is where any committed messenger of God's word starts. It is also what the conscientious voice of God's mind must stand on to be His prophetic servant.

A testimony is an eyewitness account or verification of something that happened. For an eyewitness testimony to be taken as truth, the witness must be found credible. He or she must have a long-standing verifiable reputation for being faithful, honest, and truthful. In addition to these, the faithful witness must also be known for impartiality, good judgment, and reasonable intelligence. High-strung emotionality makes for a poor witness, which is why the Lord set sober mindedness as one criterion for testifying of Him. John's Revelation calls Jesus heaven's faithful witness. God's Son embodied His Father's entire message before being dispatched to earth. Surprisingly, it was all contained in the tiny little sperm His Father planted in the womb of the Virgin Mary. Once in ministry, the Savior constantly told His listeners that His witness was true because He was among them, came from heaven, was going back to heaven, and was His Father's loyalist ally. After all, He is the first begotten Son of God. Jesus' witness, however, was not just for humans. The Savior has a host of invisible listeners standing by to hear what He says because they were just as involved in as Adam's seed was. Some of them too were victims of the dragon's attempted overthrow of heaven's government the way the earth is. See Paul's perplexing Ephesians 3:9-11 comments.

"And to make all men see what is the fellowship (really dispensation) of the mystery, which from the beginning of the world hath been hid in God, who created all things by Jesus Christ[108]: To the intent that now unto the principalities and powers in heavenly places might be known by the Church the manifold wisdom of God, according to the eternal purpose which he purposed in Christ Jesus our Lord."

WHAT PROPHECY DOES

Prophecy performs dynamically for the Lord. It does everything He appointed for His creation. It reveals, accomplishes, and imposes God's will on earth. Prophecy may be thought of as the Lord's most chief executive of Jesus Christ's testimony. It is the reason for His word and the reason His witness is immortalized in print. Jesus' eternality and prophecy's origin lay at the heart of all divine revelation. Add to these irrevocable truths John's intimate knowledge of his friend, Jesus Christ, the Second Person of the Godhead and how He incarnated Himself to embody God Almighty's word, and it all gets clearer. The three of them say why God's word, will, and way, are absolute. Unarguably, the Lord built all creation around them and He holds the secret to their operation and effects in His heavenly archives. Everything He did materialize creation, this world, and the events of its past and future revolve around Jesus Christ, to say why His testimony scripts all prophecy.

Jesus is God's Word and God's word is Jesus. John 5:39 joins Hebrews 1:2 to make this point. Speaking to His eternal life, John 1:10 says that Jesus Christ made the world. Therefore, it stands to reason that anything Scripture says to its readers pertains to Him. Since the Scriptures "testify of Jesus Christ", prophecy if it is to be legitimate in God's kingdom must do the same. Genuine prophecy must declare Jesus Christ, His incarnation, crucifixion, resurrection, and ascension. It must fully endorse Him and prove all His existences while exalting (or at least acknowledging) His power and authority as Creator and Lord at the same time. Bona fide messengers of the true and living God will perform prophetically as the Savior declares in John 6:45. It does not matter if their message is positive or negative, for or against the hearer, prophecy from Jesus' messengers (even those of His adversary) will always center on Jesus Christ: the former to prove Him and the latter to disprove Him. In a word, He is the substance of Scripture. Frankly speaking, He is God Almighty's reason for everything else too. John 1:3 puts it this way: "All things were made by him; and without him was not anything made that was made". In support of this, Paul writes in Colossians 1:16 "For by him were all things created, that are in heaven, and that are in earth, visible and invisible, whether they be thrones, or dominions, or principalities, or powers: all

---

108 Several translations omit "by Jesus Christ".

things were created by him, and for him." The Father concerning His Son continues this theme throughout the New Testament as prophecy fulfilled. In four separate passages, He designates the Lord Jesus as His Son. He is higher than the angels are, unlike any human, and the instrument of all the Almighty has done and will do. Without Jesus, nothing happens whether or not He is identified or acknowledged for it.

The first time Scriptures record God's first begotten Son as enthroned is in the second Psalm. There, the Almighty decrees Jesus as His everlasting King. "I will declare the decree: the Lord hath said unto me, Thou art my Son; this day have I begotten thee." He is the Son and He is the King because that is how it works when a sovereign begets an offspring. Acts 13:33 brings the Psalm reference forward to the New Testament. Hebrews along this line applies the same decree to Jesus as God's Son. He is unlike the angels because the Creator made Him different from the Godhead although, Scripture calls them the sons of God. That difference is what makes Christ hereditarily the Son of God. It bestowed upon Him the title Messiah, the Anointed One. Begotten is the defining word that sets Jesus apart from the angels. God birthed Jesus, while in comparison He <u>made</u> the angels. The dividing factor between the two creations is God's hands versus His Being, or reproductive Self. Angels were handmade Christ was born, brought forth from the Almighty's body, such as it is. His uniqueness is celebrated in Hebrews 1:5 and in Hebrews 5:5, Jesus Christ's Sonship forms the basis of His High Priestly office. He is installed over Melchizedek's eternal priesthood after whom Christ's new creation is named. The Bible has many references like these that immortalize the prophecies of the coming Messiah. His work and suffering dominated the Old Testament. Scripture's continuous string of revelations shares with the Church where God's true authentications may be found, how to discern and minister them. Amazingly, the Christian's Holy Bible compiled all this information for those filled with the Holy Spirit to read and understand.

A provocative question to ask in light of what has just been said, is why the Lord found it necessary to write His words in the first place, and why did He write them before time began? More often people voice questions like these as, "Why the Bible?" What is the point of the Lord compiling His words in a single book that He had to know most of His creation would ridicule, ignore, or despise? What could He hope to achieve by doing so? Surely, He knew what waited for His truths when He commissioned them to this world. Why did He do it? The answer is His Continuum that was already in motion. The Almighty passed on from eternity, His imposed will on all creation, most notably the earth, and decreed how the sin brought into existence by the dragon and his angels would be eradicated. Old Testament prophecies say much about the Almighty's history with these rebel beings. Meanwhile, Revelation 12:12 says, heaven's terrorists are now the world's antagonists. Eternal citizens expressing this somberly warn the earth that life is going to be hard. Their sentiment and sympathy together prove to this world that heaven is well able to deal with them and to defend the earth. The Most High from His world scripted for humanity how to save itself from these creatures. He forthrightly instructs the world's societies on how to evict them if they want, or at the least, how to control them so that they do not overcome the planet with evil.

SPIRITUAL COMMUNICATORS DUTY TO THE CONTINUUM

As silent as the Lord's heavenly communicators may be to humanity, they remain perpetually active guardians of His truth and custodians of His agencies. No matter how long it takes, they correct wayward messengers and admonish naïve ones to keep the Continuum's integrity. Moreover, God's ministering spirits are majorly involved in getting new messengers ready for the Lord's service. Remember, they are eternal and can neither die nor corrupt, so their presentment of His multifaceted doings is always perfectly relevant. That is why God introduces so many of His divine communicants to His angels, and why He confidently turned over Israel's care and leadership to them. See Exodus 23:23; 32:34; Judges 2:1. It is an angels' job to appear to designated messengers and teachers to guide them through their training and into their offices. His development capacitates them to say where He is and where He is not, and to verify that their detections and discrepancies are according to His Continuum; as Jeremiah did with Hananiah in chapter 28 of his prophecy. To substantiate its answer to the king about his impending war, Jeremiah turns to the Continuum's wisdom to refute an errant prophet. Although they clash over their conflicting prophecies, the Lord honors Jeremiah at the end. Jeremiah 28:8, 9 recalls the incident. "The prophets that have been before me and before thee of old prophesied both against many countries, and against great kingdoms, of war, and of evil, and of pestilence. The prophet which prophesieth of peace, when the word of the prophet shall come to pass, then shall the prophet be known that the Lord hath truly sent him." Clearly, Jeremiah is aware of his predecessors' messages and draws on them to refute Hananiah's groundless optimistic prophecy that has no basis in truth. Jeremiah logically proves his adversary's words were contrary to God's past reactions to nations' sin. Essentially, Jeremiah knows God's character well enough to deduce His disposition on national sin. Jeremiah 15:1 makes an odd statement alluding to the

Lord's celebrated intercessors, prophets who discerned God's temperament and submitted to it. Jeremiah says "Then said the Lord unto me, Though Moses and Samuel stood before me, yet my mind could not be toward this people: cast them out of my sight, and let them go forth." The Lord recalls two intercessors that moved Him, and even their interventions had their limits. He names Moses, who founded Israel and Samuel the prophet that judged it in its darkest hour. These two prophets interceded for the nation, unlike those mentioned by Ezekiel. Jeremiah's sentiments resound in Ezekiel 14, "Son of man, when the land sinneth against me by trespassing grievously, then will I stretch out mine hand upon it, and will break the staff of the bread thereof, and will send famine upon it, and will cut off man and beast from it." God's word to Ezekiel remembers what He evidently considers the world's most influential intercessors. They are named in Ezekiel 14:14: Noah, Daniel, and Job. What they have in common is that they were prophets when God did not claim any particular nation. Previously, Noah was thoroughly discussed as an antediluvian prophet. Daniel was a Hebraic prophet serving God under Nebuchadnezzar in Babylon, and Job was an ancient world prophet between Noah and Daniel. Another intriguing detail about the three is that including their names validates their role in the Continuum and reveals how far back to God's dealings with the nations go. These five (named centuries apart in some cases) not only found their way into God's Eternal Continuum but also caused the Bible's canonizers to include them in Scripture, for those who wonder how they made their decisions. The Bible canonized Job and Daniel's writings because to accept Ezekiel was to include them since the Lord expressly names them and refers to their words. Moses is a given, but of all the judges that ruled Israel, Samuel stands out as the most memorable one. Collectively, these examples indicate why the Lord has so entwined His prophets in the Continuum, and why they have a great responsibility for it. Luke 1:70 says the Lord has relied on them since the world began. What prophet goes back that far? Remember Abel?

How Prophets Guard God's Continuum

Of the many reasons given already for revering God's prophecy saturated Continuum, Moses' prediction about the coming Christ excels them all. Up until this point in history, the Continuum is somewhat obscure in Scripture. The coming of The Messiah was not as plainly detected in earlier communications. For instance, Galatians 3:8 says Abraham knew and understood it. Jude 14 says that Enoch, the seventh from Adam foretold it, apparently from his frequent visits to God's world. Balaam picks it up in his prophecy regarding Israel, and Judah as her scepter holder. Jacob before leaving the planet enlarges it a bit when he prophesies to his twelve sons. However, outside of these unmistakable links, it is only slightly detected. Yet the Continuum's chain shows up in Scripture in every area circling around prophecy, which is why it is the principal thread that holds it all together. God's Prophecy Continuum is the single contiguous revelation of the future the Lord meted out over the ages. He moves it forward through the ages, generations, and events that roll out His continuous involvement in humanity, from His world. The Lord hid His Continuum in mysteries to unveil them systematically and tactically until this present world gives way to His everlasting one. The prophets, in order to safeguard the Lord's Continuum, must know everything there is to know about God from what He has revealed so far. Modern prophets need such knowledge to uphold His Scriptures. The unfortunate thing about too many modern prophets is that they know the spirit of this world, but not necessarily the spirit of God's word, a shortfall that handicaps them as it did Balaam when he set out to curse Israel. God knew Balaam's prophetic faculties were developed enough to receive His word for Israel, and what a word it turned out to be. Momentarily, to enable the prophet to prophesy the truth, the Lord brought Balaam into the Continuum and the prophecies Jacob had earlier spoken over Judah before his death. See Genesis 49:8.

Judah is the Lion of the twelve tribes. In Jacob's prophecy, the Lord Jesus inherits the king's scepter and He will never lose it. This event decreed in heaven was prophesied on earth when the people were a tribe and not a nation, when no hint of becoming a kingdom. Yet, Jacob, Judah's father recognizes him as the Most High's lawgiver on whose shoulders all creation's government shall rest: "and the government shall be upon His shoulders". Judah, David's tribe, attracts the masses and true to Jacob's prophecy becomes king of Israel. Jesus who is born in Judah centuries later becomes all creation's Sovereign. Fulfillment of this time bound prophecy plainly displays its heavenly origins. Luke 1:69 has Zacharias, John the Baptist's father prophesying by the Holy Ghost the gospel of God. "As He spoke through all of His holy prophets since the world began, Yahweh will visit His people, raise up the strength of their preordained salvation from the house of David." The prophesied Messianic Kingship of Jesus Christ because it was long ago embedded in the world and declared by His prophets since its foundation, had to be fulfilled, as all Scripture must. Revelation 12 opens the curtain on this mysterious to recognize the precarnate Christ's preeminence in heaven's war. It is why and how the staff of leadership got between Judah's feet. The preternal prophecy spoke directly from God's world where Jesus always reigned as its King. What have the staff and feet to do with rulership? The staff guides by pointing the way and the feet lead by going ahead of followers. Jacob's symbology is typical of his day.

Earlier times record illustrious kings demonstrating their humility by riding on donkeys to connect with their people. Stallions and thoroughbreds were for racing, hunting, and war, but donkeys were working animals and only servants read them. If a king wanted to be seen as meek and lowly, he rode on donkeys to move slowly through the crowds rather than race through them as if to avoid connecting with them. Mark stresses this aspect of Christ's ministry; He enters Jerusalem before His death as prophesied, riding on a lowly donkey, the foal of a mare. To return to Judah's prophecy, John records Jesus saying, He is the vine and His converts its branches. Judah's father saw Him as Christ, binding Himself to the people and nourishing them as a vine does. Such a bond at the time symbolized monarchs' marriage to their people upon ascending the throne. Accordingly, Judah's prophecy is realized: "The scepter will never depart from Judah, nor a ruler's staff from between his feet, until the One comes, who owns them both, and to him will belong the allegiance of nations." ISV. Although Balaam's long view of the future is not as a member of God's covenanted prophetic staff, as a proximity prophet the Lord nonetheless opened him to the Continuum to see the coming of His Son. Consequently, advancing one of the prediluvian prophecies the Lord spoke. The woman's seed, spoken of in Genesis 3:15, is who Balaam saw coming to rule all the nations of the earth.

[17]

Apostles' In The Continuum

I f the prophets dominated the Old Testament, then the apostles are similarly the divinely appointed superintendents of the new. From before the expiration of Moses' Law when the Lord Jesus appoints twelve apostles to assist Him in His Israeli commission, upon the birth of the new creation church, Christ's apostles pick up where the Old Testament prophets leave off. However, before getting into the heart of this subject, it should be reiterated that the ruling powers of the Bible's formative ages were monarchs. Modern Christians forget or have failed to realize that they were not appealing to a congregation and its membership but to a nation and its citizens under a theocracy. That is why Peter identifies Christians as God's royal priesthood. His statement reflects how the Lord fused His divine offspring's royal and ministerial destinies into one heritage. It is also, why God's eternal plans for His family are that they reside with Him in a kingdom ruled by a perpetual King and not just a country under a president or prime minister. Jesus' is a kingdom that has existed forever and shall never end. To appreciate the governing climate of Jesus and His apostles' time is to envision Christianity as a growing spiritual nation and not just a church competing with the religions of this world. The future of Christ's Ecclesia and its eternal destiny depends on remembering that natural Israel, after whom God patterned the Church, is a nation and not a church. Along this line, it could be said that the writers of Scripture probably had no sense of God only ruling over a congregation and not a nation, which is why they worded everything in kingdom contexts heavily laden with poli-religious overtones. In their era, there was no separation of religion and government as deities indivisibly welded their land and temples because of how kingdoms were born.

For the Christian desiring to live a truly victorious life, laying hold of history's realities requires a giant leap. These truths are invaluable for comprehending and rightly, dividing the Lord's word. The monarchical mentality of Scripture's writers, replete with God's thoughts, is the key to how and why the Bible devolved to this generation the way it did. Adopting or at the least respecting their mindset is foremost for a healthy view of God's word. It is also helps to read and interpret it correctly to make sense the prophetic writers' sentiments on His Scriptures. Acquiring a proper mindset uncovers how the apostles illuminate and apply them in a way that is so drastically different from how other ministers do. All of this starts with appreciating, instead of disparaging the contemporary monarchical influence prevalent in the Scripture writers' era. That basic appreciation goes to why John identifies the redeemed as a nation of kings and priests in his Apocalypse, a mindset that mature apostles and prophets ultimately acquire as Christ's ambassadors. John's motivation for so naming God's people harks back to when the first apostles served Jesus Christ. He was their King, and they were glad about it. They entertained no notions of His being devious, abusive, or threatening to their liberty, nor did they consider Him conceited when He revealed His divine identity. In fact, the opposite is true; they rejoiced that the usual flaws inherent in human kings were not in their Messiah. Relieved, His disciples jubilantly saw Him as the answer to their oppression rather than another source of it. Approaching God's word with this attitude makes it easier to see how Scripture speaks to God's people and why its writers treat their audience as a heavenly nation and their canonical authority as derived from a deity and not an appointed political figure, or a national constitution.

How and Why God Entrusts His Continuum to Apostles

Ephesians 3:5 says how and why the Lord specially consecrated apostles, and prophets, to unravel and administrate His mysteries. He did it in much the same way that He separated the tribe of Levi to minister His priesthood, and from them, the sons of Aaron to perform its high priestly functions. In a manner similar to how He sanctified them to comply with His worship and service preferences spiritually speaking so too are apostles and prophets likewise consecrated. They are intrinsically constructed and separated for God's use to steward and dispense His New Testament, and new creation, mysteries and revelations. By heavenly and not natural birth, apostles get their dispensations from Jesus Christ. Paul, in this regard, said God separated him from His mother's womb, and the Scripture makes a similar statement about Old Testament Jeremiah the prophet. The Lord builds and endows apostles and prophets different from the other ministers to burden them with the powerful communication exchanges to take place between Him and the apostle. He must ensure that in the ways others miss His words or misconstrue His thoughts, they as His head messengers, do not. Conveying God's judicial mind and divulging His basilical secrets are paramount to apostles' ministries. For them to succeed, the Almighty designs and equips them quite different from the way He capacitates other ministers.

When it comes to God's divine communications, most people do not know how routine, it is for Him to impart His mind to messengers, especially the highly entrusted ones. What is imparted are His thoughts and will, His memory and vision, and His extensive experience with humanity. Other impartations include His ongoing worldly activities, along with how to articulate His thoughts and to get His will done on earth as it is in heaven. God took this approach with Moses as seen in His Deuteronomy prophecy. In that discourse, Moses sees his season ending, and yet also extending into the distant future at the same time. On his way out, He sees the Lord coming as foretold from the many ancient texts he would have had access to that confirm it. Hebrews 11:26 speaks to it. The Lord, who converted Moses from his Egyptian legacy to His Hebraic roots convinced him that he was a connecting ministry that brings forward what Abraham, Isaac, and Jacob all knew. He further tells Moses how it will all end. Until then, though, his apostolic mission is to lay the foundation for the Lord's eternal kingdom to come, and His Christ's ultimate reign on the earth. The Lord's words as spoken through Moses were authoritative, not exhortative, and yet his listeners were not offended at them. Instead, they took comfort in them. Unlike too many of today's Christian sermons, Moses is firm and decisive because he is addressing a nation and not a church. His emphases are kingdom, government, and statehood; not missions, fundraising, and church growth. Bible readers embracing this perspective grasp and properly apply the Lord's word to their faith and destiny. The only way to interpret the Scripture's sentiments and outlook accurately is to accept that Moses and other Bible contributors did not serve a church's membership but a nation's citizens under the Most High's kingship.

Consider this. As it stands today, the majority of the rules, disciplines and tenets of the Christian faith spring from and focus largely on the two to four hours a week church members spend in the pew. Countless converts spend decades learning how to worship, pray, behave in church, get the best out of God, or grow in their faith. How and why the Lord did what He did to save them, why and what He demands of them, and why what He does to keep them is left out of many people's Christian education. For the most part Christianity is all about the local church or the mission field. Apart from these two emphases, anyone with no interest or inclination to either one is almost snubbed by the Church. God in comparison holds no such myopic view of His handiwork. He loves His church as His body, but He is vaster than the institution bent on limiting Him. Apostles as His representatives foster this awareness and work to think like God to collaborate in His modern day goals and objectives, duties and responsibilities. They seek to learn what gives Christ, His right to rule and command the Almighty's people, and what it takes to fulfill His vision for His entire creation and not just the Church. For the apostle, the Lord is more than a shepherd He is a king, the King of kings. Seeing Him this way, makes them concerned with and committed to His unfolding heaven to earth activities. These they do even if many of them have yet to discover what those are, or how they should be done. Without knowing why, Paul's words in Ephesians chapter 3 speaks volumes to apostles because they relate to the mysterious revelations that brought them to Christ, and later in His ministry. It is rarely enough for this minister to be content with roaming and preaching. The apostle is driven by God's burning inward script that urges them to build His church, settle His body, increase His holdings, and secure His world dominion. As a result, faithful occupants of this office typically do not soft peddle God's truth or undermine His will as it is revealed to them. By nature, they are prone to honor what He did before being inducted into His service and pursue their calling according to the patterns set before them in His word.

APOSTLES AND GOD'S MYSTERIES

A chief mystery the Lord divulges to His apostles is the mystery of the gospel. The Old Testament prophets received it predictively, while the New Testament's apostles divulge it revelationally. Thus, the two mantles are reiterated as being the ones most suited to steward and propagate the Continuum. Their impetus, works to guard the purity of God's truths and the authenticity of His ministries. Persuaded apostles today answer best, the questions regarding the mystery of Christ disseminated by His early apostles as they received it from Jesus Christ. The Apostle Paul echoes this in Luke 24:44 in Acts 24:14 when defending the Way of God that was then being called heresy by his opposers. Paul unfolded his gospel from the Old Testament prophets' writings, the ancient scrolls that Paul calls parchments in his letter to Timothy. They are where the Risen Lord referred him to be equipped to carry His redemption to the Gentile world. Second Timothy 4:13 firmly shows Paul's commitment to the prophecies and teachings that preceded him. Being a highly trained rabbi, he no doubt was well familiar with them, which intensified is concern for the books and parchments he left behind. Paul regard for God's unbroken chain of events anchored his persuasion of others of the power of the gospels that saved Him and had the power to save his audiences too. The commission put upon him by the Risen Lord impressed upon him that that advancing His gospel was integral to his apostleship duties. The materials of his concern were probably gathered from his years in the Sanhedrin's service.

Jesus' first apostles worked through Moses Law. He named twelve, heaven ordained disciples, apostles. They, as the original twelve received the law as their first commission. Along with the prophets, it too prophesied the coming of Jesus Christ. As part of their training, the apostles' first commission dispatched them only to the lost sheep of Israel. Once they were under their eternal commission they would go into all the world to preach the gospel. Keeping with His classic patterns, the Lord Jesus' first and second commissions blended God's objectives for natural and spiritual Israel because merging the two would achieve His Father's objectives. However, before becoming the global Messiah, Jesus was sent to the Jews with His eternal apostleship activated after His ascension. Not being a Greek, but a Hebrew, Jesus did not don the title apostle until He fulfilled the Law of Moses because Moses foretold His coming as the prophet like himself who would arise from His fellow citizens. See Deuteronomy 18:14, 15.

Jesus' ministry was never strictly about this world or its inhabitants. He always had in view a world to come and a global church. [109] He knows the world He is in is passing away and there is another is to replace it as Mark 24:14 upholds. Matthew 25:34 reveals that Christ's Father prepared a kingdom for His believers, way back in the foundation of the world, while Mark 10:30 promises eternal life in the world to come. Luke 18:30 adds the promise of everlasting life. All passages indicate that apostleship began in the spirit. Anything beginning in the spirit realm means reaching outside of this world into another. For apostleship, it calls for drawing earth into the world that created it. It intimates a progressive conformance of this age to the ages to come, which are, in reality, God's eternal ages. All of Christ's apostles carry out their ministries with this mindset. Since that is the apostle's mindset, delving deeper into who and what this minister really for why the Lord saw fit to entrust the totality of His earthly kingdom duties to this office.

---

109 Matthew 12:32.

ETYMOLOGY OF APOSTLESHIP

The apostle is, generically speaking[52], "a deity or sovereign authority's specially commissioned messenger". All sources studied for this subject present apostles as Christ's deputized ambassadors. More expansively, an apostle is "A deity or sovereign's specially appointed messenger, delegated miraculous powers." "God and Christ send apostles as heaven's ambassador to overturn societal strongholds, establish its dominion, and deliver or return its nation, people and possessions to its rightful god." The apostle is the Lord Jesus' first minister. In light of this definition, refer to Acts 26:18; Revelation 11:15 and of course The Great Commission of Matthew 28:18-20. The Acts reference confirms the apostles' clash with other gods; the Revelation reference speaks to the Lord Jesus' world takeover, and Matthew's Great Commission sets forth their global mandate to make disciples of all nations. Ambassadorship, warfare, governance, and conversion all figure prominently in the apostleship. That God absorbed this mantle into the Ecclesia proves the Lord Jesus' sovereignty. That it has pre-world roots and targets solidify its indispensable place in God's Continuum.

FROM KINGDOM TO CHURCH TO WORLD

Jesus Christ sends His apostles to disciple the nations, settle or resettle His church, and to extend His heavenly mandates into present and future generations. They defend and reveal His verities, steward His mysteries, and globally demonstrate the gospel's power to save and transform. Although they emerge from the Church today discipling nations is how apostleship started out in the beginning of the Lord's ministry. His first apostles were handpicked from their nation to be dispatched to it as well. This practice underscores the uniqueness of the Great Commission's charge to all nations. When religions and their deities were localized in territories their worshippers populated, global evangelism as it is known today was uncommon to say the least. As His crucifixion and Paul's constant brushes with the law show, discipling could be dangerous as many lands treated disloyalty to their national deities as treason. Jesus' break with divine custom and in some cases divine law to dispatch His ambassadors to other gods' lands to convert their people was somewhat of an anomaly. Back then, lands were taken by incursions not preaching. However, with the gospel as their primary instrument, official New Testament apostleship popularized the Redeemer's lifestyle and embedded His world's culture in His generation and succeeding generations. This statement, along with Mark 4:23; 9:35; 24:14, seals apostleship as the Savior's bridge to all worlds. Along with governing in His name, apostles guard His kingdom and its holdings, and confirm His truths are being observed and acted on judiciously.

APOSTLESHIP IN THE CONTINUUM

Continuum apostleship, like the prophets, too, finds its origins and roots in God's world and not this one. Although Jesus introduces apostles in the New Testament, they were introduced as integral to His eternal kingdom. After all, Jesus did not have an earthly one and said more than once that His kingdom is not of this world. All that He did and everything He brought into being was marked for restoration in His world. The earth was for Him a little more than His plan's staging theatre. Scripture records His apostles as being the major launch, and a predominant branch of that plan. During their three and a half year training with Jesus Christ, the apostles learned how to discharge their office from the scrolls and the law. The Old Testament scrolls are how they recognized Him as The Messiah in the first place. Jesus often reads from these in their synagogues and He taught them everywhere. God embedded His apostles and prophets in His Continuum as Luke 11:49 shows. Jesus Christ through the wisdom of God sends apostles and prophets since the world began. Christ, who ordained them before the world says they will continue until the end of the age. Matthew and Luke quote Jesus' promise to make His apostles His eternal rulers. In this life, they are world ambassadors in Christ's future kingdom they are ordained His judicial governors.

John documents Jesus saying His Sender, God the Father instructed Him on what to speak to the world. He is to confine His message to what He heard in heaven from His Father before He became flesh. Jesus, in John 10:36, declares He is God's Son because the Godhead sanctified Him and sent Him into this world. Periodically, His disciples discerned did Martha in John 11:27. Moreover, the New Testament says repeatedly that Jesus came to save the world. John curiously reveals the Lord's disciples are not of the world just as He is not of it, and later repeats it. In John 16:28, the Savior reiterates that He came into the world from another one, soon to return to that world from which He came. Again and again, the Lord Jesus announced Himself to be from another world, merely borrowing human flesh and form to carry out a cosmic mission. He came into the world undercover to rescue His abducted creation and return them to their original Father, the one it shares with Him. That is His apostleship commission; it is why He is the Apostle and High Priest of our profession.

BEFORE THE WORLD AND THE CONTINUUM

John 17:5 records Jesus petitioning His heavenly Father to return Him to His eternal and sovereign glory after His earthly mission. He notes at the same time that He wants the followers God gave Him before He entered the world to be with Him. With this John, 17:11 agrees. John 17:24 says He prayed about a time that was before the foundation of this world. Acts 1:2 reports the first thing the Lord did when He resurrected from the grave was to give commands concerning the kingdom of God to His apostles through the Holy Ghost. Acts 1:26 adds they replaced Judas with Matthias to advance the Continuum Jesus had just shown them that they were a part of as His apostles. After they prayed to the Lord to reveal whom He had chosen to replace their fallen colleague, the text says the lot fell on Matthias. It does so according to the prophets and Psalms.[110] In Acts 2:37 Peter preaches the Gospel of Jesus Christ by reaching back to the Old Testament resources He corroborated as the Lamb of God to take away the sin of the world. Acts 3:17 also speaks of the mouth of all God's prophets that have been prophesying Him beforehand, with 3:21 going all the way back to the world's foundation. To resolve a dispute over how the Gentiles should worship the Lord, the apostles in Acts chapter 15 resorted to the prophets of old again. In Acts 15:15, their resolution agrees with the written words of the Old Testament prophets and psalmists. This passage comes from Amos 9:11, 12.[111] Acts 16:4 says that Christian dogma comes from the apostles who took their cue from the old prophets' writings. The word *decree* in that verse is the word <u>dogma</u> and means decree, ordinance, and doctrines. It comes from the official decrees issued by the Roman Senate. Acts 17:31 foresees that the Lord will judge the world on an appointed day by Jesus Christ while Romans 1:20 reveals the eternality of the Godhead and its creatorship. Romans 16:25, adds the prophets penned the mystery revealed to the Church from the Scriptures that have been unveiling God's truth since the world began.

First Corinthians 2:7 says the Lord's wisdom was ordained and kept as a mystery from before the world for the saints' glory. Ephesians 1:4 reveals the Christian was chosen by God before the foundation of the world. Ephesians 2:20 says the household of God is built upon apostles and prophets. Ephesians 3:5 says the Lord revealed His ages of mysteries to His holy apostles and prophets. That mystery is the Gentiles becoming part of Israel's commonwealth. Ephesians 3:9 reinforces the Lord's mystery was hid in God, who created all things by Jesus Christ. Ephesians 3:10 says that what

---

110 Psalm 69:25; Psalm 109:8.

111 Isaiah 8:20 says that the Lord's word and testimony is proof of His indwelling light.

the Lord is doing on earth is witnessed by and to the benefit of the principalities and powers in heavenly places. First Timothy 1:9 says the holy calling that saves the saint was given before the world began; 1:15 says Christ Jesus came into the world to save sinners. First Timothy 3:16 says, "And without controversy great is the mystery of godliness: God was manifest in the flesh, justified in the Spirit, seen of angels, preached unto the Gentiles, believed on in the world, received up into glory. Titus 1:2 talks about the hope of eternal life that God promised before the world began. In Romans 1:2 Paul says his apostleship call and the gospel are both according to the Lord's beforehand promise in the Scriptures. Again, he refers his readers to the prophets. "God's gospel, which he promised beforehand through his prophets in the Holy Scripture." Romans 9:23 says that God's preparations for the saints' glory are beforehand. Hebrews 1:6 discusses how the Almighty brought the first begotten into the world. Hebrews 3:1 calls Christ Jesus the Apostle and High Priest of the Christian's profession. Peter's first epistle, verse 11 speaks of Christ's beforehand prophecies to His Old Testament prophets. Hebrews 4:3, declares the Lord finished all His works from the foundation of the world. In Hebrews 6:5, the powers of the age to come are revealed. Jesus, in 9:26 came at the end of the world. His resurrection turned the page on His world and ushered in the Church's era. Chapter 10, verses 5 and 7 hark back to Jesus' precarnate days, declaring that a special body was prepared for Him that would grow in the womb of the virgin.

First Peter 1:20 says that Jesus Christ was foreordained before the foundation of the world. Second Peter 3:2 makes a compelling Continuum statement. *"That ye may be mindful of the words which were spoken before by the holy prophets, and of the commandment of us the apostles of the Lord and Savior."* Jude echoes this, *"But, beloved, remember ye the words which were spoken before of the apostles of our Lord Jesus Christ."* James 5:10 uses the ancient prophets that spoke in the name of the Lord as an example of patient suffering. Revelation 13:8 speaks of the *"the book of life of the Lamb slain from the foundation of the world"*. Look at how many times the words *before and beforehand* surface in the passages noted above. Collectively, they show an unfolding body of revelation that got its start in the Lord's world, some of which before the earth was, and travels in one unbroken chain down the ages to the birth of Jesus Christ, His death, resurrection and His church. They all touch, agree, and remain connected throughout an unbroken sequence of events with every successive event of the fourteen informing on or substantiating the other. In the Continuum, the event before the present one explains the event that is unfolding. The event following another sets the stage for the one behind it. The single term for such a contiguous thread and emerging cast of characters is God's Eternal Continuum. In the Old Testament, it got its start from the prophets, in the New Testament, it leaped forward, taking the whole earth with it, by the ministry of the Christ's apostles.

[18]

The Continuum's Angels

As alluded to earlier, angels figure prominently in God's Eternal Continuum. By their very nature, they would have to since they are spirit and therefore eternal. Numerous Scriptures disclose their secret activities supporting God's Eternal Continuum and the Lord Jesus' Great Commission. In the chapter that discusses the prophets in the Continuum is a section that speaks about the angels being the start of it all. Since the Continuum's fourteen events began with the Great War in heaven, it is logical to deduce that the angels were the first to be involved in the Lord's clash with those who preferred not to remain faithful to Him and His way. Owing to the fact that it was an angel that instigated the tragedy in the first place, the entire good and evil, life, and death, God and the Devil contest is rooted in that fateful event. When one reads the brief references to the frustrated angel's saga in Isaiah 14 and Ezekiel 28, their immense implications become clear. Bringing it all full circle, Chapter 12 of John's Apocalypse is an even briefer account of the war in heaven that expelled the dragon and his angels after Michael and his angels defeated them. Unrolled from eternity's archives the Creator's history explains two pivotal enigmas. On the one hand, these Scriptures disclose how things came to be the way they are on earth, and on the other, they unveil why this world was plunged in darkness and its trials and tribulations are so severe. This mystery is revealed as the angel brings the Almighty's backstory down through the ages to help people to realize that He has a history and that His history forms the basis of all that takes place in His worlds. In speaking with John, the angel recalls heaven's most shattering event, the war in heaven, and its creation wide consequences.

Phrased in an "in case you are curious about how this all began, here is the back story" way; in Revelation chapter 12 Christ's angel, fills John in on the heavenly transpirations. He is evidently an authority on the matter, no doubt having been there and so his recollections are seen by Christ as reliable. The way the Lord opens the Revelation suggests this angel may well have been Jesus' Prime Minister. A position that is typical of the servant working closest to the head of anything. With Jesus overseeing the communications and at times certifying its veracity, the angel brings John into the secrets of his world that the apostle could not otherwise have known or ever suspected. The basic theme of the conversation is that war did not begin on earth; it began in heaven. Adam was not the first being to use his free will to rebel against the Almighty; it had been done before, a long, long time ago. The laws and rules of war and peace reach back to God's world and not merely man's antiquity, despite the stage for the final clash between the two being set on earth. The way the Lord brought Moses into His past when He showed Him how He created the worlds, He repeats with John by showing Him how sin entered His eternal realms and spread to this one. The rebellion that led to a bloody revolt in heaven culminated into a violent contest between the Creator and a selfishly ambitious creature. The creature lost and forever expelled from God's supernal realms, is banished to earth until the time of the end of all things comes. However, God is not quite done with him yet. He has far-reaching plans for His new nemesis. Instead of idling him in some impenetrable prison until the end of all things, the Almighty finds the dragon still quite useful as an evil power. His new assignment is to test and sift the souls of His future species and races. The old serpent's dark visions of power and his utter self-deception qualified him for an assignment more to his liking, one that is in keeping with his new character. Since he so masterfully conceived his plan to amass an army to dethrone his Maker, the Lord thinks why not use him in that capacity repeatedly. After all, he demonstrated his deceptive ability well and definitely showed his determination and persuasiveness. With new his deceptive and persuasive skills, he successfully convinced the self-serving to join his ranks and submit to his leadership. So, why not continue to use him and just reassign him to a more compatible commission? Instead of remaining the anointed cherub that covers, which he clearly resented, Satan (his new epithet) can now function unrestricted with God's approval, as the Old Red Dragon. The red signifies the fiery war he waged against His Maker and the unprecedented bloodshed he initiated in God's kingdom. Revelation 12 voices it this way: *"And the great dragon was cast out, that old serpent, called the Devil, and Satan, which deceiveth the whole world"*. Considering his choices and losses, the name change better fit him and the new corps of rebels that joined his revolution. The havoc they have just wreaked earned them all responsibilities that made practical use of their expertise.

The logic of God's decision is based on the fact that spirit beings cannot die, which is why hell had to be created in eternity. It was designed for incorporeal creatures and used to incarcerate the Devil and his horde of destructive angels. Those that are not bound in hell are reassigned to lesser positions to perform darker, but still vital duties for the Most High. Ruling the night, the darkness, and all that is in them is essential for the same free will the Lord gave His celestial beings. The Maker extended the right of individual choice and decision to His later and lesser human creatures, exposing them to the possibility of inheriting the serpent's fate. However, free will decisions and their corresponding behaviors require a highly capable, dedicated, and experienced staff to administrate them. In the same way that believers have their celestial governors; unbelievers too must have a dedicated force of supernaturals to administer their rights. Faith and unbelief are God given, blood bought rights, and that is where the empire of unbelief enters. It is the institution fugitives from God's world built to serve their God given purpose of deceiving those rejecting Christ. Here is how Isaiah understood this divine custom,

> "Yea, they have chosen their own ways, and their soul delighteth in their abominations. I also will choose their delusions, and will bring their fears upon them; because when I called, none did answer; when I spake, they did not hear: but they did evil before mine eyes, and chose that in which I delighted not." Isaiah 66:3, 4.

Other passages that reinforce this truth are Isaiah 54:16; Job 12:16; 2 Thessalonians 2:10. These all express the Lord's attitude toward those who refuse Him, as do Titus 1:15-16 and Revelation 22:11. God is not a victim of sin, nor is He devastated by the likelihood of people rejecting His salvation. He is saddened by it, but by no means stunned. Nor is He at a loss for how to respond to unbelief. The Lord built an entire spiritual institution to accommodate those who opt out of His eternal life. An example of this is the holy angels that chose God and Christ after the cataclysmic battle that gave them a way out. They preferred to remain in heaven and along with rebuilding it after the destruction, forever serve as agents of His kingdom of light and life. These are the end time reapers the Savior mentions in His gospels. Until then, they handle His hallowed affairs. The ones who fell prey to the Devil's deception and elected to rise up against Him populated the new kingdom of darkness. The commencement of that world forever changed the landscape of eternity. From that point onward the Lord's light and dark forces; His godly and ungodly angels double as afterlife filters. Their irrevocable callings are to sift and try the professing faithful to ensure that heaven down through the ages, never has a repeat of the anointed cherub's anarchy in its territories again. The angels of light guide the faithful to the way of everlasting life. The angels of darkness bombard them with the snares and temptations that make them question the Lord and doubt His faith. Through eternally tested means, both groups certify the genuineness (and durability) of a convert's desire to dwell with the Almighty forever. It is a masterful plan that should be well understood by all who call on the name of the Lord for His salvation. He has decreed that the trying of His family's faith works patience because, the just, can only live by faith.

The Just Shall Live By Faith

Christians struggle their whole life with Christ and the issues and requisites of His faith. Many of them bristle at the idea of having to take God's word for their lives at face value. Looking forward to His world sight unseen is for some a subtle psychological strain. Unenlightened converts find it perplexing to take by faith that there is a hereafter and Jesus' side of it is the best one. That group makes up the greater part of the new creation Ecclesia. While it is true that the Holy Spirit provides prophetic snapshots of that world now and again, it is only after the saved leaves this one they discover their hope was not in vain. That wait is a large segment of the Christian life on earth. To process them for eternal life, ups and downs, wins, and losses, the senseless and the sensible all fill verifying roles in believers' readiness. Growing in God means getting comfortable with answering and living with His unknowables. It also means resolving that His well-established Scripture truths alone answer life's shock waves. Because doing so is not always an easy decision or practice, God's wisdom and foreknowledge must be embraced by faith. Additionally, the Lord's truths in the believer's life are constantly tested by both sides to separate the faithful from the faithless.

Earlier, the Lord's decision to confine all that may be known of Him to the 66 highly contested books of the Christian Bible were explored. The question posed then is why He would do so when He has the world at His disposal. What would make Him perpetually rely on the least conspicuous place to make His point? The best answer is the word faith. Taking into consideration the atrocities His world and its citizens suffered at the hands of one scheming self-willed creature, and the enormous losses they suffered for however long it lasted, one can surmise that the cost of repeating that catastrophe is just too great. The Lord's faith requirement because of this has very real value to Him. It is in His realm a preventative since the motivation behind the cherub's betrayal was independence from his Maker's government. Lust for power and preeminence drove a single trusted servant gripped by delusions of grandeur to turn on his Maker. That sinister notion moved Satan to wage war against the Almighty's kingdom and his compatriots in a brazen effort to overthrow God's rule and replace it with his own. It almost goes without saying then that those were bitter times for the Lord and the very remembrance of them warn Him against misplaced affection or familial indulgence in the future. Those who will spend the rest of His ages with Him will be thoroughly tried and cleared before He accepts them into His kingdom. And, since the betrayal inspired the transgression that blighted and terrorized His worlds for so long, He demands verification of a convert's unshakeable fidelity. God will never put Himself or His world at risk again, nor will He expose it to the abhorrent abuses it underwent while He worked through its pollution. There will be never be a recurrence of that incident again, period! Such resolve and vehement hatred on God's part for those born under the law of sin and death is difficult to conceive and for humans to grasp. Spiritually blind humanity is confused by a seeming duality in His nature. God is love and yet, despite His love, He will banish souls to hell forever.

Numerous Christians find God's eternal judgments incredulous and downplay sin's condemnation by rejecting or marginalizing them. What many of them do not know is that He has already been sending creatures to hell and has been doing so for ages. His judgments appear to be at odds with His mercy and forgiveness and so aspirants of His eternal life cannot reconcile the two. The question of how a loving God can... clashes with the immutability of His holy and righteous demands. He is unmoving on these two issues because He knows their origins and their inventor, something humans must also take by faith. Divine love and divine justice surface as contradictions of each other if one is ignorant of the backstory. Treating the Lord as single dimensional, albeit all-powerful monarch drives people to stand on one side or the other of His personhood. To them He is either almighty or He is love and the two in most believers' minds cannot possibly coexist in one being, and yet they do in the Lord. He loves what He made and hates the destructive effects of the free wills that oppose Him. Since earth has never known how pristine and how magnificent God's world is, it cannot appreciate the extent of agony it endured from the one that rose up from its ranks to overthrow it. It took much for the Godhead to restore order to its world and bring peace and harmony back into its citizens' lives. So, as humans would say on earth, sin is a raw spot for God that leaves no room for tolerance. Despite the enormous wisdom and expertise gained from His creation's dark sides, a revisit of those eras is out of the question therefore the Almighty demands that righteousness, fidelity, and obedience are all worked out in the human soul before it enters His realm. The idea that some believers have that the Lord in the end will forgive the Devil and his angels is delusional. If He intended to, He would have done so by now and not cast him out of heaven; and more importantly, never have downgraded his celestial status. Such an idea can only come from a mind that began in this world and not from one that shared His experience in heaven. Imagining that the Devil was as naïve as Adam's offspring is errant since prior to his act there was no such thing as sin. Its possibility was in no one's mind in heaven but God's. Only those who lived through the ordeal can appreciate the Godhead's resolve to guard and keep His eternal citizens from having to relive those times. Even the cherub had no way of knowing how devastating his campaign was going to turn out or how unprepared he was to live with its aftermath. Only the Creator knew what the antithesis He created would produce, and He kept it to Himself until a decision contrary to Him was conceived and acted out.

THE DEVIL KNEW WHAT HE WAS DOING

Unlike humans who must take the superlativeness of God's eternal world by faith, those that sparked the Great War in heaven knew full well what they were doing. They knew heaven's powers, its potential, and its glories, which is why they wanted it for themselves. They despised their Creator's way of life and wanted to replace it with their own government as a thorough inverse of all God originated and ordained. To accomplish that, nothing less than a total demolishment of the Almighty's kingdom would do because He constituted everything they craved. It is noteworthy that although they wanted His kingdom badly, they also despised Him at the same time. Nevertheless, the plan was to obliterate the Creator's world was hatched and implemented. A newer and less capable regime planned to renovate God's creation according to a new agenda. The revolutionaries would begin by inseminating its inhabitants with perversities and seductions that effectively weaved Satan's wishes into everyone's psyche. From their thoughts to their language, their passions and their will, everything the Creator implanted was to be erased and replaced with the way Satan saw life. His will and word would become law, obsoleting the Godhead's existence in the process and abolishing its culture. The Lord allowed that agenda to play out for everyone affected to see its outcomes. Using it as a living object lesson, the Most High permitted all of His family to witness the other side of the story. The Lord chose the dragon's shocking revolt to let everyone taste and remember its exceedingly sinful sin. His intent was that they experience and arrive at their own conclusions on its evil by living it and no longer just by His warnings against it. He further thought, it was prudent for the rest of His society to watch and feel the brunt of one of His creatures pitting himself against His Creator. Experiences of this magnitude were essential for their future safety and stability. So the struggle in heaven between God and Satan continued long enough for everyone involved to feel and etch its pain and sorrows in their memory.

The ordeal enabled every citizen of heaven to realize on their own all the reasons why God's is the best way. Beneath these objectives, there was another more indelible aim. In allowing the entire campaign to run its course, the Lord was able to let all His realm see the process of sin and discern who was with the Devil and who remained on His side. That He knew these things was irrelevant. To motivate His societies to want to safeguard themselves in the future, He permitted them to watch it unfold and observe what it took for a relative to become an enemy and an ally a foe. They had to witness for themselves the falling away that was an inevitable consequence of the rebellion. Additionally, they had to witness for themselves why sin is exceedingly sinful, live with its fallout and agree with Him that it must be eradicated and safeguards imposed to ensure no repeat of the event. Those safeguards extended to searching everyone's heart, logging the faithful from the fiendish, and confirming publicly who defected and who defended the realm. Before the purging could begin, every stage and effect of the process had to become part of the eternal record for future creatures and worlds to be guided by them.

Showing steely restraint, the Most High let His beloved kingdom languish under death and its threats to learn and appreciate His way of life beyond His warnings to them. They needed to picture and not just imagine the outcomes of displacing Him. Also, He aimed to have them catalogue for history everything that made evil what it is while they were still stinging from its assaults. Sin is evil because it robs, wounds, abuses, and kills on every scale. It was a hard lesson, but a worthwhile one as Revelation 12:12 shows. The sweeping outcome convinced all of God's worlds to stand against such reckless notions in the future. The anointed cherub had made the difference between God's way and the rebels', vividly clear. They no longer had to imagine what it would be like to do things another way, living the dragon's lie helped them understand and cherish their Maker's logic and motives. Eternity's citizens once rid of the chaos and destruction that plunged them into despair understand why they live the life they live and the rationale of the world God created for them. The reasons for His governance and standards are forever branded in their history and they harbor no delusions about the dangers of ambitious revolutions. The success of God's recovery plan inspired them to vow to never relive its lessons or undergo its consequences again. It also drives them to do all legitimately possible to warn His new worlds and creatures to take it by faith that His law and government are indeed the best and only ways to live forever in their age of light.

People often follow these revelations up with questions about why did the Lord not nip it all in the bud. Why did God not upon hearing the anarchic thoughts of the dragon's heart, judge him privately? He could have averted it all, if He had condemned the imaginations when they first formed in the cherub's heart. Why did God not simply sentence him to death, and punish him forever based on what He perceived to spare Himself and His world the tragedies of letting it all play out? The answer lies in the one-third angels that Satan sold on the idea. Killing their leader was only a temporary solution. What he sowed in his revolutionaries' hearts continued to fester and eventually, one of them would take up his vision. It was better to let it all run its course for so many judicious reasons. Once all of the effects of Satan's dream thoroughly manifested and everyone saw him for what he really is, and after suffering under his cruelty for a time, they would beg the Most High to intervene. They would not wonder when they saw the dragon's public judgment and banishment why the Lord suddenly broke out against their brother without cause. That is what would have happened had the Lord reacted to what He heard Lucifer's heart plan against Him and His creation. Beginning life in the upside of God's kingdom where everything worked and no one appeared to conceive so much as an evil thought, hid from them the effects of what would happen if they did things another way. Like Adam and Eve in the garden, God's eternal world knew only light, life, and good. They took it for granted and saw His righteousness and warnings as the antediluvians did. Heaven had never known crime, abuse, even death until the revolt came, the same way the Edenic age had never known rain before the flood. Though God is always right, heaven had never seen or felt hatred and brutality before, so the prospects of their effects were nothing more than vague ideas in their minds, if they thought of it at all. Their ability to visualize the destruction and sorrow that came with opposing their Maker was little more than a figment. They could not envision an actual admonishment against a real threat. At least that is how it was until it began to manifest. Then, like the never before rainfall that flooded the earth for the first time in response to its sin, heaven's citizens awakened to the ominousness of their alternatives too late.

Here is what God was doing while His populations came to terms with the new dark forces and contended with their powerful assaults on their world. Covertly, He worked in seclusion to quash the uprising. For a complex of reasons, it took quite a bit to address and resolve something as foreign to His world as war. For instance, since His world never had conflict before, responding to it when it arose, took time. While the revolt did not catch the Lord by surprise because He had already detected the secrets of the angel's heart, it was not that obvious to His leaders and citizens at first. Discerning the issue and realizing its compounding consequences was not a knee jerk response for eternity's inhabitants. It was all new, and for them completely out of left field. Sure, they knew the cherub had some problems, he had been grumbling about the way things were for a while. Still, nothing indicated that he had a wide scale revolution in mind. Who would have thought that he would disrupt their entire way of life to get his way? Coming to terms with something like that was difficult, and it added to the length of time it took to regroup. To act, they had to take on an entirely new consciousness to plan how they would defend their kingdom. From acknowledging that the threat is real to assessing its damage, a whole new way of thinking, planning and living emerged. God's foreknowledge was helpful and He did more with it than file it away under future possibilities. He was prepared and was set to prepare His people as well to deal with their new adversary, but again, nothing was swift. As heaven's rulers got ready to act, the assaults mounted and the citizens' suffering compounded. Operating on principles only a Creator could know, the Lord in order to respond to the treachery and sneak attacks on His realm had to bring out of His hidden repositories, resources that only He knew would one day be necessary. Up until then, the only provisions heaven's inhabitants needed to sustain their kingdom revolved around everything but weapons of war. Now those unfamiliar implements were brought out of their arsenals, and who ever suspected they existed? Like Noah's ark, their construction and necessity were unimaginable by the wider population, but that day is over and life as they knew it will be no more. The ignorance, innocence, and blissfulness that permeated their paradise were gone forever, and something more sobering was taking its place. Their exclusive knowledge of good was now to share its platform with the knowledge of evil. Pain and sorrow never thought possible before would mark their life experiences, and in God's mind it is all valid. However, hindered by the newness of the events and the first of its kind hostility, God found gathering an army and readying it for battle met a stunned resistance.

Unperceivable changes were being made and demands being put upon God's world that kept them reeling from one upset after another. Relocations, invasions, and something akin to inductions into military service unsettled their communities. Restoring peace and preserving their world was all consuming. Everything was focused on it. However, before any of it could begin, warfare strategies had to be made. After they were devised, combat tactics for carrying them out were developed. Implementations for setting it all in motion and orientating the people to all of it had to take place while other things were happening. The Almighty's faster than light, wisdom and abilities would have anticipated and performed these tasks instantaneously. His leaders, not too dissimilar would have caught on to what was happening rather quickly and recognized how He would handle it. The masses, however, would be another matter. Getting them up to speed and equipping them to act and fight called for softer and more drawn out measures. Orientating them to their new world and its new order required other impartations and trainings that extended their adjustment period and lengthened the abominations gripping their world.

How long it took for the Great War and its counteractions to complete is anyone's guess. One thing is for sure, the measures employed for its crises could not have been executed rapidly because war, recovery and restoration are tediously slow processes, especially where multitudes of beings are involved, no matter how advanced their society is. Here is a curious question. What did God do with the ruins? The combat rubble and other warfare debris, what did He do with them? Intuitively, one would think that as He rebuilt, renovated, and revived His home that He would use, perhaps invent, better materials. Materials that were less vulnerable. So what did He do with the old ones that were destroyed or depleted? How did He replenish His world? The most plausible answer to these, based on His creation practices are that He recycled the former materials and reused them elsewhere.

Spiritual Insemination Unstoppable

By the time, all the creatures of eternity realized what was at risk, the damage had begun, and the counterculture of darkness had taken hold on theirs. Once it began, there was no way to stop it. Also, the permanence of spirituality dictated that it runs its course. Averting the multiplicity of crises or the wreckage left in its wake proved to be an arduous process. These are but a few of the reasons the Lord's prudence lets His realm experience the full repercussions of their rival countrymen's rebellion. He delayed intervening long enough for the whole population to experience its damage. His delay tactic wanted everyone remaining with Him to resolve in their own free will to vow never to allow even a hint of an anarchic idea to seize their kingdom again.

Since a cherub decided in his heart to take over their world, the Lord needed every survivor of his failed attempt to settle who was who, and where they wanted to spend eternity. If He did not use the situation to force them to choose, repeated uprisings would destabilize all creation, and the only thing that would unify His masses, would be war instead of peace. For the sake of their collective future, God provoked their will to remove forever any taint of the seductions that deceived the serpent into believing he could overthrow His dominion. Once the core message had finally gotten across and its lessons fully learned, the Lord moved to rectify the entire situation, although He was not idle during their fiery trials. In the background, He aggressively plotted to rid His world of the dragon's deteriorating influences for all ages. At the most propitious time, heaven acted and the Lord's armies led by Michael, His Archangel, won a decisive victory over the Devil's revolution. In doing so, God and Christ leveraged their victory to purge his treachery from their societies and permanently evict them from the celestial realms, which is how that old serpent the Devil came to be lodged in earth's terrestrial spheres. It is also how and why he was on site in the garden to tempt the progenitors of the Almighty's final creation species, humanity.

Contrary to popular belief, the belief that the Devil and his angels were just like humans in their ignorance of the costs and effects of the rebellion, logically, could not be true. They all, unlike the earth's inhabitants began their life with God. His was their first world and the only life they ever lived. The rebels that disrupted God's world knew full well, what was at stake; later beings are deprived of that knowledge. Before Satan invented one, there was no alternative to the Almighty's perfection. Anyone wishing to have their own way had to destroy His order to do so. Defying God necessitated total overthrow of His kingdom to weaken it for invasion and takeover. This possibility is nonexistent to those who die in this world and plan to live forever with God. Human souls and spirits will not enter into His world with evil intents and errant thoughts in their hearts. The prospect of their taking up where Satan and his evil angels left off will never see the light of day again in heaven. God's purging and perfecting systems see to it. Starting out inherently full of what the Devil invented, people born on earth must work their way up to God and not do what he did, which is to fall down from his first estate. In order to dwell in the Lord's presence, humans will have to perfect their faith because the only way to inherit His eternal life is through stringently tried faith. That faith requires creation's free will agents to prove their fidelity to their Maker before getting the right to live forever as His immortal citizen. As Jesus says, those counted worthy to obtain that world, speaking of His, must be proven by the Lord and judged entirely worthy, meaning deserving, of His world. Entrance into that world begins with earning the privilege of rising from the dead and being recognized by the kingdom of life as "children of the resurrection". And, it all begins with, the trying of the convert's faith supervised by the Almighty Himself, but carried out by the kingdom of darkness into which every human except Adam and his wife is born. The unmerited favor rejected by the fallen angels is bestowed on humans in the reverse. Upon receiving Jesus Christ as Savior and Lord, and after being tried by His sufferings to conquer their carnal inherencies, people become in the Lord's opinion worthy to be received into His everlasting kingdom.

Hebrews 5:12-14 gives the premise of God's eternal life decisions. Those who would spend forever with Him in His world must know the darkness, easily recognize evil, and intimately comprehend His problems with sin. Beyond this, they must daily make conscious decisions to choose or refuse one or the other. Genesis 3:22 voices this difference, *"And the Lord God said, Behold, the man is become as one of us, to know good and evil: and now, lest he put forth his hand, and take also of the tree of life, and eat, and live forever."* The phrase "as one of us, to know good and evil" insightfully reveals God's overriding condition for eternal beings. As inheritors of His death free life, they must know good <u>and</u> evil. They must know it, not as is frequently taught, good <u>or</u> evil as if they are an either or proposition, but as equal choice options. The wise and prudent know good as thoroughly as they know evil and vice versa to make enlightened choices on the one that brings life. This is the very point Hebrews five makes. *"But strong meat belongeth to them that are of full age, even those who by reason of use have their senses exercised to discern both good and evil."* That it must be learned is early declared by Moses in Deuteronomy 1:39 *"Moreover your little ones, which ye said should be a prey, and your children, which in that day had no knowledge between good and evil, they shall go in thither, and unto them will I give it, and they shall possess it."* An intriguing statement is made by Isaiah 7:15, 16. Both verses support this teaching by ending with "to refuse the evil and choose the good". The ability to discern between good and evil and to make God's choices qualifies one for eternal life. That simple sounding ability earns one a place in heaven. Conversely, if a person chooses the darkness, Psalm 78:49 is God's response to that choice. Whenever anyone chooses God's light the Lord answers by sending Jesus Christ to them to begin their journey of preparing to enter His everlasting kingdom.

All ultimate afterlife decisions are wholly honored by God, who only wants those who crave Him to be with Him. This is true with one caveat; people on earth decide their eternal afterlife and its rewards sight unseen. Once they leave the body, their decisions are final and there are no do overs, for very good reasons. Heaven knows the root of heart decisions, for or against it. It has lived with both before. To protect itself, it is not about to relive its age of rebellion with every creation and species the Most High makes. Sin is ancient and cannot change, neither can its inventor, nor creation's Maker. All the major Continuum figures are well familiar with sin's detriments. It is why dark spirits know the outcome of their temptations and the angels of light labor tirelessly to prevent humans from succumbing to them. No immortal being is ignorant of sin's diverse manifestations, and they are seduced by none of its distortions. No celestial being has to second guess by now its motivations or implications, and that is why earth afterlife decisions are final. People who die literally fall into the hands of God's eternal system. They enter a spiritual world with an ironclad judicial process that has served Him for ages. Its justices are not only waiting to welcome human souls and spirits, but all of the implications of Matthew 25:41 and Matthew 5:22 infer eternity's justice scales are waiting to process earth's decedents for heaven or hell. Powerful realities solidify these statements as warnings for all the Maker's future beings. They are the angels that have already been judged. Evil angels have long ago been condemned for their sins and godly angels rewarded for their faithfulness to Christ and God, particularly in their most difficult periods. When Paul declares God's children will judge angels, he is not talking about their righteousness or sin. These have already been adjudicated. What saints will judge are the rewards angels will earn as the ministering spirits sent forth to minister to the heirs of Christ's salvation. Eternal judgment awaits the earth's residents, which is why Hebrews says the Lord does not give aid to angels. Spirits' forever was disposed of after the crises in their world were abated. Everything pertaining to final judgments insofar as death, hell, and the grave is concerned pertains strictly to humans. This lengthy explanation provides the serious seeker of God's truth with essential wisdom to make informed choices in this very short life. For or against the Lord Almighty, the last and most enduring choice a soul makes is the one that lands them in His Presence to welcome them into His world, or banishes them forever in His everlasting prison. That prison and its perhaps well-populated jail cells justify The Messiah's extensive discussions on hell. He knows it is real, and that it is already mandated that incorporeal criminals and aliens of His righteousness go there. Two things Peter's words in 2 Peter 2:4-5 assert.

> "For if God spared not the angels that sinned, but cast them down to hell, and delivered them into chains of darkness, to be reserved unto judgment; And spared not the old world, but saved Noah the eighth person, a preacher of righteousness, bringing in the flood upon the world of the ungodly."

Peter voices several Continuum related details in these verses. The first is that the subject is about angels, in particular the angels that sinned. Second, he is announcing that hell anciently existed in their sphere. Sinning angels were cast down from heaven to hell. Third, Peter is talking about the old world, which by implication says the world that is today is not the one of Noah's day. Interestingly, the same planet, the same earth, the same universe (assumedly) but a different world. The ancient flood that Noah escaped when he obeyed God and built the ark came upon that world and replaced it with another. Jude 1:6 supports Peter's words. The passage says angels, again referring to otherworldly beings, broke ranks with the celestial realm, and they abandoned their celestial principalities[53] for earthly reasons. Their superiority violated all of the Creator's restrictions and being judged as spiritual criminals were arrested and imprisoned in hell. Both passages note that hell is dark, it is abysmal, and it is final. Imagine what it is like for the humans who have already gone there, such as, for instance, the rich man because of impoverished Lazarus who suffered at his gate every day. Think about the puny human spirit and soul being incarcerated forever in hell with the powerful spirits and souls of the angels that sinned. The darkness, futility, and alienation aside, it must be agony to be interminably at their mercy. The Savior knows this and urges those of His era, and beyond, to avoid it at all costs. He knows from His days as Yahweh, that hell's rigid criteria were fixed long ago and conditions for avoiding it are non-negotiable. His world's penal codes and the spiritual penitentiary that serves them antedate His incarnation, which makes them as much a part of God's Eternal Continuum as the glorious paradise reserved for the righteous.[112]

So How Important are the Angels to the Continuum

From the Garden of Eden onward angels play an important role in God's earthly and heavenly events. Genesis 6 pictures them dating back to before this world began, a fact borne out by the Lord placing cherubim in East Eden to guard the way to the tree of life. Genesis 6:2 classifies them as the "sons of God" created according to His spiritual makeup. In three separate verses, Job mentions the "sons of God" as angels of which Satan was once one. The sons of God reference speaks more to the Lord's handiwork than it does His lineage to distinguish them from mankind, or the sons of man. The first of God's begotten seeds is Jesus. Until the Church, The Messiah held a sovereign position and rank equal to God. He suspended His sovereignty to bring the born again Christian into existence as a son or daughter of the living God. Spirit filled

---

112 Luke 13:38, 39.

Christians differ from the angels, and Adam's seed by being born of God and not just created, a point all of the New Testament writers underscore as the reason heaven bound souls must be born again. Those born of Christ come from His lineage and are of the Godhead's very genes, stashed in the person of Jesus Christ and reserved for the new creation. The means by which they are brought into existence makes the Christian not merely God's innovation, but His very own flesh and blood; for the blood of Christ is essential for the salvation process. Of course, none of this is to diminish the angels' work or indispensable value to the Lord. Scripture shows them having existed and functioned in their respective capacities forever. This truth firmly entrenches their place in the Continuum that holds God's history and advances Christ's destiny to the end of all ages. Despite being of different genetic makeup, the angels nonetheless are part of God's eternal family.

Tracing the Angels' Throughout the Continuum

Aside from the terms, principalities and powers the Bible mentions one or more of eternity's supernatural creatures nearly three hundred times. Most commonly, they are simply called angels, the catchall phrase people use to identify any celestial being. However, most comprehensively, the spheres of these creatures include, cherubim, seraphim, watchers, holy ones, spiritual and flaming ministers, living creatures, and the twenty-four elders. All of those references picture them as God's ministers. These are different from the human spirits made perfect. Biblically they are never portrayed as imps, naked children, or feeble errand runners. Instead, the Lord depicts His angels as powerful beings whose sole purposes are to please the Most High and handle His concerns in the realms of humanity.

The main of God's earthly ministry rests in the hands of His angels. The Most High assigns them jurisdictional authority over select regions to execute His law and administrate His government in the physical world. God uses some angels to legislate His law as they did in the wilderness when Moses received the Ten Commandments. Others are the enforcers and still more are messengers. Scripture says angels are charged with certain earthly realms, such as the watchers that judged Nebuchadnezzar for his pride. These would be a cross between the thronal and judicial angel. Daniel 10:12-21 depicts jurisdictional angels as nations' heavenly princes. The equivalent of God's royal offspring as their title sons of God implies, prince angels are granted sovereign like authority set over monarchical domains. Moreover, as issuers of God's laws, the angels communicate with prophets because as divine intermediaries they receive firsthand what He wants to publish in the natural world. The seven who stand before God functioning as the inner cordon encircling His throne have already been identified and their responsibilities discussed. According to Revelation 15:1, they are the Apocalyptic Angels of Christ's seven churches.

In addition to all that has been said about the angels, one single feature the majority of them share is fire and light. Throughout Scripture, they are described in connection with fire as if it is the predominant element of God's world. The angels appear then to be made of whatever elements and forces that produce fire. It also seems to sustain them as water does humans on earth. All of them are presented as exuding some sort of fire from their core. Not only that, but they appear able to emit fire on demand. Electricity surfaces as the self-generative agent that sustains them. It emerges as angels' life and power their supreme constituent. Furthermore, fire as their primary energy source seems to be the angels' regeneration. Each member of their class of creature hood's life appears to rejuvenate it to sustain and supply them the way air and water regenerates human cells. In the manner in which physical bodies on earth regenerate according to the earth's elements, angels' bodies do the same, according to heaven's immaterial physiology with one major difference. Theirs is entirely fire and electricity, humans are mainly air and water. With that being the case, angel's bodies are clearly composed of material that not only withstands the powers that sustains them, but is active enough to replenish it from their inner resources. More precisely, their outer sheath, comparatively human skin, cloaks their fiery or electrified bodies. The cloaking typically serves the purposes of manifesting in human form. Sometimes they exude pure light and energy and at other times, cloudy mist.

Paul's words in 1 Corinthians 15:40, 44 speak to this.

> "There are also celestial bodies, and bodies terrestrial: but the glory of the celestial is one, and the glory of the terrestrial is another... There is a natural body, and there is a spiritual body."

Couple this passage with Hebrews 7:16: Jesus

> "Who is made, not after the law of a carnal commandment, but after the power of an endless life."

Now here is a peculiar question. If Jesus when on the Mount of Transfiguration disclosed His majestic glory as the Son of Man, and that manifestation as the Son of Adam was splendorous, what must His glorified body be like? And, if that body is higher than the angels and theirs higher than humans, what awaits the Christian has to be magnificent, and it is as Paul says in 1 Corinthians 15:42-44:

"So also is the resurrection of the dead. It is sown in corruption; it is raised in incorruption: It is sown in dishonour; it is raised in glory: it is sown in weakness; it is raised in power: It is sown a natural body; it is raised a spiritual body. There is a natural body, and there is a spiritual body."

These words completely reverse Genesis 3:19 insofar as the human whose body passes from death to life as Jesus promises in John's Gospel is concerned. Nine features identify the eternal new creation body: 1) celestial 2) spiritual 3) powerful 4) incorruptible 5) immortal 6) heavenly 7) deathless 8) quickening 9) Messiah-like. These qualities the angels began their lives with, which is why they subsist on fire and electrics. They are made of it and constantly rekindle it at will. That is why the living creatures were seen as having hot coals within them. What Ezekiel saw was the internal generator that energizes the creatures of God's world in varying degrees. Fiery energy enlivens them. It drives and nourishes them, and ceaselessly powers their vessels. A hint of this is seen in the cloven tongues of fire that rested above the heads of each of the 120 present in the upper room when the Holy Spirit fell from heaven. Repeatedly, God is likened to fire as in the instance where John talks about how Jesus baptizes. The Bible's fire metaphors are important because this world's knowledge of energy and power was not available to the Scriptures' scribes. When they saw the other-worldly light, the only superior energies they could connect it with were fire and lightning. Today it is understood that they meant something akin to and greater than this universe's sun and other luminaries. To anchor these realizations biblically, recall the Lord Jesus on the Mount of Transfiguration. He shows He embodies, even in His downgraded state, the composite energy, and luminance of heaven's celestial beings, indicating that it is self-contained and auto generated. Read again, Matthew 17:1-6 and Mark 9:1-7. The Savior, it up the entire mountain from His being. Consider this episode as follows. Jesus was illuminated, Moses and Elijah appear in glory, and a cloud overshadows them that does not dim the mountain as ordinary clouds do. Instead, it brightens it further, demonstrating that light, God's world, and its citizens are all illustriously equal.

Another appreciable feature about the angels as they are depicted in Scripture is that they are servants. Servanthood seems to be the overriding consciousness of the Lord's devoted celestial beings. They exist to serve Him in whatever capacity He constructed them to do, which brings out another remarkable trait about angels. What humans would term their lot in life, angels resonate as their created purpose. They and their construction are one with their expertise. What the angels are is what they do; what angels do is what they are, which demonstrates the complete fusion of their nature with their capacities. Angels over the waters, for instance, are wholly constructed for their functions. With the ones over the elements, planets, galaxies, and luminaries, it is the same way. To watch an angel in action is to know why he was made. Fused qualities make it easier for them to, as Christians like to say, stay in their lane. Because they do not die, angels remain permanent members of the Lord's Continuum. Those that uphold its light and those that uphold its darkness equally propel creation forward from within it. However, Christ's angels resolved, long ago, any concerns and discomforts about their makeup, purposes, and the functions they perform in God's kingdom. Joining Him in His fight against heaven's revolutionaries settled any displeasure or resentment they could have about why they were made, who they are to the Lord, and what they exist to do.

The word angel shows up in Scripture nearly three hundred times to show how involved they are in the Lord's work and His administration of the earth. Falling into several classifications, named above, their duties and assignments range from messaging to ministry, governance to guardianship, judgment to leadership; from the superintendence to performance of God's word. They empower this world and its inhabitants with God's capacities so that each one born on the planet has sufficient potential to fulfill His prescribed destiny. The angels can influence or oppose human will and behavior, restraining it at God's word as one did with Balaam to warn him against cursing Yahweh's people. Angels protect those born into and residing on the earth and conduct them when their time comes to leave it. They watch over nationalities, kingdoms, countries, enterprises, humans, and their institutions. They control the elements, orchestrate divine penalties and rewards, and since the victory of the Lord Jesus Christ, they tend His church. The angels have superior power and have had it from their creation. Those in some realms or assignments take on human form, although the ones permanently stationed in God's temple do not. Occasionally, they are dispatched to earth for brief or extended periods to see to the success of the Lord's royal ventures. Jesus says the angels, as spirit beings and not flesh and blood, live forever. He also said that they do not procreate, and so exist to serve Him faithfully in His rulership of the world, and no doubt all of His worlds.

The Lord's angelic divisions[113] are traditionally known as His celestial hierarchy. It is conventionally taught that He divided His heavenly hosts into three defined spheres of supernal authority, and within each hierarchy, nine classes (choirs). The first sphere is classically known as the sphere of the heavenly counselors. The second

---

113 Wikipedia.com

sphere is called heaven's governors. The third sphere is cast as heaven's messengers. Together, these sums up the span of purposes and duties for which the Lord created and continues to employ (and deploy) His celestial creatures. Traditionally, angels' are believed to fall into nine groups. Taken largely from scripture, these are:

(1) Seraphim

(2) Cherubim

(3) Thrones or Ophanim[114]

(4) Dominions

(5) Virtues

(6) Powers or Authorities

(7) Principalities or Rulers

(8) Archangels

(9) Angels

Along with the most recognized nine angelic groups are the living creatures such as those that visited Ezekiel and the twenty-four elders who are celestial but senatorial. Their function is unlike the angels, what the term elder used to identify them implies. God's word says the angels excel in strength. That strength is not just physical, but is influential as well. As with their human counterparts, each angel has his own anointing, meaning as well as emitting energy, they exude influence a resource to succeed in their delegated tasks. The energy overrides natural technologies and the influence persuades humans to yield t their assignments. Angels have the latitude to act independently, meaning they are not obliged to clear all of their decisions or actions with the Lord before issuing or carrying them out, nor more than earthly authorities of like caliber. This includes ecclesial and secular authorities. Some angels, those close to the Most High are granted near alter ego status, meaning they are so trusted by Him that He delegates them near sovereign powers and authority. The angel He assigned to replace Himself in Exodus 23:23 and 32:34 fit this classification. He appears to have had a long service to the Lord, because the phrase used to distinguish him, "my angel" is used by Jesus a third time in Revelation 22:16 where he is sent to testify of the Lord in His churches. Speaking of the Churches, the angels are as prominent in its establishment as they are in the Savior's birth, ministry, and departure from this world. Moreover, the book of Acts says angels guided and protected the early apostles, going so far as to liberate them from jail. In respect to the Continuum goes, this brief traces firmly cements their place in it. It further exemplifies what makes them important to it. As with any institution or kingdom, a government's civil or in their case, celestial

---

114 Wheels or chariots.

servants are invaluable to its administration and effectiveness. Seeing God's world as a kingdom instead of a religion paints a clearer picture of the angel's importance to Him. They ensure His will is performed, stabilize His kingdom, and perpetuate what He does and desires to all generations.

[19]

Spiritual Protocratics

The Lord has a spiritual protocratic force that attends to Christ's Kingdom responsibilities to ensure the veracity, and perpetuity of God's Eternal Continuum. This force is guided, and regulated by hidden codes that legislate and actuate every seen and unseen aspect of the Almighty's creation. Mysterious instructions guide God's invisible messengers communicating to them their Creator's silent words and laws.[115] Sometimes they act as undercurrents and at other times their dormant cyphers await preappointed times or situations to arouse. Creator God engraved and encoded His handiworks with His divine truth and installed it them according to His predetermined will, before releasing anything to work on its own. Eternal etchings laid into this world make up the signposts that guide a lost soul to its heavenly destiny. God's eternal government, implanted throughout Scripture is imperceptibly administered by seven ruling powers set over all creation. That the seven spirits[116] are angels that oversee all creation, dominating it in the Maker's stead is stated repeatedly throughout Scripture. From Revelation 1:4 it says,

> "John to the seven churches which are in Asia: Grace be unto you, and peace, from him which is, and which was, and which is to come; and from the seven Spirits which are before his throne; to Revelation 3:1, "And unto the angel of the Church in Sardis write; These things saith he that hath the seven Spirits of God, and the seven stars; I know thy works, that thou hast a name that thou livest, and art dead." It continues with Revelation 4:5, "And out of the throne proceeded lightnings and thunderings and voices: and there were seven lamps of fire burning before the throne, which are

---

115 Psalm 19:1-9.
116 The Revelations calls them the seven spirits that are before God's throne.

the seven Spirits of God;" It ends with Revelation 5:6, "And I beheld, and, lo, in the midst of the throne and of the four beasts, and in the midst of the elders, stood a Lamb as it had been slain, having seven horns and seven eyes, which are the seven Spirits of God sent forth into all the earth." KJV

This Scripture's relevance to the Continuum is obvious. It is evident that its seven angels correlate to those appointed to the new creation church of the Lord Jesus Christ. Going from being His thronal attendants, they now extend their spiritual protocratics to His worldwide church. Nevertheless, as a rule, for any New Testament revelation to be valid it must be substantiated by an Old Testament prototype. That substantiation for John's passage is found in Zechariah 3:9 that discusses Joshua[117] the High Priest's coronation for Jerusalem's restoration. The passage reads, *"For behold the stone that I have laid before Joshua; upon one stone shall be seven eyes: behold, I will engrave the graving thereof, saith the Lord of hosts, and I will remove the iniquity of that land in one day."*

Zechariah's seven eyed stone is interesting because Ezekiel uses similar language to describe the living creatures that transport God's throne. His cherubim's endless eyes stand out to the prophet because they completely cover the creatures and their wheels. Their many eyes enable them to watch and judge all creation, hinting at the rationale for the seven eyes in Zechariah's stone. They bring to mind Zion's precious, but rejected cornerstone. Symbolically Christ, the stone and its eyes reflect His almightiness and most notably His omniscience that is figurated[118] as eyes. Seven spirits standing before the Almighty's throne could be better understood as seven specialized celestial courtiers stationed in His throne room to handle His most pressing matters. The idea that the seven spirits are nothing more than fixtures ornamenting His court is misleading. Think of Gabriel's words to Zacharias the High Priest in Luke chapter 1. When the doubtful priest disbelieved the reason for the angel's visit and what was to come of it, Gabriel declared that he stands in the presence of God. That statement hit home to a High Priest whose legitimacy, and responsibilities, rested on a similar call. Samuel too used this phrase to qualify the level of service he rendered to the Lord and to indicate the corresponding authority that came with it. Thus, the belief that the seven angels before the Lord's throne, idly stand around there is wrong. For the seven spirits, standing before the throne parallel a permanent workstation. Whatever their position requires is what the Lord delegates to them as

---

117 A type of Jesus Christ in the future.

118 Figurative of to make a good impression; represent, figure, depict, picture, imagine; appear. Figurative, pictorial, metaphorical, symbolic, allegorical.

His more immediate and therefore most trusted agents. These celestial ministers are more than attending servants and much more than assistants holding the title of servant. The seven spirits are the Lord's nearest and highest, endowed and endued, collaborators. They stand ready to handle exclusively what He would and could do personally, but finds it more efficient to delegate. Their unique standing in His Presence qualifies them to discharge the Lord's most private and critical business. More is said on this subject elsewhere. For now the link between the Continuum and the Lord's angels is the objective here.

Exodus' account of Moses receiving Israel's covenant Decalogue (The Ten Commandments) supports Zechariah's passage and its imports. As if they always existed, God dispatches the ten sayings, so they were first called, to earth by the hand of His legislative angels. His doing so demonstrates publicly, His supreme and unimpeded authority over His workmanship. Before the world was, an inviolable law encoded all creation with His logos to assure His will is done on earth as it is in heaven. The Ten Commandments and later the Christian church's canon, are but excerpts of the Almighty's pervasive laws extracted from His archetypal government. Their efficacies say God is in control, period. He maintains control because He initiated and encrypted all that humanity claims to create and rule. If He only ruled by what He wrote, the Lord's protonic[119] governors would still outstrip the most sophisticated or devious world system, but He did not stop there. He further commissioned everlasting beings to oversee and dispense His heavenly codices for Him so they span generations. These personified powers, called here spiritual protocrats, have held sway for eons. Perpetuity makes them infinitely more advanced than humans. As a result, celestial protocrats ably deter whatever the Lord rejects, and nimbly redirect humanity to prevent them from invading or discovering what is sealed for another generation or period in time. Spiritual protocratics is a term that explains the Lord's orders, ranks, hierarchies, and the human and spiritual agents co-jointly occupying and administrating His worlds. These motivated the phrase "encoded creation", identifying the spiritual regulations God's unseen rulers use to overrule earthly powers. Heaven's supernal system and its processes are, for these purposes, called God's Encoded Creation Protocratics. Although these are spiritual beings as humans use the term, the protocrats are far from ordinary messengers or simple angels. They are agents, rulers, governors, judges, episcopates, and determiners that appropriate God's powers

---

119 Preceding the tone or accent. The embryological or fundamental thing that predetermines and maneuvers everything else that follows it.

to dispense properly, what He apportions as written in the annals of their world. (See "protocratics" in The Prophet's Dictionary).

WHAT GOD MEANS BY SPIRIT

The word *spirit* speaks to what is immaterial, ethereal, otherworldly. It is what this world calls supernatural. In reality, the term designates what began with God and defines Him and His world as a result. When it comes to the Almighty, the words, celestial, supernal and sublime more precisely apply. Spiritual, as this era sees and uses the term today, falls woefully short of what it meant to early cultures. They only scarcely grasped its fullness. People cannot see spirituality as God's celestial citizens do. Spiritual for the Lord means generative and not just invisible. Everything that originates in the unseen realms and not, as this world contends, from the flesh may be classified as spiritual. What is spiritual not only transcends the flesh, but also excels its limitations. Spirituality operates on laws enacted to subject the physical world to it. It does not seek or rely on human organs or apparatuses to perform, but instead enhances them so they attain. Hither is where humanity's strict dependence on the five senses justifies the Lord's spiritual protocratics. That dependency attests to the darkness born in it. People are not born knowing, but having to learn. Knowledge is a never-ending pursuit because it is not the inherent domain of the flesh but the guarded province of wisdom. Proverbs chapter 8 says wisdom began with God and His spiritual beings. Knowledge is synonymous with light because this world is naturally devoid of light and must produce it, even with the sun, moon, and stars. Light is reserved for God's world and is a gift to the earth, as the darkness on other planets in this solar system attests. The apostle John affirms this truth when he holds that God is light and in Him is no darkness at all, and that the Lamb, Jesus Christ, and His Father Creator God are the illumination of their realm. Therefore, it should be a foregone conclusion that wherever God or any of His spirits show up, light appears with them. It does not matter if it is dim or blinding, light accompanies whatever emerges from the Lord's world, and that makes angels superior to humans. It is also why the Lord does not trust complete government of His world, or administration of its covenants and providences to people on earth alone. God charged His heavenly beings with keeping His creations intact, and they do not do so alone. He abides within them as He does the Christian to assure their success and propriety. This is in addition to keeping His Presence among them and His populaces at peace.[120]

The invisible agencies, called here spiritual protocrats, enact and enforce the Maker's laws, and the systems that administrate them. They take their cue from the very adjudications that regulate and guard their societies because principles and government has worked for them for ages. Humans way back then understood this and felt that God's sphere of law was independent and above earth's. Their ancient concept of law was not merely some philosophical ideal of territorial or tyrannical control. Law and government were viewed by them as outcomes of an unseen realm populated and administrated by spiritual authorities. All of Scripture's writings underlie this belief. Although human terms are used to mete out celestial rulers' judgments, the actions that trigger them were not seen by ancient societies as violating some human code. They did not see their misconduct as offending some indifferent (or arbitrary) behavioral script. Offending God's creational government literally meant offending the immortal beings that He delegated lordship of His kingdom. Offending them equated to offending Him because His Spirit abided in them and was as injured by violating His Law as the being He indwelt. Thus, a person and not just an institution are affronted by rebellious people. Modern people know this, which is why words like luck, karma, cause, and effect, sowing and reaping are intrinsic to every civilization's language. Something within people tells them that a greater order and government have a sort of boomerang effect on their behavior. They sense or learn early that what goes around comes around, and bounces on people in life at some time or another. God is no more out of touch with His creation than He is out of earshot when His people pray. Working mysteriously within everything He made and every leader He appoints, He rules in the background to bring what He decrees to pass. Here is a biblical example from the Lord's mouth concerning the angel that was to replace Him to lead Israel into the Promised Land:

> "Beware of him, and obey his voice, provoke him not; for he will not pardon your transgressions: for my name is in him. But if thou shalt indeed obey his voice, and do all that I speak; then I will be an enemy unto thine enemies, and an adversary unto thine adversaries. For mine Angel shall go before thee, and bring thee in unto the Amorites, and the Hittites, and the Perizzites, and the Canaanites, the Hivites, and

---

120 Further study, in light of this information: Revelation's mention of the seven angels of the Church; Zechariah, Isaiah's and Daniel's extensive interactions with these heavenly creatures; Joshua's meeting with the Lord of Host's Commander of the Armies; and the angels that worked with the apostles.

the Jebusites: and I will cut them off." KJV Exodus 23:20-23. See also Ecclesiastes 5:8.
Here is another version of these statements.

"Look, I'm sending an angel in front of you to guard you on the way and to bring you
to the place I've prepared. Be careful! Be sure to obey him. Don't rebel against him,
for he won't forgive your transgression, since my Name is in him. Indeed, if you carefully obey him and do everything that I say, then I'll be an enemy to your enemies and
an adversary to your adversaries. For my angel will go ahead of you and will bring you
to the Amorites, the Hittites, the Perizzites, the Canaanites, the Hivites, and the
Jebusites, and I'll annihilate them. Exodus 23:23 ISV

All God's invisible creatures actively superintend His natural world, whether dark or
light. According to the Bible, two angels that God seems to rely on heavily in the dispensation of His plan for humanity are named Michael and Gabriel, Although others
are named elsewhere, locating their place in the Continuum is difficult. Spiritual authority, as this passage shows, and as the people of the ancient world understood it,
comes exclusively from above. Reading Titus 3:1 with this enlightened perspective
illuminates the old world's understanding of, spiritual order and divinely delegated
authority. Jesus told Pilate, for instance, that he could have no authority over Him if it
was not given to him from above. Based on creation's design, the Lord, divided His
worlds and then set about assigning spiritual agents and authorities to care for and
defend it for Him. He inscribed custodial instructions for the earth, and gave His
spiritual agents express instructions to uphold it perpetually. He also prescribed laws
and ordinances in this world that are proven to guarantee what He made endures,
and provides for every generation. The Lord founded positions of authority to assure
those given charge over His handiwork in heaven and earth are empowered to enforce His will and achieve His vision. They carry out His rescue and preservation
mandates.

A review of Revelation 4:6 and 5:6 shows the Lord Jesus Christ fulfilled Zechariah's
vision when He dispatched the seven spirits into the world to carry out His ecclesial
ministry in the Person of the Holy Ghost. The seven spirits reach back to eternity as
participants in God's eternal government of His worlds. From Israel's inception, they
were poised to become His protocratic rulers throughout the Church age and beyond.
The Almighty always intended the body of Christ to *beaconize*[121] all creation, which is
what Ephesians 3:10 indicate and why Jesus decreed the gates of hell will never dethrone His Ecclesia. The seven spirits once exclusively occupied with God's throne are

---

121 To fire up, enlighten and illuminate; warm and guide; signal, notify and communicate; symbolize
and exemplify. The urbandictionary.com.

sent (*apostolized* was the word Scripture scribes understood) into all the earth to disseminate and superintend His church. Heaven's perpetually stationed rulers now oversee the new creation and its progressive development on earth as God's manifest sons and daughters. As such, the seven spirits equate to apostolic angels that assure the Church's stability under God's eternal government. Their chief duty is to see that His prototypical church order remains composed until it leaves the earth. Imagine what these powerful never changing beings do for Christ's global church. As heaven's layer of spiritual apostles between the Great Apostle Jesus Christ and His Ecclesia, the protocrats keep the Continuum threading throughout every age. Appreciating what their cherubic station in the on the Lord's spiritual staff mean to God's members and ministers assures what He ordained to emerge at prescribed points in history, does on time. The spiritual protocrats of creation maintain the true church of the Lord Jesus Christ until the end of its dispensation. And they do so His way, no matter what worldly trends move to pervert it from time to time. Ancient peoples called the seven eternal spirits, Revelation reveals, God's Prototypical Archons. Perhaps they are more archetypal than prototypical, either way, they are the originals.

Progressing His Continuum, Jesus shows John the archons now appearing as the seven angels of His seven churches after reassigning them to His Ecclesia's spiritual oversight. What has been said further unveils the mystery of the Church and how the Continuum verifies those entering it. Powerful unchanging agents regulated many of Israel's rituals and observances, and they do the same for Jesus Christ's church. As a throwback to Genesis 1:14, Psalm 19:1-4 shows their effect. From time immemorial, these seemingly inanimate lights ruled the earth outliving everything ever born into it and evacuate all that the Lord wants out of it. In relation to the spiritual protocrats and their actions on behalf of the Godhead, what eternalizes the revelation is that the Savior's church always existed. First concealed in natural Israel, so says Revelation chapter twelve, and upon its unveiling, becomes secreted in Christ who was hid in God. This is the mystery of the ages that was hidden until the last Pentecost that brought it into being, as the new creation church, Christ's everlasting body.

Essentially constituting creation's seven principalities, the spiritual protocrats' rule and government are weaved throughout the Old Testament. As the Almighty's protocratic authorities, they were initially unseen, though frequently felt long after they were set in motion. Once stationed in their spiritual positions, the Lord vested them with His power and wisdom to substantiate their authority. Potent governmental elements were dispensed to them to mete out the Creator's laws. Multifaceted wisdom informed them of His prescriptions, legislation, commandments, warnings, and judgments. He also assigned them superior resources to enable these indomitable beings to do their jobs. They were outfitted with eternity's implements and allotted economies from His celestial treasuries. The Lord's provisions are no different from the practices of authority figures in this world. Those put in high seats must have resources to fulfill their positions' purposes. There must be repositories for them to draw from for their rule's equipment and implements, see Jeremiah 50:25. The main tool of the Lord's government is His word. Undetected spiritual executors of that word are the multitude of angels that stand around His throne waiting to fulfill it.[122]

SEVEN SPIRITS EXAMPLES IN SCRIPTURE

1. The seven spirits before the throne of God
2. The seven spirits sent out into the entire world
3. The seven stars, as referred to by Jesus in His apocalypse
4. The ancient world knew them as the Pleiades, how they are defined in the Greek. See Amos 5:8; Job 38:31 outside of their Revelation references.
5. For Pentecost, seven Lambs were offered. Leviticus 23:15-22
6. The seven churches of the Lord Jesus Christ
7. The seven candles in the candlestick
8. Numbers 8:2 and Zechariah 3 & 4

In summary, the word protocratic comes from two Greek terms, *proto* for founding, originating, beginning, ruling; and *cratics*[123] for rule, government, dominance, sovereignty. When merged they express God superior role and ongoing grip on His creation. They establish indisputably His sovereign dominion and preeminence in all that occurs in His worlds. Spiritual applies to what is heavenly, immortal, eternal, everlasting, glorious, endless and deathless. The most frequent references that illustrate this Creator Dominion force are principality(ies) and power(s). The Lord's spiritual authorities witness and facilitate people's interaction with God's sovereignty. They uphold His dominion in seen and unseen ways. Spiritual protocratics bring the Almighty's will to bear on all worlds, and supernally override earth with eternity's government, something Isaiah 9:6-9 declares is heaven's divine order. In this capacity, they run God's natural world from outside it as His permanent regime affirming Him as the Almighty possessor of heaven and earth.

---

122 Study the following passages of Scripture for a richer understanding; Amos 5:13; Amos 9:6; Deuteronomy 32:8; Job 25:2. See also Psalm 104:1 and 103:19-22.

123 Really kratos, Strong's 2904.

SCRIPTURE REFERENCES FOR PRINCIPALITIES & POWERS

Three distinct passages of Scripture mention the two words that identify heaven's protocrats, principalities, and powers. They most frequently show up in the New Testament together. The Scriptures that present them are Ephesians 3:10, the most poignant of the three, Colossians 2:15 and Titus 3:1. The Ephesians' reference exposes the spiritual principalities and powers in the heavenlies that safeguard the Christian Church and through it, the world. The subtle implication is that there is a counterpart of these that also resist it, what is explained elsewhere in Zechariah chapter three. Later passages in the Ephesians reference, shows that principalities and powers have always existed and that they performed their functions when as yet the Church in corpus did not exist. Read how the passage is written in Ephesians 3:10, referred to above:

> "To the intent that now unto the principalities and powers in heavenly places might be known by the Church the manifold wisdom of God" (KJV)

The epistle to the Ephesians is saturated with supernatural implications that can electrify Christian spirituality, if they enlarge their perspective of the Lord Jesus' earthly mission and the real reason it was necessary. This verse, written to the Church with reference to age-old celestial powers and rulers, says much to the generations to come. A question to be pondered is what has the Lord's visit to earth in human form to redeem His lost humanity to do with the principalities and powers in the heavenly places? If God sent His Son to save only people on earth, why involve the angels or even consider their perspective on the Redemption Project? Obviously, for Ephesians 3:10 to be spoken by Paul, the Lord exposed him to something about the Church and His vision for it that taps into His world. By now, it is evident that something was the Great War in Heaven that predated the Edenic Crisis. To bridge all of the events that connect earth and its inhabitants to God's Eternal Continuum, the fourteenth and last generation of the Lord Jesus Christ is the best place to begin. This is particularly so when one remembers that Christianity is, and has always been about a king and his kingdom as much as it is about a father and his family. In a strange way, Paul's words in 1 Corinthians 2:6, 9 about the princes of this world bolsters these truths despite how calming it is to think that he is speaking in strictly human terms.

PAUL'S SPIRITUAL PROTOCRATIC RECORD

Before going any further, backtracking is needed to recall the writer of Corinthians' supernatural record. The apostle Paul recorded he had enjoyed numerous excursions to the Lord's invisible realms for the purposes of these writings. Strangely, it appears from his contexts that he met God's past, present, and future. Review, as a case in point, Paul's words in 2 Corinthians 12:1-4 where he draws on, for his authorization to handle God's heavenly things, his series of visions and revelations from the Lord. The word he uses for vision in these verses is *optasia*, which exclusively designates a heavenly vision where a mystical encounter takes place through a supernatural agent. The apostle in using the Greek word *apokalupsis* means to convey the import of the English word apocalypse. The term defines the outcome of Paul and his predecessors' supernatural encounters. *Apokalupsis* defines, "an unveiling of the spiritual world to its natural tributaries". The word <u>tributary</u> is relevant here since apocalypse means more than merely drawing back a curtain to reveal what it was hiding. Apocalypse includes triggering natural events that have come to their precoded time of eruption when (or because) the curtain is pulled back. Revelation, the English word used most often for apocalypse, in God's mind unseals, unlocks, releases, exposes, and ignites. He programed these preordained actions to happen in this world in particular generations. Therefore, when Jesus sent His angel to John with His revelation He meant to authorize His protocratic agents' ignition of cataclysmic world events scheduled to perform in their preappointed periods in time.

By design, the word <u>apocalypse</u> actualizes trigger mechanisms God placed in creation to ignite world events when apocalyptic veils are pulled back. More than sightings occur when this happens. Dormant forces are mobilized to incite situations and eruptions that propel this world toward God's ordained results. With that being the case, this world as the tributary of its supernatural counterpart is laden with embedded commands that release God's predestiny every time one or more of His invisible powers acts upon it. This is what John's Apocalypse portrays in massive degrees. Apokalupses' utterances act as catalysts that kindle all that God's messengers ever uttered or wrote at prescheduled periods in history, what He spoke by the mouths of His prophets from Enoch to John the Beloved, from Christ to the apostle witnessing the eternal events moving to perform on earth. That is why such stern warnings are attached to perverting the Revelation and why such magnanimous blessings are promised to those who regard it. The Messiah vows unending rewards for those who preach, teach, and heed the words of His Apocalypse's prophecy. Apocalyptic prophecy serves as the Continuum's turnkey. Simultaneity maps its journey to sweep earth's cycles to set in motion what the Lord decreed before the foundation of the world. Paul's repeated references to the principalities and powers and the numerous variations of this eternal agenda underscore continually what sets in motion creation's inscribed sequences. They also elevate the place of prophecy, particularly eschatological or apocalyptic prophecy that awaits the voice of the Lord's 'word triggers' to mobilize in the planet. For clarification purposes, eschatology is the end times. It refers to what is winding down to the end of the world. Apocalyptic is somewhat like it with one significant difference. It brings about what winds down the end of the world by unlocking and opening a mystery hidden in God's heavenly vault. When declared by the mouth of His divine communicant at the appointed time, apocalyptic words take on life and intelligence to orchestrate unseen events that correlate with God's edicts and decrees so they perform in the visible world.

To credential his grasp of spiritual matters, something emphatically emerges for Paul for him to take on the Church's natural affairs. He reveals he has seen, touched, and handled what is ordinarily outside the scope of this realm. Paul's call to apostleship demands that he do so to convey the reality of invisible powers and authorities behind Christ's work. Paul must acknowledge and cooperate with the Lord's celestial agents and agencies that care for His physical creation, those assigned to His church. As a result, all Paul's epistle writings (and those of the other apostles, Peter, Jude, and John) comments on heaven's supernal staff. These include angels, virtues, principalities, powers, thrones, dominions. Potent supernatural organizations behind this world, see to the events and details Creator God ordained for it, materializing His will on earth as prophesied or decreed. Ecclesiastes: 3:1, 17 and 8:6 say this very thing. To evidence this destiny objectively, spiritual principalities intervene with immaterial creatures and earthly leaders' to acquaint them with the heavenly and eternal as well as the earthly. Therefore, a thorough training in the principalities and powers of the Godhead's celestial and terrestrial worlds is imperative for all Christianity, especially its leaders.

[20]

The Holy Spirit And The Continuum

Several things reinforce the Continuum's security and perpetuity. Previous chapters talked about the numerous people or beings that contributed to its establishment and progression. Thus far, the prophets, apostles, angels, Israel, even Satan, have all been presented as key Continuum figures. Of course, it is inferred that the Lord Jesus Christ and His Father God Almighty precede them all. Nevertheless, there is one individual that has not been extensively discussed who is instrumental in all that occurs on earth is according to God's Eternal Continuum. He ensures its continuity and unity. That person is the Holy Spirit. Bringing Him into the Continuum's disclosures firmly introduces the entire Godhead.

Theologically called the Trinity because the three are equally one and the same, they are named as the Godhead by the Apostle Paul. How the Holy Spirit fits in the Continuum should be apparent. He is fully God. The Lord Jesus in Matthew 28:18-20 names them individually: The Father, The Son, and The Holy Spirit. Curiously, as much as the Holy Spirit is mentioned in Scripture, mostly in the New Testament, He remains the most overlooked of the Godhead's members. However, as the Holy Spirit proper, He crosses the entire Bible from Genesis, which opens with "the Spirit of God impressed upon the waters", to Revelation's epilogue, "the Spirit and the bride say come". Under the title The Holy Spirit, He is mentioned seven times in Scripture, three times in the Old Testament and four times in the New. As the Holy Ghost, the King James Version names Him eighty-nine times, all in the New Testament. As the Spirit of God, He is named an additional twenty-six times; fourteen of which are in the Old Testament. Thirty-one more times, He is identified as the Spirit of the Lord. Besides this, the Holy Spirit is simply called "His Spirit" five times and the "Spirit of

Christ" twice. Lastly, He is associated with the commissioned Messiah and the Lord God in Isaiah 48:16, an Old Testament allusion to the Godhead. More than one hundred and seventy-five times the Holy Spirit is brought out in Scripture besides the four times He is introduced as a member of the Godhead. That takes the full references of the Godhead's Third Person to more one hundred and eighty-five times. And what is more, there are other allusions to Him based on His attributes. Sixteen of those allusions is listed below.

The Holy Spirit's Epithets

Most notably the Holy Spirit is:

The Father's Spirit	The Spirit of His Son	The Spirit of Wisdom
The Spirit of Life	The Spirit of Grace & Supplication	The Spirit of Holiness
The Spirit of Life in Christ Jesus	The Spirit of Meekness	The Spirit of Revelation
The Spirit of Glory	The Spirit of Judgment	The Spirit of Counsel
The Spirit of Might	The Spirit of Knowledge	The Spirit of Truth
The Spirit of Adoption		

All told, the Holy Spirit is unveiled in Scripture more than two hundred times. His personified attributes express Creator God through emotion, word, action, and vitality. He acts sovereignly though never in conflict with God the Father and God the Son. He speaks and judges, commands, and convicts, heals and kills, all while conforming to the Scriptures. The Holy Spirit fused with the Almighty's other two persons, indwells people, effects salvation, and overall extends and exerts the Most High as necessary. He begets born again Christians, educates, preserves, and coaches them. Whenever God's power is put out, it is by His Holy Spirit. Whatever God wishes to communicate with His creation, He does so by His Spirit, sometimes from within people and at other times by impressing upon them. All in all, these manifest God and that is precisely who and what the Holy Spirit is, He is God. Previous discussions on spirits set the point for better comprehending the Holy Spirit. That inclusion is an important foundation that articulates His Continuum's role in the world.

Spirit Power

What God means and does not mean by the word spirit having been previously addressed, what is covered here is, what is not a spirit or spiritual. The answer begins with weeding out everything that suggests something that is nonexistent, insignificant, or inconsequential, because in God's world, none of that is true. The way Scripture portrays it, spirits are more potent than the human body because their life is not based on human blood. Physical mortality comes from Adam's blood. Therefore, anything classified as spiritual, lives forever, whereas humans age and fail. That means spirits are censured by God's law of sin and death differently and since they do not breed, they essentially leave no body to return to the dust for reuse by another creature. Humans on the other hand, are doomed to die three distinct ways: the decomposition of the body, the destruction of the soul, the eternal imprisonment (or redemption) of the spirit. All of which are imposed on the flesh through the blood. Since the soul is charged with sin and condemned for it, human mortality abides in the soul and is somehow directly connected to the blood. Otherwise, how could the soul be morally affected and mortally punished, or purged, by blood, which is what the Leviticus reference given in the footnote seems to suggest?[124] Conversely, Scripture says that the spirit gives life. What that implies is that the heart is the power source of all spirit. It revitalizes the soul to generate life properties in the blood that keeps the human body going. The spirit is the part of humans, most like the angels and God, for God is spirit. Divine and celestial essence is energetic, not organic. The life force of the spirit is light and electricity, not dark and fluid. The spirit based on this may be thought of as the soul and body's power source. The spirit of a thing is its entire self that cannot cease to be. Spirits can only be doomed, they never die, that is, they never cease to exist the way the human body does. Spiritual doom is being denied the Creator's light and power, and thereby being separated from His spirit. After all, how well long or can one live well devoid of some sort of light, however dim that light may be? The human spirit, as an everlasting creature, decrees people's hereafter. Its contamination or purity determines departed souls' afterlife abode. The condition of the spirit deports a decedent to the land of the living or the dead. And, its destiny is not just a matter of life choices, but is, moreso dictated by the life-end nature of the spirit. If the departed's spirit is of the same nature as the Godhead and the rest of its celestial citizens, then it returns to its Maker. If not, then it descends into the abyss because it lacks the conditions for ascending on high. All spirits are condemned because of what is in their nature, irrespective of what the mouth espouses. In addition, the spirit of a progenitor is the deciding factor. It is why people must be born again. The new birth changes the spirit and thus its converts' parentage. It breaks up the

---

124 Leviticus 17:11 "For the life of the flesh is in the blood: and I have given it to you upon the altar to make an atonement for your souls: for it is the blood that maketh an atonement for the soul."

mortal lineage and replaces with the divine blood of Jesus Christ. That is what John 1:12, 13 versus John 8:44 seek to transmit. The Holy Spirit turns the spirit made Christian into an heir of God and Christ. The heirship stems from the believer partaking of the Godhead's divine nature by which he or she inherit's their deathless, and sinless genetics.

For any of this to make sense, one must realize that dead to humanity is a cessation of a thing. Dead to God on the other hired man is something else completely. When things die on earth, those left alive stop being able to see them. That is not, how it is in God's world. He and His angels see the immaterial as vividly as they see the material. They must, in order to escort the disembodied to their eternal choice. God defines death as a complete withdrawal of Himself. This makes the world's definition of dead and God's definition of it somewhat contradictory. In principle, humanity views death as departing this world to go to a final resting place. That is not God's view of it, nor is it His response to people leaving their bodies. If the departed belongs to Him, the person's death is a joy. If not, it is the end of perhaps decades of wooing an impenitent life for His redemption. Death's last requirements of God is to surrender the spirit and soul to humanity's greatest enemy, the grave. In this instance, natural death gives way to eternal doom and destroys the body. God, then withdraws His life out of the soul and spirit because the person leaving this world has no more use for it. Yet, when it comes to humanity, extracting its life's spirit, merely returns a body to the grave; it does not break its spirit or individual from living on, see James 2:26.

In this world, God's Spirit bridges the gap between natural and perpetual life to give a person the chance to repent and be saved. Leaving this world permanently disconnects the decedent from the Spirit's energy source and turns them over to the invisible rulers of His kingdom. As a result, what a person worshiped on this side of eternity predicts what happens on the other side. Everyone departing this life becomes the property of the deity chosen, served, and venerated on earth. It does not matter which one it is, or how regretful one becomes at meeting their chosen deity without the flesh to mask its identity. Whatever spirit ruled the deceased in the physical body receives and controls that soul and spirit, forever.

Often the distinction between the spirit and the soul is too finite for humans to discern or appreciate. Therefore, they treat both synonymously. For instance, people often say soul when they mean spirit, and they say spirit when they mean soul. For most people the difference is inconsequential since they have never seen or cognizantly interacted with either one. However, God makes incisive differences between them that He somehow shared with Paul the apostles to the Gentiles in Hebrews 4:12: *"For the word of God is quick, and powerful, and sharper than any two edged sword, piercing even to the dividing asunder of <u>soul and spirit</u>, and of the joints and marrow, and is a discerner of the thoughts and intents of the heart."* Here the Lord makes a solid distinction between the soul that must be atoned for by blood and the spirit that must be born again. Peter declares to those who have been born again by His Holy Spirit that they still must believe the gospel brought to earth by the Holy Ghost until the salvation of their souls. Paul reiterates this in Hebrews 10:39 when he says that believers must maintain their belief "unto the saving of the soul". Clearly, both apostles understood something about the soul that made it need progressive saving despite the born again experience of the spirit that Jesus spoke of in John chapter three. So what is that something? What is that difference? The answer is Christ's conversion of the mortal soul. Psalm 19:7 tells how.

In short, people must make and maintain God's choices to protect their soul when it leaves the body. Their doomed consciences may be quarantined by the new creation spirit, but it takes the human will to eradicate the death of the soul. That does not always occur when the new spirit and God's Holy Spirit are deposited. To impart everlasting salvation into human souls, converts must exercise their own human will to live on earth the way God requires His citizens to live in heaven until the day they die. The Holy Spirit is here to help, but the determination to learn and live God's life is an individual one that even the new creation spirit cannot compel on its own. That is why Ezekiel 36 has the Lord saying, He will put His Spirit in the redeemed to cause them to live His way. Enduring to the end as the Savior exhorts happens when the heart resolves to do so. Every saved person must daily (and consciously) reinforce their commitment to eternal life until their soul is so transformed that it cannot help but to be saved. Why? Because the soul is the earthly part of the human being and the spirit is the heavenly part. Genesis says the spirit was made outside of earth and the soul was delivered on earth after the body was crafted from its dust. When Adam's body was constructed, the Lord breathed His breath into it to make it a living soul. In comparison, Jesus the last Adam has always been. That is why He is called a quickening spirit, meaning He is the life giving spirit. His spirit gives life because that is what it takes to sustain the soul, among many, many other things.

What has such extensive treatment of spirit, soul, body, life, and death to do with the Holy Spirit? And, what do all of them have to do with the Continuum? The answer is everything because the Holy Spirit is the sovereign judge of all that transports people to the hereafter. He justifies or condemns what people do on earth. He confirms the saint, disqualifies the lost, facilitates death and translates the redeemed to God's world. As the divinely sanctioned Executor of the Risen Lord's will and testament, the Holy Spirit knows what God decreed about life and dying. His Spirit holds the living blueprints for the precise type of citizen the Maker wants in His world. In addition, He is well acquainted with the grounds for the Almighty's seemingly impossible eternal life standards. After all, He shares them. But defining the Holy Spirit is as difficult as trying to catch the wind or hold water in one's hand. He is a person, He is God, and He is powerful and as divine as the Almighty who with Him created all things.

The Holy Spirit, God's Skin and Blood

So how does one define the Holy Spirit? What best describes Him, makes His invisibility tangible to a spiritually blind world? The most relatable answer to understanding the Holy Spirit is to identify Him as the equivalent of God Almighty's skin and blood. Skin being the Lord's covering and the blood symbolizing His life flows. To apprehend the depth and breadth of this member of the Godhead properly, one needs to accept that the Holy Spirit is God. To do so requires connecting Him to the biological and anatomical construction of the human body, made in God's image and likeness. This is useful because above all else Scripture regularly uses the human body to unlock the enigmas of the Lord Jesus Christ's new creation church. In preparation for what is to come, look at the Scripture passages upon which the following teaching rests, starting with the King James' rendering of Romans 12:4, 5. On that point the Apostle Paul compares the Christian church to a physical body. He uses this comparison to unify the diverse members of Jesus' Ecclesia, likening each of His member's different purposes, to the discrete functions of the human body. Paul picks up this vein again in 1 Corinthians 12:12-27, in seeking to validate the Church's identity with Christ and the Godhead. To drive his point home, he uses the Lord's highest creation, humanity to explain the spiritual nature and supernal functions of the Christian church.

Throughout the New Testament, Paul explains how the Godhead—God the Father, God the Son, and God the Holy Spirit—exist as one. They are one because an inimitable substance fuse them as a single life force. It welds their deific natures in the very same body. This existence, in effect, describes how they jointly occupy and execute the exact same office at the same time: that of creation's Sovereign. Jesus emerged from the Father; He says so more than once in Scripture. The Holy Spirit is the joint product of them both. He is what they pushed forth from themselves in unison to cover all creation, and that is what makes Him equally both of them and God. The three of them share one mind, heart, soul, and will, not three different ones. Every part of them is enwrapped in the very same essence, which is not merely identical, but verbatim and all that this word means and implies. The Godhead never split as twins do, they simply expand and extend, remaining as fused with one another afar as they do up close. Something that is not difficult for them to do since they fill all and all alike. Where one is, so is the other. There is no place the Creator is that the Son is absent. Where the Father and the Son are there also is the Holy Spirit. Their corporeal constitution is as biologically the same as Adam's seed and its physical makeup, just incomparably superior. All humanity shares the same genetic type, just as animals are characterized by their species. The Ecclesia, as the Godhead's newly engrafted members, is likewise made according to the Almighty's proprietary genetic code. The new birth makes the spirit filled church more like the Godhead than any other type of its created beings. The Godhead passing its proprietary genetics on repentant humans is how born again Christians become the Almighty's progeny, and what makes Christ's Ecclesia creation's first family. Being more like Jesus than any other creature, the Church beneath its mortal skin hides the perfect blend of eternality and deathlessness, flesh and spirit, humanity and divinity. That is its mystery, and according to Ephesians 3:10, only the principalities and powers in the heavenly places fully grasp it. Not even the long term Christians enjoying their supernal status and its corresponding privileges completely understand or comprehend it. To appreciate Christianity's uniqueness requires acceptance of, its unparalleled peculiarities. Ephesians 2:16; 4:4,5 and Romans 7:4 all say that the Church's body is none other than the glorified body of the Lord Jesus Christ that was broken for it on Calvary. God broke the Savior's human flesh to release His Spirit to distribute itself to those chosen to become the Godhead's offspring by Him. The decision, its outcome, and the procedure were all decided before the foundation of the world, which is how the Church fits into the Continuum. Ephesians 5:30 says that Jesus' eternal body is composed of flesh and bones; His mortal blood was spilt on the earth. He now lives according to what is said about His present life force in Hebrews 10:16. Christ lives today by the power of an endless life, an indestructible, invincible, deathless life that He passes on to each member of His church. The body metaphor used for the Lord's collective descendants is seen throughout Scripture. It more than substantiates what comes next.

HOLY SPIRIT'S EXPRESSIONS

Hebrews 1 says that Jesus Christ is the express image of His Father God Almighty. That word express is deliberate because it literally means to be *pressed out*. Jesus was pressed out of the Almighty's being. The same, it has been shown, is true of the Holy Spirit. As a family member of the Godhead, He is the express eminence of the two of them with two fundamental factors that distinguish Him from every other spirit. He is permeable and pervasive. The Holy Spirit encases and extends creation's Sovereigns. His encasement includes God the Father, Jesus Christ, His Son, and since Calvary, their born again spirit filled church. What He encases, He extends as God's Person to enable the Lord to act distantly as if He were actually on site. The Holy Spirit is how God is everywhere present at one time and how He controls everything, He created. The Holy Spirit does this because He is incorporeal as far as earth's physicality is defined. Despite being Spirit, He is nonetheless substantive[54] to those of His world because God is only invisible to the naked eye in this one. The Holy Spirit shares with Jesus and God the Father the exact same heredities. Whatever supremacy separates the Almighty from His creature hood is embedded in the three of them. To love God is to love Jesus Christ and the Holy Spirit. To offend God is to offend the three of them. Blaspheming[55] the Holy Spirit offends the other two members of the Godhead, which is why Jesus warns His family against it. The tragedy of doing so lies in the fact that there is no other mediator, or means, to reconcile the blasphemer back to God, since all of them are affronted by the blasphemy.[56]

The Holy Spirit as God is as omni-everything as is the other two members of the Godhead. He does not differ from them, in essence or function. The Holy Spirit does all that God and Christ do as an imperceptible omnipresent power. He performs their initiatives wholly at once with trillions of organisms at the same time. And until today, disregarding of its immateriality, the Trinity remains one and the same. No member is higher or more salutary than the other is. They have exactly the same goals, outlooks, vision, and methods. Since there is no disparity between them, there can be no conflict. Where there is no conflict there can be no division. These factors assure the Godhead is never divided. As Scripture says, "the Lord our God is one Lord" and because the Holy Spirit entwines God the Father and God the Son within Himself, what they all think is what He executes and what they all desire He achieves for their collective fulfillment. His good pleasure reflects their unanimous enjoyment of all they collectively produced. Something deeper than unity coheres them that guarantees each one always remains equal to the other in all respects. It is why the Lord

Jesus warns the earth of the gravity of blaspheming the Holy Spirit, and admonishes His church against grieving Him. The consequences of doing so are worse with the Holy Spirit, because He is the last member of the Godhead to visit and attempt to rescue the planet. He dwells in the world as God for its preservation. That God never wounds, nor injures Himself or those that He inhabits by His Spirit means the Holy Spirit and the Church leave earth before eschatological assaults on it threaten their destruction. That is the Lord's plan, and it has been recorded to be His pattern.

Prior to turning the earth over to the destroyer, the Lord and His heavenly entourage departed it in Eden. Before allowing His beloved nation to be devastated, Jehovah left the land to remain unaffected and uninjured by what was coming upon it. In John's Revelation, it says that before God's apocalyptic judgments go into full effect, the Holy Spirit who is restraining it presently will be taken out of the way. And as He abides in all the Christians left on the planet, they too will exit the world with Him. That event is called the rapture. All of this is why the Savior warns against rejecting His Holy Spirit who is reason the Lord has not pushed the earth's destruct button so to speak. The world is safe as long as the Holy Spirit is in it because God will not harm Himself and the Holy Spirit is God. The danger to humans who reject Him is that there is nothing more to be done for those who despise His Spirit. This rationale motivates the Savior's words in Matthew 12:32 and what Hebrews 6:4-6 means with it says the Holy Spirit is the last offering the Lord has to send into the world. God sent His Son to be humiliated and murdered. His Son then sent the Holy Spirit to preserve and protect it, along with saving the lost. All this talk about the Godhead raises the question of its reality and legitimacy.

ABOUT THE GODHEAD: GOD'S EXTENDED SELF

The Holy Spirit is God's extended Self. Scripture calls Him the Spirit of God, the Spirit of the Father, the Spirit of the Lord, the Spirit of Christ, the Spirit of His Son, and the Spirit of Jesus Christ. The King James calls Him the Holy Ghost to signify His incorporeal nature as distinguished from humanity's clay vessels and the other spirits in creation. The adjective holy means to accomplish this aim. As the Spirit of the Living God, the Holy Spirit imparts celestial efficiencies from God's Presence to benefit His world, to supply its inhabitants, and to separate those belonging to His Son Jesus Christ from it. The people indwelt by the Holy Spirit are sealed by Him. As habitations of His Spirit, they receive highly specialized outpourings from the Godhead, efficacies that treat worshipers before they enter God's Presence. Consider His actions and initiatives in light of the seven personified manifestations stationed before their throne and it is easy to see how the Holy Spirit figures into the Continuum. At this point, it is good to address the articles commonly used to portray the Holy Spirit including nature itself. Symbols, metaphors, and allusions are helpful because God's effects and manifestations can escape people's notice. To solidify His Holy Spirit in them, the Lord uses what they know metaphorically to illustrate Him. Unfortunately, with this approach, there is the temptation to use man-made objects to characterize God's preeminent Spirit. That is a mistake because the Lord's Spirit as the very God is best personified by His handiwork and not that of His creatures. It is impossible for anything made by human hands to portray the Almighty aptly. Hence, the best way to represent the Spirit of God is by utilizing what God made. The most graphic way to image the invisible Lord is to use what is properly His. Whatever God made and owns makes the best representation of His supremeness. Hence, the most suitable object to represent the Holy Spirit is skin, not only because He made it, but also because it is the most pervasive, all encompassing part of the human body. Imagine the Lord in whose image and likeness humanity is made possessing the seven layers of skin that covers the flesh. Imagine the revelatory worth to Him if the skin's terminology was applied to His spiritual makeup and Creator duties and obligations.[57]

The Lord's appreciation of skin-like substances shows up in all His handiwork. All of His creatures are finished with some sort of skin; the wilderness tabernacle is adorned with what He calls skin. Logically He to enshroud Himself in what the world could identify with as skin, even though it has none of the mortal properties innate to His fallen creatures. When it comes to God's Holy Spirit as skin, call up the superiority of the angel's makeup and multiply that concept infinitesimally. To make the point of this discussion, it is common knowledge that some form of skin covers every living thing, so symbolically it makes the best metaphor for the glory of the Lord. To liken the Holy Spirit's pervasiveness to skin on a body is see the Godhead's covering as their outer garment, and protective shield. Nothing says it better than skin.

What makes skin a most depictive analogy for the Holy Spirit is that skin is established as the largest organ of the body, encompassing its entire outer being and encasing its every inward part. Interestingly, there are three members of the Godhead and there are three distinct layers of the skin.[125] The Holy Spirit functioning as God's skin makes Him to the Almighty what human skin is to its bodies. Designing His Spirit as a membrane accomplishes for the Lord what human skin does for its bodies.

The way people's skin completely covers their other two sides, their spirit and soul, so too does God's Spirit cover His other two sides, the Father and His Son. The way the Almighty fills all creation is how His Holy Spirit does the same thing. He enables the Almighty God to blanket and permeate all of His created worlds. In the same fashion that human flesh protects and shields its skeleton and vital organs, is in a sense how the Holy Spirit of God sheathes the Godhead. Just think of it in this way. The skin stretches over every part of a body, and is the first point of contact between its unseeable parts and its world. Among many, many other things, the skin[58] acts like a shield, defense, sensory system, and protective cloak at once. That is somewhat how it is with the Holy Spirit. He functions similarly for God on the planet, shielding the unworthy world from the Trinity's glory. In this respect, the Holy Spirit barricades the Godhead's precious treasures from the devious and destructive, and filters everything that would access the Father's presence.

As the Lord's first line protector, the Holy Spirit decides and determines who is who in God's kingdom and ranks each one's access, interaction, and audience with Him. He blocks those who would approach the Lord unlawfully and irreverently, going so far as to blind their minds to His reality. The Holy Spirit conceals the Lord's glory, guards Him from whomever He does not want to contact Him, and processes everything before it reaches Him. In managing this, He sanctifies everything to conform it to what a Holy God can enjoy or tolerate. The Holy Spirit is how the Lord accepts or rejects what attempts to approach Him. As incredible as it may sound, this allegory is what the entire New Testament seeks to teach about creation's invisible, hallowed, and holy God. The Holy Spirit knows the Lord in ways no mortal can, because He is comprised of the Father and His Son. Equally God Himself, the Holy Spirit tells the Almighty about His creation the way people's skin tells them about their world. The way skin on the body knows its physical surroundings and transmits data about the physical world to its unseen self, God's Spirit constantly informs Him of all that lives and goes on in His created worlds, in real time. That is what the Apostle John discovered when he said the Spirit witnesses[126] from heaven to earth and earth to heaven. The Holy Spirit's pervasiveness enables seamless exchanges to take place between heaven and earth. In addition, His permeableness furthermore means instant information can be delivered to heaven and its responses returned to earth uninterruptedly. Together, these motivate Paul to say the Spirit knows all there is to know about the

---

126 See John 5:22; 8:18; Romans 8:16; 1 John 5:6.

Most High God.[127] His thoughts, feelings, needs, likes and desires along with His past, present and future are all the Holy Spirit's most intimate knowledges of the Everlasting God. It is why He encompasses the entire Continuum, from before it started.

Picture the Continuum as a sac that encases all of the vital organs of God's creation. Include in this picture, His kingdoms, their creations and their inhabitants. Envision further that sac being inseparably connected to His substance and constructed of a tissue like substance to let His life properties seep out to nourish His handiwork. Conceive of the Holy Spirit as the very same type of sac that holds human vital organs and you obtain a more realistic perception of His behavior in the Godhead. His eternal deity qualifies the Holy Spirit to be the Continuum's Chief Guardian since He lived what it contains as God and Co-Authored it along with the Almighty and His Son. He is to be credited with the Continuum the same way they are, and His their omnipresence is also duty bound to monitor it. He corrects errors and deviations from it and reassures all of its prophesied provisions and promises are carried through. Besides all of this, the Holy Spirit filters what should or should not go beyond the Lord's preset limits. In the very way the skin of an earthly body announces agents or elements seeking to contact or infect it, the Holy Spirit similarly reports to the Most High what is approaching or trying to access Him, informing Him if it should or should not access His innermost Self. Of course, the Almighty's Spirit does all of this for Him on an infinitely grander scale than people on earth can imagine. Still, there are great similarities between the two due to the Lord, having made people on earth in His image and according to His likeness. To visualize what the Holy Spirit is doing on earth for the Most High, picture all the things the skin does for its bodies in on earth.

For example, before a body is invaded, the skin senses it and alerts the rest of its makeup that something wants to access its interiors. When this occurs, the skin inspects the nature of the invader and decides if it is safe or threatening. If there are, for example, things that do not work for a body's health, the skin is the first to discover it. If the body needs or desires what wants to enter it, the human will, tells the skin to give it entrance. Conversely, if something comes from within the body, once it reaches the surface the skin shows it by some marking or eruption. The skin sends signals that announce what is happening around it from within to notify and register it as good or bad, safe or potentially hazardous. When something seeks to enter the body, to wage war against it, or wreak havoc with its systems, multiplied billions of

---

127 See 1 John 5:7, 8; See 1 Corinthians 2:10-12.

sensors on the surface and beneath the skin go into action to investigate, identify, test, approve or prevent it. The skin's sensors are its feelers. They raise defenses or drop their guard, usually as a reflex, to secure and sustain the body. In a similar manner[128], the Holy Spirit does likewise for the Godhead. When it comes to Christ's body, however, the Spirit's surveillance, screening, and shielding activities afford His church the very same advantages that Christ and the Father have, which is why it is important not to grieve or dismiss Him. Study Romans 8:11; 1 Corinthians 11:27; 2 Corinthians 2:10; Ephesians 3:16; 1 Peter 3:18; Hebrews 9:12; 10:4, 19, 20; 1 Peter 1:2; 1 John 1:7.

THE HOLY SPIRIT AS SKIN IN THE OLD TESTAMENT

The Holy Spirit as God's skin is surprisingly found in both Testaments. In the Old Testament, it is signified by the word "tabernacle[59]". The Scripture also calls it a tent, a covering that parallels skin. See 2 Peter 1:14.[60] Besides this, definitions of skin include tent, tabernacle, and covering. For instance, whenever one reads about the Tabernacle of the Lord and its all-embracing coverage of the Godhead's glory housed within it, one is figuratively meeting its skin-like substance. Jesus came and tabernacled among people as Almighty God in human skin.[129] He embodied the fullness of God within His flesh, which was also considered the Almighty's temple.[130] The glory of God manifested in the Old Testament is traditionally expressed as His *Shekinah*, a word whose original roots liken it to the skin. This true statement is especially relevant considering Moses' Wilderness tabernacle coverings were in reality constructed of animal hides. They protected what was within, hid it from unworthy and prying eyes, and typified by its three divisions, the three levels of the human body's skin. Metaphorically, the tabernacle's badger hides concealed the symbolized the Triune God, the tri-part human, and foreshadowed the Son of God's future incarnation. Its divisions are called the outer court, inner court, and holy of holies.

THE SKIN & THE BLOOD

To extend the comparison between the spiritual body of Christ and the human body, the skin has a very close partner: its blood. The skin and blood unite to provide a regular current of life sustaining information about the body to the rest of its existence.

---

128 After all, Scripture does say humans are made in the Almighty's image and likeness.

129 See Strong's G4633 and its accompanying string. See also John 1:14 when it says that He dwelt—tabernacled—among us.

130 See Strong's 4367

The life-sustaining duo also streams all sorts of supplies, nutrients, remedies, recuperative and regenerative treatments as well. Human skin and blood, warn the body of dangers, filter and screen what affects its vitality, and communicate what is healthy or harmful to its overall well-being. In effect, the skin is the network that blankets the body and the blood the transmitter that reports on all that pertains to it.[131] Both function as a cohesive intelligence unit that takes care of a person by announcing, updating, and alerting every part of the body to what is going on outside of it that may change its insides, and vice versa. Together they take messages from the spirit, soul, and organs and convey them to the outer self, repeating the process of the inner self to notify soul and spirit of what enters and is traveling through them to vital areas.

Here is but miniscule insight into the importance of the bloodline of Jesus Christ and its power in the redeemed Christian. God left it on earth to cleanse mortals from ecological (although not moral, nor spiritual) sin. Christ's blood stayed the severity of the law of sin and death engulfing the whole planet. Furthermore, it continually purges the ground out of which humans come so the frailties that marred and weakened pre-Christ generations. The efficacy of His blood working on the earth and its ecologies eventually dissipated Eden's Curse enough for good health to replace the death that shortened life spans and caused high infant mortality worldwide.[132] He could do it because it was His word that caused decreed the curse back in the garden. The world got to see the long life prophecy the Lord speaks in Isaiah 65:18-20 happen. The universality of death, sickness, and disease confounds many Christians because they cannot discern how the fatal curse pronounced on Adam works. It works because of how deadly it made the earth, a reality seen in the ground's contribution to all life. God's curse on the earth was actually brilliant despite it being also tragic because everything that exists comes from the ground. The very nutrients that go into creating a human being come from the ground from which the parents eat. Should that ground be contaminated, all beings eating from it will pass on its contaminants to their offspring because nothing on the planet is devoid of the fruit of the earth. When Christ left His divine blood on the earth, He purged it of its natural morbidity so that people could live long enough to receive His salvation. To continue mass distribute His efficacious blood, God sent His Holy Spirit to the planet to maintain the purging effect of the Savior's blood, because that is why He divinely inseminated the virgin in the first

---

131 That is besides its life sustaining actions.
132 See Genesis 3:17.

place.[133] Hence, The Messiah's blood joins the veil (skin) of His flesh by the Holy Spirit. Together they carry out for Christians in His body spiritually exactly what their natural counterparts do.

THE HOLY SPIRIT, GOD'S CONNECTOR

A very, very primitive explanation, the foregoing gives a sense of how involved the Holy Spirit is in getting converts to God and depositing them within Him. The thing to remember here is that the Holy Spirit escorts the redeemed into God's presence on His terms and not theirs. The Lord decrees how He wants to be approached, and what He calls holy, hallowed, sanctified, and reverent. These decisions He does not leave up to His worshippers. For instance, in Exodus 3:5, Moses was told by the Lord to remove His shoes because the ground on which he stood with the burning bush was holy. What made it holy? Was it the bush? No. What made that ground holy was the Lord's Presence. Moses' shoes classified him as unsanctified because they touched the earth. As a result, they were too unsanctified to remain in the presence of his holy God. To resume the skin analogy, for anything to get into the body, it must pass through the skin. It does not matter if it is a smell through the skin of the nose, sight through the eyes, or a taste in the mouth. Furthermore, the tissues beneath the surface of the skin are not excluded from these actions. To get inside a person's body everything must start at and go through some part of the skin, and the same is true for anything to get outside of it as well. Over time, based on its experience, the body's senses, learn what is most likely to hurt it. To maintain itself, it develops keenly sophisticated instincts that tell it what to admit or deny admittance to it. To reach these determinations, the senses instantly scan and approve, rank, and prioritize what to allow internally and what to ward off to protect the body. In these respects, the skin serves as a shield and the blood the briefing that informs the body of whatever is trying to contact it. Both subtly recommend what the body should receive or reject. Sometimes the skin leaves the conclusions up to the will; at other times it makes them reflexively, particularly when hurt or danger is involved. Apply these explanations to the Holy Spirit as God's skin and His dynamics become more real and regardable, especially whenever He moves to heal, deliver, or otherwise manifest as God on location.

In every way, the skin and blood are occupied with getting into and throughout the body what will do it the greatest good, and halting what will harm it. However, this explanation does not take into account the pleasure pulses that the skin uses to sur-

---

133 Luke 1:35.

vey and approve voluntary things. It merely explains in some ways what the Holy Spirit does for the entire Godhead. He vigilantly and uncompromisingly assures that only what benefits the Trinity makes it into the Godhead's presence. To this end, the Spirit of God scrupulously keeps the Almighty and His Son at the greatest advantage and sees that what they want to enter this world from theirs makes it in, as designed and intended, and on time. He also launches the proceedings that culminate in what a person does upon leaving this world.

THE HOLY SPIRIT PERFORMING AS GOD'S SKIN

Even though God is Spirit and completely different from the terracotta of this world, it is still safe to identify the Holy Spirit as His skin. Here is how and why. As said earlier, skin is the human body's largest organ. What has been said thus far explained what makes Him it all encompassing and permeating. Those explanations discussed why the Holy Spirit is the greatest extension of the Godhead, making Him all encompassing and pervasive throughout creation. The two encompassingly, and pervasively fit well with the "omni-everything" terms that typify God's Spirit. Jeremiah 23:24 has God saying that He fills heaven and earth, while Paul in 1 Corinthians 15:28 states that God Almighty is all in all. With both passages, Ephesians 1:23 agrees. Read the context in which Paul reveals these aspects of God in Ephesians 1:17-23 and 1 Corinthians 15:40. All the same, more than being celestial, the Holy Spirit, equally with the other two members of the Godhead, is unquestionably as Sovereign as they. What comprises His makeup is not the same as what everything else He made consists of, except for those who are born again in Christ Jesus.

God has <u>everything,</u> abiding within, the Holy Spirit and outside Him, nothing exists. Being spread out over all the Lord's realms and territories, since God embodies[134] all of His works, extends the Holy Spirit's housing, protection, and supervision to the Lord's entire visible and invisible, heavenly and earthly worlds. Anything that would make its way into His Presence must enter by the veil of His Spirit in the way that whatever would enter humans must do so through the veil of their skin. Even though skin can be penetrated, its layered surfaces have numerous defenders to purify it and prevent harm. Likewise, the Holy Spirit's surface can be penetrated, which is why He feels what is done to Him. Nevertheless, He too has a defense system that, unlike ours, is impervious to destruction. Furthermore, the Holy Spirit is how the Godhead holds at bay whatever He is not ready to receive until it is sanctified and approved by

---

134 Refer to Colossians 1:13-22; Ephesians 1:23.

the member of its Divine Family appointed to discharge this responsibility on its behalf. That is, by the Holy Spirit. Creator God's omniscient, omnipresent skin-like covering performs a host of tests, acceptance, and rejection duties for Him that defends, and protects creation's Sovereign from earth's ungodliness. He safeguards His Family by sanctifying whatever is approved to approach it. In this way, He shields the entire Godhead from undesirables and perfectly presents only what the Most High welcomes. In addition, constituting the veil of Christ's flesh that replaced the torn veil of the ancient Levitical Temple ripped by Calvary, God's Spirit carries out for Him and His church everything the Old Testament veils did for Israel and its tabernacle under Moses' Law. Calling to mind the wilderness tabernacle again to strengthen the skin metaphor used for the Holy Spirit, here is how it applies. The largest part of Moses' tabernacle was the outer court. Comparably, the Holy Spirit exemplifies this because, as with the tabernacle's skin, He is the largest extension of the Almighty. No one on the planet escapes Him. And, especially since the Church's first Pentecost, everyone on earth who wants to come to God must do so by way of His Spirit. The second tabernacle division was the inner court. It is where the Lord's ongoing priestly ministrations occurred. This part is reflective of Jesus as the Second Member of the Godhead. We progress to the Most High's presence through the veil of His flesh. Hebrews 8, among other passages ascribe this as the role of escorting God's worshipers to Him. The most exclusive part of the tabernacle was the holy of holies. It was the holiest of all places on earth. There the Lord's Presence dwelt as tangible as He could in this world. It held the cherubim shielded Ark covered by the gold-layered mercy seat that held His law, Aaron's budded rod, and a pot of manna to commemorate His people's wilderness provisions. These all presumably comprised the elements of the very throne of God on earth and the altar that stood before it. For these purposes, the Holy Spirit's human like skin, housed the most accessible and populated part of the Lord's tabernacle, while the holy of holies, its least accessible part was shielded by what could be called finer membranes. The most sparsely furnished section of the Lord's meeting place held what was most sacred to Him. Being a replica of His heavenly Ark, the wilderness tabernacle clad with animal skin foretokened the incarnation of His Son in the future to make Him visible and the earth more tolerable to Him. The tabernacle trained God's people how to worship, honor, and revere the Presence of their awesome God by His Spirit. Each member of God's family is veiled and protected by the Holy Spirit. In addition, contrary to some theologies, the Holy Spirit's behaviors and actions in His duties are neither static nor passive. He is supremely forceful when it comes to protecting His charges, especially when it comes to permitting or preventing what should or should not come near to God. He is scrupulously vigilant in His inspections and meticulous in His scrutiny and though He indulges God's children's weaknesses, He does not accept them fully until they are suitable for the Almighty's majesty.

As the Godhead's number one and most conscientious Guardian, the Holy Spirit becomes combative when it comes to barring anything that wants to go into the Most High's presence. Anything that fails His screening and checkpoints is prohibited from getting close to the Lord. He absolutely will not present to heaven's throne what God rejects. To block foreign or unapproved entries attempting to bypass Him to come to God the Son and His Father uninvited or disapproved, the Holy Spirit turns aggressive as any high leader's palace, regal, or presidential guard would. Whatever approaches God must remind Him of Jesus and nothing less; Jesus incarnated, crucified, and forever glorified. Rereading Uzza's tragic story in 1 Chronicles 13:9-11 shows how reflexive the Holy Spirit can be when it comes to protecting God's glory and sanctity. His conduct in threatening situations spiritually resembles human skin's defense of its bodies up to and including the muscular reflexes that instinctively act to enable or preserve it. The extreme difference between God's Spirit and His other spirits is that the Holy Spirit's invincibility assures nothing that seeks to antagonize or otherwise injure the Godhead penetrates Him, period.

HEAVEN'S EMBASSY

To better make the point, the Holy Spirit in the planet today functions as the Godhead's embassy and its Senior Ambassador. On earth, the Holy Spirit is heaven's peacekeeping force sent to see that it does not self-destruct or demonically collapse before the fullness of those to receive Christ's salvation have been born, and born again. He performs for eternity's Sovereign Divine Council every duty, task, detail and responsibility that the ambassadors of the world today performs for their senders. He represents Jesus Christ and the Father God as creation's joint heads of eternity's new creation nation state, so to speak. In the same way that abusing a political ambassador on earth is dangerous, so is abusing the Holy Spirit, which is why the Lord Jesus states that there is no pardon for those who die blaspheming Him. Within the individual human lives of the world, and the world itself, rejection of the Holy Spirit's forgiveness, salvation, redemption, and embodiment is tantamount to rejecting another country's representative on foreign soil. Many political leaders can say how that will work out. If the offended of nation recalls its embassy, it implies that relations with the abusive country are severed and there is nothing more to expect between two territories but animosity and perhaps war. That is why the Lord Jesus gave John the Revelator the Apocalypse that today is called the book of Apocalypse. The entire drama is the Lord's prediction of what will happen to earth for abusing His Spirit and His messengers, for rejecting and renouncing His righteousness, and for refusing His redemption. Unlike when Jesus restrained Himself from dispatching legions of angels against the earth to prevent His death sentence from Pilate, the Apocalypse tells a very different story. It is consistent with what happens when a sovereign of sovereigns retaliates against a nation that assaults its embassy. In political terms, such affronts are treated as acts of aggression by the stronger state, and can spell war. When retaliatory war ensues, the weaker nation is destroyed. Such is the case with heaven and earth, the Godhead and the nations of this world. In fact, Revelation 6:14-16 has the earth's world powers begging for the rocks to fall on them to hide them from the face of the Lamb of God sitting on eternity's throne. Taking the time to study ambassadorship, diplomacy, embassies and the like in relation to Jesus Christ's new creation Ecclesia as God's everlasting nation-state, clarifies two very vital things. It vivifies the role and function of the Holy Spirit on earth, and justifies His power and presence over Christ's church. Discerning the subliminal comparisons between the two means never viewing the Holy Spirit or the Spirit-filled church of the Lord Jesus Christ the same way again.

THE HOLY SPIRIT IN THE CHURCH

In the Church, the Holy Spirit acts as God's Immigration Agent, the Church's body-guard, and creation's Secretary of State all at once. He upholds the Lord's celestial government. As the Lord's Immigration Agent, the Holy Spirit certifies who is redeemed and who is not. Carrying on a study of these principles and the practices that come from them, answers what the Holy Spirit's duties and what they mean for the Lord and His church. In-depth study of this information would yield an understanding of God's reasons for stipulating the Holy Spirit's regenerative process as the only acceptable means of leaving the ranks of His created beings and becoming His begotten instead. If done thoroughly, what actually makes one a member of Christ's body will be seen to correlate with what makes one a naturalized citizen of a country in this world. The big difference is *naturalized* for earth becomes *celestialized* in His eternal nation. Since everlasting statehood and citizenship are at the center of the Lord's eternal life plan, how the Holy Spirit validates it all according to the Almighty's standard criteria is important. The Christian should remember that God's kingdom is not forming itself while waiting for the Church. Its eternality presupposes conditions for going into it already exist and terms and conditions for becoming one of its lawful citizens are fixed. God's kingdom has long-standing legal and judicial systems with codes that pertain to immortal and not mortal beings. His realm is not a republic, but a theocracy, and the reason it has always existed is the very reason why it shall ever cease. Numerous passages of Scripture assert and reassert this. Therefore, it is vital that members of Christ's body learn and accept why He does not receive people into God's kingdom the way it is done on earth as the following Scriptures show:

Romans 5:5; 8:15; 17; 9:8;15:16

Ephesians 4: 30

Galatians 3:26, 27

Philippians 4:3

Timothy 1:14; 2:19

John 3:1,2

Revelation 7:2; 21:27[61]

THE NEW BIRTH ETERNITY'S GOLD STANDARD

The Book of Proverbs likens the soul to silver and the spirit to gold. Extensive discussions on the life force that dominates God's invisible world have shown that gold is its standard because spirits due to their electrified makeup are often pictured as gold in Scripture. In addition, because of the sun and earth's dependence on it, gold is often synonymous with light or luminescence. The Lord's world on these grounds is indisputably on His gold standard. That means the dark soul must somehow be turned into purified silver and the dead human spirit must be revived to reflect the amber-like members of the Almighty's eternal world to qualify to enter it. Consequently, joining the Church, saying prayers, or performing deeds one considers to be good are on their own, inadequate for everlasting life. The kingdom of light admits only children of light.[135] It is nonnegotiable. God has archetypical immigration protocols built into His kingdom's constitution that are nowhere near as lax or flexible as the nations of this world. The first of the fourteen events in the Continuum explains why. As is often the case in some nations on earth, a departed cannot enter God's eternal kingdom apart from the Holy Spirit. A person cannot just put his or her name on heaven's roll and say to the Almighty, "I declare I am your child so treat me like a Christian, let me in". That is not how it goes in God's world. In eternal parlance, the redeemed citi-

---

135 Luke 16:8 and John 12:36.

zens of God's royal kingdom are made so by being born again[136] of the King of Glory[137]—the way all ancient nations were formed. This includes God's nation, Israel.[138] The new creature in Christ is royal and the body of Christ, His new glorified species, what 2 Peter 2:9; 2 Peter 1:3 and Revelation 1:6 all convey.

The Holy Spirit as God's sentinel watches over heaven's borders to prevent illegal entry into the body of Christ, which is what Jesus in John chapter 10 took great pains to explain. The Holy Spirit is the eternal kingdom's naturalizer. He naturalizes,[62] more accurately celestializes what the Spirit indwells to live forever as God's offspring.[63] As God's divine agency on earth, the Holy Spirit baptizes God's newcomers into His truth. He is the judge, advocate, and divine arbiter who intervenes or intercedes on the convert's behalf. He is the power that separates the Church from the world, the signature that signs off on each of its member's registration in the Lamb's book of life. Moreover, God's Spirit holds the only seal that makes those who endure to the end divine citizens of eternity when they leave this world. Beyond this, the Holy Spirit is the redeemed's uplink to the Almighty and the vehicle of download to the Church. He keeps the channels of communication between Christ and His church open and translates Christians' communications with the Lord, so they are well received, as any good ambassador would. The Spirit of the Lord surveys the kingdom's individual and ecclesial territories to assure the Redeemer's hedge of protection about His church stays secure and that predators do not encroach upon what He shed His blood to redeem. He further empowers Christian witness, verifies all testimony, and distributes the provisions and benefits of the new creation's covenant blessings as allocated by the Godhead from before heaven's primordial age. The Holy Spirit defends God's people according to His righteousness and vindicates those who are falsely accused, or attacked. In the end, the Holy Spirit will transport the Church out of this world and into the Lord's presence forever. By now it is evident that the Holy Spirit is the single all-encompassing means of contacting and connecting with God in any way. He is the Godhead's Resident Agent on the planet who interfaces, intercepts, perfects, and permits all outreaches to heaven.

---

136 John 3:6, 8; 8:23; 11:52; 1 Peter 1:23
137 And in the case of Sarah and Mary, queens (literally princesses)
138 See Genesis 17 and then Romans 4. Pay particular attention to Romans 4:13.

THE HOLY SPIRIT AND CHRIST'S CHURCH

When it comes to believers in Christ Jesus, the Holy Spirit as the Almighty's covering, defends and engulfs God's people everywhere on the planet. He does this to spread the body of Christ around the world to fulfill its salt and light mandate. In this capacity, the Spirit of the Lord conscientiously purges Christ's church to enter and dwell in God's presence. Unhappily, the casualness of His ecclesial authorities often frustrates this safeguard because they are not as discriminating about whom to welcome into God's world and whom to exclude from it. Due to indiscretion or naïveté, they populate their churches using a "come one come all" approach. God's Spirit, on the other hand, stays on task and simply spreads out the gates of Christ's salvation only to the repentant, despite His earthly ministers' indiscriminate flinging wide the doors and privileges of their churches. That view is the essence of Jesus' sermon in John chapter 10 and His declaration of Matthew 16:18. The Great Commission, notwithstanding, the Church should acknowledge that its new covenant blessings should be more responsibly guarded and prudently distributed. That is what the Continuum exists to do.

The Lord's people should accept that the Holy Spirit shields the Godhead for it and its people's benefit. Before He escorts worshipers into its presence and examines everyone thoroughly, inspecting and consecrating them inside and out for the visit. At every level before giving anyone abnormal divine audience, God's Spirit will purge, purify, and empower those the Lord receives. Not until all of the Lord Almighty's reverential requirements are met, is a worshipper or petitioner rewarded with a nearer and closer approach to His overwhelming glory. In addition, they must be covered by the Lamb's blood to survive it. This norm is followed, just as diligent when the Lord initiates the contact or summons a person to enter His Presence. As a case in point, see Exodus 19:11. It is by His Holy Spirit that the Lord purges or adjusts what would enter His Presence. According to very specific guidelines and procedures, the Holy Spirit sanctifies and transforms all overtures and efforts to what the Almighty demands and will respond to most productively. For additional examples, turn to Judges 6:19-21; 13:16-19.

As God's Agent, Sentinel, Shield, and earthly Commissioner, the Holy Spirit has the final sway over everything pertaining to the Godhead. That is salvation, healing, ministry, spirituality, life and death, redemption or damnation; they are all the administrative prerogatives of the Holy Spirit. This includes reinforcing His Godhood and the sovereignty that goes along with it. Keep in mind that He comprises God the Father and God the Son. It does not matter if the preacher, prophet, pastor, or the Church itself says otherwise; the Holy Spirit knows God's will concerning all things and will bring everything into conformance with it or block any significant access to Him. Think about all this in relation to the Lord's church. It is with this impervious incorruptible shield that the Lord Jesus declared that the gates of hell would not prevail against it. God's Spirit is the epitome of meticulousness, and as His most trusted earthly Curator, He allows nothing that belongs to the Lord or that He desires to possess to be diverted from Him. Whatever the Spirit, obtains, He contains; all that the Holy Spirit possesses, He protects; whatever belongs to Christ's body is enveloped by God's Spirit and secured for the Master's good pleasure. All of it is, sovereignly and indelibly sealed for the day that He returns for His inheritance. Here is what the New Testament Scriptures mean about the sealing of the redeemed that the Holy Spirit effects for the Godhead. He is devoted to God who as part of His very self will not let anything the Most High attains or possesses slip through the cracks or be snatched from His fingers. As an indomitable steward over the Lord's purchased possession, the Church He purchased with His own blood, the third Person of the Godhead will do all to secure whatever God holds dear. He will deliver to heaven's throne what it appointed and dispatched Him to seek, save, and sanctify from the earth.

GUARDING THE GLORY

As sovereign guardian of the Almighty's glory, the Holy Spirit enforces God's boundaries and maintains the lines of communications between God and His people. He is heaven's monitor and connection with earth and vice versa. Unfortunately, most Christians do not acknowledge this aspect of God. They dismiss any idea of His having an all-pervasive side that protects Him or that extends from His world to ours. Those who feel this way cannot imagine how exalted the Creator's technology is in comparison to the earth and spurn His antiquity as outdated and irrelevant in their times. Often, believers time-bind God's hand because His Scriptures present Him in archaic eras. They are unaware that Jesus came from the future to save them because He is Alpha and Omega. Failing to see God, as the end of all things as well as their beginning causes believers to treat His world as dragging behind this one. These explanations speak to why some saints fail to appreciate the Holy Spirit's function of screening their access to God. Aside from this, most Christians live unaware of the Holy Spirit's role in their salvation, sanctification, and spiritual life. More than a few of them cannot conceive of the Holy Spirit, as God and countless numbers of them cannot fathom what the big deal is about Him. Some Christians see Him as useful for speaking in other tongues and maybe a few other antics some zealous branches of the Church like to engage in to show off. But for the most part, those who do not like to speak in tongues or to get too deep into God prefer to dismiss Him. Despite His mixed reactions, God's Spirit keeps the Lord in touch with His creation and His creation in touch with its Sovereign Creator.

So far, extensive explanations have been given about God's Holy Spirit and what makes Him metaphorically, the Godhead's skin. All of it is to show how vital He is in the Trinity in the same way that people are useless without their skin. Its seven layers keep it them from being vulnerable to everything the world can throw at them. This metaphor says why it is vain to attempt to commune with God without the Holy Spirit. The body needs its skin and all its manifestations to make it presentable, functional, sensitive, and safe, and so does God. Skin is indispensable for healthy contact with this world. Accordingly, when it comes to the human's spiritual self and interactions with the eternal God the two likewise require His skin, the Holy Spirit. Jesus reiterated this time and again in preparing His disciples for His departure. To ease their grief over His leaving, He let them know that He would come back to them in another form, in the shape of a Comforter (Helper or Paracletos) who would be with them, and within them to assure their unhindered access to Him and the Father. That Comforter, the Lord introduced as the Holy Spirit, whom He would dispatch from heaven once He returned home. Without the Holy Spirit, one cannot even get a message to the Lord, which is why it was so important to the Father to dispatch Him into the world to indwell His church. Even the angels that traverse back and forth between the two worlds do so by God's Spirit as Ezekiel's living creatures reveal. So apart from the Spirit nothing happens. Here is the most succinct way of appreciating the Godhead and understanding its distinct unity. God the Father started it all. When He began, everything has been already in Him, the way people's reproductions and potential come into existence when they do. All that the Lord ever imagined, began invisibly (or embryonically) when He Self-manifested, including the Son. Jesus Christ can say He always existed because He has, at first in His Father's Person, and later as an extension of it. On the strength of these two truths The Messiah and His Father are forever one with the Creator and His Son's life indivisibly coexisting. It has already been shown how the Holy Spirit got started. So this is how they operate. Jesus is God's portable Self. He is how God manifests locally in actual places. The Holy Spirit is the Almighty's pervasive Self; He is how the Creator is everywhere present at once. As every single aspect of creation's only life and power source, The Maker's omnipresence is too vital to what He created to pull away from one thing to give full attention to another, no matter how critical it may be. As the cause and Sustainer of all things, God the Father is just too infinite to fit in one place, so He reproduced two other versions of Himself to handle His duties. In answer to the deficits His infiniteness caused, the Most High begot offspring to show up in some places and dispatched His Holy Spirit to assure that He manifests every place at the same time, all the time.

[21]

The Continuum and Jesus Christ: *This Same Jesus*

It almost seems superfluous to include a chapter on the Lord Jesus Christ in this book when He is its main character. Prior chapters so constantly mentions Him that one wonders what more can be said about Him. He has been presented as the precarnate, incarnate, and human-divine Son of the living God. He was unveiled as creation's Sovereign of sovereigns, Judah's Lion-Lamb; Israel's Passover Lamb, and the Founder of the Christian faith. Jesus herein has been depicted as the Shepherd of the flock and the Bishop of souls. He is Moses' Great Prophet and the Apostle of our profession. His other offices include Yahweh, Messiah, Redeemer, and everlasting King David. His story has been told from His crucifixion, resurrection, and His recovery of all that was marred in the first of the fourteen events and lost in Eden by his clay prototype Adam. So is there really any more to be said? The answer is yes, since He is the most controversial figure in history. Jesus Christ is the most beloved and despised person in any age. This chapter deals with people's inexplicable passions and hostilities toward a man who walked the earth a little over a quarter of a century who, dying ungraciously managed to take over the planet from the grave. All of these actualities make dedicating a chapter to Him worthwhile. This chapter does not simply reiterate what has been said about Him so far, it concisely unfolds His history, destiny, goals and objectives, visions and enterprises. Concentration on His most provocative roles in God's Eternal Continuum allows Christ's peculiarities to be isolated and His infinite responsibilities understood. This treatment of the Savior expounds on how He came to be and explores all of His divine offices, summing up what makes Him who and what He is in all of the Creator's worlds. Effectively, these discussions tie together Genesis 1:1; John 1:1 and Hebrews 1:10, all passages that unfold God's beginnings. If there were a theme for this section of the book, it would be,

"This Jesus". That is what its subject matter stresses, "This Jesus": what Jesus? The one Paul preached who came from heaven. The one Acts 2:32 and 17:5 refer to as Israel's promised (and prophesied) Messiah. Telling Scripture's Jesus" from other Jesuses is important to avoid being deceived in the end.

Jesus has a lot of impostors out there; He foretold they would emerge after He left. To protect His church from them, the true Jesus took great pains to differentiate Himself from His impostors. Knowing that He would be the chronic victim of identity theft, the Christ preached, Matthew chapter 24 to instruct His followers on His second advent. He is quite detailed about the conditions and signs of His return. He concludes His instructions with Matthew chapter 25. What is particularly noteworthy in His teachings is His prediction of the myriad of impostors to come who would work hard to deceive His sheep. He paints a very vivid picture of how to detect false-christs and how to reject a false advent. However, He warns that only the very elect will be able to do so. It has been a long while since Jesus left the earth and many redeemed people have come and gone awaiting His return. That return is nearer with every passing day as Romans 13:11 says. With each passing era, the Lord's return grows more imminent, making it urgent for those looking for His coming to know the true from the false. There are three passages that contain the two words; "This Jesus". They underscore that genuine and deceived seekers are watching for Messianic advent. The real offspring of the Godhead is warned against judging the signs of His coming with anything but His word. Acts 1:11 has the two angels who escort their Sovereign home say "Which also said, ye men of Galilee, why stand ye gazing up into heaven? *This _same_ Jesus, which is taken up from you into heaven, shall so come in like manner as ye have seen him go into heaven.*" Their words confirm Matthew 24:27, 30, and 31. Lightning will strike from east to west; dead carcasses will appear as translated souls leave their bodies; cosmic disasters will grip the world as the heavens fail to hold its inhabitants. Lastly, angels will flood the devastated planet collecting The Messiah's elect. Other passages support and elaborate on end time adventist signatures, but the point is made. There is but one Jesus who came to earth from heaven, left the earth to return to heaven, and who promised to return to earth from heaven for His own. He will do so, not according to cleverly contrived tales, but according to the very book that foretold His coming and passion. The one that records His pre-earth existence and exploits. Consequently, since there remains the promise and plan for Jesus's return, it is imperative that His family knows the real from the false, and there is no other way to do so outside of God's Eternal Continuum.

Jesus is God's "Faithful and True Witness" sent from eternity into time to tell heaven's story as an eyewitness. That is what is meant by His being called such in John's Apocalypse. Before addressing this one of His many titles, a point to be made about Jesus' eternality is captured in the ISV's version of Jeremiah 42:5. "Then they told Jeremiah, "May the Lord be a true and faithful witness against us if we don't do everything that the Lord your God tells us through you". It is true that this may be seen as a customary remark people of the day used to add a divine dimension to their oaths and vows. However, the idea that the invisible world's witnesses somehow record all that goes on in the physical one comes across in this passage and many others like it. Heaven is high and looks low. It is pervasive and misses nothing that goes on in the earth. Heaven's invisible cloud of witnesses is not a body of casual observers. They are a testimonial force that tracks and archives the entire birth-to-death experience of every creature to enter and exit the planet. In the end, Scripture says the books of its spiritual witnesses' will be opened and everything their record contains will be made public to those responsible for meting out afterlife judgments and rewards. The predominant figure in the process is Jesus Christ, God's faithful and true witness. Romans 14:10 and 2 Corinthians 5:10 both say that the earth's departed souls will ultimately stand before the judgment seat of Christ. As creation's Sovereign, guardian, and judge, Jesus bears witness to the souls that have departed earth to determine where each one will spend eternity.

To reinforce afterlife judgment's place in the Continuum, Daniel 7:10 foretells it in the Old Testament. It is fulfilled in Revelation 20:12. John's Apocalypse mentions a book of life that surfaces, eight times throughout the New Testament. Revelation 3:5 says Jesus has the power to blot people's names out of it; to infer being written in it before one dies is not as permanent as taught in some circles. The Messiah can blot a name out of the book of life because those registered in it must believe to the saving of their souls, which requires enduring to the end. Revelation 13:8 identifies the book of life belonging to the Lamb of God who was slain from the foundation of the world. Two other apocalyptic references shed further light on the Savior's eternal life duties. One is found in John chapter 17, called The Messiah's High Priestly Prayer. There He says His Father gave Him the power to give eternal life to whomever He wills. The last mention of the book of life comes with a somber warning because it takes in John's entire apocalyptic vision. Despite its length, the revelation is nonetheless a prophecy delivered by the glorified Jesus' angel. John's messenger says that if anyone written in the Lamb's book of life tampers with the prophecy, that person's eternal reward will be accordingly diminished. Who is it that makes such decisions? It is the glorified

Son of God, Jesus Christ, who has been administering eternity's will on earth since its origin. From the moment of His baptism, the Son of David has represented humanity to heaven. An unending duty that validates His testimony and qualifies, His as the only spirit of prophecy that God Almighty ratifies, certifying Him as the judge of the quick and the dead.

Revelation 19:10 says the "testimony of Jesus Christ is the spirit of prophecy" because prophecy is the substance of the Christian's Holy Scriptures. As a result, Jesus and His testimonies as the Old Testament's Yahweh, and the New Testament's Messiah make up the Continuum's indispensables. John's Gospel opens with why. He is the word that was in the beginning with God and as such, He is God, which is why this book portrays Him as the Continuum's principal character. From beginning to end, before all worlds and long after their demise, life in heaven and earth is all about Creator God's first begotten Son. God reproduced Himself in Jesus to delegate all of His embodiable and distant business to Him. The Almighty desired a travelable version of Himself who could manifest in ways His infiniteness prevented Him from doing. Expedience, attentiveness, and relatability[139] are why He procreated Jesus Christ. God yearned to be more than a static fixture above His creation. He always wanted to relate to and interact with His handiwork as its Maker. Doing so demanded a way for Him to remain supreme over creation and ever-present inside it at the same time. The ideal answer would enable Him to manifest to His worlds visibly and tangibly. As the Almighty, God's nature and expansiveness preclude Him from roving from place to place in order to localize as a single entity. However, His wisdom foresaw times when He should appear to His creatures to confirm His existence and cover their issues personally. The solution the Most High settled on, was an offspring, a fully contained, completely mobile version of Himself equal to Him in all regards. God's portable version could be dispatched to various realms of His creation to handle matters requiring His direct sovereignty. The Lord brought forth His first begotten Son, by His word. Jesus' birth did not come about the way so many imitative mythical deities reproduce, which is by divine marriage and sexual procreation. John 1:12 and 13 bluntly disavow this as God's way of reproducing Himself, which is not how His creatures reproduce. What John refutes is the commonly understood way new religions are born, and how encroaching deities breed themselves to populate new territories. He denounces this as the way the Almighty brought forth His first begotten Son, alt-

---

139 Able to be related to something else. Enabling a person to feel that they can relate to someone or something.

hough a modified version of it is how the Father incarnated the Christ to get Him into the earth. He did so by directly implanted is sperm in a virgin's womb.

Before creating anything else, the Lord procreated Jesus by speaking Him into existence. It is how He made Adam, which is by His word. The Most High's new creation offspring are sired likewise. He speaks and they are born again. What He speaks is forgiveness and acceptance. The point of all this is that what John stipulates in his gospel is that nothing biological achieves the new birth.[64] It is completely accomplished by God's word, what 1 Peter 1:23 affirms.

How God Engages Jesus

God in heaven uses His Son Jesus the same way a human father engages his son in this world. Earthly parents regularly use their adult children to extend or carry on the family business. Traditionally, founding fathers rely on their descendants to represent them elsewhere. History shows monarchs did so constantly with their progeny, routinely functioning in their place. To transact family business in these instances, the child is received and honored as the personification of the parent. The personification rests on the parent's word and status, nothing more. The child spoke distantly what the parent wanted to say and enforced it with whatever enforcement and performance means the parent authorized. Those means could be a rod, a signet ring, even an army. Whatever assured that the sender's will be done was attached to the person sent to assure the mission or venture's success, and it is not much different today. When it comes to expanding or extending the family enterprise, as is the parent, so is the child appointed to act as substitute. Genesis 18; Micah 5:2; and Daniel 3:25; 7:13 all mean to communicate this. Such is the case with Jesus The Messiah and Creator God. His incomparable union with the Father explains His words in John 8:49, *"I honor my Father and you dishonor Me."* What could this statement possibly mean? And then there is verse 58 of the same chapter. *"Jesus told them, "Truly, I tell all of you with certainty, before there was an Abraham, I AM!"*[140] All of the passages strongly imply God Almighty manifests in certain places that were too small or feeble for His infinite massivity.[141] Condensing His omniness allows the Self-Existent God to compact His being in a single replicant He calls His first begotten. Paul well understood this, which is why he says of Jesus that in His body dwelt all the richness of the Godhead.

---

140 ISV

141 Consisting of or forming a large mass; large in scale, amount, or degree; solid or substantial; great or imposing. A homogeneous mass.

The ISV phrases it this way, "because all the essence of Deity inhabits Him in bodily form." The Literal Translation of the Bible puts it another way, "For in Him dwells all the fullness of the Godhead bodily". The two references sound the same, but a little nuance that distinguishes them is worth noting. The ISV implies the essence of what makes God the Deity, He is fully indwelt Jesus Christ's body. His Son is as Himself. The LITV varies this a bit by implying that the Godhead's fullness prepared itself a body in which to dwell, tying it to Psalm 40:7 and Hebrews 10:7. Both renderings of Colossians 2:9 about the embodied Godhead are true, with one better expressing the other.

All of this tells how Jesus is God and how the Godhead moves around. He is the way the Most High appears to and interacts with designated creatures in His worlds. In constructing Jesus, the Maker did not stop at His body. He went on to add to His Son the power to manifest as any other thing He made. How did he do it? By intrinsically[65] embodying Jesus so that they absorbed each other to share the exact same life force and lifestyle. That is how the Father made His Son in His image. Jesus is not a copy, for that is to bring Him down a generation. He is not a clone because that is to diminish His paternal exactness. In every regard, He is as almightily divine as the Lord is, showing the richness of His Father's being and exercising limitlessly all of His forces in all worlds. John the Revelator depicts Jesus as a lion and a many-horned ram to signify the completeness of His authority as the Son of God, God incarnate, God who was raised from the dead, and the Son who returned to heaven to forever rule at His Father's right hand.[66] A persistent question is *how* God is Jesus. The answer to it could not be given before as plausibly as it can now be spoken today. Science has done a great job of enabling Christians to answer the question.

What made Jesus God in heaven has been explained. What makes Him, God in flesh is discussed here. The degree to which Jesus may be called God is the same degree that people's blood, hair, nails, skin and bodily fluids may be in essence called them. The very things that make people maternally human are what make Jesus Christ in His earthly form completely human as well. Enclosing His human form into the Godhead's divine lineage further reflects His value to the Most High. John 4:24 says, "God is Spirit." He became flesh in Christ in the following manner. To separate Jesus from the Godhead in order to make Him human the Lord changed His spiritual form. To make Him mortal He gave Him blood. To make Him physical, He gave Him a body. All of this is according to the prophecies that foretold His incarnation. The means by which the Father accomplished all of this is explained below.

Since the spirit that gives life is passed on to human offspring by their fathers, Jesus is as God as the Almighty. This is true for His heavenly and earthly births. As the Son of God, the body He received from His virgin mother, although exceptional, needed divine blood to affirm His heavenly Father's paternity. The strength of Jesus' Deity has to do with the blood of God Himself, since blood is the crux of any paternal claim. The Holy Spirit directly depositing Jesus' seed in Mary's womb makes Christ's blood sinless because all children's blood comes from the father. Blood is what makes Jesus God incarnate and what gives Him the power to purge and save those who believe in Him. His humanity made Him the Son of Man to distinguish the divinity that made Him the Son of God. The human-divine side of Him is why His blood had to be left on earth. He shed blood in this planet to mitigate the severity of the curse His Father had pronounced on the earth in Eden. When judging Adam for his transgression, Creator God cursed the ground for humankind's sake. That curse took every trace of His divine life out of the planet and left it to subsist on the rest of the fallen angels to whom Adam surrendered his person. Here is where the Lord God's providential creation of the sun and the moon prove their wisdom. To continue, back in Genesis before the Lord's Spirit left the ground, taking His life and light with Him, He forbade the earth to bring forth good fruit and condemned its farmers' to toil bitterly for what little they harvested. This is what He said, *"And unto Adam he said, because thou hast hearkened unto the voice of thy wife, and hast eaten of the tree, of which I commanded thee, saying, thou shalt not eat of it: cursed is the ground for thy sake; in sorrow shalt thou eat of it all the days of thy life; thorns also and thistles shall it bring forth to thee; and thou shalt eat the herb of the field; in the sweat of thy face shalt thou eat bread, till thou return unto the ground; for out of it wast thou taken: for dust thou art, and unto dust shalt thou return."* The curse's simple sounding words abound with implications, considering that everything on earth starts in the ground. The Edenic curse was only lifted by Jesus' death on the cross. Somehow, His death remedied a depraved wretchedness that was born in humans under the BC era. Pouring out the Son of God's sinless blood released the earth to bring forth good, and not just the cruelness it historically generated before the cross. In some mysterious way the shed blood of the crucified God so changed the planet that now souls born on it can hear and receive the gospel. That is, if they are ordained heirs of salvation. The very elect Jesus speaks of in His gospels can, by virtue of His blood drenching the planet, repent and be saved. Cosmically speaking, Jesus' shed blood deposited some agent in the BC ground that permits, chosen vessels to receive Him as their Savior and inherit eternal life as a result. Apparently, this was impossible before. It seems the barrier to eternal life prior to this time was the ground, out of which everything in this world comes. The sinless blood of its Maker alleviated a significant measure of the cruelty the earth once bred in its inhabitants, which is how Jesus saved the world. That blood, still efficacious in the earth today, gradually turned its soil into something that would cause those hid in Christ before the foundation of the world to respond to His salvation offer when He made it.[142] Of course, there are endless natural enhancements that emerged from it too. The way Jesus did this is by the abiding residence of His Holy Spirit. The power of God's life emanating from His Spirit gradually revived earth's soil. Being spread abroad delivered some semblance of heaven's type of healing to the planet. Coupling that with the eviction of the princes that so cruelly ruled it and so thoroughly contaminated gave humanity the capacity to hear the Lord, believe His gospel and repent and be saved.

JESUS' ETERNAL SERVICE TO HIS HEAVENLY FATHER

In addition to being His Father's portable Self, Jesus is also His Dad's projectable and capturable Self as well. He is how everything that was lost to the Almighty when Adam sold God's creation to the serpent is being systematically restored to the Creator's dominion. In John 16:28 the Lord Jesus says that He came forth from the Father to enter the world. He completes that thought when He is leaving the world to return to the Father. What He means by these statements *seems* obvious until His other comments about Him and His Father surface. For instance, Jesus says He and His Father are one and that He is never alone, because His Father is always with Him. If He completely left His Father, how "one" could they actually stay while He was on earth? Indeed, although He is on earth, the Savior implies that He also never left His Father. Look at what John 3:13 says about Jesus and His Father's union, and how the Son's earthly assignment did not sever but only extended them into this world. *"No one has gone up to heaven except the one who came down from heaven, the Son of Man who is in heaven."* How can He be essentially in heaven and physically on earth at the same time? It is because He never left His Father. They did not separate for His earth mission; the Father merely projected Jesus from His being into the earth, which is why the Son is the Almighty's projectable Self. As far as His being His capturable Self, here is what that means and why it is so. The answer goes all the way back to the Continuum's second event, the Garden of Eden.

Earlier discussions recalled the Bible's six days of creation; the seventh day made the full week, and on it, the Lord God rested. In that discussion, the matter of light being

---

142 Study John chapter 5.

the first thing the Lord God commanded to appear was contrasted with His creation of the two great lights to hang in the sky to rule the day and the night, the sun and the moon. If there was light and darkness, night and day, prior to their creation, then where did it come from? Of course, the light source that illuminated the world until the sun, moon, and luminaries were created was that of heaven. Reading Revelation 21:23 tells how. *"The city doesn't need any sun or moon to give it light, because the glory of God gave it light, and the lamb was its lamp."* In God's world, the Maker's glory is its utility system. Jesus is the vessel through which that glorious light beams. So powerful is their joint luminescence that they light up all the places of creation the Creator wants lit. Jesus is well aware of this and repeatedly calls Himself "the light of the world". He means it spiritually, morally, intellectually, and literally. His Spirit brought life into this world; there can be no light without some sort of life. His righteousness brought morality to the earth as heaven defines it. His wisdom lifted the dullness from the human mind to permit a measure of eternity's brilliance to enlighten its intelligence. Lastly, the Savior's claim to be the light of the world was meant literally as His Mount of Transfiguration luminosity demonstrates. To recall, the Lord Jesus Christ's very being lit up an entire mountain with heaven's light. The creation story ties it all together, what illuminated the renovated world's days 1-3 was the Creator's light. He did it that way so that later readers' of His creation narrative would be provoked to question this very contradiction. On the one hand, the light was in the world and on the other hand lights were made to illuminate it. Which one is it? The answer is, for a time it was both.

In its beginning, streams of eternal light from heaven pushed back the darkness that blanketed the waterlogged earth. Anticipating what had already occurred in His own world, the Lord God created two lights to replace His radiance when it exited the planet, which it did when Adam failed his first and only test. When that happened the Lord's Spirit withdrew, as has been said elsewhere, and left the earth to subsist on the two great luminaries and the smaller glitters in the sky. His departure plunged the world into a modified darkness until the Spirit of God received permission from the Son of God to return to earth. The darkness is called "modified" because of the two great lights and lesser luminaries that hung in the sky, as opposed to the vacuous blackness that gripped it until the Lord renovated it once again. The next question is what was so vital to the Almighty that needed His Son to capture it in bodily and spiritual form? The answer begins with Acts 3:21-24 and Peter's statements about the "restitution of all things". Here is the passage: *"Whom the heaven must receive until the times of restitution of all things, which God hath spoken by the mouth of all his holy prophets since the world began*". Immediately, the Continuum connection shows up in the phrase "since the world began". Aside from His prophets extending back to when the world began, not necessarily when the earth was renovated, two connotations emerge that are useful to the Continuum. The first is that something needs to be restituted and Jesus is primary to its restitution, and the second is that what is to be restituted precedes His incarnation and everything that came from it. Look at some hard-to-miss Continuum elements contained in these passages.

1. Upon repentance, the Lord sends Jesus. "Send you Jesus, whom he appointed long ago to be The Messiah".

2. Jesus must remain in heaven until the time of universal restitution. God announced it long ago through the voice of His holy prophets.

3. Moses spoke prophetically about the whole thing when he was on earth leading God's people.

4. Since Moses, "All the prophets who have spoken, from Samuel and those who followed him, also announced these days."

5. God not only told Moses and the prophets following him, but He first told His hope, vision and plan to Abraham.

Thayer's Greek Definitions says the word *restitution* means "restoration with a view to God's true theocratic state that He intended before the fall".[143] According to Strong, the word comes from others that mean to "reconstitute in home, health, and organization". These show the Lord had a big vision for the couple He placed in the Garden of Eden. He is now carrying that vision out globally through The Messiah's Ecclesia. Their heaven to earth reconciliation goes beyond restoring worship and fellowship with God. The Lord wants His entire kingdom back and He wants His first begotten Son to rule it for Him. He wants the Godhead's health to thrive in His people, its government to rule them from within and without, and eternity's state of existence to become that of earth. That is what the whole campaign has been about since before the foundation of the world.

How does Jesus restitute all things for His Father? It has been said that He does so by the blood He shed on the earth. Being the Most High's Messiah has been well addressed. Dispatching the Holy Spirit who encompasses them both to the planet to affect salvation is another way. Perhaps it is the most imperceptible yet universal way

---

143 Thayer on Strong's G600 and 605.

that He gathers. Jesus, who is omnipresent again, captures for God by gathering all things together within Himself; what John 11:52 and Ephesians 1:10 am plainly said.

> "And not for that nation only, but that also he should gather together in one the children of God that were scattered abroad." John 11:52. "That in the dispensation of the fulness of times he might gather together in one all things in Christ, both which are in heaven, and which are on earth; even in him." Ephesians 1:10.

Ephesians 1:11 boldly adds that the Lord chose and predestined His family, according to His own purpose. Jesus gathers for God by His Holy Spirit. The creation that was severed from them He draws back into the family of heaven. What the Father wants, the Son returns to their kingdom of life and light. Adam's body contained the world through the humans to be born from him. What the Lord Jesus captures are absorbed in His glorified Self and becomes part of the Almighty's kingdom. As The Messiah recovers what Adam lost through the people abiding in him, He recoups, converts, and sanctifies it. Once it is hallowed, He then implants it into the Godhead. When the heirs of salvation come to the Savior, what is theirs when they come and what they achieve or produce once they are saved is also what the Lord gathers. He further gathers for His Father independently as the Son of Man.

Jesus has the divine and human right to take what He wants as every monarch does.[67] That is the often unspoken and usually unperceived, issue people have with Him. It is inherited from humanity's foreparents. It is also another reason why He was born into the world; both strengthen His Father's motives for begetting Him. Each decision and solution that moved Jehovah to beget a Son reinforces Jesus as the Continuum's substance. While there are many other justifications for the Most High begetting Jesus, these explanations put forth the majority of them. To assure His Son was His precise Self, God endowed Jesus with everything that made Him Father of the first begotten, up to and including His Spirit without measure.[144] John the Baptist's statements in John 3:30-35 articulate how and why Jesus Christ is the Continuum, and what type of testimony He brings from His world.

> "The one who comes from above is superior to everything. The one who is of the earth belongs to the earth and speaks about earthly things. The one who comes from heaven is superior to everything. He testifies about what he has seen and heard, yet no one accepts his testimony. The person who has accepted his testimony has acknowledged that God is truthful. The one whom God sent speaks the words of God, because God does not give the Spirit in limited measure to him. The Father loves the Son and has put everything in his hands." ISV

---

144 Refer to John 3:34.

Eight specific characterizations are disclosed about Jesus Christ in the passage that places Him outside and before this world.

1.   He comes from above

2.   He comes from heaven

3.   He testifies about what He has seen and heard in heaven

4.   The god who sent Him is truthful (because what He disseminates is as one sent from heaven)

5.   God sent Jesus from heaven

6.   God gave Jesus, His Son the spirit in unlimited measure

7.   The Father loves the Son (Jesus Christ whom He sent from heaven)

8.   God put everything in His (Jesus Christ's) hands

Jesus' *godness* is embedded in His person. He never ceases being one thing in order to manifest as another. Despite His voluminous manifestations, another distinctive about the Son that makes Him equally God is that He never needs to reach outside Himself to become what is required to perform in a given circumstance. It is why He can say He is in heaven and on earth in the flesh at the same time. Jesus is as omnipresent as the rest of the Godhead. He is not a hodgepodge of spirits fused to appear global and diverse at once. The Savior as God's word incarnate knows the rules of godhood and the rules of flesh. He also knows what He condemned in the spirit and in the flesh. Clearly, the Savior realizes that violating His own laws invalidate His many offices as God's first begotten. He further understands His duties responsibly assure the Continuum is never broken and His Father's will marches onward. As coauthor of the Continuum, Jesus knows what is next and fully comprehends His part in it.

The Bible chronicles Christ's many coexistences and offices on the Godhead's behalf. Contiguous narratives and accounts make up its Continuum's main features and elements, enveloping the fourteen unbroken chain of events that brought this world Jesus Christ and Christianity. Scripture infers apostles and prophets are the primary stewards of the Continuum, God's first human points of contact between His Word and this world. They best authenticate and preserve its cohesiveness with integrity. What both offices provide is proof that gives evidence to the otherwise undiscoverable truths regarding Jesus Christ. Testimony is the single word that defines their high commission in Christ's service. Apostles and prophets bear witness to Jesus and all that pertains to Him. His most compelling testimony goes way outside of His three and a half year earthly ministry. It reaches all the way back through the Old Testament to the world before this one. Besides this, Jesus' testimony extends to His return home to the right hand of His Father's throne, what He left to bring heaven's history and destiny into this world.

So why is Jesus a testimony? The reason is that He was sent from heaven to earth as the Godhead's eyewitness. Jesus came to testify to heaven's existence, the reality of an afterlife, and humanity's unshakable obligation to it. Every other spirit that appeared in the planet claiming deity status alludes to another world. Some are above and others are beneath this one. God's world is classically called heaven. It is bright, free, and full of people rewarded for choosing His Son and living life on His terms. However, there is propagated a pseudo version of this heaven. It is a place where the ungodly imagines living the way they wish they could have lived on earth unencumbered by Jesus Christ and His church. In their heaven impenitents suppose they will escape hell's fire to practice the same vices and the values they loved on earth forever without restriction. These people see themselves living their eternal lives in blissful rebellion against the Sovereign God. Of course, it is a myth that cannot be achieved for all of salvation's stipulations. For starters, the new birth is a major hindrance to their vision. It is the only way dead souls and spirits rise into God's realm and do not fall into hell. Reincarnation into another mortal form precludes one from arising at death. There are other reasons, but these get the point across.

The below world is another story. For some religions, it is dark and dead. To others, it is a place of ambient light that is a mere extension of this world or a better version of it minus Christianity's prohibitions. Other deities present hell as a better alternative to heaven because Creator God is painted as boring. Some say the lower world is more appealing because it has no rules, restrictions, or retribution. Those who snubbed these attributes on the earth are well disposed to enjoying such a place forever. Still more claim that hell is no place, enticing their worshippers into going there with all sorts of promises that appeal to the heart's desires. Although hell and doom are included in many of their rituals, they are often presented as a manageable and much more attractive option than Jesus' unexciting heaven. Some people are even told that they will rule in the nether world. Of course, this is highly doubtful, considering the evil angels and other supernatural beings that have been there for eons. It is more likely that by the time, humans were created and started showing up in hell its hierarchies was already well fixed. Its prestigious posts are already filled, leaving little room for any real bestowal of power to frail human latecomers. These explanations speak to the Lord Jesus' constant discourses about hell. Coming from a world outside this one – and being one of the Creators of hell and, afterward, the God that banishes ungodly creatures to it – He is the perfect Faithful and True Witness to its existence and its horrors. His warnings to earth's citizens are not idle threats; they are serious testimonies that corroborate what He and His Father have said down the ages through the prophets, the Psalms, and lastly through the Son. Jesus testifies of many things concerning His precarnate life. He speaks about God the Father, introduces the heretofore, anonymous Holy Spirit, and divulges secrets the world has never known. He talks about bygone Bible figures as if they are historical only to earth. Jesus explains what happened to Noah, who was redeemed when He descended to hell, Enoch, who bypassed death altogether, Abraham, whose faith founded His nation's covenant, and his two sons Isaac and Jacob who progenated Israel. As a timeless witness, Jesus discusses David at length and recalls by name the long string of prophets that spoke for Him. He recalls Solomon's visit with the Queen of Sheba and David's conversations with his royal court and its subjects. Throughout His discourses, the Savior preaches from His past, present and future. He even chides Nicodemus for not believing what He revealed to him about the earth and because of it asks him how he could ever believe what Jesus would say about heavenly things. In John 5:31 He talks about bearing witness, another word for testifying. Jesus says in John 8:18 that His Father bears witness of Him.

Thirty-one times the word testimony is used in the KJV of the New Testament. It says that priestly gifts are a testimony. Preaching the gospel is a testimony; people's rejection of that gospel is a testimony. Persecution for Christ's name's sake are also testimonies. Wisdom testifies of Christ and His effect on the convert's conscience. Believing God to the end is a testimony along with spreading His word according to the Continuum. *"Who bare record of the word of God, and of the testimony of Jesus Christ, and of all things that he saw."* Revelation 1:2. Jesus' end time judgments are testimonials, and the angels who transmit the Lord's word and works to His human messengers are part of that testimony. They too advance God's Eternal Continuum. As discussed at length elsewhere, the angel in Revelation 19:10 discouraged John from attempting to worship him because he is a celestial messenger. He calls himself, John's fellow servant and his brother. Instead, the angel tells John to worship God for the testimony of Jesus is the spirit of prophecy. How is this so? The Great Commission is how.

WHAT IS A TESTIMONY?

A testimony is a witness. Its Hebrew word is *eduth*. Essentially, it means <u>witness</u>. Testimonials are witnessed events that are taken as true because of their witnesser's stature and reputation. Only the historically trusted made credible witnesses. Another word for testimony used in the Old Testament comes from Ruth 4:7. It is the word *teudah*, an obvious variant of *eduth*. It adds testimonial acts to the first word's meaning. Eduth's verbalizing is legitimized by teudah actions on the part of some official attesting to something or confirming it. In respect to the prophecy, this word includes a prophetic injunction. A use of the word resurfaces in Isaiah 8:20. The word teudah there is a legislative response to testimonies. These include a ban on certain behaviors and practices, divine orders issued as edicts from the prophets, and sanctions that restrict the actions deemed threatening to the population. Embargo, another type of ban, is an injunction on business and trade. It restricts one nation's exchange with another. Such actions stem from testimonies; documented witnesses to the incidents that caused them and brought them to the attention of the authorities. Together, these pertain to the prophet's enforcement role in the land. When God issued a new command or returned to a constantly transgressed one, He usually began with the prophets who called His people back to the Law of Moses. They witnessed two things. The first is that God set a standard for His people to follow that directly related to His law. The second thing they witnessed was that the law was violated by God's people. The prophecies in Scripture in this regard serve as heaven-to-earth testimonies from God to His messengers and His messengers back to their God, whose law (Scripture asserts) testifies for or against them. God's law is for them when their compliance released His blessings and provisions to them, which flow unimpeded. It is against them when they violate it, and its punitive measures are activated. Then the blessings stop and the Lord appear to turn a deaf ear to their distresses for a season.

The Greek word for testimony is *marturion*. It comes from roots that explain a civil, judicial, or religious witness. By definition, it is a formal statement about something seen, known, or experienced, usually given in a court of law or before another deliberative body. Testimonies rely on witnesses. In a legal case, testimonies are written or spoken, but are always made a matter of record. These definitions establish that Jesus' redemption work was more than religious; it was legal. Divine courts monitored and scrutinized His work. Before God and His court and the invisible spirits of this world, Jesus was on trial every step of the way. On earth, He was judged by the very prophecies that He uttered when He was the sovereign Son of God. Throughout His passion, experience, He was required to prove to His world that He is the same Son of God that ruled them, and to this world, that He was its promised Savior. Calvary was the most critical of His proofs as it verified His eternal call to be the Lamb of God slain from the foundation of the world. Besides these, His death was to justify His Father's faith in Him by paying the most horrendous price anyone could pay for sin. He had to give His life as a ransom for the souls abducted in Eden. All of this, the Messiah was obliged to do in strict incontestable accordance with the gospel preached to the serpent, the woman, Enoch and Noah, Abraham, Isaac, and Jacob. These all make up the Christ's prediluvian and antediluvian witnesses. In this realm, His work was judged by the Law of Moses, the Psalms, and the Prophets that all foretold this period of His life. Typically, when it comes to the Church and Christianity, a testimony is a public declaration regarding a religious experience. However, when the Lord God launched His campaign on earth, there was no church or Christianity. There were families, communities and, as time progressed, nations and kingdoms. These are what the Lord ruled in heaven. They provided the premises for the governmental systems He inspired and instituted. In prior ages, testimony was felt to carry weight with councils seen and unseen. The heavens were appealed to for affirmation, intervention, exposés, and when human judgment failed retribution. Therefore, human testimonies were received under spiritual auspices and vows made concerning them treated as spiritually and legally binding. Testimonies were not always taken at face value; sometimes they needed evidence to verify them as true.

Generally, evidence is part of a testimony and asserts something exists or is true. Moses' stone tablets containing the Almighty's Law along with the ark that held them are two examples of testimony fitting God's classification. The tabernacle and its services are other testimonials of the Most High's involvement, care, and provisions for His people. Testimonies rely on evidence. They are strengthened by oaths and legitimized by authorities. When agents or representatives of institutions (such as courts or governments) hear and can corroborate a testimony, they record it as truth. In this vein, the Lord's divine decrees function as testimonies since they attest to His intervening activities in the world, and verify His supremacy over all its governors and governments. God's testimonies are solemn declarations that openly announce or acknowledge His experience with His creation and their experience with Him. It seems from Scripture that the way the Lord views, and values testimonies compared to how the earth perceives and handles them, are quite different. God views a testimony and the one giving it (along with its nature) as one inseparable package. The character of the testifier, the reliability of the eyewitness, and the legitimacy of the testimony and its proceedings all carry equal weight. The witness must be credible. The testimony must be veracious. The incident must be real and worth the time and money invested in hearing it. The Savior met these criteria when He incarnated and verified events as one who lived and ruled before anything took place in His world or this one. The Lord's perpetual governance standardized what was to become the testimony of Jesus Christ later. Those standards regulate the Continuum. They see to it that what heaven measures and how it measures it conform to creation's eternal archives, as well as to earth's ancient ones. Both sides' recorded accounts are superintended by celestial and terrestrial institutions founded by the everlasting God to oversee His creatures' successive life spans. The reason is because in Jesus' world, the Continuum's spiritual protocrats discharge this responsibility. In this world His Holy Spirit, His Ecclesia, and the world ministers of Psalm 68:18 and Romans 13:1-4 see to it.

UNDERSTANDING GOD'S WORLD

God did not just bind humans to His law and government; He also bound His invisible intermediaries to them as well. Often in Scripture, more so in the Old Testament, the Lord called heaven and earth to record or witness something He did or said. In the New Testament, Jesus makes a seemingly ridiculous statement about rocks crying out as a witness to His eternal Lordship. The Most High often treated what humans call the invisible atmosphere as if it were populated with real but invisible beings, ones that had as much responsibility for what happened on earth as the people they were charged to oversee. Invisible authorities that keep the most accurate records. They are as much a party to the Lord's will and human conduct as the human authorities serving beneath them. The Lord relies on unseen governors for true reporting produced with honest motives. They are the Continuum's true stewards and guardians. It is their testimony that takes precedence over human witnesses because of their longevity, experience, and lack of incentive to indulge violations of God's laws. Theirs is a truer witness than all earthly records because they are not confined to the five senses, or clouded by human sentiments and purposes. The Lord's protocrats keep a different sort of record that may not have a third of what humans document. Theirs contain a host of little insignificant events that the typical citizen of this world would dismiss. That is because what God assigns them to judge is much broader and specific to eternal life. What offends human leaders or violates their laws only marginally reflects God's laws because, as Psalm 71:9 says, His righteousness is very high.

Therefore, what heaven's protocrats witness actually ripples throughout eternity, and probably contains little of what this world is concerned with or is willing to restrain. God's eternal kingdom, as has been explained, is fixed. It is not looking for flesh and blood, so to speak, to revive or to revamp it. He is sure that His established institutions work, that they function according to His will, and collectively manifest His vision for all His worlds. His celestial witnesses are comfortable with this and record what conforms to their culture. In their minds, this world and its systems – since they are passing away – are already passé. Subsequently, God's spiritual protocrats focus on the imperishable treasures of this life. They sift and sort people's beliefs, pursuits, events, and actions that reveal candidates for their world of eternal light and not everlasting darkness. Thus, there witness is likely to look a great deal different from human documenters.

How Heaven Works

The whole substance of the Continuum's teaching is Jesus Christ, and not just as the sacrificial Lamb slain for the salvation of the world. It emphasizes His Davidic roots and His destiny as creation's eternal Sovereign of sovereigns, which is how Matthew 1:1 and 17 substantiates it. The Continuum traces His life and all of His dignities as God's first begotten Son. Much of His family on the other hand limits His purpose in their lives, to the day they got saved, or to their latest misadventure. Such attitudes tend to cause Christians to reject Jesus' benefit to any other area of their life, most of all, overlooking His primary authority as King of kings and Lord of lords. In this respect, many ministers, sadly, downplay His potencies, to make Him touchable and more tenable to those He saved. Instead of trusting in Jesus' authority to intervene on their behalf, countless Christians overestimate the carnal world's powers in life's pressing issues. Most are unaware of The Messiah's world authority. Few Christians think Jesus should be involved in world affairs when, in fact, the world belongs to Him. Christian intellectuals so buy into Satan's separation of church and state delusion that they actually maintain it means, entirely eliminating Jesus Christ from world affairs. Oddly, though, they have no problem blaming Him when things turn out unfavorably for them as a result. Psalm 24:1 says it best. "*A Psalm of David. The earth is the Lord's, and all it contains, the world, and those who dwell in it.*" NAS. In light of the extensive Continuum teaching just presented, this declaration certainly makes more sense. The earth is the Lord's; it is not the Devil's. The Devil did not create this world, nor does he own it. Everything in the planet belongs to the Most High God and His first begotten Son. Both of them are familiar with how to run worlds and intimately acquainted with what makes them and their creatures live or die. First Samuel 2:8 says about God's ownership of the world, *"He raiseth the poor out of the dust, and lifteth the beggar from the dunghill, to set them among princes, and to make them inherit the throne of glory: for the pillars of the earth are the Lord's, and he hath set the world upon them."* Webster's Bible Translation. The pillars of the earth are its archetypical, and prototypical supports and these too were created and appointed by the Most High God. Other Scriptures related to the pillars include:

- For the foundations of the earth are the Lord's; on them he has set the world. NIV
- For all the earth is the Lord's, and he has set the world in order. NLT
- The foundations of the earth belong to the Lord, and he has placed the world on them. NET
- For the poles of the earth are the Lord's, and upon them he hath set the world. DRB
- For the pillars of the earth are Yahweh's, He has set the world on them. WEB
- For to Jehovah are the fixtures of earth, And He setteth on them the habitable world. YLT

The above versions of Hannah's prayer reinforce the Continuum's pre-earthly existence, along with its record of how the Lord's life went before He created the earth and its inhabitants. It also says why the earth reacts violently when human sin weighs too heavily upon it. Before there were humans on it, the natural world was programmed to evict uncleanness no matter its source. The preceding Scripture clearly states the Lord owns everything and His kingdom rules over all.[68] Read Psalm 47 and zero in on verse 9 where it says in comparison to the pillars of the earth, that the earth's shields likewise belong to the Almighty. *"The princes of the people are gathered together, even the people of the God of Abraham: for the shields of the earth belong unto God: he is greatly exalted."* Magen is the Hebrew word for shield; basically, it speaks to the hedge of protection surrounding the earth to defend it. Based on what the verse says, the hedge is comprised of human, natural, and spiritual forces. It also speaks of the earth's spiritual rulers, God's people in collaboration with them, and God Himself whose kingdom rules over all. Nebuchadnezzar's conflict with Babylon's appointed spiritual watchers demonstrates this collaboration well. Below are other ways to view this truth from various Scripture renderings of it.

- Rulers of peoples are brought together with the God of Abraham. For by God the strong ones of the earth exceedingly were lifted up. ABP.

- The princes of the people are gathered together, even the people of the God of Abraham: for the shields of the earth belong unto God: he is greatly exalted. KJV, BRG.

- The princes of the peoples are gathered together to be the people of the God of Abraham: For the shields of the earth belong unto God; He is greatly exalted. ASV

- The nobles of peoples gather together, the people of the God of Abraham. For the shields of the earth *are* God's; He is greatly lifted up. LITV

- The rulers of the peoples have come together, with the people of the God of Abraham; because the powers of the earth are God's: he is lifted up on high. BBE

- The rulers of the people are assembled with the God of Abraam: for God's mighty ones of the earth have been greatly exalted. Brenton

- The rulers of the peoples are gathered together, the people of the God of Abraham; for the shields of the earth *are* God's; He is lifted up on high. MKJV

- The willing-hearted of the peoples have gathered together, *with* the people of the God of Abraham. For unto God *belong* the shields of the earth: he is greatly exalted. Darby

- The princes of the people are gathered together, with the God of Abraham: for the strong gods of the earth are exceedingly exalted. DRB

- Nobles of peoples have been gathered, *with* the people of the God of Abraham, For to God *are* the shields of earth, greatly hath He been exalted! YLT

- The nobles among the nations have joined the people of the God of Abraham. For the shields of the earth belong to God; he is greatly exalted. ISV

These passages show the people of God are meant to collaborate with the intermedial[145] powers of His world because they oversee this one. Heaven's supernal powers, though they are earth's spiritual shields, defenders, and protectors – originated with the Almighty and, because of that, are owned by Him. The pillars are earth's prototypical supports. They assure its institutions do not collapse until the Most High is ready for them to. The same is true with the shields. Where the pillars uphold the earth and its governments, the shields surround and defend it. Earth's celestial pillars are councilists and its shields are militarists. The primary difference between them is this. The pillars of the earth are somewhat passive; they are its maintainers and sustainers. In this capacity, the spiritual watchers are guardians more than defenders. Defense de-

---

145 Occurring or situated between two points, extremes, places acting as an intermediary. Collins.

tails are left to the shields of the earth. They are more aggressive because shields, are articles of defense and not structural supports as a pillar would be. Both are how celestial creatures extend the Most High's institutions into this realm and how He reigns over it. They are how He instructs and governs the nations individually and collectively. As dual[146] beings and forces, they further show how the Most High guarantees His will is achieved on earth as it is in heaven. When the time comes for Him to act, there is no power on earth that can subvert His purposes. Ezekiel chapter nine is a powerful example of this.

A) **KJV**: *He cried also in mine ears with a loud voice, saying, Cause them that have <u>charge over the city</u> to draw near, even every man with his destroying weapon in his hand.*

B) **ISV**: *Then the Spirit shouted right in my ears with a loud voice! "Come forward," he said, "you <u>executioners of the city</u>, and bring your weapon of destruction in your hand!"*

C) **YLT**: *And He crieth in mine ears--a loud voice--saying, `Drawn near have <u>inspectors of the city</u>, and each his destroying weapon in his hand.'*

D) **DRB**: *And he cried in my ears with a loud voice, saying: The <u>visitations of the city</u> are at hand, and every one hath a destroying weapon in his hand.*

E) **BBE**: *Then crying out in my hearing in a loud voice, he said, let the <u>overseers of the town come near, every man armed.</u>*

F) **LITV**: *And He cried in my ears with a loud voice, saying, let the <u>overseers of the city</u> draw near, even each with his destroying weapon in his hand.*

Five distinct functions are ascribed to the invisible watchers over God's city in the different translations. Each one indicates the scope of the invisible angels' responsibilities. That they are angels may be deduced from the task the Lord assigned them, to go and mark the foreheads of those who share His grief and indignation over the wickedness that is done in their city. If they are not angels, how else can one account for their speedy marking of a city full of people to spare them from the coming judgment?

Charge over the city	Executioners of the city	Inspectors of the city	Visitations of the city	Overseers of the town

All of the five phrases speak to officials empowered to judge, correct, punish, as well as protect the city or town in question according to what an authorizer commands.

---

146 In a dual manner; doubly. Collins English Dictionary, online.

Inherent in the statements are laws, government, standards, regulations, ordinances, and the like. The chart below illustrates what the writers of this passage had in mind when they penned this verse of Scripture.

Charge	Executioner	Inspectors	Visitations	Overseers
Custody	Killer	Examiners	Examinations	Managers
Care	Slayer	Checkers	Inspections	Administrators
Control	Assassin	Superintendents	Checkups	Chiefs
Trust	Slaughterer	Assessors	Disasters	Bosses
Burden		Supervisors	Benefits	Superintendents
Safekeeping			Blessings	
Duty	This chart shows how God remains in control of His world and assures His will on earth is carried out even when humans do not want to hear or obey Him. The spiritual protocrats He assigns do the work for Him, with or without earthly leaders' approval or cooperation.			
Care				
Command				

That is not the end. There is the 11th verse to examine and consolidate this teaching with the Continuum. The 11th verse reads, *"And, beholds, the man clothed with linen, which had the inkhorn by his side, reported the matter, saying, I have done as thou hast commanded me"*. "I have done as thou have commanded me" is the report that the celestial being had to bring back to the Lord who delegated him his task. Here is how the other translations surveyed above phrase his report.

- **ISV**: Then I noticed the man dressed in linen, who wore the writing case by his side as he brought back this message: "I've done as you have commanded me".
- **BBE**: Then the man clothed in linen, who had the inkpot at his side, came back and said, I have done what you gave me orders to do.
- **LITV**: And, behold, the man clothed with linen, with the inkhorn at his loins, reported the matter, saying, I have done as you commanded me.

Pulpit Commentary on Ezekiel 9:11: *"And, behold, etc." The speaker in the previous verses had been none other than the Presence, which remained upon the cherubic lotto, while the seven ministers did their work. The captain of the seven now returns to report, as an officer to his king, that the work has been accomplished."[69]* Gill adds, *"As if he should say, there is nothing wanting of all that was commanded".[70]*

God is confident because the invisible forces He installed in the planet see that His word never returns to Him void.[147] His word, accepted as Jesus in voice, spirit and substance, performs the Father's will, no matter how the wicked misrepresent them

---

147 See Deuteronomy 32:41. Read also Ezekiel chapter 9 and pay particular attention to verses 1 and 11.

or the resentful attempts to resist them. Humanity has no choice but to obey its Maker's commands, and He does not alter them because people agree or disagree with Him. It does not matter if they rant and rave, or rejoice and praise. Everything was resolved before the Lord God replenished the planet with its new species and world institutions. Jesus advances this reality further in John 18:36. There He says to Pilate, *"Jesus answered, "My kingdom does not belong to this world. If my kingdom belonged to this world, my servants would fight to keep me from being handed over to the Jews. But for now my kingdom is not from here."* When standing before Pontius Pilate and certain death, Jesus asserts He is not of this world. Unmoved by the gravity of the situation, He boldly informs His interrogator that in His world He is creation's highest authority. His doom, the Savior explains, is fully sanctioned by the Almighty. Consequently, Pilate *must* sentence Him the death, despite His guilt or innocence. Both men knew they were somehow caught in the grip of a cosmic tussle that neither one of them would come out of the same. Jesus could not declare His innocence, and Pilate – though he sensed that innocence – has to put Him to death anyway. To help things along, Jesus jabs at the man's ego and tells Pilate that His unearthly authority actually supersedes his. The Lord declares that His world is a kingdom and there He is, a king, with an angelic guard that would never allow Him to be arrested (let alone killed). Scripture documents this with its constant references to the hosts that accompanied Him wherever He went. They allude to a massive entourage of attendants, ministers, and soldiers that escorted Him throughout His realm unmolested. Jesus claimed to come from a supernal kingdom that dates back to when there was no earth. Its perpetuity well-disposed His army, since the Great War, for protecting their King when He entered the world as God incarnate. Then again, this earth mission is a little different. He came to this hostile place in a vulnerable state to be abused and, to their dismay, to die at the hands of creatures He made. As much as it anguished them, this time Christ's royal guard could not intervene and fight for their King.

The mission compelled them to witness their sovereign being brutally beaten and savagely crucified as part of the Godhead's plan. Had they not been restrained, the Messiah said, the twelve legions of angels He commanded would have certainly destroyed the entire region; but in obedience to His purpose, they had to stand down. The earth and those assaulting its Creator never knew how close they came to being destroyed that day. The earthquake that marked His death suggests it, and if His angels had been incompliant, they would have moved to rescue Him out of love and affection. However, Jesus their sovereign had come to earth to save it and not destroy it, so heaven's hosts stood by watching the bigger picture play out. Compassion for human ignorance and suffering locked everyone into the Almighty's wisdom. Ignoring adversity and its tragedies, everyone pressed onward, with neither Christ nor His angels fearing Pilate or the masses that wanted Him dead. In verse 37 of John's Gospel, Jesus repeats His reason for being on earth. He reiterates again that He is tantamount to being an alien, something apparently not considered strange in that day. He says He came to bear witness to the truth that only speaks to everyone that belongs to the God of truth. Nonetheless, He is resigned to the fact that the ones who can hear His words as truth are those belonging to it.

The Continuum connection is frankly expressed in these words; Jesus says He, "came into the world" to testify, to bear witness to the truth. In Pilate's response, we see that Jesus' truth was as alien to this world as He was. Pilate answers Christ with a sarcastic question: "What is truth?" The question justifies Jesus' declaration in John 14:6; He is "the way, the truth and the life". He is a way of life the world has never known, a living truth that had to come from outside of it, and a life that takes humanity all the way back to the creation's sixth day before He breathed into Adam into his clay body. When it comes to the Continuum, everything begins outside the earth with its Maker who annexed it, to replicate His world on it before this one began. In archetypal ways, heaven and earth operate similar in structure, government, institutional, and civilization. Jesus Christ – before He became the New Testament's Messiah – governed, guided, and protected His Father's worlds long before He took charge of this one. Taking on the Calvary mission expanded His divine offices to that of Israel's Messiah. As Creator with His Father, Jesus is concentric to all that is, was, and will ever be. Worshippers and scholars cannot envision invisible worlds and their ages or generations, and separate them from Christ. There is nothing outside of Him as John 1:1-3 certifies. When he wrote in the beginning was the word, the word was with God and as such the word is the very God that made heaven and earth, John did so with direct knowledge of what he wrote. Verse 1:14 of his gospel clarifies it further.

The Word became flesh and dwelt among us. Jesus as the Old Testament Yahweh, Jehovah, has always been active on earth in some form or another. In John 6:46, He said no man has seen His Father except Him. That means all of the Old Testament references to people who saw God actually saw Jesus, His Son, the second Person of the Godhead, not God the Father Himself. The Son reinforces this in John 14:9 by saying, "He that hath seen me hath seen the Father". Here is where the Son is essentially saying, He is God's spitting image. Moreover, Jacob's declaration that he saw God's face actually refers to Jesus. Judges 13:22 implies that seeing an angel is tantamount to seeing God personally because that is as close as they expected to migrate to the divine world and its citizens. John 1:18 stresses that the only one to see God is His only begotten Son. In his first epistle, John reiterates that no man has seen God at any time. Along this line, Micah an Old Testament prophet in 5:2 of his prophecy foretells the coming one to be the ruler of Israel. He is from Judah and has been traveling back and forth between this world and eternity from of old. The Lord God dispatched Jesus from heaven on various missions long before time. He entered and left the planet routinely up to His Calvary mission, the culmination of a string of earthly visits to handle this world's matters on His Father's behalf. Jesus' Calvary mission differed from the others in one major respect; He appeared in the world not as spiritual God but as God in the flesh. Unlike His visit to Abraham in Genesis 18 and His years as Yahweh, The Messiah appears to Israel as the Son of Man. In that manifestation, Jesus does not break through the barriers separating this world from His but through the womb of a woman. The prophets of old prophesied His incarnation and validated it by witnessing His precarnate Messianic existence.

Back in Isaiah 43:10-12, the Lord says of Himself "You are My witnesses, says Jehovah, and My servant whom I have chosen; that you may know and believe Me, and understand that I am He. Before Me no God was formed, nor shall there be after Me. I, I am Jehovah; and there is none to save besides Me. I have declared, and have saved, and I have shown, when there was no strange god among you; therefore you are My witnesses, says Jehovah, that I am God. Yea, before the day was, I am He; and no one delivers out of My hand; I will work, and who will reverse it?" He concludes this revelation with Isaiah 44:8 "Fear ye not, neither be afraid: have not I told thee from that time, and have declared it? Ye are even my witnesses. Is there a God beside me? Yea, there is no God; I know not any." These passages illuminate John 8:58. They reveal how Galatians 3:8 happened and what the Holy Spirit means by Hebrews 4:2. Moreover, Genesis 15:13-21 presents itself as part of the gospel that Jehovah preached to Abraham. More than 400 years before the Exodus, the Almighty God told Abraham what would take place and how it would translate to endless global blessings in his name. He detailed how his seed would end up as slaves when he had yet to have a child. He then followed up that prophecy with what would happen to his descendants and their captive nation as a result. Abraham's children will be freed and their captors destroyed. God preached the gospel to Abraham His friend quite a bit, and the New Testament affirms it as the very gospel He dispatched to earth in the Person of His Son. When Abraham saw the Lord, it was actually Jesus He saw. Furthermore, this Continuum reinforces, that Jesus is seen as Yahweh in 1 Corinthians 10. Scripture makes it plain that the Father of Jesus Christ does and has always done everything through and for His Son, with the Bible incessantly witnessing Jesus' activities before earth, on earth, and after earth. That witness is what He as The Messiah delivered to His prophets, from Abel to John's two witnesses to perpetuate for Him, and for His apostles to reveal through His churches. Many prophets down through the ages pick up on Jesus' incarnated Messiahship mission, but only a few can pierce the veil on His precarnate life.

This book probed in detail actual and inferred accounts of Christianity's Jesus Christ and His world. It tapped into fourteen specific occurrences that govern and guide the world events that brought Jesus Christ and Christianity to the earth. The events uncovered an unbroken chain that traces and links the fourteen sequential events of God's world to this one and circle back to His own. The events and their unbroken chain are identified as God's Eternal Continuum and they culminate in the Almighty's eschatological end of all human ages. The part of His story that brings Him into this world, this work proves, did not begin with His incarnation. It began with the Great War in heaven and ends with the Lord's righteous war that removes the wicked, rewards the faithful, and enthrones Christ and His body as God's everlasting family. The war started it all and, as distasteful as it is for the unenlightened of earth, war is what will end it; so says Revelation 19:11, *"Then I saw heaven standing open, and there was a white horse! Its rider is named Faithful and True. He administers justice and wages war righteously."* The Book of Revelation long ago scheduled the Revelation 19:11 battle to settle for the last time who is the Lord, whose kingdom reigns, and the winner of the ageless contest between creature and Creator.

Meeting the Devil on his own turf for the last time (the first when He met him in the wilderness after John's baptism, and the second in the pit of hell), the Christ finally executes the last phase of Genesis 3:15. He crushes the serpent's head for humanity the same way He did for the celestial citizens of His world, and the pre-Ecclesia souls in hell. The eviction of the dragon and his angels from heaven was accomplished by the Lord Jesus Christ in His world. His eviction from the rest of creation, decreed by the Most High's appointed time, is likewise achieved by the Messiah according to Revelation chapter 12. *"And I heard a loud voice saying in heaven, now is come salvation, and strength, and the kingdom of our God, and the power of his Christ: for the accuser of our brethren is cast down, which accused them before our God day and night."* The Lord Jesus Christ, the name He had to bring to earth with Him as the one that defeated the old Draconic serpent in eternity, concludes it all on earth. He defeated Him in heaven and He defeated him in hell. The only place left to end the contest is earth, and that defeat is fast approaching.

Conclusion

Before the Garden: God's Eternal Continuum tells His story at times unattractively but always gloriously. It covers God, Christ, and Christianity with one aim in mind; to tell the Almighty's backstory, His way. Taken from the pages of Scripture and at times reading like a contemporary novel, the book achieved its purpose by meticulously scouring the Bible, searching traditional doctrines, and exploring a broad theological spectrum. Combing these, it fills in the nagging blanks people have on these subjects. It frankly answered some age-old questions about God that have perplexed people since time began. This work articulated the often-muted answers the Lord has been giving to these questions as He progressively publicized His story over the ages. Written as an exposé, this work disclosed Jesus' life and career prior to His incarnation and since His return to His heavenly throne. What He did before He took on flesh and what He is doing today and forever now that He has procreated multiplied billions of souls comprise its major themes. Expanding His life's story to include what He has done before as well as since the Garden of Eden, the book expounds on many myopic thoughts and beliefs about Him that confine His Messiahship to a mere three and a half years on earth.

Nailing His reputation down to such a brief period leaves too little information for the long term Christian or the new convert to discover about Him. Confining the Christ to traditionalism's narrow window short changes high thinkers, especially those that must bear witness to Him. Deliberately, the gospels only minimally summarize His life to impel serious seekers to delve deeper. However, if left on their own, their seemingly splintered narratives can prove too sketchy without another way to piece His story together for a fuller picture; and there is one. It is God's Eternal Continuum, repository of the mysteries the Lord kept secret from before the world's foundation. Tapping into these, the book reconstructed the story of what brought Jesus and Christianity to the world to disable its greatest conflict using His wisdom. The faith's primary conflict stems in part from seeming to be "almost like; similar to;

sounding or worshipped like", primeval religions did before Christianity was born". Scattered revelation and interpreter-edited truths did little to ease its struggle. These along with numerous afterlife and dying deity myths made its journey even more difficult. Their rituals are also weaved throughout the Continuum and they will continue to resurface until all is fulfilled. Their hindsight value is that they paved the way for the Son of God and His true faith.

While Jesus was en route to the planet, primitive religions that predated His mission provided useful anecdotes to the truths that would once and for all be revealed in Him. Tactically speaking, antiquity's religions served the dual function of exploiting the Creator's free will granted to all humans. They also provided Christ's rejectors alternatives to His salvation. Jesus came to earth as God disguised as a man. He left it with a criminal record, executed for the very reasons He came. Both are His cover story that if people believed leads to salvation. If on the other hand, they reject His redemption cover story, they will as He put it, die in their sins. Learning first the alternatives to Christ plan inspired an otherwise bleakly darkened humanity to envision a world outside its own. Until His time to appear arrived, God let the world consume itself with other religions. [148] Although they were contrary and subversive, they tutored His world on the ABC's and the 1, 2, 3's of spirituality and unsuspectedly primed it for His Son's arrival. With a view to His global redemption, the Almighty permitted crude, and often, vicious religions brought to earth by His fallen angels to school humanity in the elementaries of worship, ritual, divine service, and the laws of cause and effect. It was how He penetrated their darkness for them to receive His real faith when Jesus brought it to earth. That line upon line, precept upon precept approach worked in God's favor the way the alphabet and arithmetic benefit its learners. The way they lay the foundations of advanced and ultimately profitable education, false religions in a similar manner laid the foundation for the Creator's eternal life. It does if the worshipper is really a child of the truth. [71]

Once Christ accomplished His mission, Christianity's seemingly imitative narratives set the stage for the last phase of His Father's plan. Faith in Him actually delivered. Instead of promising an overly glamourized afterlife, Jesus returned His elect back to their Creator God. Subordinate deities and substandard religions had carved the framework for His faith's message, death, and resurrection in His chosen ones' minds, with a major advantage. Jesus abolished death and brought immortality to light. The archaic gods' constantly recycled death and resurrection commemoratives

---

[148] Acts 17:30.

are what made belief in His salvation possible. Years of hearing and attempting to comply with them accustomed people to the idea of a supernatural being dying and returning to earth. Exploiting the advantage the dissatisfactions this delusion bred, the Lord Jesus' once only death and resurrection did more than fascinate zealous devotees. A single trip to the grave enabled Him to change the world and replicate Himself until the end of time. Faith in His death and resurrection actually converted souls, unlike the hollow ceremonies of His impostors. Their empty rituals burdened worshippers with cyclical actions that as Hebrews puts it, had no effect on their conscience. Contrary to them, not just a deity died on the cross, nor was it just a man. It was both. Jesus really did die and He did so very publicly and very humiliatingly. He went to hell to win the right to return to heaven; it was the only way for Him to get back home to eternity. Because He did, His converts only have to enter His salvation once. They do not have to relive their repentance and conversion again and again.

While indisputably originating in His world, Jesus' redemption appears at first glance to imitate the false religions that precede Him. This fact is why He says in John chapter 3 *"Except a man be born again, he cannot see the kingdom of God."* Until people have Christ within, salvation's key elements remind them of a popular philosophy, belief, or doctrine they heard before. It takes the Holy Spirit to show them otherwise. The truth is, when it comes to world religions, supernally speaking, it is the other way around, earth's faiths tend to mimic God's, and no wonder. He is the first and only model to imitate. Nonetheless, Scripture anticipates people's indifferent attitudes toward His Son's salvation and responds to those seeing it as something they encountered before with words like *"once for all, since the beginning or the foundation of the world; before the world was, never to die again"*. These phrases vow that what the Son of God did in coming to earth as a doomed human, He will never do again. It was hard, it was successful, and it is final. Jesus is now occupied with the business of populating His Father's world with new creation offspring from the Godhead, all according to the word of God.

Unabashedly, the chapters of this book unfold the Maker's past under the brutal light of truth, His own world's truth. It tells God's side without glossing over His history's horrible details, as some good news only messengers, are accustomed to do. Before the Garden flaunts the Almighty God's well deserved glory because He triumphed over His enemies and captured humanity's victory. The Messiah's faith world as told in Scripture does not paint a rosy picture of His past, but instead hints at a calamitous spiritual climate created by a ruthless angelic regime bent on destroying His and His Father's worlds. In Jesus' eternity, there are wars, attempts at political overthrow, and brutalized citizens mercilessly pummeled by cruelly ambitious angels. Out of the blue, a peaceful, pristine world is thrown into chaos. The Creator who is responsible for bringing the worlds into existence ekes out His experience throughout the Bible. He recalls His creatures' suffering during that period and confides how He worked quietly to rid all universes of the problem once and for all. Unflatteringly, this book told the Holy Spirit's truth about how things got to be the way they are on earth. It is because they started in heaven. The Scriptures strip naked God's world and its otherwise undiscoverable past. The Bible exposes His once crime riddled kingdom and the criminals responsible for it. It admits to gangs and gang wars, thefts, murders, betrayals and aberrant sexuality. Idolatry, bestiality, hatred, and all sorts of molestations span its pages. Power plays, attempted political coups, and violent seditions dating all the way back to before the Garden of Eden found their way into this world from God's spiritual kingdom. Eternity's tragedies and triumphs are revealed by a holy, loving God forced to take the most annihilating measures to contain the rampaging and restore peace to His planets. The Most High's history, as His account of it shows, is magnificent, but it is also brutal and bloody. His dreams get smashed, His heavens get ravaged, and His worlds are devastated by self-serving subjects convinced they can run His kingdom better than He could. Yet for all this, He does not surrender, but takes full responsibility for it, if for no other reason than that He is the Creator. He moves to stop The devilish storm ransacking His handiwork and triumphs over His enemies. The entire campaign the Lord carries out with the help of His first begotten Son and the Holy Spirit, along with His most faithful angels. He not only lives to tell His story today and forever, but He also gets to boast about how powerfully He squelched His uprisings and regained indomitable control over His creation. Greatly affected by the ordeal, God shares how He restored peace and warns the future of the dangers of ignoring a threat just because it never happened before. That is how the antediluvians were shut out of Noah's Ark. Because it had never rained before, they ignored the warning and scoffed at Noah's obedience.

Before the Garden bluntly lays blame for humanity's troubles where it belongs and at the same time, acclaims what Jesus Christ and Christianity recouped for His Father. It captivatingly unravels the mysteries of all ages. This book unveiled fourteen specific events that run through God's eons. They are the Fourteen Events Continuum that forged the unbroken chain of Creator experiences that affirm Christianity's legitimacy and perpetuity. Through the fourteen events, Before the Garden supplied answers that filled the gaps in believers' faith. It gave them more profound reasons to stay with their redemptive God. Christ's salvation is true because it brings life, hope, and genuine wellbeing. People are not debased by their faith in Jesus, but are rather inspired to transform into His superior version of them. World religions cannot offer this because the transformative codes and powers needed to regenerate people are not available to it, no matter how wonderful or liberating their faiths makes them feel. In the end, it will be seen that religious experience is no match for the Godhead's nature and that is what the new birth bestows. The Lord's converts get a new spirit, a new heart, and constant indwelling of their Savior by His Holy Spirit. Christ's redemption authenticates itself by aligning with humanity's beginnings. Think about the Garden of Eden. God's way was first and life under the Maker started out good. Sadly, the first couple did not realize it until too late. Since the fall until the Church, the Most High's goodness has been obscured by Adam's inherited law of sin and death born in all flesh, and is only part of the story.

By no means incontrovertible, Jesus Christ and the Bible never are, these wisdoms urge readers to revisit the Scriptures in the Christian Bible. The book exhorts readers to rethink their beliefs and reexamine their faith practices, if for no other reason than to confirm they are right. Before the Garden challenges truth seekers to choose either Paul's or Agrippa's side of the argument. Those called to Jesus Christ believe the way Paul did; they believe the prophets, what he asked Agrippa in Acts 26:27. Paul's question referenced the very prophets that Jesus drew on to validate His earthly mission. The prophets, He attests to have been speaking to the earth since the foundation of the world. These are the very Old Testament prophets that Peter talks about who prophesied, who by the Spirit of Christ who was in them prophesied God's world as it is today. The Lord's credible prophets also include the antediluvian ones that sparked the Continuum, the angelic, and the human ones altogether. Should Paul's side of the matter be found unappealing, the reader can stand on Agrippa's side of the argument and almost be persuaded to become (or remain) a Christian. Whichever side of the question the readers chooses, what fills these pages supplies a wealth of information upon which to base such far-reaching afterlife decisions.

Index

ABOUT THE AUTHOR

Author of the renowned *Prophets' Dictionary*, Paula A. Price is a strong and widely acknowledged international voice on the subject of apostolic and prophetic ministry. She is recognized as a modern-day apostle with a potent prophetic anointing. Active in full-time ministry since 1985, she has founded and established three churches, an apostolic and prophetic Bible institute, a publication company, consulting firm, and global collaborative network linking apostles and prophets together for the purpose of kingdom vision and ventures. Through this international ministry, she has transformed the lives of many through her wisdom and revelation of God's kingdom. Her programs, curriculum and material are used in both secular and non-secular environments worldwide. Although she has written over 25 books, manuals, and other course material on the apostolic and prophetic, she is most recognized for her unique 1,600-term Prophet's Dictionary, and her concise prophetic training manual entitled The Prophet's Handbook. Other releases include The ABC's of Apostleship, a practical guide to the fundamentals of modern apostleship; Divine Order for Spiritual Dominance, a five-fold ministry tool; Eternity's Generals, an explanation of today's apostle; and When God Goes Silent: Living Life Without God's Voice.

In 2002, Dr. Price created one of the most valuable tools for Christian Ministry called the Standardized Ministry Assessment series. It is a patent pending, destiny discovery tool that tells people who they are in God, what He created them to do, and how He created them to do it. The assessment series pinpoints those called to the church, its pulpit or other ministries, and those who would better serve the Lord outside of the church. Beside this, Dr. Price has also developed credentialing tools for ministers and professionals, commissioning criteria and practices, along with ceremony proceedings for apostles and prophets. To complement these, she designed extensive educational programs for the entire five-fold officers and their teams. In addition to her vast experience, Dr. Price has a D.Min. and a Ph.D. in Religious Education from Word of Truth Seminary in Alabama. She is also a wife, mother of three daughters, and the grandmother of two.

For full biography details, please visit www.drpaulaprice.com.

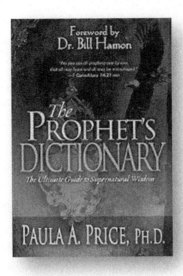

The Prophets Dictionary:
The Ultimate Guide to Supernatural Wisdom

The Prophet's Dictionary by Paula Price is an essential tool for laymen, prophets, prophesiers, pastors, intercessors, and dreamers of dreams. As an all-in-one dictionary and reference book containing over 1,600 relevant definitions of terms and phrases for the prophetic realm of Christian ministry, it exposes ancient religious seductions and how they have infiltrated movies, television, and books. Prophetic visions and clues to interpreting their symbolism, imagery, and signs are also included. People from all walks of life can benefit as this book aids in the understanding of what may be expected from prophets or the prophetic ministry.

USD $25.95

To purchase visit www.drpaulaprice.com.

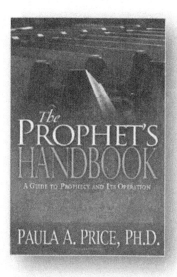

The Prophets Handbook:
A Guide to Prophecy and Its Operation

The prophetic gifts are still operating today. Discover Gods divine plan for them and how they are meant to benefit and not hinder the body of Christ. The Prophets Handbook details the roles and duties of the prophetic in the church and clearly explains its necessity. As an indispensable reference, this comprehensive text is something no church leader should be without. Dr. Paula Price intelligently and skillfully explains the function and responsibilities of local church prophets and those who prophesy. Her years of research and ministry have led to the ultimate guide to prophecy in the local church.

USD $16.99

To purchase visit www.drpaulaprice.com.

Eternity's Generals:
The Wisdom of Apostleship

It has been said that one cannot explain the apostle without using reams of paper. Eternity's Generals disproves that belief. The time to understand and receive God's apostles in the church has come, but how can one know who is or is not a real apostle? This text will show you how. Book one of a two-book series, it soundly answers a broad range of questions. With crisp practicality, every apostle or apostolic minister can glean volumes of insight from this one text.

USD $29.95

To purchase visit www.drpaulaprice.com.

The Standardized Ministry Assessment Series

Fulfilling Your Purpose: Take the guesswork out of discovering destiny.

How would you like to take the guesswork out of discovering your purpose and call by using one simple tool? A dynamic instrument, our assessments offer a variety of solutions for all aspects of ministry, particularly for people just like you who are seeking sound wisdom and guidance that will help you get into your place.

The Standardized Ministry assessments, created by Dr. Paula Price acclaimed author of The Prophet's Dictionary and more, were designed to help you identify, articulate and better utilize your ministry gifting or five-fold office. Discover the full potential of your ministry strengths, abilities, aptitudes, character and assets, including your level of emotional intelligence and how it affects your abilities, ministry readiness and your most suited ministerial environment. It offers a total snapshot of you as an existing or potential minister.

The Minister's Assessment (MAQ)

More than ever, modern ministers and Christian professionals require a way to accurately place their prospective ministers in their proper offices or learning programs. Determine your dominant gifts and faculties, the temperaments that best fit them, character assets, competence level and reliability, mastery, accuracy and more.
USD: $65.00 (Includes Advisement + Complimentary Assessment)

The Prophets Assessment (PAQ)

The Prophets assessment is a unique, specialized assessment tailor made to represent the unique demand on the mantle of a prophet or prophetic type. It will identify your mantle, sphere, emphasis, classification, communication style, delivery, maturity, readiness and more.

For full details, or to book your online assessment, please visit
www.ppmglobalresources.com or www.drpaulaprice.com.

Notes

[1] For clarification purposes, apostles promulgate while prophets propagate. Often the two terms are confused and treated as synonyms, but they are not. Promulgation is the act of formally proclaiming or declaring a new statutory or administrative law after its enactment. In some jurisdictions, this additional step is necessary before the law can take effect. After a new law is approved, it is announced to the public. National laws of extraordinary importance to the public may be announced by the head of state on a national broadcast. Local laws are usually announced in the local newspapers and published in bulletins or compendia of municipal regulations. See extensive footnote definitions and comparisons.

[2] Albert Barnes' Notes on the Bible (Barnes) makes a perceptive comment on this: "Here the angel says that, in the capacity in which he appeared to John, he belonged to the general rank of the prophets, and was no more entitled to worship than any of the earthly prophets had been. Like them, he had merely been employed to disclose important truths in regard to the future; but as the prophets, even the most eminent of them, were not regarded as entitled to worship on account of the communications which they had made, no more was he."

[3] Barnes, "With ten thousands of saints - Render, from amidst ten thousands of holy ones: literally from myriads of holiness, i. e., holy Angels (compare Zechariah 14:5). God is represented as leaving heaven where He dwells amidst the host of the Angels 1Kings 22:19 and descending in majesty to earth Micah 1:3." This reputable scholar discovered from his research that the angels were there when God descended to Mount Sinai and gave Moses His law. Hebrews 2:1 supports this *"For if the word spoken by angels was steadfast, and every transgression and disobedience received a just recompense of reward"* to say that the Sinaitic Law was promulgated by angels. The innumerable assembly of angels is pictured in Hebrews as members of the Lord's general assembly.

[4] Something written; a writing; sacred writ. In early English law, for example, any formal document in letter form, under seal, and in the sovereign's name. An archaic term for a piece or body of writing, such as a Holy Writ.

[5] 1 Samuel 28:19. Note that tomorrow in a world with even the second has yet to be measured that is completely ruled by the seasons and luminaries' rotations, the word *tomorrow* can have broader meanings. Also, Samuel is speaking from outside this world and not from Saul's time. If today's worlds dozens of time zones, what Samuel meant could be something else entirely. Here is one thought about time zones. "There are currently 40

time zones in the world. There are 24 standard time zones and 16 areas that use time zones divided into 15-30-45 minutes increments. Each time zone represents where the sun is at a certain point of the day. It literally is 5 o'clock somewhere am or pm. For more information, visit: http://www.ask.com (Wikipedia, 2014) /wiki/Time zone. Ask.com. However it is claimed that time measured by sundials could be different for every settlement and either Saul's time (earths) or death's time (outside of the earth from where Samuel spoke) were different. Considering there was no rotation of the planets where Samuel was, the question is whose tomorrow he was referring to in the prophecy.

[6] **Note**: In this work the words 'eternal' and 'everlasting' are not used interchangeably. The selection of one over the other is deliberate in that it is meant to differentiate that which had its beginning with God in His world and extends throughout every other world, and all creation. Everlasting pertains to what He made from what is born within this world but is nonetheless created to exist forever. So there is the eternal—without beginning or ending and the everlasting—having a beginning but no ending. Although the Church of Jesus Christ is eternal, having existed in God since before the world began, its emerging populace got is incarnate start on earth. Thus, the spirits to enliven the souls that make up the New Creation ecclesia are eternal. The souls to earn the right to merge with those spirits are eternal. Refer to Genesis 1:26; Genesis 2:7 and 1 Corinthians 15:45. Adam was created spiritually on the 6th day, embodied on earth and given his soul on the 8th day because the Lord rested on the 7th day.

[7] Meaning literally intended to push out the dead spirit they entered the world with and replace it with the new one hidden in Jesus Christ until they decide to receive His salvation in order to be born anew. That is, born from above.

[8] The same is true for those who reject Christ's eternal life and trample under foot His redemptive blood. These are apostate, and so comprise the people, who turn away from the faith, blaspheme the Holy Spirit, and renouncement of Jesus's saving grace.

[9] *"And if the righteous scarcely be saved, where shall the ungodly and the sinner appear? "* 1 Peter 4:18. "The word (*molis* used for scarcely) implies that there is some difficulty, or obstruction, so that the thing came very near not to happen, or so that there was much risk about it." "The apostle (Peter) in this passage seems to have had his eye on a verse in Proverbs, Proverbs 11:31 and he has merely expanded and illustrated it: *"Behold, the righteous shall be recompensed in the earth: much more the wicked and the sinner."* By the question, which he employs, he admits that the righteous are saved with difficulty, or that there are perils which jeopardizes their salvation, and which are of such a kind as to make it very near not to happen. They would indeed be saved, but it would be in such a manner as to show that the circumstances were such as to render it, to human appearances, doubtful and problematical." Albert Barnes Notes on the Bible.

[10] Design: preliminarily sketched plans and preparations for a work to be done or an official act to be executed by a delegated subordinate or team. Such a plan includes, stylizing, structuring, projecting resources especially skill sets, and meticulously defining intended purposes and ultimate outcomes. Typically, designs get their start in the mind in the form of visions. Once the desired image is conceived, true visionaries initiate steps to plan how the vision is to become a reality. The plan devised comprises the processes, procedures, and means by which the vision makes its way from the mind's eye to the handiwork that materializes it. Throughout its journey, the visionary's thoughts are exercised to sculpt the final product as designed in a manner that achieves its purpose. Therefore, visionary sketches are minute because they must start broad and end specific, going so far as to include outlines, machinations, construction, executions, and other compositions that combine to depict the minutest details featured in the plan's project. The most coherent of plans goes so far as to devise the patterns, elements, and schemes to be followed to assure the design is fully produced. In respect to the Almighty and His continuum, this explanation takes much of the typical magic ascribed to His enterprises and in its place injects the essential logic that portrays Him as a deliberative Creator instead of an irrational bullying wizard wielding His power and wisdom for the sake of show and oppression.

[11] To mark or point out; define and design, to indicate or show; to specify beforehand; to denote; signify in advance all the way up to stylizing, entitling, naming and even nominating what is to happen at a later time and most often in a different place altogether. To preselect for an office, preappoint for duty, prepurpose* for an assignment before actual installation or recognition, activities ensue. These include the acts and procedures involved in delegating and deputing the prenominated. Example: a preappointed though not yet placed in office ambassador, minister or other designate. *Prepurpose is fixing the reasons, setting the bounds, and deciding how something is to be made, used, viewed, and rendered affective to its end user or recipient. Ends, goals, intentions, determinations, and desired results all factor into prepurpose as these are decreed and scripted as part of the prepurposed object's makeup to assure that it inherently performs as desired and produces as envisioned.

[12] Supervene Word Origin & History: 1594 (implied in supervenient), from L. supervenire "come on top of," from super "over, upon" (see super-) + venire "come". Online Etymology Dictionary, © 2010 Douglas Harper.

[13] On the word Logos: First, and foremost, the Word of God, creative powers and the wisdom behind it. the eternal thought or word of God, made incarnate in Jesus Christ: John 1. Logos, "the divine Word, second person of the Christian Trinity, the divine Word, Christ. From Greek logos "word, speech, discourse", also "reason", from PIE root *leg- "to collect" (with derivatives meaning "to speak," on notion of "to pick out words. The word or form, which expresses a thought, also, the thought, French for to speak. The rational principle

that governs and develops the universe. A word; reason; speech. <u>Etymology</u>: C16: from Greek: word, reason, discourse, from *legein* to speak. Origin: Latin logos < Gr, a word: see logic. Also from Ancient Greek λόγος (lógos, "speech, oration, discourse, quote, story, study, ratio, word, calculation, reason"). G3004—lego, Logos identifies something said, especially including the thought that provoked it. In theology the divine word or reason incarnate in Jesus Christ. John 1:1–14. The word implies the topical subject of discourse, along with the reasoning used by the mental faculties and their motivation. Hebrews 4:12 makes this case best. Logos' meanings extend to the actual thinking processes and their logistics. In respect to the Almighty, logos as used in John's Gospel refers to the Divine Expression of Christ. As much of a calculative term as it is a communicative one, the logics of doctrine, its effects, intents, and spoken matters concerning preaching, treatises, God's word and work and the reckoning processes used to answer questions, reasoning their responses, and the methodology speakers use to prepare and deliver their speeches that persuade others. Includes ration, reasoning, prudence and so forth. Logos encompasses cogent arguments and their justification. It is the divine word of God; the second person in the Godhead, the incarnate Jesus in His Sovereign governance of all creation. The plural is *logoi*: the divine wisdom manifested in creation, its government, and the redemption of the world, often identified with the second person of the Trinity. In comparison to logos, rhema, a noun means word; verb. rheme, n. speech element expressing an idea. Rhematic a variant of the word is an adjective that pertains to the formation of words; derived from verbs. Rhematology is a study of rhemes. Rheme is a speech element expressing an idea. rhematic, a. pertaining to formation of words; derived from verbs. rhematology, n. study of rhemes. Origin 1890–95; < Greek rhema saying, In linguistics, compare theme as the constituent of a sentence that adds most new information, in addition to what has already been said in the discourse. The rheme is usually, but not always, associated with the subject.

[14] Rhema, from c.1300, Old French rethorique, Latin rhetorice, from Greek rhetorike techne "art of an orator," from rhetor (genitive rhetoros) "orator," <u>related to rhema "word</u>," literally "<u>that which is spoken</u>," from PIE *wre-tor-, from root *were- "to speak" (cf. Old English word, Latin verbum, from Greek *eirein* "to say;"). Online Etymology Dictionary. (Online Etymology Dictionary)

[15] From Latin rhetorica, Ancient Greek ῥητορική (rhētorikē), feminine form of ῥητορικός (rhetorikos, "concerning public speech"), from ῥήτωρ (rhētōr, "public speaker").

[16] To grasp God's perception of eternity, think of it this way. God says He is the beginning and the ending, the first and the last, the beginning that is with the last and on it goes. His name Jehovah, or Yahweh as the Hebrew knows Him, says that He is the "Self-Existent

One". That means He caused Himself to come into being and after that caused everything else that is, was and will be. The implication is until God manifested Himself nothing was. As obvious as that conclusion sounds, what it means to God is not what it means to people. He does not mean that before Him nothing existed because in the context of who He is and He Himself being the first something, the Almighty's thought is that He created nothing because there had to first be a something. Therefore, eternity to God is Himself because His existence is everything and nothing predates or outlives Him. He shrewdly contained all existence within His being. Read, in view of this explanation, see Isaiah 43:10 *"Ye are my witnesses, saith the Lord, and my servant whom I have chosen: that ye may know and believe me, and understand that I am he: before me there was no God formed, neither shall there be after me."* To this add, Isaiah 44:8 *"Fear ye not, neither be afraid: have not I told thee from that time, and have declared it? Ye are even my witnesses. Is there a God beside me? Yea, there is no God; I know not any."* These two passages show a being that scanned His entire world, reached as far back in His memory as possible and saw no other being like Himself, which is why everything since Him is a creature. He looked for what preceded His and found that before Him, not even emptiness existed.

[17] Initially, spelled capitol, it refers to a building or complex of buildings where a state's legislature meets. Identifies a group of buildings in which the functions of state government are carried out; literally, the place of the head seat, or the headship's seat. When the government seat comprises an entire city or country or similar region as opposed to being just a complex of buildings situated in a designated precinct it is classified as the capital city. The idea goes back to highly developed ancient cities that credited their opulence and influence to their god. The most notable of these is Jupiter's capital temple site in ancient Rome. The capitol region within the city as the seat of his temple reflected deities thought to rule where they received and were petitioned by worshippers who were there in turn rewarded for their homage and obeisance. However, to be most specific, the Lord's capital city, Jerusalem although it held His main temple, also contained the palace and other governmental facilities. Since God is and always has been a King, His capital is more precisely a basilical city rather than where elected officials meet. He currently resides in His heavenly Jerusalem where His eternal temple containing the everlasting Ark of His Covenant with creation abides. Thus, when He replaces this earth with His eternal version of it, the New Jerusalem to replace the demolished one on earth will serve the same purposes for Him, this time forever and uninterrupted.

[18] Abel's was the second blood to be shed on the planet, the first being the animal the Lord slew to flay its skin, tan it, and give it to Adam and his wife for coverings. Down the line it became known that the animal was a lamb, something the death and resurrection of Jesus Christ revealed. It seems to answer the Old Testament writers, at least in the version pop-

ularized today, why the shed blood of animals, most notably the blood of lambs or sheep, figured so prominently in their sacrifices. Both Luke's Gospel and the Epistle to the Hebrews divulge the rest of the story that Moses appears to have left out. Abel was a prophet, the real reason he was killed, and not just for being Cain's irritating younger brother. In addition, the reason Moses gives for his death is more profound than first believed. Abel's God-approved sacrifice that so enraged Cain suggests that he also had priestly functions, making his shed blood more of a sacrifice because it began The devillish tradition of slaughtering His ministers of righteousness.

[19] A) Eternal from heaven in the beginning before time began. B) On earth until Abraham and Moses. C) Eternal under the High Priestly ministry of Jesus Christ. D) Everlasting through the new creation saints that inherit eternal life in Christ. E) Lastly eternal once and after being raptured from the earth and permanently stationed in God's temple as His ministers.

[20] Judges 5:20 is worth examining with respect to the Lord's supernal intervention into earthly affairs.

This reference and the language of its different translations are in complete keeping with Daniel chapter 10 that discusses the archangels Michael and Gabriel fighting with the angelic counterparts to the earthly rulers rising and falling in the earth. Their inclusion in the Continuum is pertinent given that they do not die, age, or abandon their posts as humans are inclined to do, except the angels in Jude's epistle that in Genesis 6 opted to forego their celestiality to become progenitors through the daughters of men. It is important to read the Bible as if it were only written for this world and not as if its record rigidly subject to it.

[21] "Here is my servant, whom I support, my chosen one, in whom I delight. I've placed my Spirit upon him; and he'll deliver his justice throughout the world. He won't shout, or raise his voice, or make it heard in the street. A crushed reed he will not break, and a fading candle he won't snuff out. He'll bring forth justice for the truth. And he won't grow faint or be crushed until he establishes justice on the mainland, and the coastlands take ownership of his Law." This is foreshadowing the impending ministry of the Lord Jesus Christ.

[22] This is what the Lord says to his anointed, Cyrus, whose right hand I have grasped to subdue nations before him, as I strip kings of their armor, to open doors before him and gates that cannot keep closed: "I myself will go before you, and he will make the mountains level; I'll shatter bronze doors and cut through iron bars. I'll give you concealed treasures and riches hidden in secret places, so that you'll know that it is I, the Lord, the God of Israel, who calls you by name. For the sake of Jacob my servant, Israel my chosen, I've called you, and he has established you with a name, although you have not acknowl-

edged me. I am the Lord, and there is no other besides me: and there are no gods. I'm strengthening you, although you have not acknowledged me, so that from the sun's rising to the west people may know that there is none besides me. "I am the Lord, and there is no other. I form light and create darkness; I make goodness and create disaster. I am the Lord, who does all these things. Shout, you skies above, and you clouds, and let righteousness stream down. I am the one who says to the earth, 'Let salvation blossom, and let righteousness sprout forth." Isaiah 45:1-8, ISV.

[23] "They won't build for others to inhabit; they won't plant for others to eat—for like the lifetime of a tree, so will the lifetime of my people be, and my chosen ones will long enjoy the work of their hands." Isaiah 65:22, ISV.

[24] This principle was evidently well known and traditionalized as a divine practice in Jesus' and the apostles' time because of what Paul writes in Hebrews chapter 7: *"And as I may so say, Levi also, who receiveth tithes, payed tithes in Abraham. For he was yet in the loins of his father, when Melchisedec met him."* Hebrews 7:9, 10. It seems that whatever a father does outwardly is ascribed to his seed while it is still in his loins. This principle links human behavioral dispositions to the parent's genes, which makes sense when one considers the Savior's words in John 8:44 and 1 John 3:8.

[25] This example fits what Paul understood about Jesus as Abraham's seed in Galatians 3:16 where verse 17 reinforces the Continuum's before all time premises. *"Now to Abraham and his seed were the promises made. He saith not, and to seeds, as of many; but as of one, and to thy seed, which is Christ. And this I say, that the covenant, that was confirmed before of God in Christ, the law, which was four hundred and thirty years after, cannot disannul, that it should make the promise of none effect."* Galatians 3:16, 17. A revisit to Matthew 1:1 and Isaiah 53:8 It fortifies these principles.

[26] More accurately *"from eternity or the eternal ages"*. Thayer G165 translates the word *aion* for eons or ages. The use of this term reinforces the concept of the Continuum for it means "forever, an unbroken age, perpetuity of time, eternity; the worlds, universe; period of time". Note the constantly implied tenor of succession, continuous, contiguous, and so forth. Strong's definition of this term adds to the previous, perpetuity, age, an eternal never-ending course, the beginning of what is without end. A continuing duration with no designated, defined, or provided for end. An incessant perpetuity that never varies at any time but resumes itself consistently the same way every time regardless of circumstances. Thayer.

[27] Dictionary.com.

[28] Idio: A combining form, a prefix attached to a word that comes from the Greek 'i`dios, meaning private, personal, peculiar, distinct used to form compound words having the sense of individuality, peculiarity, separateness. One's own; private; personal. Distinct;

separate. A peculiarity that pertains to an individual person or thing. An element in compound words of Greek origin, meaning 'one's own,' 'private,' 'peculiar.' Greek, from idios, personal, private; see s(w)e- in Indo-European roots. (American Heritage® Dictionary of the English Language, Fourth Edition). Idios represents a combining form of Ancient Greek ἴδιος ("own, personal, distinct"). As used in this work, refers to the Almighty's communication Himself to others in whole or part, for whatever reason in predetermined measures.

[29] Gill's commentary: Concerning "what is said in Heb_11:3, and the same says Philo the Jew, who not only calls him the archetype, and exemplar of the world, but the power that made it: he often ascribes the creation of the heavens, and the earth unto him, and likewise the creation of man after whose image, he says, he was made (t). The Ethiopic version adds, at the end of this verse, "and also that which is made is for himself". JFB Commentary: "He is the archetype of the Church, from whom and according to whom, as the pattern, she is formed. He is her Head, as the husband is of the wife (Romans 6:5; 1 Corinthians 11:3; 1 Corinthians 15:45). Christ will never allow any power to sever Himself and His bride, indissolubly joined (Matthew 9:6; John 10:28, John 10:29; John 13:1)." "As being "the Son of God, higher than the heavens" (Heb_7:26): the archetype and antitype of the legal high priest." McLaren: "that He is the Archetype of all excellence, the Ideal of all moral completeness: that we can know enough of Him to be sure of this that what we call right He loves, and what we call right He practices."

[30] "Generally, to contextualize (Houdman): An idea, statement or event is to place it within its larger setting in which it acquires its true and complete meaning. Contextualization aids comprehension." Read more: http://www.gotquestions.org/contextualization.html#ixzz2vPRptxhR

As with the previous string of translations, the ones above give a student of Scripture the opportunity to explore the full scope and depth of the Lord's mind when He released these revelations to John the Apostle. For the sake of comprehensiveness, the Apostolic Bible handles the passages this way. Note: Some compositional adjustments are made to increase coherency. These have not disturbed the revelations to be gained from the passages, nor do they disjoint its contexts.

Revelation 12:7-12: "And there was war in the heaven; Michael and his angels to wage war with the dragon, and the dragon waged war and his angels; and it (the dragon's army) did not prevail, nor was a place found for him any longer in the heaven. And the dragon great was cast out, the serpent ancient, the one being called the Devil and Satan; the one misleading the inhabitable world entire was cast unto the earth, and his angels with him were cast. And heard voice a great in the heaven, saying, and now is come the deliverance, and the power, and the kingdom of our god, and the authority of his Christ; for was cast down the accuser of our brethren, the one accusing them before our god day and night. And they overcame him through the blood of the lamb, and through the word of their testimony, and they loved not their life until death. Because of this be glad, heavens, and ones in them encamping! Woe to the earth, and the sea, for is come down the Devil to you, having rage great, knowing that a short time he has."

[32] Tail as mentioned in Revelation 12:4, was understood in John's day to refer to the tail of an army, representing the dignities, office, and rank of soldiership. On the ministry side, it refers to the prophetic. In this context, dark spirituality is meant, which is why the serpent's tail is highlighted. False prophecy is typically what is being referred to, which says much about what the dragon did to convince one third of the stars (messengers of heaven) to defect from the light and truth to become members of his regime. Isaiah 9:15 confirms this: *"The ancient and honourable, he is the head; and the prophet that teacheth lies, he is the tail"*. The tail is the slave to the head, the performer of the mind's thoughts. See also Revelation 9:10, 19; 12:4.

[33] Many people are unaware of the Lord's practice of letting people's behaviors and effects name or rename them. Far from being merely identification, names are also epithets. That is, a word or phrase applied to a person or thing to describe an overwhelming or attributed quality; a characterizing word or phrase firmly associated with a person or thing and often used in place of an actual name, title. These complements are added to a name to show the namer's sentiments, opinion, or experience with the one named. Hence, Lucifer being renamed as the serpent, dragon, deceiver, and adversary are all due to his manifest actions and attitudes. They separated him from the masses in heaven, the rest of God's citizenry. Using devious tactics and implicatively false prophecy or empty promises, he appealed to the disgruntled to achieve in his own right what he was either never created for him, or what he was deprived of based on the divine cultural and customs in which he lived. This explanation enhances the relevance of Jesus' words in John 8:44.

[34] Bringing forward Psalm 109 to their New Covenant apostleship, Peter quotes it to substantiate selection of one of their most faithful followers to take Judas' office. Furthermore, Peter understands the office that David foresaw was apostleship. The Douay Rheims and Webster's Bible calls it a bishopric, Darby calls it an overseership and Young's Literal Translation Bible calls it oversight It includes oversight care, watch, or charge as an army or civil officer. The translation most widely accepted is that of the bishopric. John Gill's Exposition of the Entire Bible adds that Judas occupied "the office of an apostle, a high and honourable one, the chief office in the Church: it was a charge, as the word signifies; a charge of souls, an oversight of the flock... There being a change of the priesthood, law, and ordinances, there was a change of offices and officers; new ordinances were appointed by Christ, and new officers created, on whom gifts were bestowed suitable to

their work." Henry's Commentary on the Whole Bible says it this way "Consequently all his places should be disposed of to others, and they should enjoy his preferments and employments: Let another take his office. This Peter applies to the filling up of Judas's place in the truly sacred college of the apostles, by the choice of Matthias, Acts 1:20." Albert Barnes' Notes on the Bible expressly says that Matthias was chosen to replace Judas in the "the office, or portion of apostolic work." There is no question in his mind that Peter and the rest of the eleven installed him to "the apostolic ministry." Clarke likewise saw that Judas " abandoned the ministry and apostolate;" the office and dignity of an apostle. Regarding Acts 1:25, he says "That he may take part of this ministry and apostleship,.... Of the ministry of the apostles, or of the apostolical ministration; which lay in preaching the Gospel, administering ordinances, planting churches, and working miracles; and which part, lot, or inheritance, Judas had by betraying his Lord, whose apostle he was, he was turned out of his office, and had no longer part in the apostolical ministry: see Acts 1:17.

[35] Refer to the following as well. Matthew 2:5 manifests Micah 5:2. God fulfills Hosea 11:1's prophecy in Matthew 2:15 while Jeremiah in Matthew 2:17 explicitly names, Jeremiah in particular. See 31:15. Matthew 3:3 records fulfillment of Isaiah 40:3, as does Matthew 4:14 in reiterating Isaiah 9:1-2. This recollection draws on Moses' words in Deuteronomy 1:1 and 4:49 and how Esaias the prophet's words (Isaiah 53:1-12) foretell Jesus' healing and deliverance ministry.

[36] 1 Corinthians 2:6, 8, "Howbeit we speak wisdom among them that are perfect: yet not the wisdom of this world, nor of the princes of this world, that come to nought...which none of the princes of this world knew: for had they known it, they would not have crucified the Lord of glory. Compare these comments with the spirit of Ephesians 3:10.

[37] Progenic Web Definitions: As variant of the word progeny it means offspring. The immediate descendants of a person; "she was the mother of many offspring"; "he died without...wordnetweb.princeton.edu/perl/webwn. The immediate descendant or descendants of a person, animal, etc., a result or outcome (C13: from Latin progenies lineage; see progenitor). (Wordnet.Web.Princeton.edu) Progeny: breed, children, descendants, family, issue, lineage, offspring, posterity, race, scions, seed (chiefly biblical) stock, young. English Collins Dictionary.

[38] About the word news and its application to the gospel: ETYMOLOGY: Middle English newes, new things, tidings, pl. of newe, new thing, new, and the Latin nova. Middle English newis, plural of newe new thing, novelty (see new); on the model of Middle French noveles (plural of novele), or Medieval Latin nova (plural of novum); see novel. Hence, the gospel divulged to the world the new thing the Most High was doing and the means and messenger through which He was doing it. Synonyms for news include information, advice, report, intelligence, notice, tidings, word and broadcast. They are also intelligence,

updates, good word. What they share is that they all refer to information about hitherto unknown events and happenings. Even when the gospel is preached contemporaneously, it is still news to those hearing it for the first time. Despite its agelessness, the interminableness of the Holy Spirit's inhabitation of humans to pass them from death to life and pass them into the kingdom of the Lord Jesus Christ, because it is ongoing, keeps the gospel's effect new and so its message fresh. The following definitions are useful to appreciate the role ministers of the gospel fills as the Savior's messenger in their times. The timelessness of their message and ministry aside, there are some definitive points of knowledge and therefore service the meanings below that speak to the evangelist's training and communications.

1) Information about something that has happened recently; 2) new information of any kind; 3) interesting or important information not previously known or realized; 5) something having a specified influence or effect; 6) reports of current events; 7) newly received or noteworthy information, especially about recent events; 8) a person or thing considered interesting enough to be reported in the news; 9) a report of a recent event; intelligence; 10) information; 11) includes a bearer of news; a courier; 12) a report of recent occurrences; 13) information of something that has lately taken place, or of something before unknown; 14) fresh tidings; recent intelligence; 15) a strange or new happening; 16) new information about specific and timely events; 17) recent account; fresh information of something that has lately taken place at a distance, or of something before unknown; 18) tidings; informal information of any kind that is not previously known to someone.

[39] In respect to the gospel, this reference other translations are worth noting. Psalm 40:7-11 "Then I said, Lo, I come, in the roll of the Book it is written of Me; I delight to do Your will, O My God; and Your Law is within My inmost soul. I have announced righteousness in the great assembly; behold, I will not restrain My lips; O Jehovah You know. I have not concealed Your righteousness in My heart; I speak Your faithfulness and Your salvation. I have not hidden Your loving-kindness and Your truth from the great assembly. Do not withhold Your tender mercies from me, O Jehovah; let Your loving kindness and Your truth always watch over me." LITV.

[40] Forensic is generally an argumentative exercise; the art or study of argumentative discourse; scientific analysis of physical evidence. Of, relating to, or used in debate or argument; rhetorical. An exercise in debate; a forensic contest; an argumentative thesis. From Latin forēnsis ("of the forum, public"), from forum (Wiktionary). From Latin forēnsis, public, of a forum, from forum, forum; see dhwer- in Indo-European roots. (American Heritage® Dictionary of the English Language, Fourth Edition). From Latin forēnsis ("of the forum, public"), from forum. Pertaining to, used in, or fit for public discussion or debate; rhetorical. the study or practice of formal argumentation or debate. Word Origin & History:

forensic from L. *forensis* "of a forum, place of assembly," from forum. Used in sense of "pertaining to legal trials or public debates," as in forensic medicine. The word *forensic* comes from the Latin *forēnsis*, meaning "of or before the forum. This origin is the source of the two modern usages of the word *forensic*–as a form of legal evidence and as a category of public presentation.

[41] Pertaining to, or suitable for exhibition in a cinematograph; of or pertaining to or characteristic of the cinema. Relating to movies; presented as a motion picture.

[42] To make celestial or divine; to make supremely good; sublime. To make or qualify to become a heavenly citizen. To render divine or spiritual. To beautify for the Lord's world. To make compatible with or comparable to the Lord and His angels.

[43] John 11:52 and Ephesians 1:10.

[44] John 3:17; 1 Thessalonians 2:16; Psalm 78:4; 108:18.

[45] Exodus 30:32; Psalm 69:28; Isaiah 41:4; Philippians 4:3; Revelation 3:5; 13:8; 17:8; 20:12; 20:15; 20:27.

[46] Generatively, reproductively, conducive to producing in abundance.

[47] Jesus precarnate, incarnate, and eternal, speaking to His Scriptures.

[48] Capable of being understood through study and observation; comprehensible; open to or able to be understood by scrutiny, decipherable. Etymology: Late Latin *scrutabilis*, searchable C17; from Latin *scrūtārī* to inspect closely; straightforward and articulate.

[49] "Who has known the mind of the Lord? Or who has become his adviser?" Romans 11:34. 1 Corinthians 2:11; Isaiah 40:13. "Who hath directed the Spirit of the Lord, or being his counsellor hath taught him?" It is designed to express the infinite wisdom and knowledge of God, by affirming that no being could teach him, or counsel him. Earthly monarchs have counsellors of state, whom they may consult in times of perplexity or danger. But God has no such council. He sits alone; nor does he call in any or all of his creatures to advise him (Barnes).

[50] Prognistically: foreknowledge, beforehand as it relates to prediction; having value for making predictions; Serving to predict the likely outcome of; predictive of something in the future; a forecast, predictive; a sign of a future happening; a portent.

[51] Deuteronomy 4:25: "I call heaven and earth to witness against you this day..."; Deuteronomy 30:19: "I call heaven and earth to record this day against you, that I have set before you life and death, blessing and cursing: therefore choose life, that both thou and thy seed may live." Deuteronomy 31:28; "Gather unto me all the elders of your tribes, and your officers, that I may speak these words in their ears, and call heaven and earth to record against them."

[52] Eternity's Generals, by this author.

[53] Another term for the word estate, which is unquestionably the abode of angels. In this regard, prince angels assigned to territories to watch over the earth. Barnes on Jude 1:6. The use of the word habitation comes from Strong's G3613 that means residence or house. Since angelic homes would be invisible to humans, it reasonable to conclude that bodily house is meant. Thayer's definition of this word considers this likelihood and adds to this definition, "habitation of the body as a dwelling place for the spirit".

[54] Of considerable size, quantity, or amount, something that is substantial and based in fact. Not imaginary, actual, real--Important, serious, or related to real facts; being the essence or essential element of something; having practical importance or value. Of the essence or essential element of a thing that makes it solid in foundation or basis, firm, thus having independent function, resources, or existence. Independent in existence or function and so not subordinate in addition to being a word naming or referring to a person, place, thing, or idea. What has substance and prompts thought. Militarily substantive is considered actual or real, as rank, having the actual rank of something. Having a firm basis in reality and being therefore important, meaningful, or considerable. Relating to the essential legal principles administered by the courts, defining rights and duties as opposed to giving the rules by which rights and duties are established. V2 Vocabulary Builder: "Substantive is derived from the Middle French substantif, "having or expressing substance." Having major substance or quantity is the common meaning of substantive. If something has substance, it is real, it's serious, its legitimate--its substantive. In business, substantive is used to discuss a productive meeting or a meeting with substance that covered important issues: "It was a substantive meeting--we finalized next year's marketing budget". In law, substantive refers to the essential principals of a court's work." from Late Latin substantīvus, from Latin substāre to stand beneath.

[55] It should be understood that unsaved people cannot actually blaspheme the Holy Spirit and suffer irrevocable damnation for doing so, because they do not know Him. Living lost to God is the inherent condemnation everyone born into this world receives as Adam's seed. Never receiving His forgiveness and saving grace comes with being born mortal. That is damnable enough. Truthfully, blasphemy or not, one cannot suffer any worse fate than dying unredeemed. The unsaved and the blasphemer's punishment have the same eternal outcome. They both end up in hell. Therefore, the unregenerate can curse and insult God forever. He will just treat it as nothing more than what is to be expected of those living without His Spirit because such behaviors typify the unsaved soul. That is why the Lord Jesus came in the flesh. Before the immitigable damnation of blaspheming the Holy Spirit can come into effect, the blasphemer must first have received and rejected Jesus Christ, otherwise, the blasphemy is useless. God is already at odds with blasphemers, which everyone born into the planet is naturally. That is why He demands all people get

saved to escape death and its eternal damnation. When salvation deposits a measure of God's Spirit within the soul, insulting His Spirit and remaining impenitent about it becomes condemnable. Those that die in such a state return the death sentence that Christ's blood ransomed them from when they received Him as their Savior.

[56] It should be understood that unsaved people cannot actually blaspheme the Holy Spirit and suffer irrevocable damnation for doing so, because they do not know Him. Living lost to God is the inherent condemnation everyone born into this world receives as Adam's seed. Never receiving His forgiveness and saving grace comes with being born mortal. That is damnable enough. Truthfully, blasphemy or not, one cannot suffer any worse fate than dying unredeemed. The unsaved and the blasphemer's punishment have the same eternal outcome. They both end up in hell. Therefore, the unregenerate can curse and insult God forever. He will just treat it as nothing more than what is to be expected of those living without His Spirit because such behaviors typify the unsaved soul. That is why the Lord Jesus came in the flesh. Before the immitigable damnation of blaspheming the Holy Spirit can come into effect, the blasphemer must first have received and rejected Jesus Christ, otherwise, the blasphemy is useless. God is already at odds with blasphemers, which everyone born into the planet is naturally. That is why He demands all people get saved to escape death and its eternal damnation. When salvation deposits a measure of God's Spirit within the soul, insulting His Spirit and remaining impenitent about it becomes condemnable. Those that die in such a state return the death sentence that Christ's blood ransomed them from when they received Him as their Savior.

[57] There are _three main layers_ of skin in humans. They are the epidermis, the dermis, and the subcutaneous tissue. There are *seven sub divisions* of the epidermis and the dermis. They are (1) stratum basale, (2) stratum spinosum, (3) stratum granulosum, (4) stratum licidum, (5) stratum corneum, (6) the upper papillary layer, (7) the lower reticular layer; Ask.com.

[58] The skin is an ever-changing organ that contains many specialized cells and structures. The skin functions as a protective barrier that interfaces with a sometimes-hostile environment. It is also very involved in maintaining the proper temperature for the body to function well. It gathers sensory information from the environment, and plays an active role in the immune system protecting us from disease. Understanding how the skin can function in these many ways starts with understanding the structure of the three layers of skin: the epidermis, dermis, and subcutaneous tissue. Skin Anatomy, and www.about.com). (Heather Brannon)

[59] In relation to human skin symbology, the word tabernacle is translated from the common Hebrew for skin, 'ohel.' In this context, it refers to the skin that covered the skeletal

structure of Moses' wilderness tabernacle. That is the wooden pillars and such that formed it that were dismantled and enmantled whenever it was traveled or reassembled. The Tabernacle of David, Kevin J. Conner, pages 9-11. (Conner, Tabernacle of David, 1976)

[60] Tabernacle there is from Strong's G4638, the word skenoma, skay'-no-mah. It means, among other things, the Temple (as God's residence), the body (as a tenement for the soul):--tabernacle.

[61] As mentioned, on earth the Holy Spirit is definitely heaven's peacekeeping force, sent to see that it does not self-destruct, or demonically destruct before the fullness of those to receive Christ's salvation have been born and born again.

[62] To admit (adopt) an alien to the rights of a country by a naturalizing process that enables his or her acclimation and adaptation to its government, customs, culture, practices and such as a natural born citizen. To confer upon (an alien) the rights and privileges of a citizen by introducing and converting him or her to a region, establishing and causing the alien to conform and flourish as a native in a land, country, kingdom, etc. To bring into conformity with the nature, environments, and circumstances of a new surrounding after, or in order to grant full citizenship to one of foreign birth to a new place as a native.

[63] See 2 Peter 1:4 that identify the Spirit indwelt that makes the new creature product of the new birth a Christian. In this way, they are made partakers of God's divine nature. The word nature includes, to make it clear, a lineal descendent, a genus or sort, a dispositional offspring of a particular lineage, of natural constitution by imparting the very same nature.

[64] The expression "born again" of the King James Version, John 3:3, John 3:7; 1 Peter 1:23, translating the Greek "a no ˉthenˇ" and "ana" in composition, becomes in the Revised Version (British and American) "anew," i.e. "over again." As these particles mean "from above" and "up", their use as indicating repetition is sometimes disputed, but without further foundation than that "again" does not exhaust the meaning. ISBE. See Thayer on Strong's G1080 for further insight. ISV: "Jesus replied to him, "Truly, I tell you with certainty, unless a person is born from above he cannot see the kingdom of God". John 1:12,13 talks about the new birth as being from above and later in chapter 3 records Jesus describing how it happens. In today's world of voice activation, it is much easier to grasp how this is done by God with those who are heirs of His salvation before the foundation of the world.

[65] Something that is intrinsic is an essential part of a whole, so *intrinsically* describes something closely connected to or inseparable from something. Vocabulary.com. That which constitutes the fundamental nature of a thing.

[66] Colossians 2:10, "And having been filled, you are in Him, who is the Head of all rule and authority. ISV. The KJV adds the word 'complete'. "And ye are complete in him, which is the head of all principality and power." The Apostolic Bible Polyglot has an interesting variation of this passage that speaks to who Jesus is and the extent of power and authority He wields. "And you are him being fulfilled], who is the head of all sovereignty and authority." See also Revelation chapters 4 and 5.

[67] "Just as the Father has life in himself, so also he has granted the Son to have life in himself, and he has given him authority to judge, because he is the Son of Man." John 5:26, 27.

[68] Psalm 103:19, "The Lord hath prepared his throne in the heavens; and his kingdom ruleth over all". Daniel 4:17 adds, "This matter is by the decree of the watchers, and the demand by the word of the holy ones: to the intent that the living may know that the most High ruleth in the kingdom of men, and giveth it to whomsoever he will, and setteth up over it the basest of men."

[69] The Pulpit Commentary, Electronic Database. Copyright © 2001, 2003, 2005, 2006, 2010 by BibleSoft, inc., Used by permission.

[70] Jamieson-Fausset-Brown Bible Commentary on Ezekiel 9:11: "I have done as thou hast commanded—The characteristic of Messiah (John 17:4). So the angels (Ps 103:21); and the apostles report their fulfillment of their orders (Mark 6:30)."

[71] "It is written in the Prophets, 'And all of them will be taught by God.' Everyone who has listened to the Father and has learned anything comes to me." ISV. "It is having been written in the prophets, And they shall be all taught of God; every one therefore who heard from the Father, and learned, cometh to me." YLT. "It is written in the prophets: And they shall all be taught of God. Every one that hath heard of the Father and hath learned cometh forth me". DRB "The writings of the prophets say, And they will all have teaching from God. Everyone whose ears have been open to the teaching of the Father comes to me." BBE "It has been written in the Prophets, They "shall" all "be taught of God." So then everyone who hears and learns from the Father comes to Me." Isa. 54:13 LITV While there appears little difference between them it is helpful to pay attention to the slight variations to expand the text's meaning.